MANAGERIAL ECONOMICS

MANAGERIAL ECONOMICS

Professor V. P. Gupta

Dr. M. C. Sharma

RESEARCHCO BOOK CENTER

NEW DELHI - 110 005

First Published 2006

ISBN : 81-902320-7-X

Published by :

Researchco Book Center
25B/2, New Rohtak Road
(Near Liberty Cinema)
Karol Bagh
New Delhi-110005

Printed at :

Salasar Imaging Systems
New Delhi

TABLE OF CONTENTS

1

Nature and Scope of Managerial Economics

Introduction

A primary emphasis of managerial economics is the application of economic theory and methodology to the practice of business decision-making. An important secondary emphasis in managerial economics is the study of how managerial decisions are affected by the economic environment. Managerial economics is applied economics; it is the use of economics theory and methodology to solve practical decision problems.

How do managers make good decisions? What pitfalls must be avoided? What to produce? How to produce, for whom to produce? When are the characteristics of a market, a line of business, or an industry so attractive that entry becomes appealing? When are these attributes so unattractive that growth is not warranted and exit is preferable to continued operation? Why do some professions continue to pay well, while others offer only minimal financial rewards? All of these questions involve important economic issues that pose a continuing challenge to the managerial decision making process. Providing a logical and consistent framework that can be used to derive an appropriate answer to each of these questions is a task for which managerial economics is ideally suited. Managerial economics tells managers how things should be done to achieve objectives efficiently, and helps them recognize how economic forces affect organizations.

Definition

Managerial economics is the application of microeconomic tools and techniques to the key decisions firms need to make e.g. pricing, output, investment and advertising. McNair and Meriam, gave the definition, Managerial economics consists of the use of economic modes of thought to analyze business situation. According to Spencer and Siegelman , Managerial economics is the integration of economic theory with business practice for the purpose of facilitating decision-making and forward planning by management.

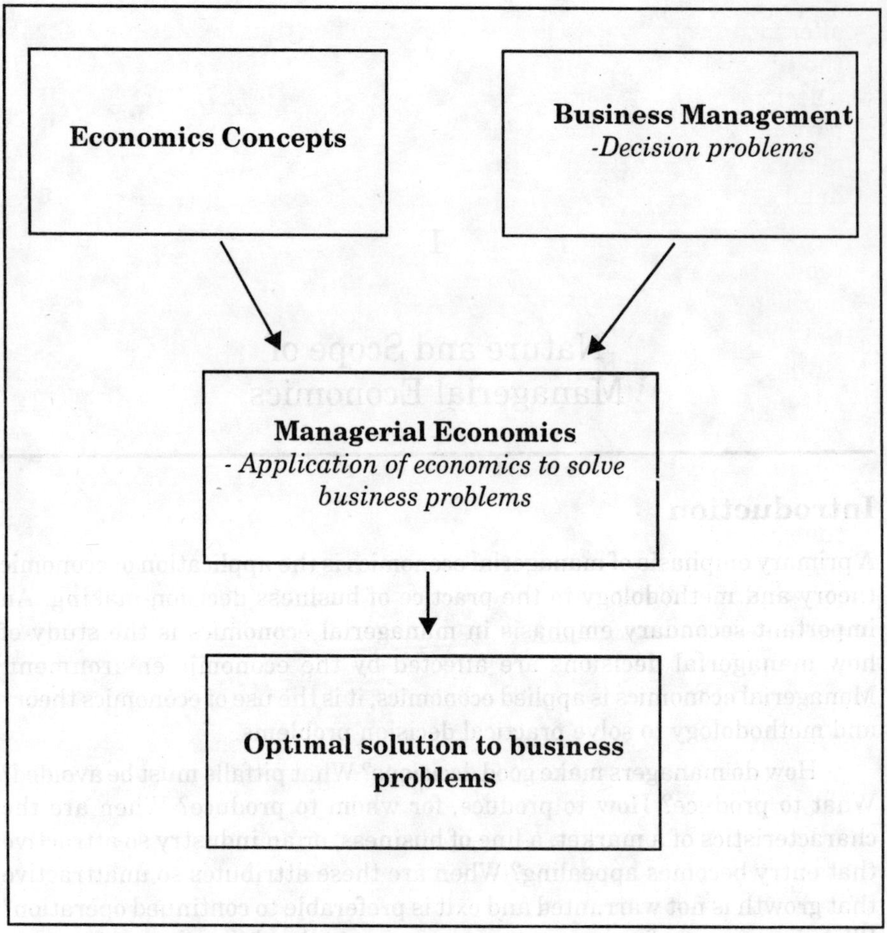

Figure1.1: Relationship between managerial economics, economics and business management.

Nature of Managerial Economics

Business Decision Making

Robbins has defined Economics as "the science that studies human behaviour as a relationship between ends and scarce means which have alternative uses". Human wants are virtually unlimited and non-satiable, but the means to satisfy them are limited. Managerial Economics hence has evolved as a discipline of choice making

The prime function of a management executive in a business organization is *decision-making and forward planning*. Decision-making means the process of *selecting one course of action from* two or more *alternative courses of* action whereas forward planning means *establishing* plans *for the future.* The question of choice arises because resources such as capital, land, labour and management are limited and can be employed in alternative uses. The decision-making function thus becomes one of making choices or decisions that will provide the most efficient means of attaining a desired end, say, profit maximization. Once a decision is made about the particular goal to be achieved, plans as to production, pricing, capital, raw materials, labour, etc., are prepared. Forward planning thus goes hand in hand with decision-making.

A business organization has to work and take decisions under the condition of uncertainty. And this fact not only makes the function of decision-making and forward planning more complicated. If knowledge of the future were perfect, plans could be made without error and hence without any need for subsequent revision. In the real world, however, the business manager rarely has complete information about the future sales, costs, profits, capital conditions, etc. Hence decisions are made and plans formulated on the basis of past data, current information and the estimates about future predicted as best as possible. As plans are implemented over time, more facts become known and if needed plans may have to be revised, and a different course of action adopted. Managers are thus engaged in a continuous process of decision-making through an uncertain future and the overall problem confronting them is one of *adjusting to uncertainty*.

Economic theory can be used considerably in fulfilling the function of decision-making in an uncertainty with considerable advantage. Economic theory deals with a number of concepts and principles relating, for example, to profit, demand, cost, pricing production, competition, business cycles, etc., which aided by allied disciplines like Accounting, Statistics and Mathematics, can be used to solve the problems of business management. The way economic analysis can be used towards solving business problems constitutes the subject-matter of Managerial Economics.

The decision making process involves the following steps:

Step 1: Establish the objectives -Identification of objective of the organization is necessary to make a decision. Unless one knows what is to be achieved, there is no sensible way to make a decision.

Step 2: Define the problem – Problem should be clearly stated with all the specifications so as to make right decision. The problem may arise due to firm's planning process or may be prompted by new opportunities.

Step 3 : Identification of alternatives -Once the problem is defined, possible courses of action should be identified. After addressing the question, "What do we want?", it is natural to ask, "What are our options?" The decision maker should identify the factors which are under his control and the constraints that limit his choice.

Step 4 : Selection of best alternative -Having identified the set of alternative possible solutions, revenues and costs associated with each course of action should be estimated and stated. Then the best possible alternative should be selected, taking into consideration the goals of the firm.

Step 5: Implement the decision -Once an alternative is chosen, it must be implemented in order to be effective.

Basic characteristics of managerial economics are

- It is concerned with 'decision making of an economic nature'
- It is micro-economic in character
- It largly uses the economic concepts and principles of 'theory of the firm'
- It is goal oriented and prescriptive
- It is both conceptual and metrical

Scope of Managerial Economics

From the point of view of a firm, managerial economics, can be defined as the economics applied to the allocation of resources available to a firm or a unit of management among the activities of that unit. An analysis of scarcity of resources and choice making poses three basic questions which managerial economics provides answers for so as to help management of a firm to make rational decisions. The three questions are:

Q.1. What to produce and how much to produce?
Q.2. How to produce?
Q.3. For whom to produce?

The first question relates to what goods and services should be produced and in what quantities. Demand theory guides the manager in the selection of goods and services for production. It analyses consumer behaviour with regard to:

- Type of goods and service which they are likely to purchase in the current period and in the future,
- Goods and services which they may stop consuming,
- Factors influencing the consumption of a particular good or service, and
- The effect of a change in these factors on the demand of that particular good or Service.

A detailed study of these aspects of consumer behaviour help the manager to make product decision. If firms decide to launch new goods and services or stop providing a particular good or service, methods of demand forecasting help in deciding the quantity of a good or service to be produced.

How to produce the goods and services is the second basic question. It involves selecting inputs and techniques of production. Decisions are made with regard to the purchase of items ranging from raw materials to capital equipment. Production and cost analysis guides a manager in personnel practices such as hiring and staffing and procurement of inputs. For example, the decision to automate clerical activities using PC network results in a more capital-intensive mode of production. Capital budgeting decisions also constitute an integral part of the second basic question. Allocation of available capital in long-term investment projects can be done through project appraisal method.

Third basic question relates to segmentation of market. A firm has to decide for whom it should produce the goods and services. For example, it has to decide whether to target the domestic market or the foreign market. Production of a premium good is another example of market segmentation. An analysis of market structure explains how price and output decisions are taken under different market forms.

As observed in the above discussion study of managerial economics essentially involves the analysis of certain major subjects like:

- The business firm and its objectives
- Demand analysis, estimation and forecasting
- Production and cost analysis
- Pricing theory and policies
- Profit analysis with special reference to break even point
- Capital budgeting for investment decisions
- Market competition

Demand analysis and forecasting help a manager in the earliest stage in choosing the product and in planning output levels. A study of demand elasticity helps a firm in fixing prices for its product. The theory of cast also forms an essential part of this subject. Estimation is necessary for making output variations with fixed plants or for the purpose of new investments in the same line of production or in a different venture. Theories regarding price determination under various market conditions enable the firm to fix prices for its product. Control of costs, proper pricing policies, break –even analysis, alternative profit policies are some of the important techniques in profit planning for the firm which has to work under conditions of uncertainty. Thus managerial economics with the help of economic tools and techniques tries to find out which course is likely to be the best for the firm under a given set of conditions.

Economic Analysis

Economic activity is a constant effort to satisfy wants with the optimal use of resources available. A firm has to allocate the available resources among various activities of the unit. Resource constraints can be in form of limited supply of men, machines, money and managerial ability. The objective in all the cases has been to maximise the attainment of ends given the means and the priorities. *How* to maximise the output level or to minimize the use of resources, thereby, the cost of production, is regarded as the optimal solution to economic problem.

Decision-making by management is economic in nature because it involves making choices out of available set of alternatives. The optimal decision-making is an act of optimal economic choice, considering objectives to be fulfilled keeping the given constraints in mind. This justifies an evaluation of managerial decision through concepts, percepts, tools and techniques of economic analysis of the following types-

a) Micro and macro analysis: In microanalysis the problem of choice is focused on single individual entity like a producer, a customer, or a market. Macro analysis deals with problems on larger framework like national income, general price level etc.

b) Partial and general equilibrium analysis: In partial equilibrium analysis to attain the state of stable equilibrium, the economic problem is analyses part-by-part one at a time assuming 'other things remaining same'. In general equilibrium analysis the assumption of other things remaining same is relaxed and interdependence or interaction among variables may be allowed.

c) Positive and normative analysis: In positive economic analysis, the problem is analyses in objective terms based on principles and theories i.e. in simple words it means positive analysis is 'what it is'. In normative economic analysis, the problem is analyses based on value judgment (norm) i.e. normative analysis is 'what it should be'.

d) Static, comparative static and dynamic analysis: This analysis is done in reference to time dimension. In this a problem can be analyses

- Allowing no change at a point of time (static)
- Allowing once for all change at a point of time (comparative static)
- Allowing successive changes over a period of time (dynamic)

Basic Economic Tools Used in Managerial Economics

The most significant contribution of economics to managerial economics lies in certain principles, which are basic to

The entire gamut of managerial economics and helps the manager in decision-making process. The basic principles may be identified as:

1. Opportunity cost principle,
2. Incremental principle,
3. Principle of time perspective,
4. Discounting principle, and
5. Equi-marginal principle.

Opportunity Cost Principle

The opportunity cost of a decision means the sacrifice of alternatives required by that decision. This can best be understood with the help of a few examples

a) The opportunity cost of the funds employed in one's own business is the interest that could be earned on those funds had they been employed in other ventures.

b) The opportunity cost of the time an entrepreneur gives to his own business, is the salary he could earn by doing a job in some other company.

c) The opportunity cost of using a machine that is useless for any other purpose is zero since its use requires no sacrifice of other opportunities.

d) If a machine can produce either X or Y. the opportunity cost of producing a given quantity of X is the quantity of Y, which it would have produced. If that machine can produce 10 units of X or 20 units of Y, the opportunity cost of 1X is 2Y.

e) The opportunity cost of holding Rs. 1000 as cash in hand for one year is the, eight percent rate of Interest, which would have been earned had the money been kept as fixed deposit in a bank.

For decision-making, opportunity costs are the only relevant costs. The opportunity cost principle may be stated as: *The cost involved in any decision consists of the sacrifices of alternatives required by that decision. If there are no sacrifices, there* is no cost.

Points to Remember

1. The opportunity costs of a given sum of money can never be zero.

2. Decisions that involve choice must involve opportunity cost calculation.

3.Opportunity costs may be either real or monetary, either implicit or explicit, either Quantifiable or non-quantifiable.

4. Economist's different concepts of trade off such as Indifference curves, Isoquants, Phillips Curve are all an opportunity cost reasoning.

5. Opportunity cost concept is directly applicable to manager's different decision areas such as make or buy decision, breakdown or preventive maintenance of machines, replacement or new investment decision, direct recruitment from outside or departmental promotion to man a post.

6. Minimization of opportunity costs should be the decision principle of a manager for optimal allocation of resources, given his objectives and constraints.

7. The accountant always considers the explicit costs only and never considers opportunity Costs.

8. If there is unutilized plant capacity , or if workers do not have sufficient work to engage them for requisite number of hours, the opportunity cost of unutilized plant capacity (or workers) is zero.

Incremental Principle

Incremental concept is closely related to marginal costs and marginal revenues. Incremental concept involves estimating the impact of decision alternatives on costs and revenues, emphasizing the changes in total cost and total revenue resulting from changes in prices, products, procedures, investments or whatever may be at stake in the decision. The two basic components of incremental reasoning are: Incremental cost and incremental revenue. Incremental cost may be defined as the change in total cost resulting from a particular decision. Incremental revenue is the change in total revenue resulting from a particular decision. For instance, if a firm decides to go for computerization of market information, the additional revenue it earns will be termed incremental revenue and the extra cost of setting up computer facilities will be termed incremental cost. The incremental principle may be stated as : *"A decision is obviously a profitable one if- (i) it increases revenue more than costs, (ii) it decreases some costs to a greater extent than it increases others,(iii) it increases some revenues more than it decreases others, and (iv) it reduces costs more than revenues."*

Some businessmen are of the view that to make an overall profit, they must make a profit on every job. The result is that they refuse orders that do not cover full cost (labour, materials and overhead) plus a provision for profit. Incremental reasoning indicates that this rule may be inconsistent with profit maximization in the short run.

A refusal to accept business below full cost may mean rejection of a possibility of adding more to revenue than to cost. The relevant cost is not the full cost but rather the incremental cost.

Principle of Time Perspective

The principle of time perspective may be stated as: *"A decision should take into account both the short-run and long-run effects on revenues and costs and maintain the right balance between the long-run and short-run perspectives."*

Managerial economists are concerned with the short-run and long run effects of decisions on revenues as well as costs. A significant problem in decision-making is to maintain the right balance between the long run and the short-run considerations. A decision may be made on the basis of short-run considerations, but as time elapses it may have long-run repercussions, which make it more or less profitable than it first appeared to be. *For example*:

Suppose there is a firm with temporary idle capacity. An order for 5,000 units comes to management's attention. The customer is willing to pay As. 4.00 per unit or Rs. 20,000 for the whole lot but no more The short-run incremental cost (ignoring the fixed cost) is only Rs 3.00 Therefore, the contribution to overhead and profit is Rs 1.00 per unit (Rs 5,000 for the lot).

Analysis of the problem

Following long-run repercussions of the order ought to be taken into account as well.

1. If the management commits itself with too much of business at lower prices or with a small contribution, it may not have sufficient capacity to take up business with higher contributions when the opportunity arises.The management may be compelled to consider the question of .expansion of capacity and in such cases, even the so-called fixed costs may become variable.

2. If other customers come to know about this low price, they may demand a similar low price. Such customers may complain of being treated unfairly and feel discriminated against. The reduction of prices under conditions of excess capacity may adversely affect the image of the company in the minds of its clientele ultimately affecting its sales.

Discounting Principle

One of the fundamental ideas in economics is that a rupee tomorrow is worth less than a rupee today. Following example would make this point clear .Suppose a person is offered a choice to make between a gift of Rs. 100 today or Rs. 100 next year. Naturally he will choose the Rs. 100 today. This is true for two reasons. *First,* the future is uncertain and there may be uncertainty in getting Rs. 100 if the present opportunity is not availed of. *Secondly,* even if he is sure to receive the gift in future, today's Rs. 100 can be invested so as to earn interest say, at 6 per cent so that one year after the Rs. 100 of today will become Rs. 106 whereas if he does not accept Rs. 100 today, he will get Rs. 100 only one year hence. Naturally. he would prefer the first alternative because he is likely to gain by Rs. 6 in future. Another way of saying the same thing is that Rs. 100 one year hence is not equal to Rs. 100 of today but less than that. But then how much money today is equal to Rs. 100 one year hence? To find it out, we shall have to find out the relevant rate of interest which one would earn if one decides to invest the money. Suppose the rate of interest is 6 per cent. Then we shall have to discount Rs. 100 at 6 per cent in order to ascertain how much money today will become Rs. 100 one year after. The formula is:

$$V = \frac{\text{Rs.}100}{1+i}$$

where V = present value

i = rate of interest

Now, applying the formula, we get

$$V = \frac{\text{Rs.}100}{1+i} = \frac{100}{1.06} = \text{Rs } 94.33$$

As a cross-check, if we multiply Rs. 94.33 by 1.06, we shall get the money which will accumulate at 6 per cent after one year:

94.33 x 1.06 = 99.98= Rs. 100

The same reasoning applies to longer periods. A sum of Rs. 100 two years from now is worth

$$V = \frac{Rs.100}{(1+i)^2} = \frac{Rs.100}{(1.06)^2} = \frac{Rs.100}{1.1236} = Rs.\ 88.99$$

The principle involved in the foregoing discussion can be called the discounting principle and may be stated as : *"If a decision affects costs and revenues at future dates, it is necessary to discount those costs and revenues to present values before a valid comparison of alternatives is possible."*

Equi-marginal principle

This principle deals with the allocation of the available resources among the alternative activities. According to this principle an input should be so allocated that the value added by the last unit is the same in all cases. This generalization is called the equi-marginal principle.

Suppose a firm has 100 units of labour at its disposal. The firm is engaged in four activities, which need labour services *viz* A, B, C and *D*. It can increase any one of these activities by adding more labour, but only at the cost of other activities.

It should be clear that if the value of the marginal product is higher in one activity than another, an optimum allocation has not been attained. It would, therefore. be profitable to shift labour from low marginal value activity to high marginal value activity, thus increasing the total value of all products taken together. To take an example. if in activity , the value of marginal product of labour is Rs. 20 while that in activity *B,* it is Rs. 30, is profitable to shift labour from activity *A* to activity *B* thereby expanding activity *B* and reducing activity *A.* The optimum will be reached when the value of the marginal product is equal in all the four activities or, symbolically expressed when

$$VMP_{LA} = VMP_{LB} = VMP_{LC} = VMP_{LD}$$

whereby, the subscripts indicate labour in respective activities.

Certain aspects of the equi-marginal principle need clarification.

1) The values of marginal products are net of incremental costs. In activity B we may add one unit of labour with an increase in physical output of 100 units. Each unit is worth 50 paise so that the 100 units will sell for Rs. 50. But the increased output consumes raw materials, fuel and other inputs so that variable costs in activity B (not counting the labour cost) are higher. Let us say that the incremental costs are Rs. 30 leaving a net addition of Rs. 20. The value of the marginal product relevant for our purpose is thus Rs. 20.

2) If the revenues resulting from the addition of labour are to occur in future, these revenues ought to be discounted before comparisons in the alternative activities are possible. Activity A may produce revenue immediately but activities B, C and D may take 2, 3 and 5 years respectively. Here the discounting of these revenues will render them comparable.

3) The measurement of the value of the marginal product may have to be corrected if the expansion of an activity requires a reduction in the prices of the output. If activity B represents the production of radios and it is not possible to sell more radios without a reduction in price, it is necessary to make adjustment for the fall in price.

4) The equi-marginal principle may break under sociological pressures. For instance, due to inertia, activities are continued simply because they exist. Again, motivated by empire building, managers may keep on expanding activities to fulfill their ambition for power. Departments which are already over budgeted often use some of their excess resources to build up propaganda machines (public relation offices) to win additional support. Governmental agencies are more prone to bureaucratic self-perpetuation and inertia.

Table: Business Application of equi- marginal principle

Multi-market seller	$MR_1 = MR_2 = MR_3 = \ \ldots MR_n$
Multi-plant monopolist	$MC_1 = MC_2 = MC_3 = \ \ldots MC_n$
Multi-factor employer	$MP_1 = MP_2 = MP_3 = \ \ldots MP_n$
Multi-product firm	$M\pi_1 = M\pi_2 = M\pi_3 = \ \ldots M\pi_n$

Note: MR= Marginal revenue, MC= Marginal Costs, MP = Marginal Products and Mπ = Marginal Profits

n refers to n markets, plants, factors and products respectively.

Points to remember

1. **Managerial economics deals with** " how decisions should be made by managers to achieve the firm's goals - in particular, how to maximize profit" (Also government agencies and nonprofit institutions benefit from knowledge of economics.)

2. **What is managerial economics?**
   - Managerial economics is the application of microeconomic tools and techniques to the key decisions firms need to make e.g pricing, output, investment and advertising.
   - Managerial economics is the application of economic theory and methodology to business administration practice.
   - Managerial economics is use of economic analysis in the formulation of business policies

3. **Why Managerial Economics?**
   - ➤ Managerial economics organizes information for decisions
   - ➤ Managerial economics leads to better understanding of a company's environment
   - ➤ Managerial economics deals with the role of business in a market economy
4. **Management Decision Problems**
   - a) Product Price and Output
   - b) Make or Buy
   - c) Production Technique
   - d) Stock Levels
   - e) Advertising Media and Intensity
   - f) Labor Hiring and Training
   - g) Investment and Financing
5. **Economic Tools in managerial economics**
   - a) Opportunity cost principle
   - b) Incremental principle
   - c) Principle of time perspective
   - d) Discounting principle
   - e) Equi-marginal principle
6. **The Three Basic Economic Questions: What, How, and For Whom?**

   From the standpoint of a country:
   - ➤ What goods and services should be produced and in what quantities?
   - ➤ How should these goods and services be produced?
   - ➤ For whom should these goods and services be produced?
7. **The Three Basic Economic Questions: What, How, and For Whom?**

   From the standpoint of a company:
   - ➤ The product decision (what)
   - ➤ The hiring, staffing, procurement and capital-budgeting decisions (how)
   - ➤ The market segmentation decision (whom)
8. **There are essentially three ways or processes to answer these questions:**

   Market process: let supply, demand and material incentives (=profit motive) answer the three basic questions

Command process: let government or some other central authority answer the three basic questions

Traditional process: let customs and traditions answer the three basic questions

Questions

1. Discuss the nature and scope of managerial economics.
2. Explain how managerial economics is economics applied in decision-making.
3. "Managerial economies is the integration of economic theory with business practice for the purpose of facilitating decision-making and forward planning by manager". Explain and comment.
4. Discuss the various economic tools and techniques used in managerial economics. What is managerial economics? How does it differ from traditional economics?
5. Discuss the nature and scope of economics in relation to business.
6. "Managerial economics is the integration of economic theory with business practice for the purpose of facilitating decision-making and forward planning by management." Explain.
7. "Managerial. economics is the discipline which deals with the application of economic theory to business management." Discuss.
8. Distinguish between macro economics and micro-economics. How is macro-economics useful in managerial decision-making?
9. Show the significance of economic analysis in business decisions.
10. "Economic theory and the theory of decision-making appear to be in conflict, each based on a different set of assumptions. Which theory shall we choose? It is unnecessary to make a black and white choice. Managerial economics is useful in the choice of better decisions." Discuss the statement.
11. Discuss the application of basic economic theory to the practical problem of a business firm.
12. 'Managerial Economics' is prescriptive rather than descriptive in character? Examine this statement.
13. "Managerial economics is the study of the allocation of resources available to a firm or other unit of management among the activities of that unit." Explain.

14. "Managerial economics is economics applied in decision-making." Explain.

15. "Managerial economics is the discipline which deals with the application of economic theory to business management." Also point out how managerial economics differs from economics.

16. "Managerial economics is a special branch of economics bridging the gap between abstract theory and managerial practice. Its stress is on the use of the tools of economic analysis in clarifying problems, in organising and evaluating information and in comparing alternative courses of action." Comment on the statement.

2

Business Objectives and Models of the Firm

Introduction

Managerial economics is the application of microeconomics tools and techniques to the key decisions firms need to make eg. Pricing, output, investment and advertising. Therefore its important for a manager to know what a firm is, what are its functions and objectives, the structure of the industry within which the firm is located (the number of firms in competition, the nature of competition, etc). Knowledge of objectives of a firm helps the manager in decision-making process and in profit maximization. A manager has to make rational decision in face of constraints due to scarcity of resources. Thus a well-defined and clear statement of goal of a firm would help him produce efficiently and maximise profit.

A **firm** is an organisation that produces a good or service for sale. Most of the firm's attempts to make a profit with an exception of a few like NGO' s, which are non, profit making firms working for social welfare. Firms can be classified on the basis of number of owners, investment limits and participation of government in business. Classification of firms differs from country to country depending upon their individual company laws. Broadly firms are classified as follows:

- Proprietorship (owned individually),
- Partnership (owned by two or more individuals) and corporations (owned by stockholders)
- **Public sector, private sector and joint sector**

The firm changes hired inputs into saleable output. An input is defined as anything that the firm has used in its production process. The inputs are divisible into two categories

1) Human resources which includes labour resource and entrepreneurial resource

2) Capital resources, which include land, man, made capital etc.

Thus the four major factors of production are land, man made capital, labour and entrepreneur (organisation) while the remuneration they get is rent, interest on capital, wage and profit.

The function of a firm is to buy inputs or factors of production like labouring services, capital and raw material and converting them into goods and services for sale. Individuals and firms are highly interdependent therefore there exist a circular flow of economic activity between them.

Firms can not keep on producing goods unless there is demand for them in the market similarly labour has no value in the market unless there is a firm willing to pay for it .

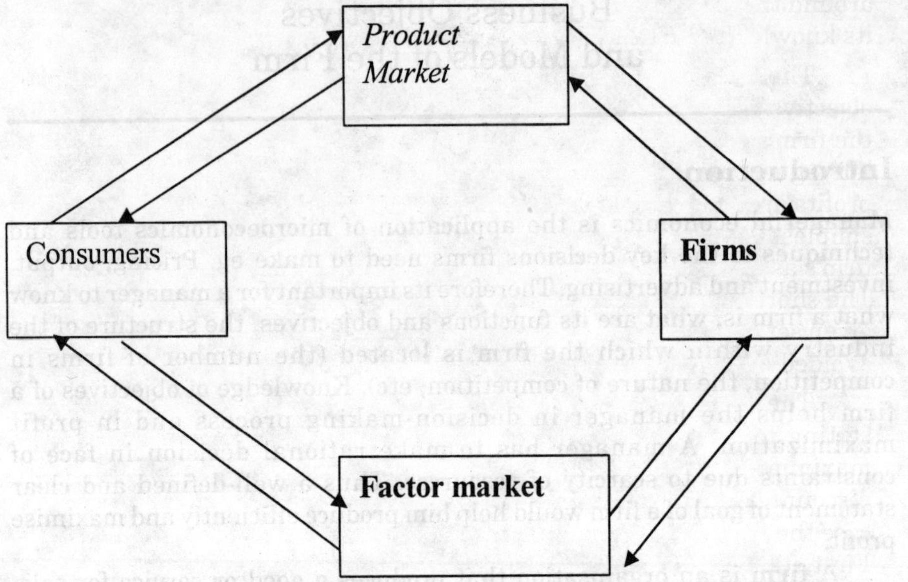

Rationale for the existence of a firm is firstly it lowers transaction cost as entrepreneurs enter into long term contracts with labour and to perform a number of task for a specific wage and doesn't have to make a new contract for every new task assigned to labour at each step of production process. Similarly long term contracts are made with owners of other factors of production.Secondly a firm exist to internalise transaction costs. Sales tax is imposed on transaction done between firms and not transaction within a firm . A firm can save sales tax and reduce its total cost of production by performing many functions within firm eg .a construction company can hire a carpenter to make wooden racks instead of buying it from some other company.

However, the size of the company has to be limited because cost of internal transaction becomes equal or greater than the cost of transaction between firms as a firm grow larger. Also the cost of services like lawyers and medical facilities (which are needed occasionally) within the firm exceeds the cost of purchasing these facilities from other firms which has expertise in these. Manager's ability to control the firm is also limited therefore if a firm grows larger effective allocation of resources also becomes difficult thus company could face internal disadvantages of larger size. To fulfil the quest of a firm to grow further few big companies have recognise the problem of large size and decentralise by establishing a number of separate divisions or profit centres that act as individual firms.

The Neo-classical Economical Model of the Firm

The orthodox, neo-classical or traditional model assumes profit maximisation as the only objective pursued by the firm. This model centres around three basic sets of assumptions concerning the aim of the firm, and its knowledge of the cost and demand conditions.

The first component of orthodox model is the assumption that the objective of the firm is to maximise profits,defined as the difference between the firm's revenues and its costs. In this simple form the assumption is a bit vague because it makes no reference to the period of time over which profits are to be maximised. This may be resolved in one of two ways. The simplest is to see the model as a one-period or short-run model, where the firm's assumed aim is to make as much profit as possible in the short-run. The short-run is defined as the period in which the firm is restricted to a given set of plant and equipment and has some fixed costs which cannot be avoided even by ceasing production.

The slightly more complex version which establishes a multiperiod setting for the model is to assume that the objective of the firm is to maximise the wealth of its shareholders, which in turn is equal to the discounted value of the expected future net cash flows into firm. In this case the firm can be thought of facing two inter-related kinds of decisions. First, it has to take long run or investment decision on the level of capacity and the type of plant it wishes to install. Second, it has to decide upon the most profitable use of that set of plant and equipment. These short run, capacity utilisation, decisions are essentially the same as those facing the firm maximising profits in the short run, and the same analysis applies. The value of the firm or wealth is given by

$$PV = \frac{\pi_1}{(1+r)} + \frac{\pi_2}{(1+r)^2} + \ldots\ldots + \frac{\pi_n}{(1+r)^n} = \frac{\Sigma \pi_t}{(1+r)^t}$$

where t=1,2,........n

where PV is the present value of all expected profits of the firm, π_1, π_2,.....π_n is the expected profits in each of the n years considered, and r is the appropriate discount rate used to find the present value of future profits.

The assumption of profit maximisation gives the basic model of the firm a number of characteristics, which distinguish it from other models. In the first place, it identifies the model which is 'holistic' in the sense that, however large and complex, the firm is seen as a single entity which can be said to have objectives of its own which can be said to take decision. This in mark contrast to the 'behavioural' model of the firm, where it is argued that 'only people can have objectives, organisations cannot', and the 'managerialist' model where it is agued that managers and shareholders have different and conflicting objectives. The second characteristic of the model is that it is an 'optimising' model, where the firm is seen as attempting to achieve the best possible performance, rather than simply seeking 'feasible' performance which meets some set of minimum criteria.

The second component of the traditional model of the firm concerns the nature of firm's production and the behaviour of costs. The firm is assumed to produce a single, perfectly divisible, standardised product for which the cost of production is known with certainty. In the short run, when costs are fixed, the average cost curve will be U-shaped as shown in the figure 2.1 below. Cost per unit falls over the range A to B as the fixed costs are spread over a larger number of units, but begins to rise beyond B as the principle of diminishing returns leads to increasing variable costs per unit.

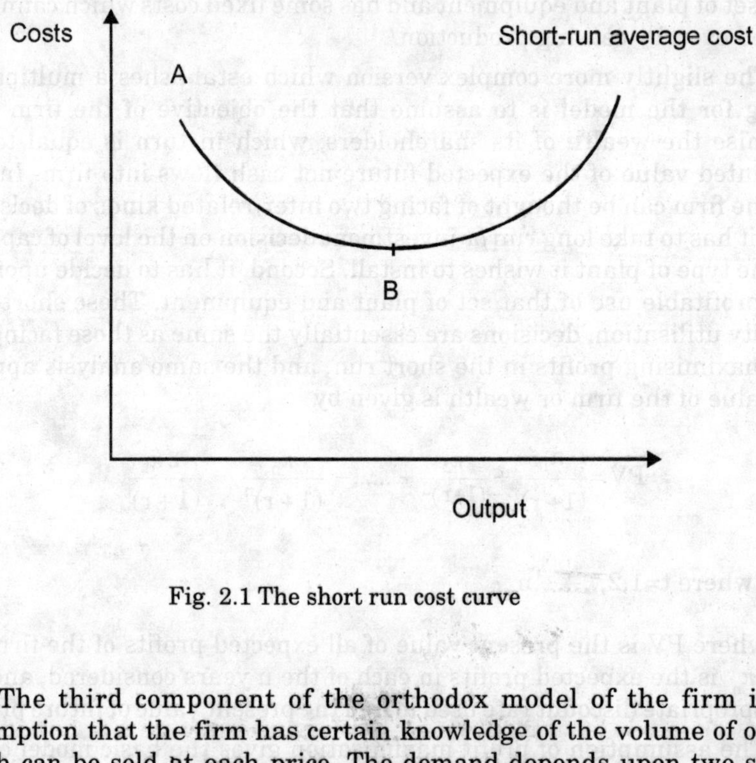

Fig. 2.1 The short run cost curve

The third component of the orthodox model of the firm is the assumption that the firm has certain knowledge of the volume of output which can be sold at each price. The demand depends upon two sets of factors first, it depend upon the behaviour of the consumers, which determines the total demand of the product. Second. It depends upon the structure of the industry in which the firm is operating, and the behaviour of rival sellers. The simplest example is that of the monopolist, where there is only one supplier of the product. In that case consumer demand of the product can only be met by the single firm in the industry and there is no distinction between the total demand for the product and the demand for the individual firm. There is only one demand curve for the firm and the industry. The shape of that curve depends upon the nature of the product, the number of consumers in the market and their incomes, wealth and tastes.

The mathematical formulation is :

Maximise \$ (q)
where \$ (q) = R (q) – C (q)
where \$ (q) = profit
R (q) = revenue
C (q) = costs
q = units of output sold

Profit would be maximised if following conditions hold

1. $d\$ / dq = dR / dq - dC / dq = 0$ or $dR / dq = dC / dq$
2. $d^2R / dq^2 > d^2C / dq^2$

In words above two conditions can be stated as, profit will be maximum if the firm produces the level of output such that marginal revenue (dR/dq)equals marginal cost (dC/ dq) and when the slope of the marginal cost curve exceeds the slope of the marginal revenue curve.

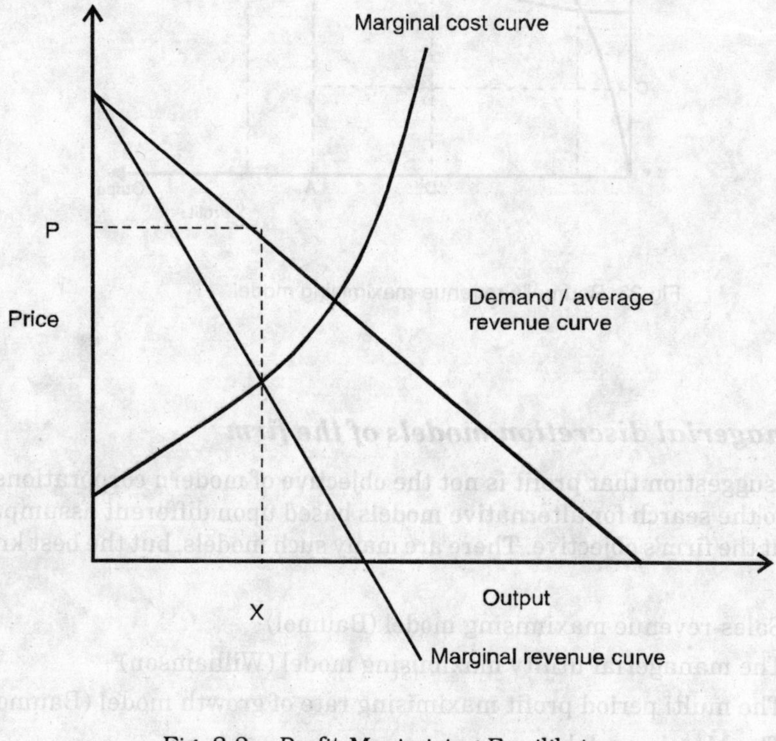

Fig. 2.2. : Profit-Maximising Equilibrium

It will pay the firm to produce any unit of output for which the extra revenue earned (marginal revenue) exceeds the extra cost (marginal cost). In the figure 2.2 at level of output X which is also profit maximising level of output all such units are produced. If output is increased further, the additional units produced will add more to costs than to the revenues, and the level of profit will fall. The diagram and the equations set out above identify the profit maximising equilibrium for the firm. In the short run, under the assumptions made, the firm will produce the indicated level of output and sell it at the indicated price. If cost and demand conditions remain the same, the firm has no incentive to alter its price or output, and the firm is said to be in equilibrium.

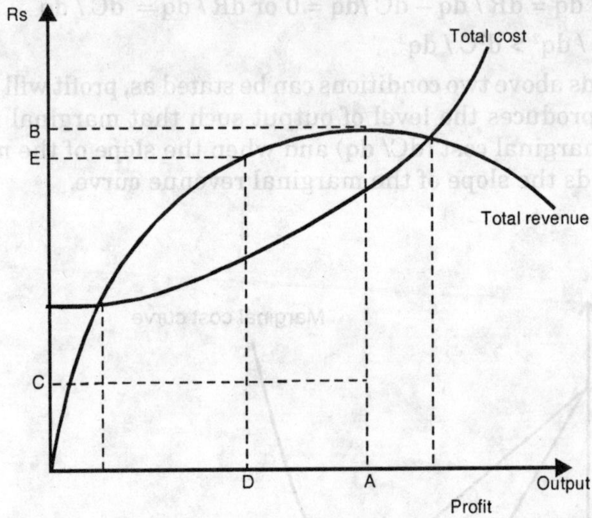

Fig 23: Baumol's revenue-maximising model

Managerial discretion models of the firm

The suggestion that profit is not the objective of modern corporations has led to the search for alternative models based upon different assumptions about the firm's objective. There are many such models, but the best known are:

1. Sales-revenue maximising model (Baumol)
2. The managerial utility maximising model (Williamson)
3. The multi period profit maximising rate of growth model (Baumol)
4. The Marris model

Baumol's sales revenue-maximising model

Baumol's model stems from the observation that the salaries of managers, their status and other rewards often linked to the size of the companies in which they work, measured by sales revenue, than to their profitability. Therefore managers are more concerned to increase size than to increase profits, and the firm's objective will be to maximise sales revenue rather than profits. In many respects sales revenue maximisation model shares fundamental characteristics with profit maximisation model, as it is also an optimising model in whicha single product firm aims for a single objective, having perfect information about its cost and demand conditions. The figure below shows the basic version of model, using total revenue, total cost and profit curves.

In figure, the firm will choose to produce level of output A, giving total revenue B and profit C. This implies a higher level of output, and therefore a lower price, than the equivalent profit-maximiser, which would produce output D and earn revenue E. A straight forward revenue maximiser will always produce more and charge less than a profit-maximising firm facing the same cost and demand conditions for the following reasons:

- for revenue maximisation marginal revenue = 0
- for profit maximisation marginal revenue = marginal cost
- as marginal cost must be greater than 0, then for a profit maximiser marginal revenue must be greater than 0.
- therefore marginal revenue for a profit maximiser must be greater than marginal revenue for a revenue maximiser.
- as marginal revenue slopes downwards to the right, equilibrium output must be higher for a revenue maximiser than for the profit maximiser.

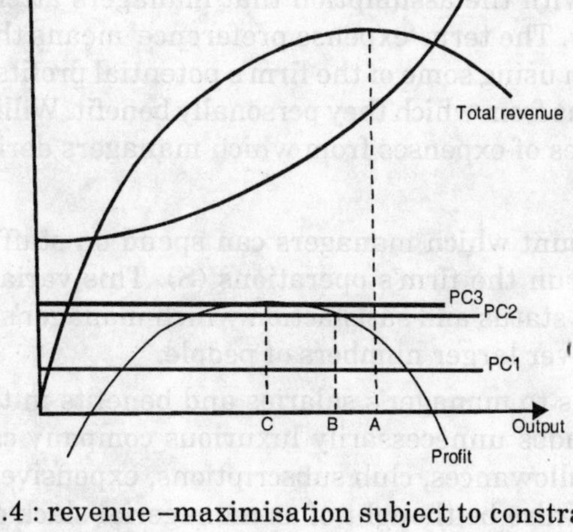

Fig 2.4 : revenue –maximisation subject to constraints

As can be seen in figure, the sales maximiser will also make some profit. However, this may not be enough to satisfy the shareholders, and in many cases maximisingrevenue may imply making losses. As a result the simple revenue maximising model is implausible, and the model needs to be amended to include a profit constraint. Instead of simply assuming that the firm aims for maximum revenue, without regard to the implications for profit, it is assumed that the objective is the maximisation of sales revenue, subject to meeting a minimum profit constraint as shown in diagram below

There are three possible cases in this amended version of the model. The first is where the profit constraint is shown by line PC1. At the level of output which maximises revenue enough profit is made to satisfy the shareholders. The second case is where the profit constraint is shown by PC2. In this case, at the revenue maximising level of output, insufficient profit is made to satisfy the shareholders and output is reduced until that constraint is met, at level of output B. The third case is where the minimum profit required to satisfy the shareholders is equal to the maximum profit which can be made, in which case the firm has to reduce its output to C. In third case, the firm behaves in exactly the same way with respect to its output and price as a profit maximiser, despite the fact that it has set itself a different objective. If shareholders insist upon the maximum level of profit being earned, then profit maximising model will provide accurate predictions of the behaviour of a firm whose management prefer to maximise sales revenue. If the purpose of the model is to predict the firm's behaviour the fact that managers see their aim as maximising sales revenue, and not profit, is irrelevant. The firm behaves like a profit maximiser.

The managerial utility maximising model

Williamson's managerial utility maximising model takes into account a wider range of variables by introducing the concept of 'expense preferences' and beginning with the assumption that managers attempt to maximise their own utility. The term 'expense preference' means that managers get satisfaction from using some of the firm's potential profits for unnecessary spending on items from which they personally benefit. Williamson identified three major types of expenses from which managers derive utility, which are:

1. The amount which managers can spend on staff, over and above those neede to run the firm's operations (S). This variable captures the power, prestige, status and satisfaction which manager's experience from having control over larger numbers of people.

2. Additions to manager's salaries and benefits in the form of perks (M). These includes unnecessarily luxurious company cars, extravagant entertainment allowances, club subscriptions, expensive office buildings. Such items may also be thought of as managerial slack or X-inefficiency.

They appear as costs to the firm, but are not necessary for the efficient conduct of its activities and are infact coming out of profits.

3. Discretionary profits (D). These are after-tax profits over and above the minimum required to satisfy the shareholders. They are therefore available to managers as a source of finance for projects and allow the managers to invest in developing the firm in direction which suit them, enhancing their power, status and satisfaction.

The basic form of the model is as follows:

U = f (S, M, D) – managerial utility (U) depends upon the levels of S, M and D available to managers.

With the utility theory of consumer behaviour it is also assumed that the principle of diminishing marginal utility applies, so that additional increment to each of S,M and D yield smaller increment of utility to the management.

If R= revenue, C= costs and T = taxes then

Actual profit = R-C-S

Reported profit = R- C- S- M

If the minimum post-tax profit required by the shareholders is Z, then:

D= R-C-S-M-T-Z

The solution to the model uses calculas in order to maximise the utility function. If managerial utility is to be maximised, the last rupee spent on S,M and D must yield the same marginal utility i.e.

$MU_S = MU_M = MU_D(1-t)$ where t is the rate of tax on profits.

If demand declines, then at every level of output D will decline. On the assumption of diminishing marginal utility, MU_D will rise, so that the equilibrium condition is no longer fulfilled. To regain equilibrium the available profits wiil be redistributed towards D and away from S and M. The level of output will fall. Similarly for a rise in fixed costs, or a lump-sum tax. If the tax on profits increases then $MU_D(1-t)$ will fall and so there will be a shift towards S and M, accompanied by increasing output.

The profit-maximising rate of growth model

Both the models given above are static as they give no reference to developments over time and the equilibria identified involves sales, profits and utilities remaining constant unless preferences or outside circumstances change. In addition to such static models there are a range of dynamic models which consider growth over time in multi –period setting.

One such model is profit- maximising rate of sales growth model, developed by Baumol. In this analysis the aim of the firm is to maximise the present value of expected future profits, which is simply the difference between the present value of expected future revenues and the present value of expected future costs, as shown in figure 2.5 below.

The present value of costs (PVC) is made up of two components. First there are costs of producing output, including both the fixed and variable costs of operation. Secondly, there are the costs associated with expansion, especially those concerning the development of a management team capable of controlling a larger organisation, and those involving raising a finance.

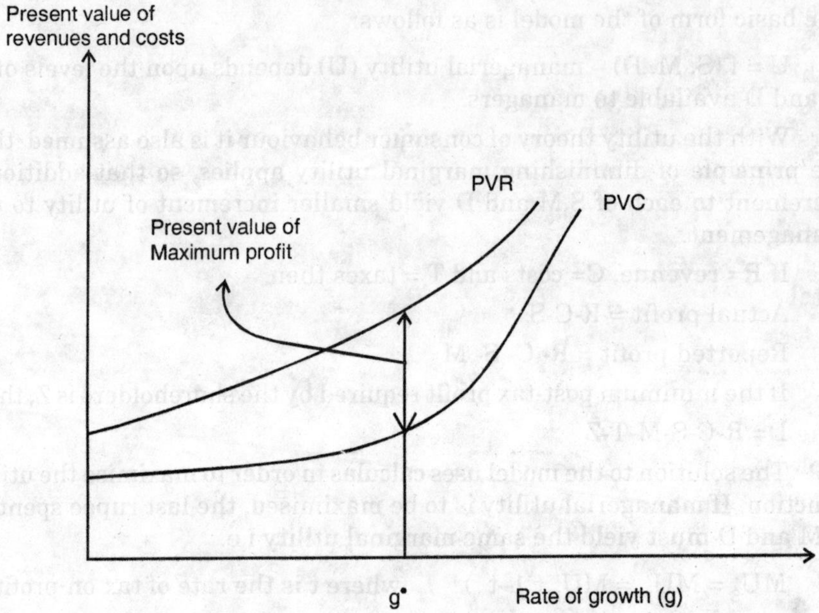

While the costs of production may rise proportionately with growth it is assumed that expansion costs will rise more than proportionately as the growth rate rises, so that PVC has the shape as in the figure, becoming increasingly steep.

The curve showing the present value of expected future revenues will also tend to be upwards sloping, with an increasing slope. Whatever the discount rate used to calculate present values, the present value of future revenues will be larger as the growth rate of sales volume is larger. A relatively simple mathematical manipulation will show that the slope of the line increases with the growth rate.

Here, the decision variable is not the level of output, but the growth rate of output, selected in order to maximise the present value of future profits, given by rate of growth g*, where the vertical distance between the revenue and cost curves is at its greatest.

The Marris model

The Marris model is also dynamic in that it concerns growth rates, but it shares the basic assumption of the Williamson model that managers aim to maximise their utility. In this model it is assumed that managers utility depends upon the rate of growth of the firm instead of utility from expense preference. While growth is their main aim, managers are also motivated by the need for job security, which depends upon the satisfaction of the shareholders, who are assumed to be wealth –maximisers concerned to keep share prices and dividends as high as possible. Growth and profitability are therefore the key variables in this model.

Growth in the Marris model is assumed to take place through diversification into new products, rather than an increase in the output of existing products, and the relationship between growth and profitability has two dimensions. First, there is the 'supply-growth' dimension where growth is a function of profits. A higher level of profits provides more funds directly for reinvestment and also allows more funds to be raised on the capital markets and therefore allows a higher rate of growth to be funded. This gives a direct and positive relationship between growth and profits, shown in figure above as a straight line.

Secondly, there is the 'demand-growth' relationship which operates in the other direction, with growth determining profits. This is more complex. As growth consists of diversification into new products the links between profits and growth are seen as different at different levels of growth. At low levels of growth it is argued that the relationship is a positive one, with more growth providing more profits. At these levels it is argued that the firm will be introducing the most profitable new products from those which are possible and managers will be motivated to be more efficient by more growth. However, as the growth rate increases, with ever greater diversification, the relationship changes and becomes negative. The management team has to cope with increasing burdens, including the development of a larger management team, the higher rate of diversification can only be maintained by proportionately higher expenditures on advertising and research and development. As a result, beyond a certain growth rate, higher growth leads to lower profitability. The resulting relationship is shown in the figure below. As both the supply-growth and demand growth relationship must be satisfied, the combination of growth and profitability, which the firm achieves, must be where the two curves intersect, at point X.

In the figure 2.6 the combination of profitability and growth chosen is not one where profits are maximised. The manager's desire for growth, from which they gain utility, has encouraged them to seek more growth than is consistent with profit-maximisation. However, the extent to which they do this depends upon the strength of their desire for job security, which may be threatened if the shareholders feel that their wealth is not being maximised and if there is an active threat of take-over by other firms.

This will affect the position of the 'supply-growth' relationship, through the retention ratio and the price of the firm's shares.

If the retention ratio is very low, so that nearly all profits are distributed to the shareholders, then at every level of profitability, growth will be low, as there is limited finance for expansion. The supply-growth curve will be very steep, as shown by SG1 in the figure. The equilibrium of the firm will be at a point like A, where less than maximum profit is earned and growth is relatively low. As the retention ratio rises, the supply-growth curve becomes flatter as more growth can be financed from retained earnings at each level of profitability. As a result, as the retention ratio rises, so does the equilibrium combination of growth and profitability until

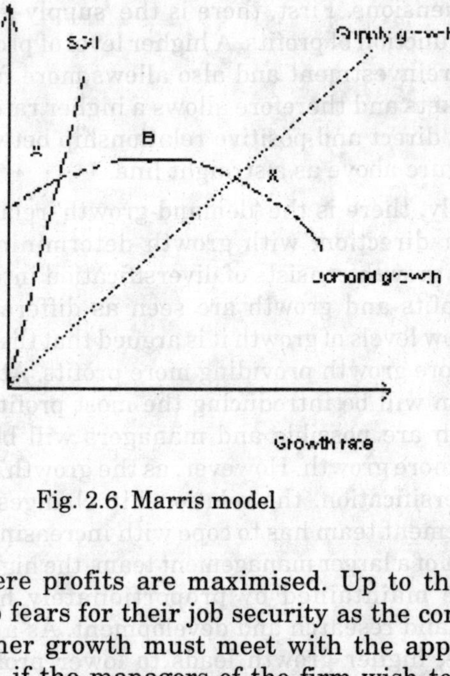

Fig. 2.6. Marris model

it reaches point B where profits are maximised. Up to this point the managers need have no fears for their job security as the combination of higher profits and higher growth must meet with the approval of the shareholders. However, if the managers of the firm wish to adopt even higher retention ratios, giving even higher growth then they need to pay careful attention to the impact on the wealth of the shareholders. A further increase in retentions will reduce dividends because profits will be lower and the proportion of those distributed in dividends will be lower. In so far as share prices are determined by both dividends and the firm's growth rate it will probably be possible to go some way beyond point B without the firm's share price beginning to fall. However, at some point the effect of still higher retentions, creating an even flatter supply-growth curve and yet lower profits and dividends will be to reduce the share price and the value of shareholder's wealth, rendering the firm vulnerable to take-over and threatening the job security of the incumbent management. The actual position of the supply-growth curve will depend upon how real the threat of take-over is perceived to be and the relative preferences of managers for job security and growth. If the threat of take –over is perceived to be very powerful, and managers place a high value on the job security then they will not push the firm beyond the point where shareholder's wealth and the share price is maximised. However, if the threat of take-over is perceived to be weak, and managers place a high value on growth relative to job security, they will adopt retentions policies which give higher growth and lower profits than those which would be optimal for the shareholders.

The behavioural model of the firm

'Behavioural' criticisms of models of the rum

The 'managerial' models of the firm stem from criticism of the profit-maximising assumption, on the grounds that in an era when ownership and control are separate and many firms compete in relatively comfortable oligopolistic market structure managers are able to direct the resources of companies towards their own ends.In many other respects the managerial models share similar characteristics with the orthodox textbook model of the firm. It is assumed that the firm is a single entity being capable of having objectives, even if these are held by a group of managers and the firm is seen as taking and implementing decisions. The models outlined above are all optimising models and it is also assumed that the firm has certain knowledge of the cost and demand conditions facing it. In many respects the managerial model differ from the orthodox only in that they begin with a different assumption with respect to the firm's objective.

A much more radical attack on the orthodox model of the firm, which also implies criticism of the managerial models, has been made by a group of theorists referred to as the 'behavioural school', building on seminal work by Simon, Cyert and March . In this approach attention focuses on behaviour within the firm, which is not seen as a single entity, but as a set of shifting coalitions among individuals, each of which has their own set of objectives. The fundamental argument is that organisations cannot have objectives, only people can, and that to perceive a firm as having an objective is an example of 'reification', confusing an abstract concept with a real entity.

In addition to rejecting the notion that a firm can have objectives, the behaviour theorists also reject the assumption that those taking decisions are perfectly informed. The assumption of certainty is abandoned and emphasis is placed on the idea that most organisations are so complex that the individuals within them have only limit information with respect to both internal and external developments.

The behavioural alternative

The behavioural model of the firm is therefore very different from either the orthodox model or the managerial models. It is not a 'holistic' model in that the firm is not seen as a single entity. It is not an optimising model where the firm achieves the best possible performance with respect to its objective, and it is not based upon the assumption of certainty. In place of these features of the other models it contains a number of key elements.

First, the 'firm' hardly exists, consisting as it does of a group of individuals who form coalitions and alliances amongst themselves based upon common interests or characteristics, departmental loyalties or simple personal affinity. As a result the firm has multiple objectives which are in conflict with each other and which cannot be reconciled through a concept like the utility function, which gives a weight to each objective and allows an overall 'score' to be achieved. The accountants in a firm may wish to keep the level of stocks down in order to reduce the costs of holding them. At the same time the sales force may wish to hold a high level of stocks in order to be able to meet orders quickly. The research department may wish to employ a large number of qualified scientists, while the marketing department would prefer to spend more on advertising. Longer established employees may wish to avoid interruptions to their routine while newly employed executives may be anxious for change. Each individual will themselves have multiple objectives, arising from their personal histories, preferences and position within the firm and these multiple sets of objectives cannot be reduced to any simple overall statement which explains what the organisation as a whole is attempting to achieve.

The second major feature of the behavioural model, which distinguishes it from those outlined above, is that decision-makers exhibit 'satisficing' behaviour, rather than 'optimising' behaviour. Neither the firm nor its component coalitions, nor individuals, are seen as attempting to maximise or minimise anything. Instead, each person or group has a 'satisficing' level for each of its objectives. If these levels are reached, they will not seek for more, in the short term at least, but if they are not met action will be taken in order to remedy the problem.

An important consequence of satisficing behaviour is that firms acting in this way will not keep costs down to a minimum. Instead they will exhibit 'organisational slack', incurring higher costs than are absolutely necessary.

A third feature of the behavioural model is that action within the firm takes the form of 'problem-oriented search using rules of thumb'. If one of the multiple objectives is not met, so that someone within the firm is dissatisfied, a search will take place for a means of meeting that objective. However, the search will be fairly-narrow, relating solely to the objective which is not being met, and the firm will use rules-of-thumb to attempt to put the problem right. These rules-of-thumb are not arrived at through any detailed analysis, but are a function of the past experience of the firm and the people within it. For instance, if revenue falls, the firm may automatically raise its price, because that has been tried in the past, and appeared to be successful.

Fourthly, the aspirations of the individuals within the firm, which determine the levels of each objective with which they will be satisfied, change over time as a result of 'organisational learning' .If a firm succeeds in meeting all of its objectives for a period of time then eventually the individuals and groups will raise their aspiration levels, demanding more of whatever it is they care about. Eventually a situation will be reached where not everyone achieves 'satisficing' levels with respect to all of their objectives, at which point a problem-oriented search will take place to seek a solution to the problem. If one is found, the process of gradually increasing aspirations continue. On the other hand, if a solution is not found despite a number of search aspiration levels with respect to the particular variable concerned will have to reduced.

Clearly, the behavioural model is very different to the others which have b considered, and describes a number of very familiar features of organisational life. In many respects it is descriptively more realistic than either the orthodox or the managerial models and is very attractive for that reason. However, it also has to be recognised that it has relatively limited use-value in addressing the questions with which managerial economics is concerned. If we consider the positive question 'how do firms respond to changes in their environment?' the model offers little assistance, as it focusses entirely within the firm. If we consider the normative question 'can we identify the decision-rules which firms should follow in order to meet their objectives?' that question is not addressed either by the behavioural model. On the other hand, a firm which conforms well to the description set out by the behaviour theorists could behave in exactly the same way with respect to price and out decisions as the profit-maximising firm, or the firm described by one of the manage , models. If the shareholders are a powerful group within the firm and will only be satisfied with maximum profit, and if employees and managers are concerned for the firm's survival, the process of organisational learning may lead the firm towards profit-maximisation. For the purposes of managerial economics, then, the behavioural model is of relatively limited usefulness.

The concept of X-inefficiency

A useful concept which links the behavioural model, and the managerial utility model is that of 'X-inefficiency'. In profit-maximising model it is assumed that the firm incurs the minimum cost achievable for the level of output , being produced, given the set of plant and equipment which has been installed. In terms of the diagram, the firm is on its cost curve. Such a firm may be described as being 'X-efficient' or 'operationally-efficient' .However, this may not be the case. A firm which is maximising managerial-utility, for instance, will tend to spend more on staff and on 'perks' for the management than is necessary, in which case it may be said to be 'X-inefficient'. In terms of a diagram, it will be above its cost curv as shown in figure. Similarly, a firm which conforms to the behavioural model will incur higher costs than are strictly necessary and be X-inefficient, or have 'organisational slack'.Liebenstein (1966) emphasises the importance of X-inefficient and considers the factors which are likely to encourage or discourage it. This analysis draws together a number of issues already considered above.

In the first place, the degree of X-inefficiency will be partly determined by factors which are internal to the firm. If contracts between principals and agents (the owner managers and workers) are not as efficient as has been suggested above then workers and managers will not be motivated to keep costs down, and the firm will be X-inefficient. If larger firms are more difficult to control, with a greater degree of bureautic rigidity, then they will also tend to be more X-inefficient.

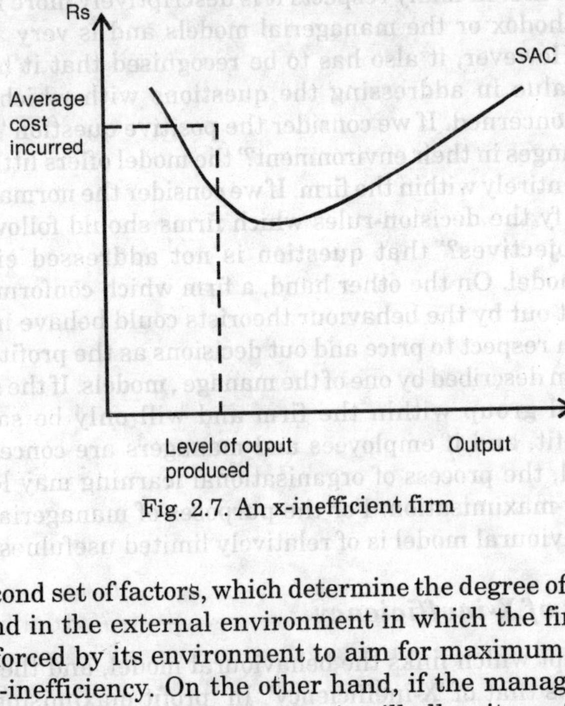

Fig. 2.7. An x-inefficient firm

The second set of factors, which determine the degree of X-inefficiency, is to be found in the external environment in which the firm operates. If the firm is forced by its environment to aim for maximum profit, it must eliminate X-inefficiency. On the other hand, if the management has the discretion to avoid profit maximisation it will allow its costs to rise above the level, which is strictly necessary. The environmental factors, which lead to X-inefficiency, are therefore the converse of the factors, which force the firm to aim for maximum profits. If shareholdings are diffused amongst a large number of relatively ill- informed small shareholders there will be little pressure from that direction. If the threat of take-over is limited, perhaps because the firm is too large to be under serious threat, or because anti-trust legislation prevents take-over, then the likelihood of X-inefficiency is correspondingly higher.

Similarly, the degree of X-inefficiency will tend to be higher as the market structure in which the firms operate is less competitive. If there are a small number of competitive rivals who

are able to avoid direct competition with each other, and they are protected by barriers to entry into the industry, then there will be few penalties for slackness and X-inefficiency is correspondingly more likely to result.

Alternative to profit Maximisation Policy

Different economists have suggested a variety of profit policies which business ftrms may pursue as an alternative to profit maximisation. These alternative profit policies are :

1. K. Rothschild has suggested that the primary motive of an enterprise is long-run survival. Decisions, therefore, aim at maximising the security of the organisation. The desire for a secure profit is a dominant motive in oligopolistic industries.

2.M. Reder has argued that an entrepreneur may have two objectives:

a) to maximise profits, and

b) to maintain financial control of the firm.

Under the circumstances, he may not maximise profits in order to achieve the second objective, say, by financing firm's expansion with own funds or retained earnings.

3. Donaldson and Lorsch found that "career managers preferred policies that favoured the long-term stability and growth of their enterprises to those that maximised current profits To assure survival, self-sufficiency and success, these top managers strive continuously to conserve and augment corporate wealth Top managers seek the maximisation of wealth, the more the wealth, the greater the assurance of the means of survival.

4. W. Felh1er has similarly argued that fimrs are Interested In 'safety margins'.

5. T. Scitovsky had introduced leisure as a variable. The entrepreneur depending on his character may choose to maximise his profit and forgo leisure or choose total leisure and forgo all profit or may decide on some combination of profit and leisure.

6. W.W. Cooper has introduced another variable, *viz.,* liquidity, Businesses attempt to maintain liquidity enough to ensure the firm's financial position and retention of control.

7. H.A. Simon has put forward the view that the entrepreneur may not care to maximize profits but may simply want to earn a return that he regards as satisfactory. In other words, he will attempt only to 'satisfice'-make satisfactory profits-rather than maximise profits.

8. W.J. Baumol, basing his view on his extensive management consulting experience, has suggested that firms attempt to maxi mise sales subject to profit constraint-that is, profits do not fall short of the minimum level which is just on the borderline of acceptability.

Questions

1. Examine critically profit maximisation as the primary objective of the business firms. What other objectives can business firm have? Explain with examples.
2. Discuss why profit maximization is not always the aim of a business firm.
3. Compare and contrast the behaviour theory with the economical theory of a firm.
4. Earlier economists made a fundamental assumption that 'profit maximization' is the basic objective of every firm. .In recent years 'profit maximization' has been extensively qualified by theorists, Bring out these qualifications.
5. Explain the differences between the neo-classical theory and the X-inefficiency theory of the firm.

3

The Importance of Risk and Uncertainty

This chapter introduces the problem of imperfect information. Techniques for decision-making in the presence of risk and uncertainty are outlined and the chapter then goes on to consider the broader implications of uncertainty for the analysis of the firm.

Alternative states of information

There are three alternative states of information. The first is **certainty**, where the decision-maker is perfectly informed in advance about the outcome of his decisions. For each decision there is only one possible outcome, which is known to the decision-maker. Realistic examples are difficult to find, but it is important to remember that the simple model of the firm, is based on the assumption that the firm has certain knowledge of its cost and demand conditions.

The second state of information is known as **risk**. In this situation a decision may have more than one possible outcome, so that certainty no longer exists. However, the decision-maker is aware of all possible outcomes and knows the probability of each one occurring.

The third state of information is that of **uncertainty**. In this situation a decision may have more than one outcome and the decision-maker does not know the precise nature of these outcomes, nor can he objectively assign a probability to the outcomes.Various techniques exist to assist decision-making in conditions of risk or uncertainty, which may be considered in turn.

Techniques for decision-making in risky conditions

The use of expected monetary values

If a decision-maker knows the possible outcomes which may result from a decision, and can assign probabilities to each of those outcomes, then expected monetary values may be substituted for certain values in choosing between alternative courses of action. The expected monetary value (EMV) of a particular course of action may defined as:

$$EMV = \Sigma piVi$$

where:

Pi = the probability of the i'th outcome

Vi=the value of the i'th outcome

And Σ pi = 1

Expressed in words, the EMV is equal to the weighted sum of the possible outcomes when each outcome is weighted by its probability, and all possible outcomes are tok into account.

To take an example, an ice-cream shop may know that its sales vary with the weather, which may be sunny (with a probability (p) of 0.2) or cloudy (p = 0.4), or raining (p = 0.4). In this case, the EMV is calculated as shown below:

Weather conditions	Probability	Sales
Sunny	0.2	Rs 500
Cloudy	0.4	Rs 300
Rainy	0.4	Rs 100

Expected monetary value = Rs 500(0.2) + Rs 300(0.4) + Rs100(0.4) = Rs 260

In the example given here there are only three possible weather conditions and three probabilities, which sum to 1. This is known as a discrete probability distribution shown diagrammatically in Fig. 3.1.

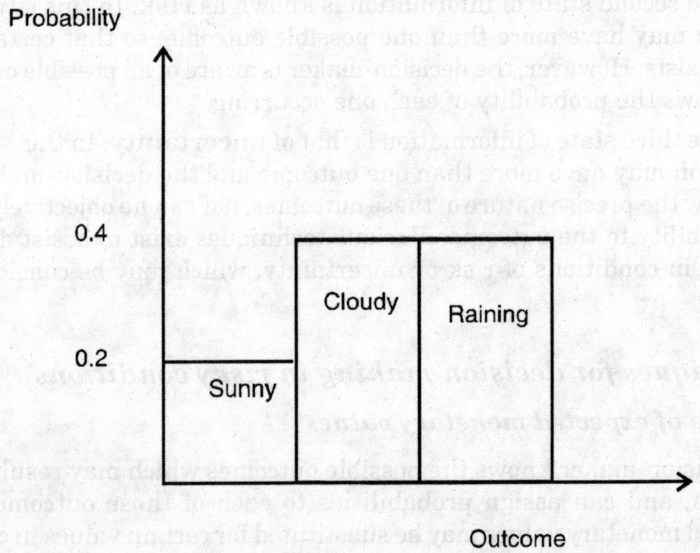

Fig. 3.1 A discrete probability distribution

As the figure indicates, there are no weather conditions which come in between those specified, and no level of sales are possible apart from those given. A slightly more difficult case is where there is a continuous probability distribution, as shown in Fig. 3.2.

If the sales of the ice-cream shop can take a very wide range of values, graph of sales against probabilities will be a smooth curve, rather than a set discrete points. There are a wide variety of such distributions, and a detailed analysis of them lies outside the scope of this chapter. However, if the distribution of ice-cream shop sales is characterized by the normal distribution, then the expected monetary value of the takings is given by the mean of the distribution

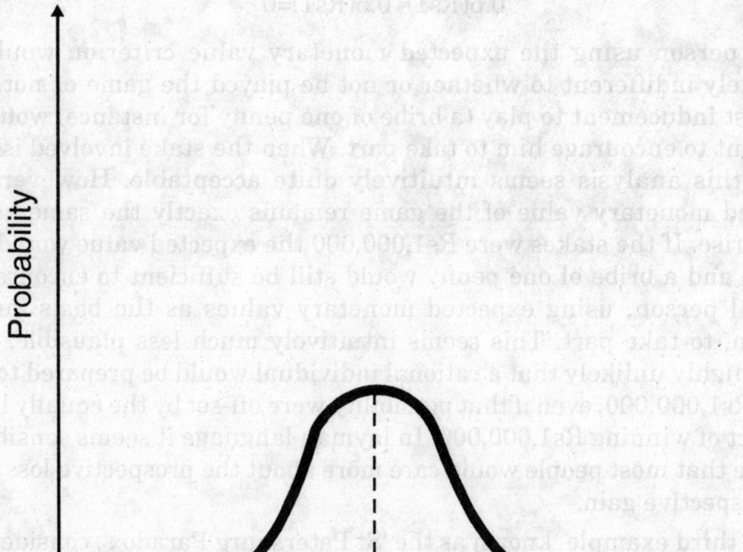

Fig. 3.2 A continuous probability distribution

The limitations of expected values

If expected monetary values are used as the decision criterion, then a rational decision- maker deciding between two alternatives will always choose the course of action which yields the highest expected monetary value. However, while this may appear an intuitively sensible way in which to take decisions, a number of examples show that its application can lead to a number of quite clearly absurd conclusions. Consider first a person's decision to insure their house against destruction by fire. If the house has a value of Rs1000,000 and the probability of it burning down in a year is one in ten thousand

(0.0001) then the expected value of the loss is Rs 100. A decision-maker employing the expected value approach would be willing to pay Rs100 for insurance, but no more. However, it seems intuitively quite clear that many rational people would be willing to pay much more than Rs100, in order to be absolutely certain that they will never be faced with the prospect of having to lose their house without recompensation. In some sense, people 'care' more about the possible loss of Rs1000,000 than they do about the certain insurance cost of Rs100. The same point can be made through another example. Imagine that a rational person is asked to take part in a game with another player which consists of tossing a coin for a stake of Rs1. If the coin lands with 'heads' up the there is a gain of rs1. If it lands 'tails' up, there is a loss of Rs1. Provided that the coin is a fair one, so that 'heads' and 'tails' are equally likely, the expected value of this game is equal to:

$$0.5(Rs1) - 0.5(Rs1) = 0$$

A person using the expected monetary value criterion would be absolutely indifferent to whether or not he played the game or not. The slightest inducement to play (a bribe of one penny for instance) would be sufficient to encourage him to take part. When the stake involved is very small, this analysis seems intuitively quite acceptable. However, the expected monetary value of the game remains exactly the same as the stakes rise. If the stakes were Rs1,000,000 the expected value would still be zero and a bribe of one penny would still be sufficient to encourage a rational person, using expected monetary values as the basis for the decision, to take part. This seems intuitively much less plausible, as it seems highly unlikely that a rational individual would be prepared to risk losing Rs1,000,000, even if that possibility were off-set by the equally likely prospect of winning Rs1,000,000. In layman language it seems sensible to suppose that most people would care more about the prospective loss than the prospective gain.

In third example, known as the 'St Petersburg Paradox', consider the situation where a coin is tossed and payment is made to the player, depending upon which toss of the coin first come up heads. If it comes up the first time, the payment is Rs2. If it does not come up until the second toss, the payment is Rs2^2 = Rs4, and if it does not come up until till nth toss, the payment is Rs 2^n. How much would a rational person be willing to pay to take part in this game? The expected monetary value of the game is given by;

$$EMV = 0.5(2) + 0.5^2(2^2) + 0.5^3(2^3) + \ldots\ldots + 0.5^n(2^n) + \ldots\ldots\ldots$$
$$= 1 + 1 + 1 + \ldots\ldots + 1 \ldots\ldots 1$$
$$= \text{infinity}$$

In other words, the expected monetary value is infinity, and a person using the EMV as a means of decision-making would be willing to pay everything they have to take part in the game!

These examples illustrate a major problem with expected monetary values as a means of taking decisions. Individuals will not accept fair bets involving large amount of money because they care more about the possibility of loss than they do about the possibility of an equal gain. In the language of economic analysis, the utility lost as a result of losing Rs100 may be more than the utility gained by winning Rs1.

Utility and attitudes to risk

The analysis above suggests that expected monetary value has serious limitations a criterion on which to base decisions. It seems intuitively likely that the value, or 'utility', placed on a loss of Rs100 by a rational individual may well exceed the utility' arising from a gain of Rs100. This suggests that an explicit examination of the links between utility and income may help to provide an alternative means of assess' decisions in situations of risk. Fig. 3.3 shows three different possible relationships between an individual's level of income, and the utility they experience as a result of having that income. Each can be seen to illustrate different attitudes to risk the part of the individual concerned.

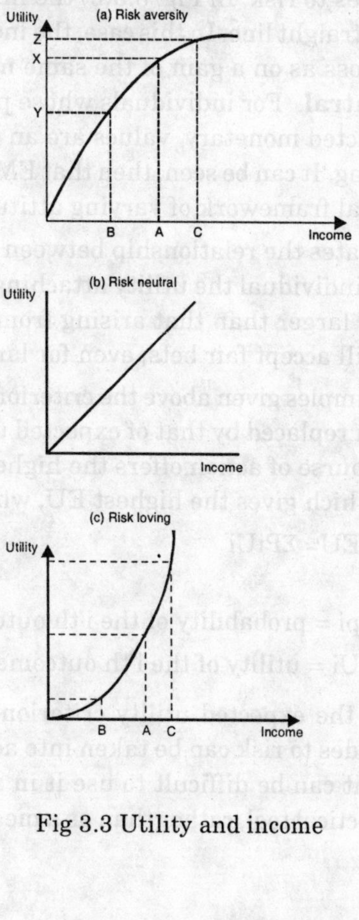

Fig 3.3 Utility and income

In Fig. 3.3(a), the curve linking utility and income becomes less and less steep at higher levels of income, indicating decreasing marginal utility of income, If such an individual is at level of income A, which gives him utility X, and is considering whether or not to accept a fair bet with a 50/50 probability of either increasing his income to C or reducing it by an equal amount to B, he will consider the impact on his utility. If his income is reduced to B, his utility falls to Y. On the other hand, if his income is increased to C, his utility rises to Z. However, as Fig. 3.3(a) clearly shows, the decrease from X to Y is substantially larger than the increase from X to Z. If these are equally likely, as in the example given, the individual in question will not accept the bet offered

The type of behaviour illustrated in Fig. 3.3 (a) is known as risk averse behavior and it is frequently assumed that most individuals and companies behave in this way, as implied in the examples considered in the section above. Nevertheless, an individual or a firm's attitude to risk depends essentially upon their personal preferences, or the preferences of their shareholders, and not everyone may be risk-averse. Fig. 3.3(b) and 3.3(c) illustrate the relationship between utility and income for individuals who have different attitudes to risk. In Fig. 3.3(b) the link between utility and income is drawn as a straight line. In this case, the individual places exactly the same value on a loss as on a gain of the same monetary value, and is described as **risk neutral**. For individuals whose preferences conform to this relationship expected monetary values are an appropriate reflection of their decision-making. It can be seen, then that EMVs represent a special case within the general framework of varying attitudes to risk.

Fig. 3.3(c) illustrates the relationship between income and utility for a **risk lover** For this individual the utility attaching to the gain in income from A to C is clearly larger than that arising from the loss from A to B. Such an individual will accept fair bets, even for large amounts.

In each of the examples given above the criterion of expected monetary value (EMV) has been replaced by that of expected utility (EU). Instead of choosing whichever course of action offers the highest EMV, the decision-maker chooses that which gives the highest EU, where:

$$EU = \Sigma PiUi$$

where:

pi = probability of the i'th outcome

Ui = utility of the i'th outcome

The adoption of the expected utility criterion provides a means by which different attitudes to risk can be taken into account when modeling decisions. However, it can be difficult to use it in a normative way, as a prescription and a practical tool, rather than as a means of predicting firms' behaviour in a general way, as it involves estimating the relationship between utility and income for a particular decision-maker (or for the shareholders on whose behalf he is taking decisions, which adds to the difficulties).

One approach to solving this problem is to use a technique involving what are known as 'standard gamble comparisons'. This procedure can be set out as a series of steps. First, utility values are assigned to two different money values. As utility has no obvious unit of measurement this can be entirely arbitrary, provided that the larger money value is assigned the higher utility value. For example, let a money value of Rs 0 yield a utility of 0 and a money value of Rs100,000 yield a utility value of 1. The aim is now to find the utility values of monetary amounts between Rs 0 and Rs100,000 for a particular decision-maker. Imagine that the aim is to find a utility value for Rs 50,000. In this case, the decision-maker is asked to consider the choice between:

a) receiving a certain Rs 50,000

b) taking part in a lottery whose outcome will be either a gain of Rs 100,000 with probability P, or a gain of zero, with probability (1-P).

At very low values of P, the decision-maker will prefer the certain Rs 50,000, but at some higher value he will change his view and will prefer to take part in the lottery. Clearly a knowledge of that value sheds light on the individual's attitude to risk, which can be used to solve the problem in hand. If, for instance, the decision-maker in question becomes indifferent between the two alternatives at a probability of 0.6 then it can be inferred that at that value the utilities attaching to the certain Rs 50,000 and the risky Rs100,000 or Rs0 are the same. Therefore:

$$U(Rs50{,}000) = 0.6(U(Rs100{,}000)) + 0.4(U(Rs0))$$

But we have assigned values to the utility arising from Rs100,000 and Rs0, and can therefore evaluate the equation given, on the same scale.

$$U(Rs\ 50{,}000) = 0.6(1) + 0.4(0) = 0.6$$

This exercise could be repeated to find the value of utility attaching to any amount between Rs0 and Rs100,000.

If the aim is to identify the value of utility (or dis-utility) attaching to losses, rather than gains, the technique can be used in a similar way. In order to evaluate the utility loss arising from a monetary loss of Rs60,000 the decision-maker is asked to choose between a certain pay-off of Rs0 (whose utility has been assigned a value of zero) and a lottery involving probability P of losing Rs60,000 and probability (1 -P) of gaining Rs100,000 (whose utility has been assigned a value of 1). Once the value of P, at which the decision-maker is indifferent is known, then the utility value of losing Rs 60,000 is the only unknown remaining in the equation, which can therefore be solved. For example, if the decision-maker declares himself to be indifferent between Rs0 and the lottery when P = 0.1, then:

$$U(Rs\ 0) = 0.1(U(-Rs\ 60{,}000)) + 0.9(U(Rs100{,}000))$$

or

$$0 = 0.1(U(-Rs60{,}000)) + 0.9(1)$$

therefore

$$U(-Rs60{,}000) = -9$$

This method of estimating utilities suffers from the fact that it relies upon the decision- maker's ability to answer hypothetical questions in the same way in which he would answer real ones. Nevertheless, it offers a means of making the analysis operational.

Indifference curves and attitudes to risk

The analysis above shows how attitudes to risk are reflected in different relationships between utility and income. However, it does not provide a direct measure of the riskiness of any particular course of action. The most common measure of the riskiness of an action, or the risk associated with a particular financial asset (a share, a portfolio of shares, or a foreign currency, for instance) is the **standard deviation** of the returns , accruing to it. This is simply a measure of the variability of the returns, and is defined " as:

$$SD = P_i(X_i - X)^2$$

where:

P_i = probability of outcome i

X_i = value of outcome i

n = number of possible outcomes

X = mean value of all outcomes

When considering choices between alternative courses of action, decision-makers may be thought of as deciding on different combinations of return on the one hand, measured by the expected value of the returns, and risk on the other, measured by standard deviation of those returns. In this case, indifference curves can be drawn up , showing the different combinations of risk and return which will leave an individual equally satisfied. If individuals are assumed to be risk-averse, which is the assumption generally made, then the indifference curves will be as shown in Fig3.4. below, rising from left to right, with the more desirable combinations being as indicated by the arrow, having higher returns and lower risk.

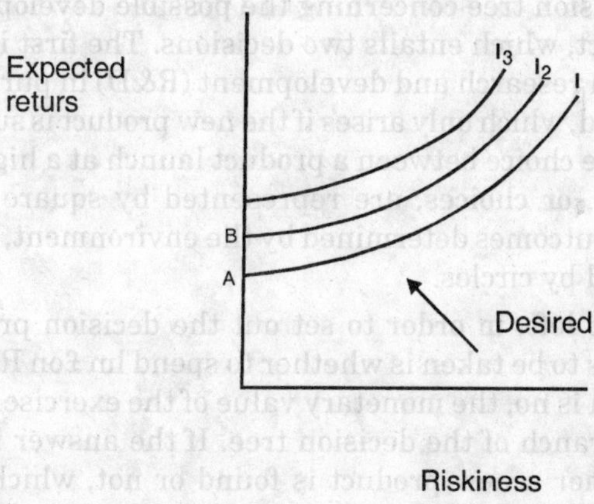

Fig. 3.4 Indifference curve for risk and return (risk averters)

The extent of an individual's risk aversion will be reflected in the slopes of indifference curves. An individual who is very highly risk averse will be prepared to sacrifice a large amount of return in order to secure a small reduction in risk and will therefore have relatively steep indifference curves, relative to one who is only slightly risk averse. (A risk neutral individual will have horizontal indifference curves.For a risk lover, for whom both risk and return are desirable characteristics, the curves will slope downwards from left to right, rather than in the other direction)

The concept of the certainty-equivalent

The most important applications of the risk versus return (or mean/variance) indifference analysis concern the construction of portfolios of financial assets and therefore lie beyond the scope of this book. However, there is one useful concept which should be noted, which is that of the **certainty-equivalent** of a course of action involving risk. This is defined as the sum of money, available with certainty, which would leave the decision-maker as satisfied as if he had undertaken the risky action. This may be interpreted, in terms of the indifference curves, as the vertical intercept of the curve which includes the course of action concerned. In Fig. 3.4, for instance, RsA is the certainty equivalent of any combination of risk and return in the indifference curve I_1 and Rs B is the certainty-equivalent of any combination on curve I_2,I .

The use of decision trees

Another well-known technique which can be helpful in analyzing situations involving risk is the use of **'decision trees'**. These are particularly useful when a number of related decisions need to be made in sequence and where the outcome of each decision depends upon the response of the environment. Fig. 3.5 shows the decision tree concerning the possible development and launch of a new product, which entails two decisions. The first is whether or not to spend £1 m on research and development (R&D) in pursuit of the new product. The second, which only arises if the new product is successfully developed, concerns the choice between a product launch at a high price or a low price. Decisions, or choices, are represented by square boxes, or decision nodes', while outcomes determined by the environment, or 'chance nodes', are represented by circles.

Working from the left, in order to set out the decision process, the first decision which has to be taken is whether to spend lm £on R&D. If the answer to this question is no, the monetary value of the exercise is zero, as shown in the lowest branch of the decision tree. If the answer is yes, the next question is whether a new product is found or not, which depends upon factors in the environment outside the control of the firm. The chance node shows that there is a probability of 0 .7 that a new product is found, 0.3 that it is not. If no new product is found, the £ lm has been wasted and the monetary value of the activity is –£lm. On the other hand, if a new product is found, the firm then has to decide whether to launch it with a high price or a low price. Whichever decision is taken, there is a range of possible outcomes, depending upon the economic circumstances of the time. Each of these is shown as an eventual profit, and the probability of that profit.

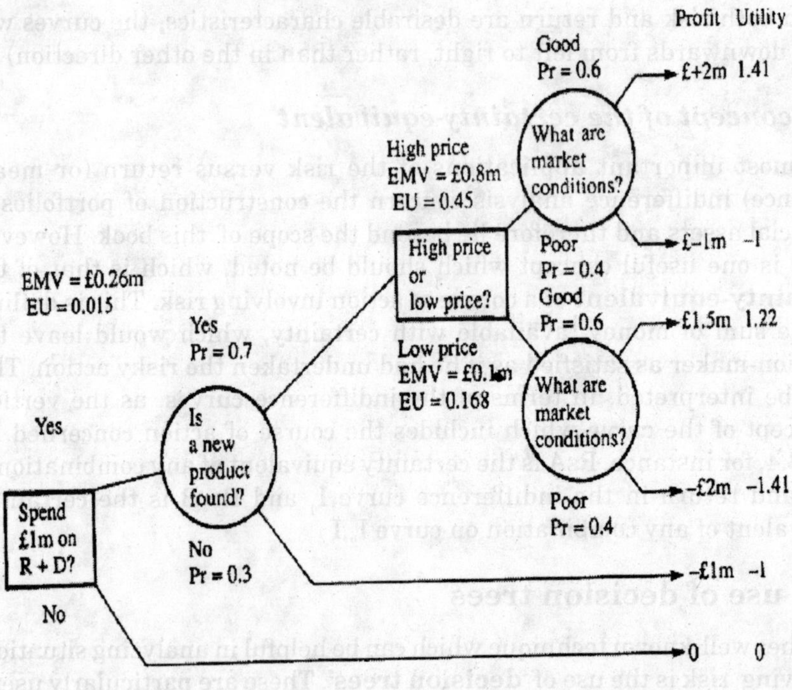

Decision trees of this kind may be used in conjunction with either the *expected monetary value* (EMV) or *expected utility* (EU) *criteria.* In either case, the basic method involves working backwards through the decision tree from right to left. For each of the possible routes through the tree a monetary value, or utility, is calculated as shown. Each of these is then worked back to the next chance node, and an EMV or EU calculated at that point. In the example shown, for instance, if the product is launched at a high price, the expected profits are equal to £.8m. If it is launched at a low price, the expected profits are £.lm. As the expected profits arising from a high price exceed those for a low price, this is the decision which will be taken, if the choice is made on the EMV criterion. If the search for a new product is successful, it will be launched at a high price, with expected profits of £8m. However, this will only be possible if the search for a new product has been successful, which itself has a probability of 0 .7. If the decision is taken to spend Rslm on R&D, then the expected value (in £) is:

$$EMV= 0.7(0.8)+ 0.3(-1)= 0.26$$

As the expected EMV is positive, the firm should decide to make the investment in R&D, if EMV is the criterion to be adopted, which implies risk neutrality.

If the firm is risk averse, which is the usual assumption with respect to attitudes to risk, the same process can be gone through using expected utilities (EUs) rather than EMVs. This requires some knowledge of the firm's utility function. In the example shown in Fig. 3.5 it has been assumed that for this firm utility is equal to the square root of the monetary return, for gains, and minus the square root of losses. In that case, re-working the example, the EU if the product is launched at a ' price is 0.45, but if it is launched at a low price, EU is equal to 0.168. The choice of price remains the same and the EU if the product is launched is equal to 0.45. The EU of spending the £ lm on R&D is given by:

$$EU = 0.7(0.45) -0.3(1) = 0.015$$

In the example given the EO criterion yields the same decision as EMV. However, it can be seen that if the degree of risk aversion were higher then both the decision on price and the decision on whether to proceed with the R&D project could alter.

Alternative types of probabilities

A situation of risk is one where the probabilities of different outcomes are known to the decision-maker. There are a number of different ways in which such probabilities might be arrived at.

A first useful distinction is between probabilities which are calculated or known **'a priori'** and those which are only known **'a posteriori'**. An 'a priori' probability is one which can be calculated through prior knowledge.

For instance, if a coin has two sides and is fair it is known that the probability of it landing on either side is 0.5. 'A posteriori' probabilities are only known after a sample of events has occurred and the frequency of each outcome is known. For instance, if it has rained on 10 out of every 30 days in June for the past 20 years, the 'a posteriori' probability of it raining on a day in June may be said to be 0.333.

Both 'a priori' and 'a posteriori' probabilities may also be described as '**objective**' probabilities in that they arise from an agreed analysis of fundamental principles or from observation of past events. The effective use of many statistical techniques depends upon such probabilities being available. However, many business decisions are non-repetitive and unique, so that objective probabilities are not available. If the environment is changing then a probability drawn from past experience may no longer be applicable. In that case, resort has to be made to '**subjective**' probabilities, based upon the decision-maker's own expectations, preferences, experience and judgment about the future. Such preferences may be quantified by asking the decision-maker to make comparisons between the real world problem being considered and a hypothetical gamble whose objective probabilities are known. This can provide some assistance in allowing a probability to be estimated but it is clear that different individuals in an organisation may ascribe different probabilities to the same outcome, or that the same individual may arrive at different probabilities for the same outcome if asked at different times. As different individuals in a firm will all have slightly different information relevant to the decision, and as it is possible that no single individual has all the relevant information, the use of subjective probabilities can be a dangerous guide to decision-making.

If satisfactory probabilities cannot be ascribed to outcomes, or if the possible outcomes are not even known, then the situation is not one of risk, but of uncertainty.

The expected value of information

It is clear from the discussion above that information is valuable and that a firm may wish to improve ita knowledge of a particular situation by gathering additional information. However, in order to do so cost effectively decision maker need to know the value of acquiring additional information, in order to judge how much additional expenditure is worthwhile. Two different cases may be identified. The first is where it is possible to acquire perfect information about the future and the second is the more general case where it is only possible to secure imperfect revelation of which future states of nature will occur.

If it were possible to acquire perfect advance state revelation then the expected value of that perfect information could be measured as the difference between the expected value of future actions, given the information currently available, and the expected value of future actions given that perfect advance state revelation had been acquired. Foster (1978) uses the example of a bank which is deciding whether to make a $1 million loan at 10 per cent to a company which might default, or whether to use the same funds to purchase risk-free government securities at 7 per cent. If the loan is made to the firm, and it does not default, the bank's wealth in respect of the action is valued at $1.1 million. If the firm defaults, the bank's wealth is reduced to $900,000. If risk-free government securities are purchased, the bank's wealth is valued at $1.07 million with certainty. It is estimated that the probability of the firm defaulting is equal to 0.2. Fig.3.6 sets out this basic information in tabular form.

Alternative	**Alternative outcome**	
	Firm defaults (Pr = 0.2)	No default (Pr = 0.8)
Lend to firm	$ 900,000	$1,100,000
Buy govt stocks	$ 1,070,000	$1,070,000

Fig. 3.6 A bank lending decision

S'ource: G. Foster, Financial Statement Analysis

If a decision is made on the basis of the information currently available, the bank will compare the expected monetary values of the two alternative courses of action, using the method outlined above. This gives the following calculation:

Expected value if the loan is made to the firm:

EV = (0.8)($1 ,100,000) + (0.2)($900,000) = $1,060,000

Expected value of a risk-free investment in government stock:

EV = $1,070,000

As the action with the highest expected value is investment in government stack this is the option which will be taken up and the expected value of the action, with the information currently available is equal to $1,070,000.

If it now proves possible for the bank to acquire 'perfect state revelation' so that it will know for certain whether the firm will default or not, the situation changes. In this case, whichever outcome occurs, the bank will have been able to choose the optimal action. If it is discovered that the firm will default, the bank will choose to invest in government stock. If it is discovered that the firm will not default, the bank will choose to make the loan.

In order to calculate the expected value in this case, it is noted that the probability of default is 0.2 and that if default takes place, the bank will have invested in government stock. The probability of the firm not defaulting is 0.8, in which case the firm will have made the loan. This gives the expected value of the bank's wealth as:

$$EV = 0.8(\$1.1m) + .2(\$1.07m)$$
$$= \$1.094m$$

This can be compared with the expected value of the optimal action in the situation where the bank has not acquired perfect information about the future, which has been calculated above as $1.07 million. The difference between the two values, $24,000, is the expected value of perfect information (EVPI).

The circumstances under which perfect information about the future is available are very rare indeed and in most cases the purchase of additional information will not provide absolutely certain advance state revelation. Nevertheless, the calculation of EVPI is still a useful tool in such situations because it provides an upper limit to the value of additional information which might be collected. The first step which should be taken when considering the purchase of additional information is to consider whether the cost of acquiring it exceeds the EVPI. If it does, the information should not be acquired as its expected value could not possibly exceed that of perfect information.

If the cost of acquiring additional information is less than the EVPI then it may be worth acquiring that information. The basic principle involved in placing a value on the extra information is essentially the same as that involved in calculating EVPI. The value of the information is equal to the difference between the expected value given currently available information and the expected value with the additional information which has been acquired. This can be difficult to calculate in practice.

Techniques for coping with uncertainty

The problems considered above have all related to situations of risk, where the probabilities of different outcomes are known. If probabilities are not known, the situation is one of uncertainty, rather than risk, and the techniques outlined above cannot be applied. Nevertheless, there are a number of different strategies which may be adopted in order to make decisions on rational criteria.

The maximin criterion

A firm making a decision may be characterized as choosing between alternative courses of action, whose outcomes depend upon which 'state of nature' happens to be in force at the time of the action. In a situation of uncertainty the probabilities of the

different states of nature are not known. In order to begin analyzing the problem of pay off matrix may be constructed as ahown in fig 3.7 below

	States of nature		
Actions	A	B	C
1	20	40	180
2	-40	100	220
3	60	70	90

Fig 3.7 A pay off matrix

Each cell in the matrix shows the pay-off, which could be in terms of monetary' or utilities, for the given course of action, given the state of nature indicated.

If the maximin criterion is adopted, the decision-maker examines the worst pay off for each action and then chooses the action for which the worst pay-off is highest. In the example given in Fig. 3.7 the worst pay-offs are:

- Action 1:20
- Action 2: - 40
- Action 3:60

In this example,

Action 3 is selected, guaranteeing that the lowest pay-off' received will be 60.

The maximin rule ensures that the worst possible outcomes are avoided and may be described as a pessimistic, conservative, or highly risk averse strategy. The obvious difficulty with it is that it ignores the higher value pay-offs which may imply foregoing some possibly very large gains.

The minimax regret criterion

In the case of the minimax regret criterion the decision-maker considers the extent of the sacrifice made if a particular state of nature occurred but the best action for that state of nature was not chosen. In the example shown in Fig. 3.7 for state of nature A, Action 1 involves a 'regret' of 40, Action 2 a 'regret' of 100 and Action 3 a 'regret' of 0. Fig. 3.8 shows a complete 'regret matrix' for all actions and states of nature.

	States of nature		
Actions	A	B	C
1	40	60	40
2	100	0	0
3	0	30	130

Fig 3.8 Regret matrix

Having set out the regret matrix, the action is chosen for which the largest regret is a minimum, leading to the choice of Action 1, Such a strategy ensures that the maximum regret is not experienced, and is also a relatively pessimistic basis on which to make a decision.

As in the case of the maximin criterion a major criticism of this technique is that it only makes use of a very limited amount of the information which is available, ignoring everything else. Actions which are rejected may have much smaller regrets than the one which is chosen, apart from their largest regrets. It is also possible that use of this approach could lead to inconsistent decisions in that if an action is chosen from a group of alternatives and then one of the rejected actions is deleted from the options, a different action may now be chosen, despite the fact that the original 'best' option is still available.

The maximax criterion

This criterion is the opposite of the maximin criterion in that the best outcomes of each action are identified, and then the action is selected for which the best outcome is largest. In the case set out in Fig. 3.6, this would lead to the choice of Action 2. This is clearly an 'optimistic' criterion to use in that it selects the action which provides a possibility of making the highest possible return. As in the case of the other criteria considered, its main failing is that it only takes a limited amount of the available information into account. The action which offers a prospect of the highest possible return may also be the one which offers the prospect of the largest possible loss (as in the example shown), but this is ignored.

The Hurwicz 'alpha'-criterion

The Hurwicz approach is an attempt to use more of the information available by constructing an index (the 'alpha-index') for each action, which takes into account both the best and worst outcomes and the extent to which the decision-maker wishes to adopt a pessimistic or optimistic posture.

The index is defined in the followmg way for each action:

$$I_i = al_i + (1 - a)L_i$$

where:

I_i = the index for action i

a = an optimism/pessimism index

l_i = the lowest pay-off for action i

L_i = the highest pay-off for action i

The action which has the largest alpha-index is the one selected. The optimism/pessimism index may vary from between 0 and 1 and may be estimated by increasing the value of x in the situation shown in Fig. 3.9 until the decision-maker is indifferent between the two actions.

	States of nature	
Actions	A	B
1	0	1
2	X	X

Fig. 3.9 Estimating the optimism/pessimism index

A very pessimistic decision-maker will be indifferent between the two actions at very low value for x (he will be quite happy with a small certain gain compared with the prospect of either 0 or I, because his pessimism leads him to suspect that the outcome of Action 1 would be zero). On the other hand a very optimistic decision maker, who suspects that the outcome of Action 1 is likely to be 1, will only be equally content with a certain amount which is almost as large as 1.

Once the value of x has been estimated, through direct questioning of the decision maker, it is assumed that as the decision-maker is indifferent between Action 1 and Action 2 they both have the same alpha-index. From the formula given, Action 1 has an index of $(1-a)$ and Action 2 has an index of x. It follows, therefore, that

$$(1-a)=x$$

and the value of a can be calculated from the known value of x, arrived at by experiment.

It should be noted that if x has a value of 1, so that a takes the value of 0, this indicates that the decision-maker is very highly optimistic, and the alpha-index criterion is exactly the same as the maximax criterion. Similarly, if the decision-maker is highly pessimistic, so that a takes the value of 1, the alpha-index criterion is equivalent to using the maximin approach. The Hurwicz technique therefore has the rather elegant property of encompassing maximin and maximax as special cases, each at a different end of a spectrum of decision-making attitudes which may vary from highly optimistic to highly pessimistic. As the technique also makes use of more information than either maximin or minimax it may be said to be superior to either of them in that respect but nevertheless, like them, it also wastes some of the available information concerning the possible outcomes of actions, using only that for the best and the worst outcome.

Combinations of different strategies

There is no reason to suppose, of course, that firms do, or must, adopt any single criterion in taking decisions under uncertainty. They may adopt different strategies on different occasions, or may consciously combine different strategies in order to 'spread the risk' associated with any single approach.

The broader implications of uncertainty for the theory of the firm

While techniques to assist decision making under uncertainty are potentially useful they are clearly very limited and there is a danger that they may obscure the fact that the existence of uncertainty has very profound implications for the theory of the firm. In a situation of uncertainty firms and the individuals within them cannot calculate the probabilities of the outcomes of their actions. In many situations their ignorance may extend even further than this and they may not even be aware of what the possible outcomes are for any particular action. Recognition of this important limitation on firms and individuals has led to a number of significant insights into the workings of the firm.

Uncertainty and 'bounded rationality'

If a firm is operating in a situation of uncertainty its ability to act rationally is limited because of its lack of information. The 'hyper-rational' firm represented by the neo- classical model, in which the firm has perfectly accurate knowledge of its cost and demand conditions, has to be replaced by a model in which decision-makers exhibit ;= 'bounded rationality'. That is not to imply that they are simply irrational, they are 'intendedly rational, but only limitedly so', to quote Simon's phrase.Each decision-maker attempts to seek rational answers to his problems in the contextof his limited knowledge and experience. Instead of 'optimising', as in the neo-classical model, decision-makers 'satisfice' as in the behavioural model of the firm. Instead of immediately identifying the appropriate course of action, or solution to a problem, actions and solutions are arrived at through a process of searching through sequences of possible alternatives, using past experience and rules-of-thumb as guidelines. Clearly, the concept of 'bounded rationality', which is important in situations of uncertainty, leads away from the orthodox picture of the firm as a fully-informed optimiser, and suggests the usefulness of a much more behavioural approach.

Uncertainty and transactions costs

Another implication of uncertainty is that it makes it difficult and expensive to draw up complete contracts between individuals. If all future contingencies are known, then a contract between two individuals could specify how each should behave in the event of each contingency, and that contract could be enforced by law. However, as Williamson (1986) points out, if the future possibilities are not all known, contracts will have to be incomplete and there is a difficulty in deciding how to resolve any conflicts which may arise in an unforeseen situation. This need not matter if all parties to all contracts behave without guile towards each other, because in that situation a contract may be thought of as 'a promise, rather than a plan' and each party could agree not to take advantage of the other in unforeseen situations. Unfortunately, in a situation of uncertainty some parties to incomplete contracts may behave 'opportunistically', taking advantage of circumstances to the disadvantage of their partners to the contract.

This is a much more fundamentally important issue than it might appear at first sight, because it reaches to the heart of the question 'what is the firm?', and is important for the understanding of such apparently different phenomena as vertical integration, licensing agreements, and the existence of the multinational enterprise. If contracts between individuals could always effectively and cheaply bring about transactions there would be no need for firms to even exist. All economic activity could be organised through contracts between individuals or households. Only when some transactions are organised by management authority, instead of the market mechanism, does a firm come into being. If there were complete certainty, or even just risk, then market transactions organised through complete contracts could cheaply co-ordinate economic activity. Only when there is uncertainty is a substitute for market transactions required and the firm has a role to play.

Kay (1984) makes a similar point in a particularly graphic way by noting that most 'real world' firms are organised into functional departments, usually including production, marketing, finance, and research and development. However, if perfect knowledge were actually available, and there were no information problems, none of these departments would be needed. Marketing departments only exist because consumers are not perfectly informed of the firm's products, their characteristics and their prices. Finance departments are only needed because the firm does not have perfect access to financial information. Research and development (R&D) is only required because perfect technological information is not available. Production departments would continue to exist, but they would only need capital and direct labour because the functions of foremen, managers, clerks and typists would not be needed. Furthermore, only one category of labour would exist, because the basic difference between different types of labour is *informational* in that each type of labour -manager, welder, fitter, electrician -is distinguished from the others by the information that each has with respect to their own specialist function. In a world of perfect information where everyone has access to the all the knowledge required every worker would be able to fulfil any function!

Uncertainty, entrepreneurship and innovation

Textbook models of the firm, which assume certainty or risk, present the firm as a relatively passive entity, having an objective and responding to an environment which is given and over which it has no control. Cost conditions are determined by factor prices and the state of technology and demand conditions are determined by consumers' preferences, which are internal to themselves. The firm has no capacity to change the world in which it operates.

Questions

Q1. Distinguish between certainty, risk and uncertainty and explain how utility theory might be used to assist decision-making in the presence of risk.

Q2. Define decision tree and how it's used in risk analysis?

4

Demand

Introduction

The ... "*successful operation of any economic organization requires a thorough understanding of demand and supply conditions for its products.*"

The demand for a good or service refers to the amount of a product that people are willing and able to buy at various prices during a given period of time. Need or desire is a necessary component but must be accompanied by financial capability before a demand is created.

For example one might like to own a luxury car like mercedez but inability to pay for it is not regarded as demand. Similarly, the desire of a miser to own a big house is not demand as he is not willing to pay for it, despite affordability Therefore, a want becomes effective demand when there is i)desire to buy, ii) ability to pay and iii) willingness to pay.

The demand function

The demand function specifies the relation between quantity demanded and all of the variables that determine demand i.e. the demand function sets out the variables which influence the demand for a particular product. These variables are different for different type of product but a generic demand function is given below which includes some of the most common variables that affect demand of a good or service. The demand function can be written as:

$$Qd = f(P_O, P_C, P_S, Y_d, T, A, CR, R, E, N, O)$$

The first three variables in the demand function relate to price. They are the own price of the product (P_O), the price of complements (P_C) and the price of substitutes (P_S). For the good's own price , the expected relationship would be, the higher the price the lower the demand and the lower the price the higher the demand (Law of demand). In the case of complementary good, if the price of complementary good increases, the demand falls both for it and for the good that it is complimentary to. As fewer people would now desire to buy either good given that the complimentary good is now more expensive and this would reduce the demand for the good its complimentary to as well. If the price of a substitute good rises, then demand for the good that it is substitute for would be expected to rise as people would now buy the latter than its more expensive substitute.

The fourth variable Yd in the demand function stands for disposable income, i.e. the amount of money available to people to spend. The greater the level of disposable income, the more people can afford to buy and hence greater the level of demand for the goods. There is an assumption that they are normal goods, consumption of which increases with rising levels of income, as oppose to inferior goods that are consumed less as income rises.

Here disposable income is considered because the total income undergoes tax deductions and other such deductions thus a person finally gets some percentage of total income in his hand which he could spend.

The fifth variable T stands for tastes of consumer. Over a period of time, tastes of consumer may change significantly. For example, in case of food items, greater availability of alternatives may have a significant effect in changing the national diet. In India , the demand for bajra has fallen over last ten years as people have switched to eating rice and wheat instead. Factors like social pressures, technology change etc. may also change tastes hence demand for a product.

The next set of variables, A stands for the level of advertising (own advertising as well as the advertising of substitutes and compliments). The relationships here are as follows. The higher the level of own advertising for good, the higher demand for that good would be expected, other things being constant. Likewise, the higher the level of advertising of a complimentary good, the higher the demand for it and the goods which it is complimentary will be, given their symbiotic relationship. Conversely, the higher the level of advertising of a substitute, the lower the demand for the good for which it is an alternative and consumer would buy heavily promoted good. The overall effect of advertising will depend on the extent to which each of these forms of advertising is used at a given period of time as they may, at least in part, cancel each other out. This is something a firm should also have knowledge of so as to determine its optimum advertising strategy.

The variables CR and R represent the availability of credit and the rate of interest, i.e. the price of credit. These variables play an important role in the demand for consumer durable goods, eg cars. A person's ability to buy a car will depend on his ability to raise money to pay for it. This means that the easier credit is to obtain, the more likely they are to be able to make the purchase. At the same time credit should be affordable i.e rate of interest must be such that its easy to repay.

The variable E stands for expectations, which may include expectations about price and income changes. For example if consumers expect the price of a good to rise in future then they may bring forward their purchasesof it in order to avoid paying the higher prices. This increases the demand in short run, but the demand would fall as the prices increases. The firm would have to adjust its production accordingly. Expectations about income may also be important. For example people who expect their income to rise may buy more goods, where as those who expect their income to fall will but less. At the individual consumer level this may not be significant but when aggregated across the country's population it can be. Thus during boom in the economy the additional expected purchasing power of consumers will lead to increase in demand for a significant number of products. Conversely, the during recession in economy, demand reduces as consumers become more cautious.

The variable N stands for the number of potential consumers. Each product is likely to have a target market whose size may vary. The number of potential consumers may be a function of demographic profile of consumer or location etc. The variable O represents any other miscellaneous factors which may influence the demand for a particular product. For example it could be used to represent seasonal changes in demand for a particular product like ice cream, umbrellas etc.) if demand is subject to such fluctuations. Thus each product will have its own particular demand function depending upon the variables which influence the demand for it.

Determinants of Demand

For different types of goods there are different variables or determinants of demand thus resulting in different demand function for each product and services. The most important determinants of demand are a product's price , income, taste and preferences and the price of complementary or substitute products. In section below determinant of demand for three kinds of goods are discussed.

Non-durable Consumer Goods

There are three basic factors which influence the demand for these type of goods:

Purchasing Power

Purchasing power is determined by disposable personal income (personal income -direct taxes and other deductions) . Some people suggest the use of discretionary income in place of disposable income. Discretionary income can be estimated by subtracting three items from disposable income namely, (a) imputed income and income in kind, (b) major fixed outlay payments such as mortgage debt payment, insurance premium payments and rent, and (c) essential expenditures such as food and clothing and transport expenses based upon consumption in a normal year Discretionary income can be quite an important determinant in case of consumer non-durables which are luxuries.

Price

The price factor is another important variable which should be included in demand analysis. Here, one has to consider the prices of the product and also its substitutes and complements. One may also consider the price differences between the product concerned and its substitutes and complements.

Price as a determinant of the volume of sales of consumer nondurables is sometimes more important through cross-elasticity (involving substitute products) than it is directly in terms of price elasticity. Direct price elasticity can be expected to be more important with respect to those consumer non-durables, which are capable of storage and free from risks of changes in styles.

Demography

It includes characteristics of the population, human as well as non-human. using the product concerned. For example. it may pertain to the number and characteristics of children in a study of the demand for toys or the number and characteristics of automobiles in a study of the demand for tyres or petrol. In fact. it involves distinguishing between the total market demand and market segments. Such segments may be derived in terms of income, social status, sex, age, male-female ratios, urban-rural ratios, educational level, geographic location, etc. The segment when quantified can be used as an independent variable affecting the demand for the product in question.

Demand can be forecast by employing the following formula:

$$d=f(Y,D, P)$$

where d is demand, y is disposable income,D is demography, and P is price. The various determinants of the demand for cotton textiles can provide a good illustration. The demand for cotton cloth is a function of the price of cotton cloth, prices of substitute commodities and the income of consumers. It bears a negative relationship with the price of cotton cloth and with the prices of complementary commodities: on the other hand, a positive relationship exists with the prices of substitute commodities and with income. However,over a period of time, a change may take place in some or all of these factors. For example, population may increase and fashions and consumer preferences may undergo a change. But in a developing country like India, prices of food grains constitute an important determinant of the demand for cloth. Since the demand for food is inelastic, any increase in the food prices leads to a corresponding increase in the expenditure on food reducing the part of income available for purchasing other goods including cotton cloth. This leads to a cut in the demand for cloth. Thus food prices exert a negative influence on the demand for cloth.

Durable Consumer Goods

The important considerations in the forecasting of demand for durable consumer goods are as under:

(A) The consumer has to make a choice between either using the goods longer by repairing it, if necessary , or disposing it of and replacing it with a new one. The choice may depend upon non-economic factors like social status, prestige, etc. or on economic factors like income and obsolescence.

In periods of shortage. there is no alternative but to continue using the old product.

(B) These goods require special facilities for their use. e.g., roads for automobiles. and electricity for refrigerators etc. The existence and growth of such facilities is an important variable for determining their demand.

(C)Consumer durables are used by households rather than an individual, therefore the decision to purchase may be influenced by family characteristics such as size of family, income of family, distribution of number of adults and children in family etc.

(D) Price and credit facilities available also effect the demand for durable consumer products. If the credit is easily available and at less rate of interest then demand for consumer durable goods eg. car etc would increase.The ratio of price to the average life of the product should also be considered If average life of the product is high, the principle effect would be to dampen the influence of price .The availability of hire purchase facility also tends to push up the demand for these products.

Capital Goods

Capital goods are the goods, which are used for further production. As the demand for capital goods is a derived one, it will depend upon the profitability of industries using the capital goods (called user industries), the ratio of production to capacity in the user industries, and the level of wage rates. When wage rates rise in relation to other costs, the management will seriously consider further investment in labour-saving equipment.

In the case of particular capital goods. Demand will depend upon the markets they serve and the end uses for which they are bought. The demand for textile machinery will, for example, will be determined by the expansion of textile industry in terms of new units and replacement of existing machinery. New demand as well as replacement demand will have to be considered. The demand for commercial vehicles depends upon: (i) the scrappage rate. (ii) the availability of vehicles; (iii) economics of movement by road vis-a-vis rail, (iv) availability of bank finance to the prospective customers, and (v) growth pattern of the economy.

The factors, which would affect the demand for capital goods, are:

(a) The growth prospects of the user industries (demand estimates for the end-use products in the case of intermediate goods).

(b) The pattern of consumption of capital goods per unit of installed capacity (per unit of each end-use product in the case of intermediate products). It is assumed that patterns of consumption would remain stable. For example, for construction purposes mild steel maybe in use in place of construction steels which are more suitable, because of the latter's non-availability or high costs. In such cases, as the pattern of availability changes, norms of consumption would also change.

Types of Demand

A classification of demand for goods and services is essential to make a meaningful demand analysis. Numerous goods and services available in an economy can be classified on different grounds. Table 3.1 classifies the goods with regard to different criteria. Major demand distinctions have been discussed here.

Demand for Consumers' Goods and Producers' Goods

Goods and services used for final consumption, like food items, clothes, services of doctors, and residential houses are called consumer goods. Demand for these goods depends mainly on the disposable income of the consumer, price of goods and size of the population. Demand for consumer's goods is also called as direct demand. Direct demand is the demand for goods meant for final consumption.

Producers' goods or capital goods refer to the demand for goods required for production of other goods. This is also known as derived demand as it is derived from or tied to the demand for consumers' goods they produce. Demand for raw materials, plant and machinery and a car to be used as a taxi is demand for producers' goods. Their demand varies with the level of production. Thus, the demand for an input/ factor of production is a derived demand as it depends on the demand for final output. The derived demand for an input can be assessed on the basis of quantity of demand for the final output and the degree of substitutability / complementarity between inputs. For example, the demand for sugar in a soft drinks industry depends on the quantity of soft drink to be produced and substitutability between sugar and high fructose corn syrup (HFCS).

Demand for Perishable and Durable goods

Both the consumers' and producers' goods can be further classified into perishable (non-durable goods) and durable goods. Perishable goods are single- use goods whose utility perishes after using them only once. Cold drinks, pizzas, cement and services of teachers are such examples. Durable goods are repeated use goods like clothes, car and machinery. They can be used repeatedly arid continuously over a period of time.

Durable goods present more complicated problems for demand analysis than perishable goods. Perishable goods meet only the current demand but sales of durable goods depend on both current as well as future demand. Demand for them depends on their current prices, income and preferences of the consumer. Durable goods are more costly and their demand can be prepose or postponed depending on the market conditions. They are demanded to replace old stock and to expand the total stock. Credit facilities, technological changes, business conditions, speculation and price expectation are some factors that influence their demand.

Individual and Market demand

Individual demand is demand by a single buyer in the market at a particular price per time period. Market demand is the demand by all the buyers of a particular good or service in the market. In other words, it is the aggregate demand of individual buyers of a specific product at a particular price per time period . This distinction is helpful for formulating sales strategy for different income groups.

Demand by Market Segments and Total Market

Individuals can be grouped in a market segment on the basis of some criteria. Distinction can be made in terms of income, product use, age, geographical regions, different distribution channels and so on. If any of these differences is important in terms of prices, profit margins, seasonal pattern, competition and cyclical differences, then it is worthwhile to make the distinction, as market strategies can be formulated for each market segment. Segmenting helps the companies to focus on a particular area..

The total market demand will be aggregate demand for the product from all segments while market segment demand would refer to demand for the product in that specific market segment. The Apollo Tyres segments the tyre market on various basis as shown below and caters to such segments with differentiated products:

Geographical criteria -XT 9 is launched for trucks in the south and west India while Flash is made for the northern region.

Application criteria -Amar front wheel tyre to be used in southern India, Rock master for mining and Haulag for underload applications.

Mileage and loading criteria -Hercules for medium mileage overloading application. Milestart XT 7 for high mileage and medium load.

Company Demand and Industry Demand

Industry demand denotes the total demand for the products of a particular industry. Cars in India are manufactured by MUL, Daewoo, Hyundai, Fiat and others companies. Demand for Maruti cars is company demand or firm demand, whereas demand for cars produced by all firms is industry demand. In other words, it includes the demand for differentiated products produced by all the companies that are close substitutes. Similarly demand for refrigerators produced by Whirlpool or BPL or Samsung is company demand and their aggregated demand (for all brands) is industry demand. The main factors influencing company demand are technology, market leadership and financial position.

Market share is the expression of company demand as a percentage of industry demand. Therefore, market share is a relative term and company demand is an absolute concept. Managers are concerned with the market share of the company as it is under the control of the firm. Differentiation, promotional schemes and other methods can be adopted to increase the market share of the company.

Autonomous and Induced Demand

Autonomous demand is independent of demand of any other good whereas **induced demand** for a product is tied to the purchase of a parent product. Induced demand is also called as derived demand as it depends on the demand of the final output. Demand for basic needs like food, clothing and shelter is autonomous demand. Demand for raw materials, machines, money, labour and managerial ability come under the purview of induced demand. Demand for tyres is induced demand as it depends on the automobile industry.

Short-Run and Long Run Demand

Distinction is made between short and long run demand on the basis of time element (refer section 1.6.4 for detailed explanation). Short run demand refers to the current demand which is based on the prevailing tastes and technology and influenced by a change in the prices and income. Demand for seasonal goods like cold drinks and ice creams is short run demand. Long run demand is the demand likely to exist in future. It depends on product improvement and changes in tastes and technology overtime. This distinction is useful in control and management of demand.

Law of Demand

The **law of demand** states that, " higher the price, lower the demand, and vice versa other things remaining the same". In other words as price of a good or service increases, its quantity demanded would decrease. The law shows that there is an inverse relation between price and quantity demanded. Managers should be aware that the law indicates that a price change will have an impact on a firms' sales volume and total volume and thus, its profitability. It should be noted that the law is applicable when other factors influencing demand are taken as constant and only price is changed. The law can be depicted in the form of demand schedule and demand curve.

The **demand schedule** for a good is a table that shows the total quantity of a good that will be purchased at each price.

Price (in Rs)	**Quantity demanded by buyer 1**	**Quantity demanded by buyer2**	**Market demand**
100	60	40	100
80	120	100	220
60	180	160	340
40	240	220	460
20	300	280	580

The Law of demand is also shown graphically in the form of chart which is called demand curve. Demand by buyer 1 and buyer 2 are individual demands. Total demand by the two is market demand. Thus, the total market demand can be derived by adding the quantity of a good demanded by all buyers, at each price.

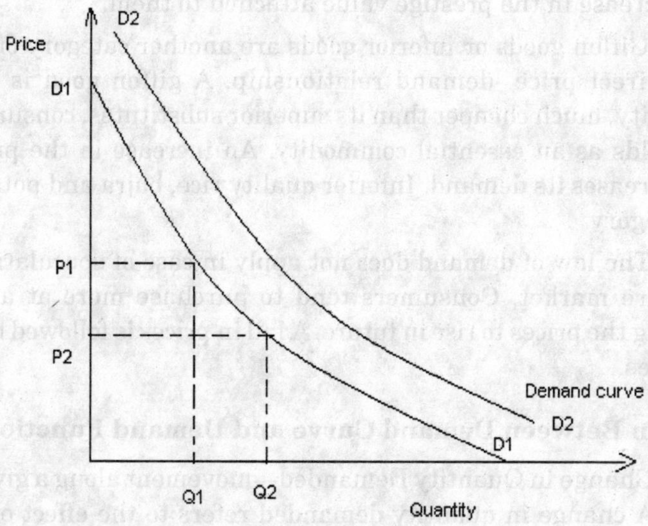

Figure: Demand curve

In figure, D_1 and D_2 are individual demand curves and Dm is the market demand curve which is derived by horizontal summation of individual demand curves. Each point on the demand curve shows a unique combination of price and quantity. It can be observed from figure that the demand curve slopes downwards to the right indicating that when price rises, less quantity is demanded.

The inverse relationship between price and demand as indicated by law of demand can be explained in term of two reason. A) Income effect : The fall in prices of a commodity leads to an equivalent increase in the income of the consumer because now he has to spend less for purchasing the same amount of commodity. When prices rises, consumer's income, in effect reduces as aresult he would control his expenditure on all commodities including the commodity whose prices have increased. (b) When the price of a good falls, the consumer tendsto substitute that commodity for other commodity which is not relatively dear. Substitution effect is due to consumers' inherent tendency to substitute cheaper goods for the relatively expensive ones. For instance, the purchase of relatively more oranges, when the price of apples increases is due to substitution effect.

Exceptions to the Law of Demand

The law of demand is not applicable in certain cases:

(a) The law of demand is violated in case of veblen or conspicuous goods. Some goods are purchased for snob appeal, ostentation and prestige value. As a result higher their price, the greater their demand. Diamonds, antique pieces and rare paintings are purchased more at a high price due to an increase in the prestige value attached to them.

(b) Giffen goods or inferior goods are another category of goods that depict direct price -demand relationship. A giffen good is an inferior commodity, much cheaper than its superior substitutes, consumed by poor households as an essential commodity. An increase in the price of such good increases its demand. Inferior quality rice, bajra and potatoes fall in this category.

(c) The law of demand does not apply in case of speculative markets like share market. Consumers tend to purchase more at a high price expecting the prices to rise in future. A fall in prices is followed by a smaller purchases.

Relation Between Demand Curve and Demand Function

1. Change in Quantity Demanded—movement along a given demand curve. A change in quantity demanded refers to the effect on sales of a change in price, holding constant the effects of all other demand-determining factors.

2. Shift in Demand—a shift from one demand curve to another, reflects a change in one or more of the nonprice variables in the product demand function.

The task of demand analysis is distinguish between changes in the quantity demanded (movements along a given demand curve) and changes in demand (shifts from one demand curve to another). The process is complicated by the fact that not only prices, but also income, population, interest rates, advertising, etc. vary from period to period.

Elasticity of Demand

Price elasticity

The law of demand tells us that as the price of a commodity falls, the quantity demanded increases, and *vice versa.* The law of demand tells us only the direction of change, but not the rate at which the change takes place. To know about the latter, we should know the price elasticity of demand, or elasticity of demand. Elasticity of demand is based upon the law of demand itself. The price elasticity of demand may be measured by the following formula:

$$ep = \frac{\textbf{Proportionate change in the quantity demanded}}{\textbf{Proportionate change in price}}$$

Or

$$\text{ep} = \frac{\text{change in quantity demanded /quantity demanded}}{\text{change in price / price}}$$

$$= \frac{(Q_2 - Q_1)/Q_1}{(P_2 - P_1)/P_1}$$

where Q_1 = quantity demanded before price change
Q_2 = quantity demanded after price change
P_1 = price charged before price change
P_2 = price charged after price change

Types of Price Elasticity

1. Perfectly elastic demand-where no reduction in price is needed to cause an increase in demand. If this be the case, a firm can sell the quantity it wants at the prevailing price but none at all at even a slightly higher price. Here the shape of the demand curve is horizontal.

2. Perfectly inelastic demand-where a change in price, howsoever large, causes no change in quantity demanded. Here, the shape of the curve is vertical.

3. Demand with unity elasticity-where a given proportionate change in price causes an equal proportionate change in the quantity demanded. Here the shape of the demand curve is that of a rectangular hyperbola.

4. Relatively elastic demand-where a reduction in price leads to more than proportionate change in demand. Hence the shape of the demand curve is flat.

5. Relatively inelastic demand-where a decline in price leads to less than proportionate increase in demand. Here the shape of the demand curve is steep.

Table presents the characteristics of various types of price elasticity.

Type	**Numerical Expression**	**Description**	**Shape of curve**
Perfectly Elastic	∞	Infinite	Horizontal
Perfectly Inelastic	0	Zero	Vertical
Unity Elasticity	1	One	Rectangular hyperbola
Relatively Elastic	> 1	More than one	Flat
Relatively Inelastic	< 1	Less than one	Steep

In real life we generally come across cases 2,4 and 5.

Notable Points Regarding Price Elasticity

A. When Demand Curve is Linear

1. Price-elasticity can range between O or completely inelastic demand and infinity, or perfectly elastic demand. These are known as limiting cases.
2. The elasticity will be zero if demand curve is a vertical straight line.
3. The elasticity will be infinity if demand curve is a horizontal straight line.
4. The elasticity of demand can also be ascertained by the formula:

   $$e_p = \frac{\text{Lower segment of the demand curve}}{\text{Upper segment of the demand curve}} = \frac{L}{U}$$

   where L and u mean lower and upper segments respectively.
5. At the mid-point of the linear demand curve, *e* = 1
6. The-price-elasticity of a linear demand curve decreases as one travels down the curve.
7. The price-elasticity is never 1 throughout the linear demand curve.

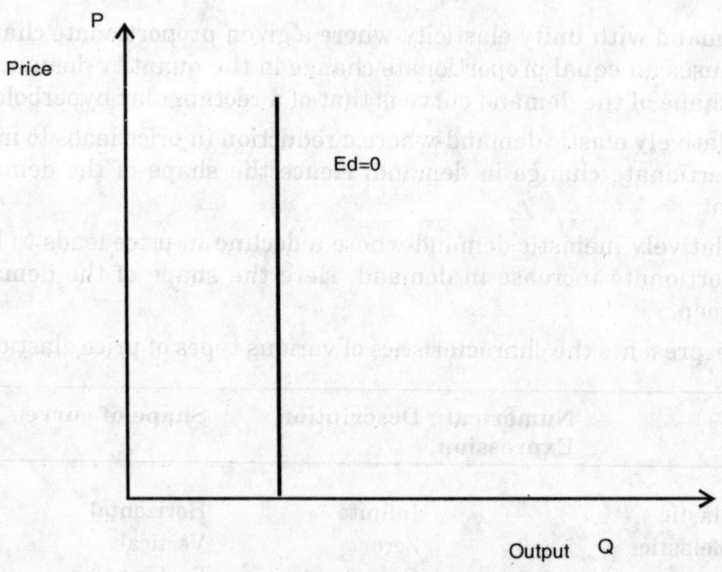

(a)

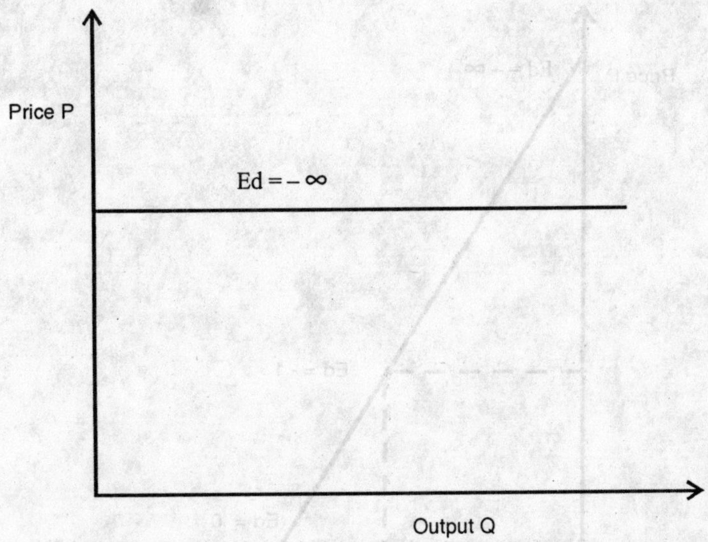

(b)

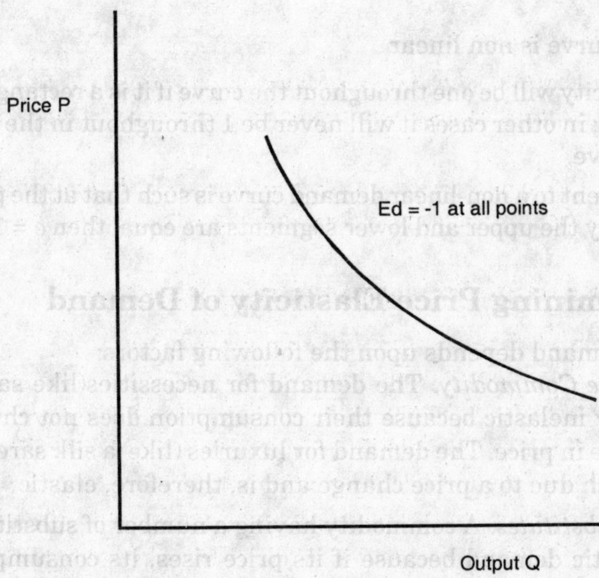

(C)

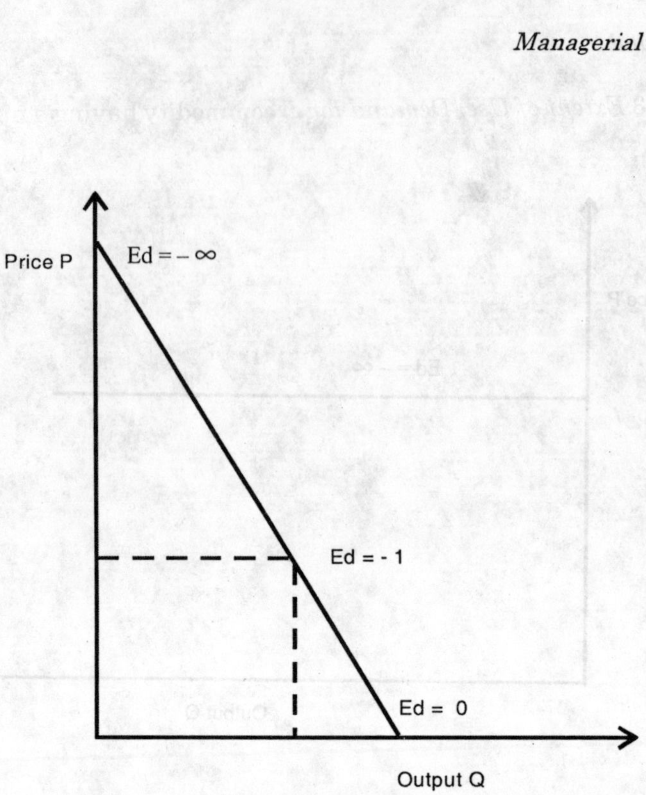

(d)

Figure 4.2 Price elasticities ofdemand

B. When demand curve is non linear

1. The elasticity will be one throughout the curve if it is a rectangular hyperbola: in other cases it will never be 1 throughout in the non-linear curve.
2. If the tangent to a non-linear demand curve is such that at the point of tangency the upper and lower segments are equal then $e = 1$.

Factors Determining Price Elasticity of Demand

The elasticity of demand depends upon the following factors:

1.*Nature of the Commodity.* The demand for necessities(like salt or wheat) is generally inelastic because their consumption does not change much with a change in price. The demand for luxuries (like a silk saree, or a car) changes much due to a price change and is, therefore, elastic

2. *Range of Substitutes.* A commodity having a number of substitutes has relatively elastic demand because if its price rises, its consumption can be curtailed in favour of the substitutes. A commodity with no substitutes or with weak substitutes has relatively inelastic demand.

3.*Extent of Use. Demand for a* commodity having a number of uses is comparatively elastic. For example, steel can be used for many purposes. A slight fall in its price will bring forth demand from many quarters and hence demand is elastic. On the other hand, a commodity having a limited use will have a comparatively inelastic demand.

4. *Income Level.* People with high incomes are less affected by price changes than people with low incomes. A rich man will not curtail consumption of fruits and/or milk even if their price rises significantly and will continue to purchase the same quantity as before. But a poor man cannot do so. Hence the demand for fruits or milk is inelastic for the rich but elastic for the poor.

5. *Proportion of Income Spent on the Commodity.* Where an individual spends only a small part of his income on the commodity, the price change does not materially affect his demand for the commodity , *e.g.,* match box, salt. etc., and the demand is inelastic.

6.*Durability of a Commodity:* The more durable and repairable a commodity is, the higher is its elasticity of demand likely to be because if the price rises considerably, one is likely to use the commodity for a longer time, if necessary, after getting it repaired eg. shoes

7. *Purchase Frequency of a Product* If the frequency of purchase of a product is very high, its demand would be more price elastic than in the case of a product which is purchased less often.

Revenue Relationships

For purposes of demand analysis, it is useful to differentiate between various types of revenue.

Average Revenue means the total receipts from sales divided by the number of units sold { i.*e* AR = TR /Q },

Total Revenue means the total sales proceeds. It can be calculated by multiplying quantities sold by price *[ie, TR = p times Q].*

Incremental Revenue simply measures the difference between the new total revenue and the existing total revenue. Its formula is: $IR = R_2 - R_1 = \Delta R$.

Marginal Revenue is the additional revenue which would be earned by selling an additional unit of a firm's product. It thus shows the change in total revenue when one more or one less unit is sold. Algebraically, it is the addition to total revenue earned by selling *n* units of a product instead of *n* -1, where *n* is any given number. Alternatively, marginal revenue refers to the addition to total revenue earned by selling *n* + I units instead of *n* units.

In actual business, it is rare that output is increased by only one unit. What happens is that additional inputs result in additional output. The extra revenue for this additional output can be determined by finding out the change in total revenue as a result of the sale of this output. This is known as incremental revenue. However, to find out the marginal revenue, the incremental revenue will have to be divided by the increase in output. This will give the extra revenue for the additional unit of output. The marginal revenue over the entire range of extra output will be constant.The formula for marginal revenue, thus, is:

$$MR = (R_2 - R_1) / (Q_2 - Q_1) = \Delta R / \Delta Q$$

The reason for dividing by the difference between the old quantity and the new quantity is to convert the *total* change in revenue into per unit change of output.

Incremental revenue differs from marginal revenue in the following ways:

1. Incremental revenue is the change in total revenue irrespective of the change in sales whereas marginal revenue is the change in total revenue per unit of change in sales.

2. Incremental revenue is not confined to the effects of price change. It rather -measures the effect of any kind of managerial decision on total revenue

Relationship between price elasticity of demand, total revenue and marginal revenue are as follows:

1.When price elasticity of demand > 1 , the marginal revenue is positive and the total revenue rises as price falls.

2.When price elasticity of demand = 1, the marginal revenue is zero and a change in price will not change the total revenue.

3.When the price elasticity of demand < 1, the marginal revenue is negative and the total revenue falls as price falls.

Relationship between average revenue, marginal revenue and price elasticity of demand: Joan Robinson has given the following formulae which shows the relationships of three at any output:

1.Average revenue = marginal revenue x e / (e – 1)

2.Marginal revenue = average revenue x (e – 1) / e

where e = price elasticity of demand on average revenue curve.

Price Elasticity of Demand and Business Decisions

The price elasticity of demand concept has important practical applications in managerial decisiòn-making. A good knowledge of the elasticity of demand of a commodity as well as the brand produced by the company and "the way total outlay responds to price changes, is essential for the effective analysis of a wide range of business problems specially pricing and marketing problems. Often a businessman has to consider whether a lowering of price will lead to an increase in the demand for his product, and if so, to what extent and whether his profits would increase as a result thereof. Here the concept of elasticity of demand plays an important role. If the increase in sales is more than proportionate to the decline in price, firm's total revenue, will increase and profits might be greater. However. if the increase in sales is less than proportionate, the total revenue will decline and profits will also be less. A knowledge of the nature of the elasticity of demand for his products will help a businessman to decide whether he should cut his price in a particular case or not. Such a knowledge would also help a businessman to determine whether and to what extent the increase in costs could be passed on to the consumer. In general. for items whose demand is elastic it will pay him to charge relatively low prices, while on those products whose demand is inelastic, he could charge higher price. A monopolist would not be able to increase his price if the demand for his product is elastic.

Elasticity mainly depends upon the desire for the commodity and upon the availability of substitutes for it. If the desire for a commodity is urgent, a higher price will not result in a great decrease in the quantity sold unless there are many substitutes available. If there are many substitutes available (i) a decline in the price of the product will lead to product replacing its substitutes, and (ii) an increase in its price will lead to its substitution by the substitutes, provided the prices of substitutes do not change at the same time and to the same extent. The most immediate substitutes for the product of any company are the products of its competitors. Also, the demand for a product is more elastic over a period than it is at a particular time because the process of substitution often takes time.

The price elasticity of demand for a certain commodity and the price elasticity of demand for a certain brand of that commodity may be radically different. For example demand for cigarettes is highly inelastic (that is, elasticity approaching zero}, but the price elasticity of demand for the product of a firm, say, a particular brand of cigarette, is generally greater than one. The reason for this is weak brand loyalty and the availability of substitutes.

In practice its difficult to have an accurate estimate of the probable response of volume of sales to price changes. Moreover, the cost of the statistical analysis required in some cases may exceed the benefits especially when uncertainty is great or when the volume is too small to provide a reasonable return on the amount spent on research. Also, the subjective judgements of certain managers, based on years of experience, sometimes are more accurate than results of the best statistical techniques. Due to these reasons, businessmen need not make very precise calculations of the numerical size of the elasticity of demand; instead, subjective estimates of experienced businessmen may serve the purpose.

Income elasticity of demand

Income elasticity of demand is defined as the degree of responsiveness of quantities demanded to a given change in income. Its formula is:

$$e_y = \frac{\text{Proprotionate change in quantities demanded}}{\text{Proportionate change in income}}$$

$$= \frac{Q_2 - Q_1}{(Q_2 + Q_1)} \div \frac{Y_2 - Y_1}{Y_2 + Y_1}$$

The size and sign of the income elasticity of demand for a product depends to a great extent upon the nature of the product in question and the level of income which consumers have reached. In the case of *necessities,* consumers will purchase a certain amount even at very low levels of income, but they will not increase their spending on these goods as their income rises. The Engel curve showing the relationship between income and demand for the product will be relatively flat, as shown in Fig, (a) and income elasticity of demand will be positive but less than 1, indicating income inelasticity of demand.

In the case of *luxury goods,* little or nothing will be spent at very low levels of income, but once a threshold level has been passed, as at Y_1 in Fig.(b) consumption of such goods will increase rapidly, indicating that demand is income elastic, having an income elasticity greater than 1.

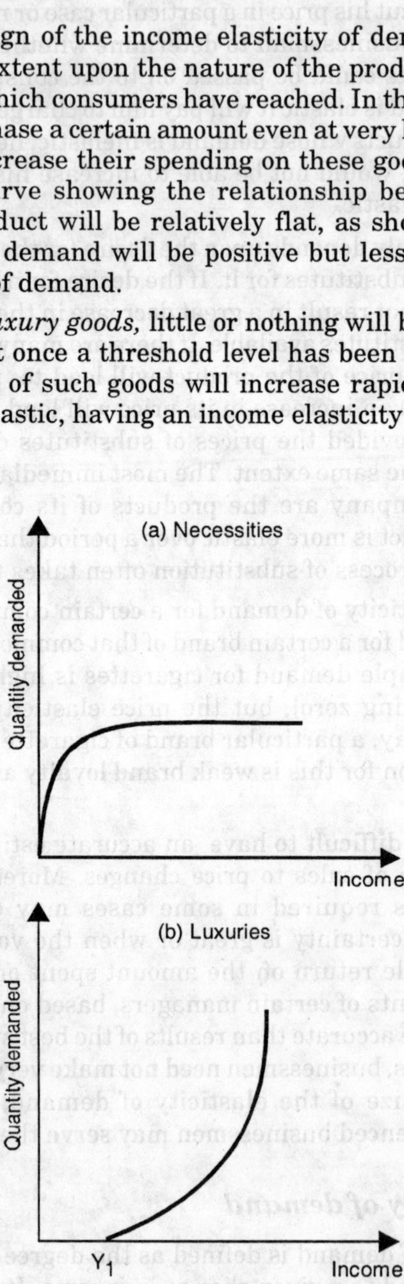

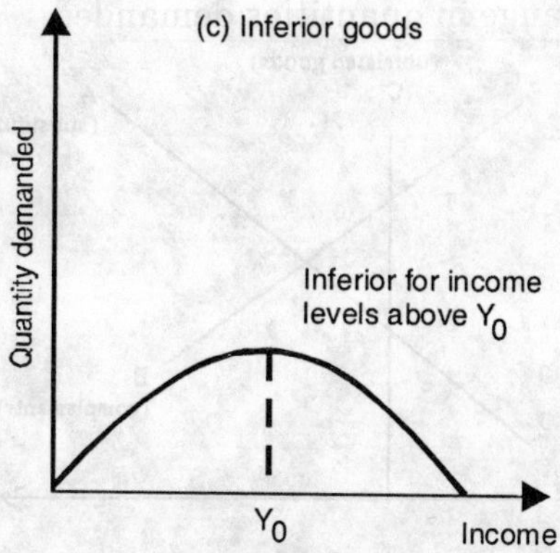

Fig: Engel curves

For *normal goods,* including both necessities and luxuries, income elasticity is positive, as consumption increases with income. For *inferior goods,* income elasticity is negative as consumers chose to purchase less of such commodities as they have higher incomes, as shown in the Engel curve in Fig.(c).

Cross elasticity of demand

Cross elasticity of demand indicates the responsiveness of the demand for a commodity to change in the prices of other goods, the most important other goods to consider being close substitutes and complements. In other words cross elasticity is the proportionate change in the quantity demanded of a particular commodity in response to a change in the price of another related commodity. Suppose the price of one commodity, say y is the independent variable whereas the quantity of another commodity, say x, is the dependent variable. The cross elasticity of demand is calculated by the following formula:

$$e_p = \frac{\text{Proportionate change in quantity purchased of x}}{\text{Proportionate change in price charged for y}}$$

$$= \frac{(Qx_2 - Qx_1)/(Qx_2+Qx_1)}{(Py_2 + Py_1)/(Py_2+Py_1)}$$

The goods are substitutes if cross elasticity is positive and the goods are complements if cross elasticity is negative.

And the cross elasticity of demand for unrelated goods is zero. Figure below shows some possible relationships between the quantity demanded of x and the price of y. Function A shows the demand for x rises as Py rises, implying that x and y are substitutes. Function B shows that the demand for x falls as Py rises, implying that x and y are complements. Function C indicates there is no relationship between x and Py.

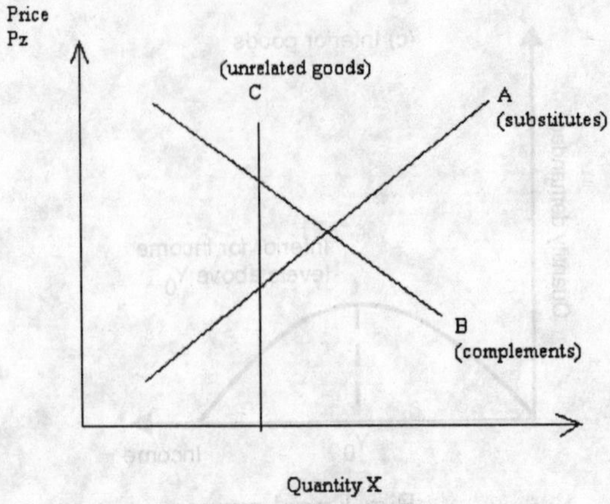

Figure: Cross elasticities of demand

Advertising elasticity of demand

Advertising elasticity or promotional elasticity is used to measure the increase in demand for a product by means of advertisement and other promotional activities. The advertising elasticity measures the responsiveness of demand to changes in advertising or other promotional expenses. The formula for advertising elasticity is:

$$e_a = \frac{\text{Proportionate change in sales}}{\text{Proportionate change in advertising expenditure}}$$

$$= \frac{(Q_2 - Q_1) / (Q_2 + Q_1)}{(A_2 - A_1) / (A_2 + A_1)}$$

where Q and A stands for sales and advertising outlays.

Factors determining advertising elasticity of demand are

1.Type of commodity: Advertising elasticity will be higher for luxury goods than for necessities. Also advertising elasticity would be higher for new and growing products than for old products.

2.Market share: The advertising elasticity would be lower for firms having larger market share and vice-versa.

3 Rival's reaction: If rivals increases their own advertising spending in reaction to an increase in a firm's advertising expenditure, the expenditures will tend to cancel each other out thus reducing advertising elasticity of demand.

4.Economic conditions: If economic conditions are good and household have more spending power, they are more likely to respond to advertising than when incomes and expenditures are tightly constrained.

The demand curve for an individual firm

The analysis above has been solely concerned with the market demand curve for goods, and the elasticity of that curve, which depends upon the existence of substitutes, the importance of the commodity in consumers' total spending, and upon the length of time in which consumers are able to adjust their purchasing patterns. While information on market demand is useful for individual firms they will tend to be even more concerned with the demand conditions for their own individual product, rather than that for the output of the industry as a whole. This in turn depends upon the *competitive structure* of the industry. A number of different cases may be distinguished.

The first is where the industry is a pure monopoly in that there is only one firm producing the product in question, and there is no possibility of entry by other firms into the industry. In that case the demand curve for the individual firm is the market demand curve for the industry as a whole, and there are no further complications.

The second case, at the other extreme of the spectrum of market structures, is perfect competition, where there are a large number of firms in the industry, all producing identical variants of the product. In this case, the price will be set by the interaction of supply and demand and each individual firm will be able to sell as much as it wishes at that price, but none at higher prices. The demand curve for the individual firm will be a horizontal straight line, as shown in Fig forEd = - ∞in price elasticity.

In the case of market structures which are neither pure monopolies nor perfectly competitive, demand conditions for the individual firm will depend upon a number of factors.

The first is the elasticity of market demand for the product as a whole. Clearly, if demand for the product as a whole is perfectly elastic, individual firms will be unable to sell their product at anything apart from the indicated price.The second determinant of the elasticity of demand for an individual firm is the degree of product differentiation or brand loyalty on the part of purchasers. If products are highly differentiated and purchasers are extremely loyal to a particular firm, the demand curve will be downward sloping, rather than horizontal. Each firm is essentially a 'mini-monopolist', producing a product for which there are no very close substitutes. On the other hand, if products are identical, and consumers exhibit no brand loyalty, demand curves will be horizontal lines, as no consumer will be prepared to pay more for the product of one firm than for the product of another.

The third factor which will determine the elasticity of demand for the individual firm's output will be its share of the market. If a firm has a very large market share, a reduction in its price will need to attract a substantial proportion of other firms' customers if the proportionate increase in its demand is to be large. On the other hand, a firm with a very small market share will be able to induce a large proportionate increase in its sales by attracting a relatively small proportion of its rivals' customers.

Fourthly, the elasticity of demand for an individual firm's product will depend upon its rivals' reactions to its changes in price. If rivals react to a price reduction by increasing their output (and reducing their own prices) then clearly demand will be less responsive than if rivals maintain or even reduce their output.

For the case of undifferentiated products, Needham identifies the following simple equation linking the various different determinants of the demand for an individual firm's product:

$$Ef = (E_m + E_s . S_r) / S_f$$

where:

E_f = elasticity of demand for the firm's product
E_m = market elasticity
E_s = elasticity of rival's supply with respect to changes in the firm's price
S_f = the firm's market share
S_r = rivals' market share

As the formula confirms, elasticity of demand for the firm's product is partly determined by rivals' reactions to its own actions, which cannot be known for certain, and which are therefore sometimes referred to as 'conjectural variation'.

Control or Management of Demand

In practice, demand forecasting may not be enough. At times, control or management of demand may become necessary. In that case, demand forecasting may, of course, make the way for effective demand management.

Bigger firms in industrial countries usually plan their production well in advance. If there are uncontrolled price movements, there will be total uncertainty as to whether there will be profit or loss and in what dimension. Naturally there is a tendency to regulate (control) prices. It would, however, be quixotic for the firm to seek control over its prices and then leave purchases at these prices to the random fate of taste and accident. So, the need arises to control what is sold at these prices. As a result, the control or management of demand has become a vast and rapidly growing industry in itself. The purpose of demand management is to ensure that people buy what is produced. Although advertising is certainly important as the central theme of this management, much more is involved. Included among the managers are those who sell goods and design the strategies by which they are sold.

The key to management of demand is the effective management of the purchases of final consumers. Again, the effective management of the consumer demand requires management not only of how income is spent but also of the amount of income that is available for spending on specific goods. Though a hungry man cannot be persuaded as between bread and a movie, a well nourished man can be. The faster a man satisfies his physical needs, the more open he is to persuasion- or management - as to what he buys because he moves on to next level of satisfaction i.e. emotional satisfaction.

The management of demand consists in devising a sales strategy for a particular product. It also consists of devising a product, or features of product, around which a sales strategy can be built. Product design, packaging, bringing new models and performance reflect the need to provide strong selling points.

Consumer Behaviour and Demand

In this section, we will understand how the market demand curve for a consumer is linked to and based on the tastes and preferences of consumers in the market for his good. An analysis of consumer behaviour is significant as it forms the basis of individual demand which in aggregate constitutes market demand. Two theories of consumer behaviour have been taken into account to explain how the demand curve for a good is derived. The two appoaches are:

(a) Marginal utility analysis or cardinal utility approach, and

(b) Indifference curve analysis or ordinal utility approach

Both the theories are important in their own right as a basis of downward sloping demand curve. Perhaps their greater significance lies in building a model of rational choice. That is, an optimal decision made either by a consumer or a manager by a careful analysis of preferences and trade offs among available alternatives. The cardinal approach asserts that utility is quantitatively measurable like length and weight. While the modern theory or ordinal concept is based on ordering of preferences. The modem economists are of the view that utility cannot be measured in absolute terms rather a consumer can only express his satisfaction in terms of 'less than' or 'more than' or rank his preferences.

Marginal Utility Analysis

A goods is desired as it gives the consumer satisfaction or utility. Utility is the want satisfying power of a goods. It is a subjective entity. Utility is 'ethically neutral.' Like liquor and drugs may satisfy need of a section of a society but they are socially immoral.

Assumptions of the Marginal Utility Theory

The marginal utility analysis was developed by Marshall on the basis of certain assumptions.

(1) Utility is a cardinal concept -This implies that utility is measurable and quantifiable. Money is regarded by Marshall as the measuring rod of

utility. The price which each consumer is willing to pay for each unit of a good rather than go without it is the measure of utility it derives from that good.

(2) Rationality -A consumer is rational as he tries to maximise his satisfaction subject to the constraint posed by his budget or limited income.

(3) Constancy of marginal utility of money -The marginal utility of money remains constant throughout when the individual is spending money on a good.

(4) Utility is additive -The utility derived from the consumption of good X, Y and Z depends on their consumption i.e., Ux = f (Qx), Uy = f (Qy) and Uz = f (Qz). The total utility function now is: U = Ux + Uy + Uz. Thus, total utility is the sum of independent utilities derived by an individual from the consumption of different goods.

The Law of Diminishing Marginal Utility

The law of diminishing marginal utility is the basis of the marginal utility approach. Marginal utility refers to the change in satisfaction when a little more or little less of that good is consumed. The law of diminishing marginal utility states that 'the additional benefit which a person derives from a given increase in stock of a thing diminishes with every increase in the stock he already has' (Marshall). The utility decreases with additional consumption because the intensity of need of the consumer goes on decreasing.

The law of diminishing marginal utility recognises that wants of an individual are unlimited and each single unit is satiable. Therefore, when a person consumes additional units of good, his total utility increases till a certain level while the extra utility derived fron the consumption of successive unit of the good decreases. Total utility is maximum when marginal utility approaches zero and then starts decreasing. Table below shows the total utility and marginal utility derived from cups of coffee consumed per day.

Coffee consumed (units) (cups /day)	**Total utility (units)**	**Marginal utility**
0	0	-
1	12	12
2	21	9
3	27	4
4	27	0
5	23	-4
6	16	-7

When one cup of coffee is taken per day, the total utility derived by a person is 12 units and marginal utility derived is also 12 units. With consumption of second cup per day total utility increases to 21 units and marginal utility decreases to 9 units. Total utility is maximum at 4 cups a day and marginal utility is zero, beyond this level marginal utility becomes negative. The downward sloping diminishing marginal utility curve depicts the law of diminishing returns. The law applies to all goods and services except in case of money, music and hobby. But in these cases also after a certain level marginal utility declines.

Hypothesis of Utility Maximisation: Consumer Equilibrium

Income of a consumer is a constraint that consumer face. In order to maximise satisfaction, he allocates his limited income among various goods in such a way that marginal utility of each good is proportional to its price. We also know that, the marginal utility derived from consuming various goods is subject to diminishing returns and some goods yield greater satisfaction than others. As a rational consumer, an individual selects a good with highest utility followed by others in preference. Consumer switches his expenditure from one good to the other in accordance with their marginal utility.

The consumer attains utility maximising equilibrium when he spends his income in such a way that the utility derived from the last rupee spent on each good is equal. Suppose, there are two goods X and Y. The consumer will exchange his money income for good X as long as marginal utility of X is greater than constant utility of money weighted by the price of the good. That is, the consumer will get more utility by increasing expenditure and the level of satisfaction is where;

$$\mathbf{MU_x = P_x\ (MU_m\}}$$

where MU_m is marginal utility of money expenditure, MU_x is the marginal utility of good, X and P_x is the price of good X. Since the law of equi-marginal utility states that a consumer will spend his money income on various goods in such a way that marginal utility of each good is proportional to its price. The consumer will spend his money income on purchase of X and Y such that,

$$MU_x / P_x = MU_y / P_y = MU_m$$

The consumer reaches equilibrium when the marginal utility derived form each rupee spent on goods X and Y are same. The equality can be achieved at different levels of expenditures.This equation is applicable in case of more than two goods as well.

Indifference Curve Analysis

The starting point of indifference curve analysis is the assumption that although consumers cannot assign a precise utility value to different amounts of commodity, they are able to decide which combinations of the commodities they prefer to others. The consumer's aim is not to maximize cardinally measurable 'utility' but to achieve the highest possible level of ordinally measurable 'satisfaction'. In this case consumers will not be able to count the number of utils arising from the consumption of different units of a commodity but they will be able to decide which combinations of goods they prefer to others. Consumers know which combinations of goods give them most satisfaction. They also know when they are indifferent between two different combinations of commodities. Therefore it will be possible to draw indifference curves for any pair of commodities, showing the combinations of different amounts of the two goods which consumers are indifferent between. Figure below , has been arrived at by first randomly selecting a combination of apples and oranges, at a point A, then considering which other combinations of apples and oranges would leave the consumer feeling equally satisfied.

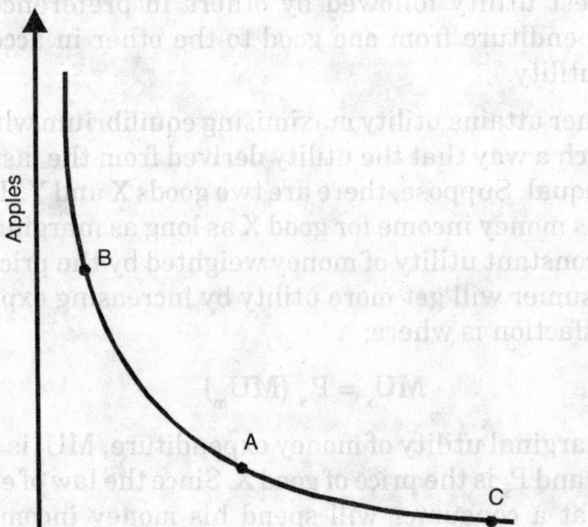

Fig: An indifference curve

The shape of an indifference curve will depend upon a number of factors. If both the commodities are such that consumers get satisfaction from both, the indifference curves will slope downwards from left to right, showing that if a consumer has less of one they will require more of the other in order to remain equally satisfied. If the basic principle behind the concept of diminishing marginal utility also holds true, so that consumers experience successively less additional satisfaction from each additional unit of a good, the indifference curves will be concave as shown in figure above.

If the consumer has a large number of apples and a small number of oranges as at point B, then they will be prepared to sacrifice quite a large number of apples (which are giving them relatively little satisfaction at the margin) for a small number of oranges (which give them a high level of satisfaction). The indifference curve will therefore be relatively steep at a point like B. On the other hand, at a point like C, where the converse is the case and the consumer has a large number of oranges and few apples, the curve will be relatively flat, showing that if they gave up a large number of oranges they would need relatively few apples in order to compensate. This idea is similar to the principle of diminishing marginal utility, known in the context of indifference analysis as diminishing marginal rate of substitution.

Indifference analysis generally assumes that indifference curves are concave upwards and also they are smooth and continuous , implying that the goods in question are very highly divisible and that levels of satisfaction also change in a continuous fashion.

If the consumer has a choice between two goods and increasing amounts of a commodity yield diminishing marginal satisfaction, indifference curves will take the general shape as shown in figure above. Their precise shape depends upon the strength of the consumer's relative preferences for the two commodities in question. If the consumer is an apple-lover with a great liking for apples and a lesser liking for oranges, the curve will be relatively flat, as shown in figure (a) below, because the consumer would be willing to sacrifice a large number of oranges in return for a small number of additional apples. On the other hand, if the consumer is an orange lover the curve will be relatively steep as in figure (b) below.

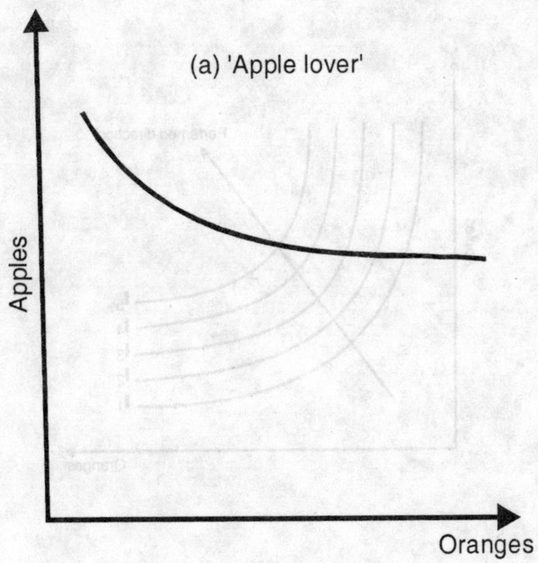

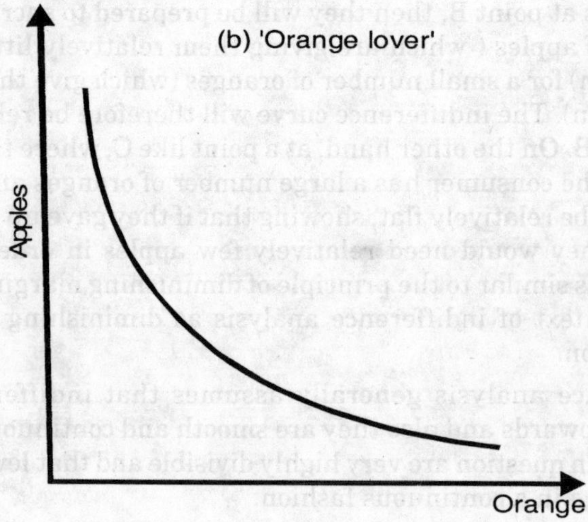

Fig: Indifference curves and consumer preferences

A single indifference curve gives a great deal of information about a consumer's preferences for the commodities concerned. However, it concerns only one level of satisfaction, showing as it does all the different combinations of apples and oranges for which the consumer is indifferent to the combination at point A. As point A was chosen at random therefore there are an infinite number of a number of indifference curves. The diagram showing a number of indifference curves is called indifference map as shown in the figure below.

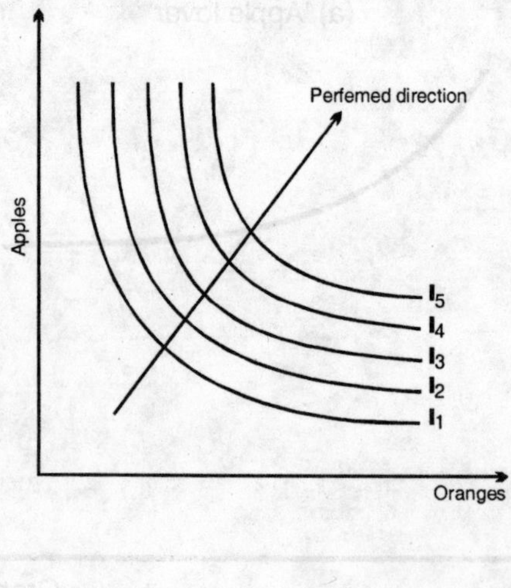

Important properties of indifference curve are

1. The curves which are further away from the origin represents higher levels of satisfaction. Consumer would prefer to move from lower indifference curve to higher indifference curve.

2. Indifference curves will not cross each other. If they did as shown in figure below, a logical contradiction would be implied. Poin X on indifference curve I_1 must indicate a higher level of satisfaction than point Y on indifference curve I_2, as it lies further from the origin. But point Z, which lies on both indifference curves, yields the same level of satisfaction as both Y and X. Clearly this can not be the case and indifference curves cannot cross.

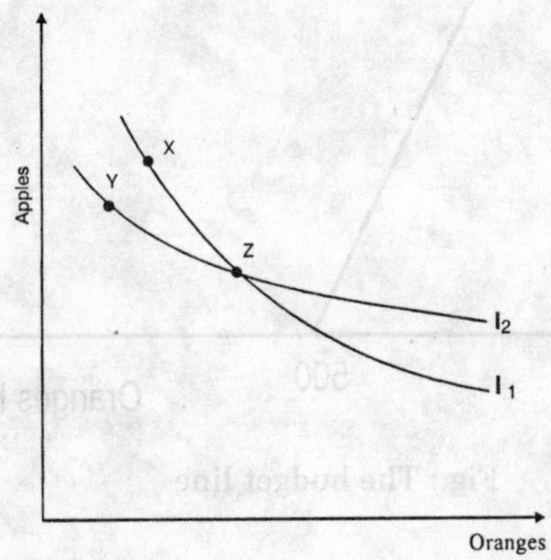

Consumer equilibrium

Having established the concept of the indifference map it is then possible to analyse the consumer's choice between alternative combinations of commodities. As the aim of the consumer is to reach the highest possible level of satisfaction, this can be represented in the analysis by noting that the consumer will choose the combination of commodities which is located on the highest possible indifference curve. However, the consumers are restricted in their choice of combinations of commodities by their income, which only allows them to purchase a limited amount of goods. The combinations of goods which consumers are able to purchase depends upon their income and the price of goods and can be represented in the diagrammatic analysis by a **budget line,** as shown in figure below.

If the consumer has an income of Rs 1000, apples cost Rs10 per kilo and oranges cost Rs 20 per kilo, then the combinations of apples and oranges which the consumer can buy are given by the straight line shown in figure above. If all of the consumer's income were spent on apples, they could consume 1000 kilos of apples and no oranges. Conversely, by spending all of the available income on oranges the consumer could have 500 kilos of oranges and no apples. Intermediate combinations of apples and oranges

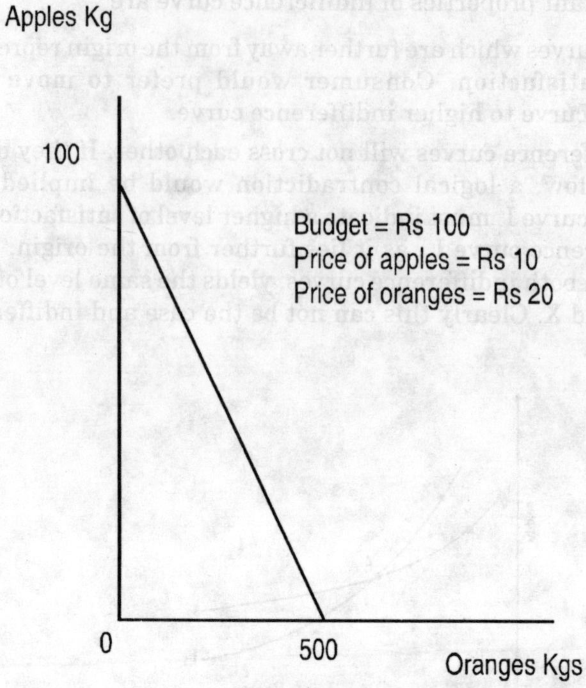

Fig.: The budget line

which the consumer is able to purchase are given by the straight line joining the two intercepts, which is simply the line given by the equation:

$$Y = P_A.A + P_O.O$$

where:

Y	=	consumer's income
P_A	=	price of apples
P_O	=	price of oranges
A	=	amount of apples
0	=	amount of oranges

It may be noted that the slope of this line is equal to the ratio of the prices of the two commodities. It is assumed that all of the consumer's income must be spent on the two goods in question, which are the only commodities available. The analysis can easily be extended to cover a larger number of goods but in that case diagrams have to replaced by mathematical workings.

The budget line shows the combinations of goods which the consumer is able to purchase and the indifference map shows the combinations which give the highest level of satisfaction. Bringing the two together makes it possible to identify the equilibrium combination of goods, which gives the highest level of satisfaction. This is shown in the figure below at point X.

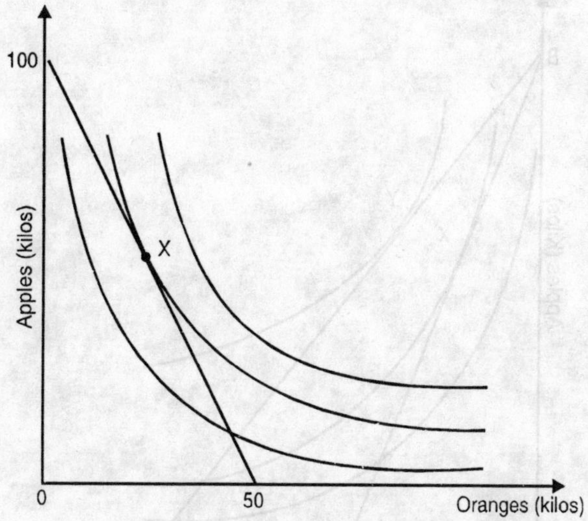

Fig: Consumer equilibrium

As the figure shows, at the equilibrium position the slope of the budget line, which is equal to the ratio of the prices of the two commodities, is equal to the slope of the indifference curve to which it is a tangent, which may be interpreted as the marginal rate of substitution between the two commodities in question.

Income and substitution effects

Having identified the equilibrium position for the consumer it is possible to consider how changes in prices will affect consumer behaviour and the implications of the analysis for the shape of the demand curve for commodities. Fig. below shows the same initial equilibrium position as in Fig above but also illustrates the change which takes place if the price of oranges falls from Rs20 to Rs10.

The most obvious effect of the change in the price of oranges is to shift the budget line from BB to BB_r. As a result of that change, the optimal combination of apples and oranges shifts from X to Y.

In the example shown, more oranges are bought when their price falls (indicating a downward-sloping demand curve for oranges) and more apples are also bought. This is clear enough in the specific example given, but it remains to consider whether this is a general result which must always hold, or whether it is simply a function of the particular circumstances indicated in the diagram. In order to analyse this issue effectively it is necessary to carry out a careful examination of the factors involved in the shift from the original equilibrium X to the new position Y.

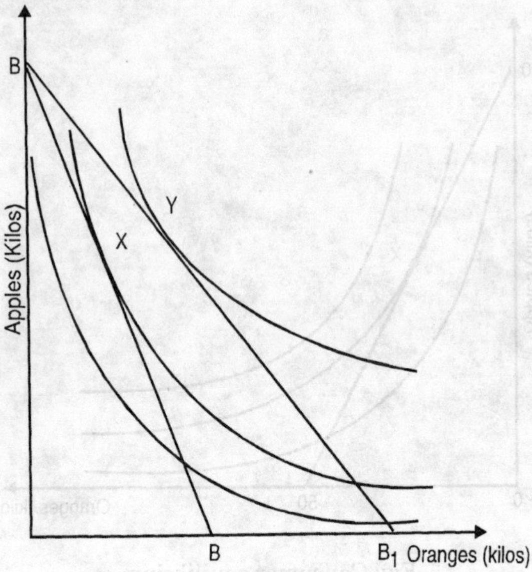

Fig. The impact of a price change

When the price of a good falls, leading to a change in the optimal basket of goods chosen by a rational consumer, two separate events may be said to have taken place. First, the fall in price has led to an increase in the real income of the consumer and this change in income will alter the goods which the consumer chooses to purchase. That change is known as 'the income effect.' Second, the relative prices of apples and oranges have changed, which will also alter the choice of purchases. That change is known as 'the substitution effect.' These two phenomena may be examined separately, by extending the diagram set out above as shown in Fig. below.

The overall change induced by the fall in the price of oranges is indicated by the shift from X to Y, which is known as 'the price effect.' This can be subdivided into two separate components, as indicated. In order to isolate the income effect it is necessary to ask 'how would the basket of goods purchased change if the consumer's real income rose by the amount which it has, but relative prices stayed the same? The answer can be found by recognising that the change in the consumer's real income is represented by the shift from the lower indifference curve I_1 to the higher one I_2 and that relative prices are represented by the slope of the budget line. In terms of the diagram the answer can be found by examining how the basket of goods would change if the consumer were on indifference curve I_2, enjoying the higher level of income, but relative prices were as given by the original budget line BB. This can be found simply by shifting the line BB outwards, parallel to its original position, thereby indicating the same

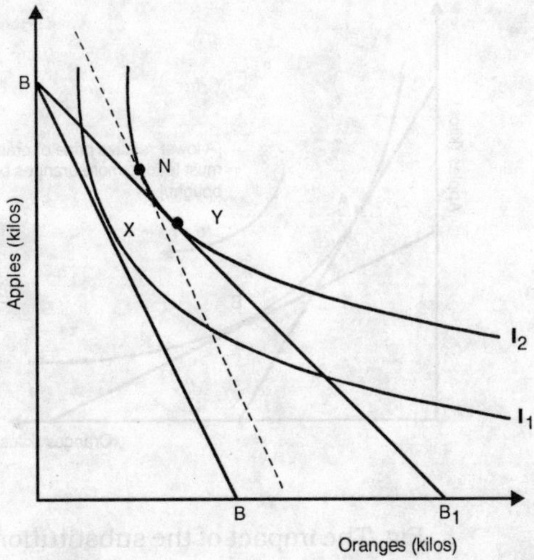

Fig. The income and substitution effects

relative prices, until it is tangential to the higher indifference curve I_2. Point N, where the two lines meet, shows the combination of goods which the consumer would purchase if their income rose sufficiently to place them on I_2 but relative prices remained unchanged. The shift from the initial equilibrium position X to N is the income effect.

The substitution effect may be found by a similar process. It may be defined as the change in the basket of goods which would be purchased if relative prices changed, at a constant real income. This may be interpreted as the movement around the indifference curve I_2 from N to Y. The total 'price effect', then, may be disaggregated into its two components, the income effect changing the basket of goods from X to N and the substitution effect taking it from N to Y. Each of these may then be examined separately in order to illuminate the links between price changes and the level of demand for a good.

If the substitution effect is taken first, it is clear that its impact must always be to increase the demand for a good whose price has fallen. As indifference curves slope from left to right, with the slope decreasing to the right, then a fall in price of the commodity measured on the horizontal axis, which makes the budget line flatter must mean that the point of equilibrium shifts to the right, as illustrated in Fig below.

While the direction of the substitution effect is unambiguous and supports the notion of a downward-sloping demand curve, the income effect is much more uncertain. It is feasible that for some goods increases in income lead to less, rather than more, being bought. Such commodities are known technically as 'inferior goods'.

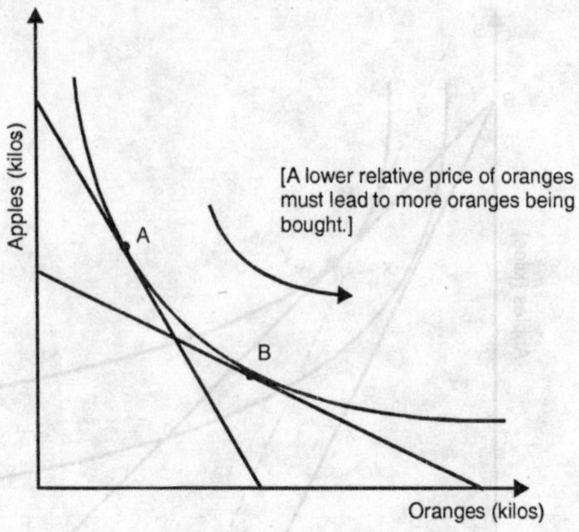

Fig. The impact of the substitution effect

In the case of inferior goods, the consumer's overall response to a fall in price depends upon the balance between the income effect and the substitution effect. If the substitution effect is larger than the negative income effect then a lower price will lead to more of the good being bought, as in the case of normal goods. However, in the extreme case where the negative income effect is larger than the substitution effect a fall in price will actually lead to less of the commodity being bought, rather than more, in contradiction to the downward-sloping form of the demand curve. Such goods are known as 'Giffen goods' example bread in nineteenth century. If consumers were spending a very high proportion of their income on the very cheapest foodstuffs then a fall in their price would lead to a very substantial increase in their real income. That increase in real income could lead them to substitute other types of food for the bread which they previously relied upon, thereby reducing the demand for bread as its price fell.

Revealed preference theory

The major advantage of indifference analysis over utility theory is that it involves making a much less restrictive set of assumptions about consumers' decision processes. Instead of assuming that every consumer can assign a cardinally measurable utility score to every unit of every commodity consumed, it assumes that they have a consistent set of preferences and know which combinations of commodities they prefer to others. Nevertheless, it has been argued that this is still a very restrictive set of assumptions to make, and theorists have sought alternative means by which a theory of consumer behaviour may be constructed. One such alternative approach is known as revealed preference theory.

The starting point for revealed preference theory is the assumption that the consumers are consistent in the way they make choices.

Consistency may be said to require the fulfilment of two conditions. The first is known as two term consistency, which simply requires that in a ranking of alternatives any two are always consistently placed relative to each other. In other words, if option A is placed above option B, then B can never be ranked above A. The second condition is transitivity, which simply means that if A is preferred to Band B is preferred to C, then A must be preferred to C.

For any given consumer, a budget line may be constructed, in exactly the same way as for indifference analysis, as shown by the line AO in Fig. below.

The line shows all the different consumption possibilities facing the consumer in question. In the case of revealed preference theory no knowledge of indifference curves is assumed, so there is no way of predicting where exactly the consumer will choose to be on the line AO. Instead the consumers' behaviour is simply observed as a means of revealing their preferences. Suppose that the consumers in question chooses the combination of goods indicated by point X. Now imagine that the price of oranges falls, so that there is a new budget line AO_1. As the consumers will now choose to be somewhere on the new budget line, they will choose a new combination of apples and oranges, perhaps point Z. In the example shown, point Z involves the purchase of more oranges than before, and the lower price of oranges has led increased demand for them. The demand curve slopes downwards. However, the analysis thus far has given no reason to suppose that this must necessarily be the case. Point Z was chosen arbitrarily, in order to illustrate the point. In the case indifference analysis the move from one consumer's equilibrium to another was explained in terms of an income effect and a.substitution effect, each of which could be seen to have certain characteristics. A similar procedure can be carried out using the assumptions of revealed preference theory, without having to assume detailed knowledge of preferences.

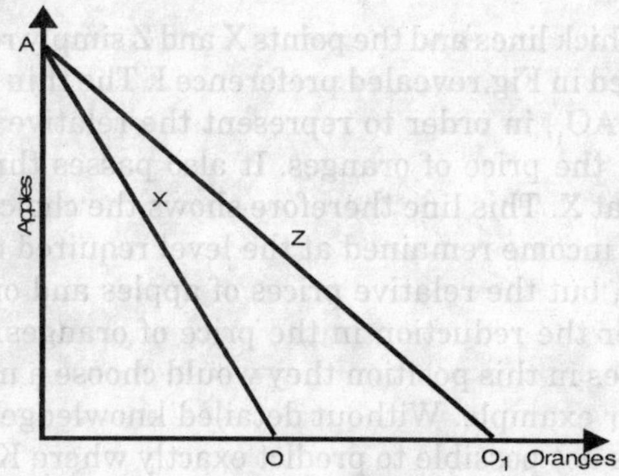

Fig. Revealed preference I

The example has shown a consumer moving from point X to point Z as a result of a change in price. This is the 'price effect', which may be divided into an income effect and a substitution effect. In the case of indifference analysis it was possible to isolate the substitution effect by defining 'a constant level of real income' to mean 'being on the same indifference curve', so that a movement around an indifference curve could be seen to represent a pure substitution effect, with changes in real income having been cancelled out. Clearly, this cannot be done within the framework of revealed preference theory, because no knowledge of indifference curves is assumed. However, there is an alternative way forward, which can be explained with the help of Fig below.

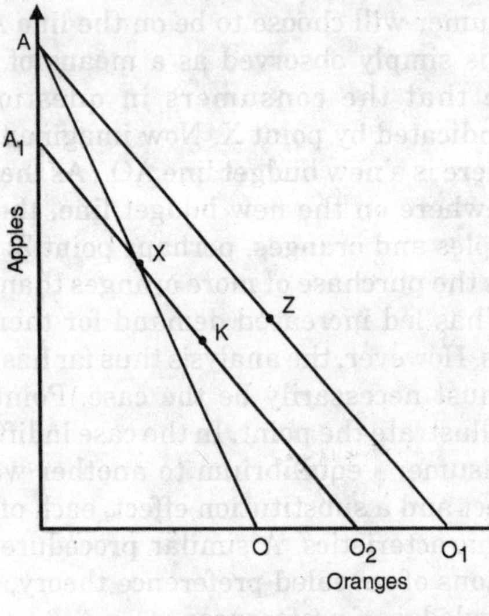

Fig: Revealed preference II

In Fig the thick lines and the points X and Z simply repeat the situation already described in Fig.revealed preference I. The thin line A_1O_2 is drawn parallel to line AO_1, in order to represent the relative prices which hold after the fall in the price of oranges. It also passes through the original choice of goods at X. This line therefore shows the choices available to the consumer if his income remained at the level required to buy the original basket of goods, but the relative prices of apples and oranges were those which hold after the reduction in the price of oranges. If the consumers found themselves in this position they would choose a new combination of goods, like K for example. Without detailed knowledge of the consumer's preferences it is not possible to predict exactly where K will be. However, on the very limited assumptions made about the consistency of consumers' choices it is possible to be certain that the point K must lie on or to the right of point X, between X and O_2. This is because the consumer's initial choice of point X indicates that it is considered superior to all the other combinations between A and X. As the combinations between A_1 and X are all inferior to those between A and X, consistency ensures that the consumer must choose to be either at X or to the right of it.

If the consumer selects point K such that it coincides with X then it could be said that there is no substitution effect. The change in relative prices leads to no change in the basket of goods selected. In this case, the whole of the shift from point X to point Z must be an income effect. On the other hand, if point K lies to the right of X (as shown) it is more difficult to unravel income and substitution effect. Certainly the move from K to Z is entirely due to the income effect, because it takes place without any change in relative prices. However, the move from X to K is a combination of substitution effect arising from changing relative prices and income effect arising from the fact that the consumer now faces a higher real income,

Revealed preference theory does not, therefore, allow a clear division of the price effect into a pure substitution effect and a pure income effect, except in the extreme case where the substitution effect is zero. What it does achieve, though, is essentially the same general conclusion as indifference analysis, without having to claim a detail knowledge of consumers' preferences. As the consumer will never choose a point on A_1O_2 which is to the left of X, the substitution effect can never lead to less of a good being bought when its price falls. The effect must always be to increase the amount bought or, in the very extreme case, to leave it constant. The income effect may, of course, operate in either direction, as was shown in indifference analysis and the overall effect of a price change, which determines the shape of the demand curve, depends upon the interaction of the two effects. Demand curves will slope downwards except in the case of Giffen goods where the income effect is negative and powerful enough to outweigh the substitution effect.

Managers with practical concerns may find the usefulness of an abstract exercise like revealed preference theory, difficult to discern. Nevertheless, it has the theoretical advantage of allowing us to make at least limited general predictions about consumer behaviour without having to assume that we have detailed knowledge of consumer preferences, and it also provides a basis on which statisticians and econometricians can build empirical models of demand behaviour which could provide estimates of consumers' responses to price and income changes which would be of practical help to decision-makers.

Limited information and conspicuous consumption

Each of the analyses above has tended to confirm the original commonsense notion that demand curves slope downwards, except in some identifiable and extreme cases. As a result this book will use such downward sloping curves whenever a demand curve is needed. However, it is worth noting that there may be some situations where this will not be the case. If consumers are ill-informed about the performance characteristics of a product they are purchasing, which may be the case for goods which they buy infrequently, or for goods where quality may vary in an unobservable way from batch to batch, it is possible that they may use the price as an indicator of quality, in which case consumers concerned to buy high quality merchandise may buy more of the same product at a higher price than at a lower price, mistakenly presuming that they are receiving a better quality product. (Colleges offering short courses for industry, for instance, commonly report more demand for the same product at higher prices than at lower prices.) However, for consumers to continue to behave in this way implies that they never learn and can always be seduced into parting with more of their hard-earned income than they need. If there is active competition between firms and easy entry into the industry, if there are consumer organisations and standard setting bodies, or if consumers simply share their experiences with each other, it is difficult to argue that such behaviour will be common or long-lasting. It is certainly not a sufficiently important phenomenon to suggest that the analysis of the firm should rest upon upward sloping demand curves, or that firms seeking profits should raise their prices in order to generate a greater volume of sales. In addition to the case where consumers mistakenly interpret high prices as indicators of high quality, there is another situation where the demand curve f product may slope upwards. This is where consumers take satisfaction in 'conspicuous consumption', enjoying the fact that the goods they purchase have a high price, and deriving less satisfaction from the same goods if they are available at a lower price.

In this case consumers are not simply deriving utility or satisfaction from the performance characteristics of the commodity in question, and seeing the price as the sacrifice they have to make, but seeing the price itself as one of the characteristics which directly gives them satisfaction. For some types of luxury goods this is a phenomenon which should not be ignored.

Questions

1. What is meant by 'demand'? Everyone desires a luxurious house, Does this mean that the demand for luxury houses is large?
2. Calculate price-elasticity of demand if:

   $Q_1 = 4{,}000 \quad P_1 = \text{Rs, } 20$

   $Q_2 = 5{,}000 \quad P_2 = \text{Rs, } 19$
3. Examine the role of price, income, prices of related goods and advertising as factors determining demand.

4. State and explain the Law of Demand, What are its exceptions?
5. What is the significance of demand analysis to a sales manager of a business firm? Explain the important determinants of demand, Demand Curve and Demand Function? Show how market demand is calculated from individual demands.
6. Explain the difference between shifts in demand curve and shifts along a demand curve. What causes the market demand curve for a commodity to
   (i) Increase (shifting up)
   (ii) Decrease (shifting down)
7. The market demand function of a commodity is given by $Q_A = 20 - 2P_A - 0.5\,P_B + 0.01Y$ where Q_A is quantity demanded of A and P_A is the price of A , P_B is the price of B and Y is the consumer's income. Calculate the price elasticity of demand for the A where $P_A = 5$, $P_B = 10$ and Y= 1000
8. Define and explain price elasticity of demand.
9. Distinguish various types of price elasticity of demand. Discuss the factors on which the elasticity of demand depends.
10. Calculate price-elasticity of demand for different years from the following data:

Year	Percent change in quantity	Percent change in price
1999-2000	Zero	1.3
2000-2001	-2.2	3.1
2001-2002	4.5	-1.2
2002-2003	-7.4	7.4
2003-2004	6.4	-2.4

11. What is meant by elasticity of demand? Explain giving a suitable illustration. How elasticity of demand determines the price policy of a firm.
12. State the relationship between price-elasticity of demand, average revenue. marginal revenue and total revenue.
   (a) Distinguish between incremental revenue and marginal revenue.
   (b) Suppose the price of a commodity falls from Rs, 10 to Rs, 9 per unit and its sales go up from 2,000 units to 3,000 units. Calculate incremental revenue and marginal revenue.
13. What do you understand by 'Shift in Demand Schedule' (Change in Demand)? Distinguish it from elasticity of demand. Give the reasons for demand shift.
14. If demand is elastic, it will pay a businessman to charge relatively low prices: if demand is inelastic, he would be better off with a higher

price." Discuss and point out the role of price-elasticity in business decisions.

15. Explain the utility of demand analysis for a firm.
16. Explain the concept of income-elasticity of demand and explain its role in business decisions.
17. Define cross-elasticity of demand and state its importance.
18. Would you expect the cross-elasticity of demand to be positive, negative or zero for each of the following pairs of products:

    (i) Hawkins and Prestige pressure cookers,
    (ii) Desks and chairs, and
    (iii) Kwality ice-cream and men's socks?
19. What general rule can you give to base your answers?
20. Define advertising elasticity of demand and discuss the factors affecting it.
21. What is advertising elasticity of demand? Explain the different approaches in determining the advertisement budgets. Discuss briefly the approach to measure effects of advertisement on sales.
22. State the utility of demand analysis for business firms and explain with illustrations how the following concepts are useful tools for managerial decisions:

    (a) Promotional elasticity,

    (b) Cross-elasticity, and

    (c) Demand schedules *vs.* Demand functions.
23. List the factors which appear to be most important for estimat1hg the demand for cement in the next 5 years.
24. Suppose that aluminium producers find that they are now able to sell more aluminium than they did last year at the same price. Suggests at least two reasons why this might occur. Is this a shift of the demand curve or movement along the curve?
25. Distinguish between the 'substitution effect' and the 'income effect' of a change in price and show the relative importance of these two effects in the law of demand.
26. Four of the 5 events described below might reasonably be responsible in shifting the demand curve for tea to a new position. Point out the one which would not shift that demand curve and why?
    (i) A rise in the price of some good which some consumers regard as substitute of tea.
    (ii) A fall in the price of tea.
    (iii) An increase in the money income of tea consumers.
    (iv) A widespread advertisement campaign undertaken by the producers of cofJi (v) A change in the people's taste with respect to tea.

27. Over the years the demand for textiles in India has grown in spite of considerable rise in prices. How do you reconcile this fact with the law of demand?
28. Distinguish between the following:
    (i) Producer goods and consumer goods.
    (ii) Durable goods and non-durable goods.
    (iii) Superior goods and inferior goods.
    (iv) Complementary goods and substitutes.
    (v) Company demand and industry demand.
29. Distinguish between derived demand and autonomous demand. Explain how derived demand has less price-elasticity than autonomous demand.
30. Explain the market share concept of demand and state its significance for forecasting company's sales. Point out the factors which determine the market share of a company.
31. Discuss the factors affecting the demand for *(a)* non-durable consumer goods and *(b)* capital goods.
32. *(i)* Why is demand analysis essential for successful production planning and capital expansion?
    (ii) If you have to analyse the demand prospects of *(a)* steel, and *(b)* automobiles, what factors would you take into consideration? Do you anticipate the importance of price elasticity of demand to be identical for both the products?
33. What are the various factors affecting the demand for durable consumer goods? Why is the problem of forecasting the demand of such goods more complicated?

5

Estimating and Forecasting Demand

In the process of business decision–making the concepts of demand curve and elasticities of demand play a very significant role. However, the theoretical concepts can only be of practical application if reliable quantitative estimates can be made of the level of demand and of elasticity. This is a difficult task, which can be approached in a number of ways as explained in this chapter. The most fundamental difference between **estimation**, which attempts to quantify links between the level of demand and the other variables which determine it, and **forecasting** which simply attempts to predict the level of demand at some future date.

Estimation can be done in following ways:

1) Simple estimation of arc elasticity: it is done by observing the quantity of the product sold before and after a price change and assuming that the two known combination of price and quantity are points on the same demand curve and demand could be estimated from the standard formula. For eg. if 100 units of output were sold at a price of Rs 10 and 120 units were sold when the price fell to Rs 8 then elasticity of demand can be estimated from the standard formula i.e. (change in quantity/ change in price). (price/quantity) which comes to (20/ - 2).(10/100) equals –1.

Advantage of this technique is that its simple and estimates can be made on the basis of a single price change. The disadvantages are that adjustments have to be made to compensate for speculative building up or running down of stocks in anticipation of a price change and there is no guarantee that the two price/output combinations observed lie on the same demand curve. It could quite easily be the case that both supply and demand curves shifted in the movement from A to B.

2) Econometric estimation of demand curves: its a more sophisticated approach to demand estimation. Econometrics is the statistical analysis of economic data using techniques like multiple regressions, which allow empirical data on demand and its determinants to be used to estimate the co-efficients of demand function. The general form of demand function has been taken as :

$$Q_d = f(P_{o,} P_{c,,} P_{s,} Y_{d,} T, A_{o,} A_{c,} A_{s,} I, C, E)$$

This equation simply states the quantity demanded is a function of each of the determinants, without specifying any particular functional form for the relationship between the dependent variable (Q_d) and the independent variables ($P_{o,} P_{c,,} P_{s,} Y_{d,} T, A_{o,} A_{c,} A_{s,} I, C, E$)

If the size of the coefficients linking the various independent variables with the level of demand is to be estimated a particular functional form needs to be chosen. The two most common forms are the **linear demand function** and the **exponential demand function.**

i) **The linear demand function** can be written as

$$Q_d = a+b_1P_o+b_2P_c+b_3P_s+b_4Y_d+b_5T+b_6A_o+b_7A_c+b_8A_s+b_9I+b_{10}C+b_{11}E$$

If data is available on each of the variable s, and there are sufficient observations to apply the statistical technique of multiple regression then the co-efficient for the intercept (a) and the co-efficient showing the impact of each determinant upon the quantity demanded (b1 to b11) can be estimated. Once they have been estimated it is possible to predict the level of demand for any set of values for each of the determinants by simply inserting these values into the equation.

In the case of the linear specifications of the demand curve,estimating the coefficients of the demand functions does not provide a direct estimate of the elasticity of demands. However it could be simply calculated as shown below. The definition of price elaticity of demand can be written as:

$$e_d = \frac{dQ}{DP_o} \cdot \frac{P_o}{Q}$$

However it could be seen from the demand function that :

$$\frac{dQ}{dP_o} = b_1$$

So that:

$$e_d = b_1 \cdot \frac{P_o}{Q}$$

Other elasticities ,including income elasticity, cross-price elasticity and advertising elasticity can be calculated in the same way. The linear form embodies the assumption that a given change in price always has the same effect on the volume, regardless of the level of price. This assumption conflicts with most economic reasoning , including theories of consumer behaviour, so that alternative methods are often used to estimate demand.

ii) **The exponential form** is one of the most popular alternative to linear form , which may be written as:

$$Q_d = P_o^a . P_s^b . P_c^c . A_o^d . A_s^e . A_c^f . Y_d^g . I^h . C^i . E^j$$

In this form the elasticities are the exponents (the co-efficients a to j) and the equation can be rewritten in a linear form by taking logarithms. This gives the equation:

$$\text{Log } Q_d = a\log P_o + b\log P_s + c\log P_c + d\log A_o + e\log A_s + f\log A_c + g\log Y_d + h\log I + i\log C + j\log E$$

This equation can be estimated using the method of multiple regression, giving different elasticities of demand directly. The exponential form is the most common used method however it should be noted it takes the assumption that elasticities are constant, in place of the assumption in the linear form that the marginal impact of price (and the other factors) on volume is constant.

Forecasting demand

Forecasting is the prediction of demand for a good or service, for the forecast period ,on the basis of present and past behavior patterns of some related events .Forecasting involves predicting future economic conditions and assessing their effect on the operations of the firm. Accurate demand forecasting is essential for a firm to enable it to produce the required quantities at the right time and arrange well in advance for the various factors of production, viz., raw material , equipment, machine accessories, labour etc. thus forecasting is an aid in effective and efficient planning. Forecasting can also help in providing information on the product mix for a company producing a number of goods. Demand forecasting is very popular in industrially advanced countries where demand conditions are always more uncertain than the supply conditions. In developing countries however instead of demand , supply is often the limiting factor. High prices and black markets point to supply bottlenecks.

A good forecast should be accurate, simple, economical, consistent and timely. A sound estimate of future demand should be based on adequate knowledge of relevant past. The forecast should be simple to under stand, made with allocated budget and consistent with the objectives of the firm. It should be made within the time limit.

Steps of demand forecasting

Demand forecasting should be done in a scientific manner following the steps given below:

1) Identification of objective: First step is to decide about the period of forecast, whether it is for short – term or long- term purpose. A short term forecast is generally for a period of three months and it provides data on

a) Operational needs for production (raw material, equipment, warehousing, labour)

b) Marketing needs (sales force, promotional campaigns, and distributional network)

c) Personnel required by firm.

Long-term forecast is for more than an year and it provides information on expenditure on plant and equipment to meet the strategic goals of a firm.

2) Nature of the product: Selecton of forecasting technique to be used depends to a great extent on the nature of the product for which the demand forecast is to be made. For example, obsolescence and demographic changes influence demand forecasting for consumer durables, while demand foı capital goods can be forcasted on the basis of growth prospects of thє industries consuming those products, demand for consumer perishable: depend on the price, population characteristics and disposable income Therefore its very important to do a thorough analysis of all th determinants of demand for a product before making a demand forecas for that product.

3) Selection of forecasting technique: the choice of forecastir technique depends on the level of accuracy desired, objectives of forecas availability of data, type of product and time period of forecast. Survey a useful when high degree of accuracy is desired and to forecast the dema for a new product. Barometric techniques are used for short term foreca

4) Accuracy of forecast: To avoid the margin of errors in a forec various methods of testing of accuracy are applied.

Demand forecasting techniques

Extrapolation and time series analysis

One of the simplest techniques is to believe that some aspect of I behaviour of the variable being forecast will continue to be true in future, thereby providing the basis for the prediction. At its elemen stage it includes naïve method of forecasting such as the assumption next year's volume of sales will be equal to this year's figure. A r sophisticated version is to identify any trends over the recent past then to extrapolate those trends forward into the future as illustrat the figure.

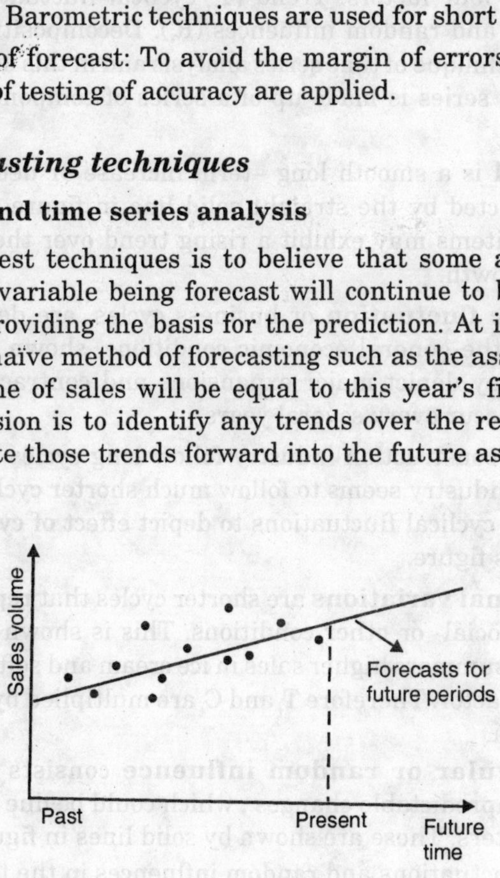

Figure 5.2 Forecasting by extrapolation

The scatter of points in the figure shows the level of sales in recent time periods, and the solid line is provides the 'best fit' to those points, fitted either by eye or by simple linear regression. The dotted line marks the extension of that relationship into the future and provides the forecast of sales level for future periods. Major disadvantage of this method is that they make no reference to the casual factors which demand the volume of demand, in effect assuming that time is the only determining factor which needs to be taken into consideration. They also assume that the relationship between time and the variable being forecast is a very simple one consisting only of long –term trend.

Time series analysis is a much more sophisticated type of extrapolation and it includes a wide range of different techniques. Time series data refers to the value of variables arranged in chronological order by date, weeks, months, quarters or years. It usually exhibits four different types of components which can be written in the form of equation $Y_t = T_t.C_t.S_t.R_t$

Changes in actual values of economic variables (Y_t) are determined by product of four factors: Trend (T_t), cyclical fluctuations (C_t),seasonal variations(S_t) and random influences (R_t). Decomposition method is the best known technique of time series analysis and in this method its assumed that any time series is made up of a series of components which are as follows

a) **Trend** is a smooth long –term increase or decrease in the time series as depicted by the straight solid line in figure (a) below. For eg. Sales of food items may exhibit a rising trend over the years due to the population growth.

b) **Cyclic fluctuation** or business cycles, are deviations from the trend due to the general economic conditions, shown by broken line in figure (a). They depict major expansions and contractions in economic activity that occur every several years.

Housing construction industry follow long cycles 15-20 years while automobiles industry seems to follow much shorter cycles. Trend value is multiplied by cyclical fluctuations to depict effect of cyclical fluctuations on firm's sales figure.

c) **Seasonal variations** are shorter cycles that repeat each year due to seasonal, social or other conditions. This is shown by broken line in figure (b) . In summers higher sales in ice cream and soft drinks companies is due to this factor. Therefore T_t and C_t are multiplied by seasonal index S_t in the formula.

d) **Irregular or random influence** consists of non recurring essentially unpredictable changes , which could be due to strikes, wars or natural disasters. These are shown by solid lines in figure (b).

Cyclic fluctuations and random influences in the time series can not be examined systematically, therefore trend is used to forecast values. A trend line can be fitted through a series either graphically or by least squares method.

1) Graphical Method: The annual sales data is plotted on a graph and a line is drawn through plotted points. This line could be extended to obtain sales forecast for a future period. Major limitation of this method is that the accuracy of the forecast depends on the ability of the analyst to fit a curve to the data.

2) Fitting trend equation: Least square method is used to fit the trend line on the data available. The trend equation is of the form

$$S = a + bT$$

Where a and b are constants , S and T are variables representing annual sales and time (in years) respectively.

Suppose the annual sales data for a firm for past 5 years is given and the sales revenue is to be estimated for next two years.

Table: Sales revenue of a firm

Year	Sales (S) in Rs crore	Time (T) year number	T_2	ST
1991	46	1	1	46
1993	55	3	9	165
1995	78	5	25	390
1997	44	7	49	308
1999	75	9	81	675
N=5	$\Sigma S = 298$	$\Sigma T = 25$	$\Sigma T^2 = 165$	$\Sigma ST = 1584$

The coefficients a and b are estimated by solving the equations based on least squares

$\Sigma S = Na + b\Sigma T$

$\Sigma ST = a\Sigma T + b\Sigma T^2$

By substituting values from table we get

$298 = 5a + 25b$

$1584 = 25a + 165b$

By solving the equation we get the trend equation as

$S = 47.85 + 2.35T$

Sales for next two years 2000 and 2001i.e 10th and 11th year can be estimated by substituting values in trend equation. The forcast sales for next two years will be Rs 71.35 crores and Rs 73.7 crores respectively.

Barometric forcasting technique

Time series analysis uses information about the past in order to make forecasts of future. Barometric forecasting uses indicators of current activity in order to provide forecasts for the future. Most common barometric technique is the use of leading indicators. A leading indicator is a variable which is known, or believed to be correlated with the future behaviour of the variable for which the forecast is required. For example to forecast the number of children who will be entering the school for the first time in five years time , the number of children born this year will provide a very useful leading indicator. Similarly increase in stock prices, permits for new buildings, corporate profits after tax, and index for industrial prices indicate an increase in general economic activity. Decrease in contracts for plant and equipment usually precedes a slowdown in economic activity.

Variables that coincide or move in step with general economic activity are coincident indicators. Unemployment rate, GNP at constant prices and sales of retail stores are such indicators.

Variables that follow or go down after the peak and go up before the trough are lagging indicators. Bank rate on short – term business loans and outstanding loans are examples of such indicators. Corresponding to these three we have leading series, coincident series and lagging series. They precede, move in step and follow turning point in business cycles respectively. To discover the turning points in business cycles, some countries use diffusion indices. These indices are formed by a combination of a number of indicators in the leading series.

The leading indicator method is used for short term forecasting. In this method Sometimes it becomes difficult to find out the leading indicator and the lead-time itself can change with the passage of time.

Econometric Method

For forecasting demand for a product or the economy as a whole statistical tools like regression and simultaneous equations are used. In simple regression analysis , a single variable is used to forecast demand for the dependent variable. Multivariate regression is used where demand of the product is a function of many variables. The method of using a number of simultaneous equations is a very systematic and complete approach to forecast demand for a product as it considers simultaneous interactions between dependent and independent variables.

Smoothing techniques

Smoothing techniques are a higher form of naïve method. There are two typical forms.

a) Moving average: moving averages are averages which are updated as new information is received. With the moving averages a manager simply employs, the most recent observation and drops the oldest observation, in the earlier calculation and calculates the average, which is used as the forcast for the next period.

Let us assume that tha sales manager has the following sales data:

Date	Actual sales Y_t (in Rs thousands)
Feb1	54
Feb2	49
Feb3	46
Feb4	53
Feb5	49
Feb6	58
Feb7	45

Taking a six day moving average, we get

$$Y'_7 = \frac{54+49+46+53+49+58}{6} = 51.5$$

$$Y'_8 = \frac{49+46+53+49+58+45}{6} = 50$$

The moving average is simple to use but it has the short comings that a great deal of data has to be retained from forecast period to forecast period. Also equal weightage is given to all samples, if new data are more valid why not they are given greater weightage.

b) Exponential smoothing : it is a popular technique for short run forecasting. It uses a weighted average of past data as the basis for a forecast. The procedure gives more weight to more recent data and smaller weights to observations in more distant past. The reason for this is that the future is more dependent on the recent past than on distant past. The method is known to be effective when there is randomness and no seasonal fluctuations in data.

New forecast = Last period's forecast + a (last period's actual demand – Last period's forecast)

Where a is a smoothing constant or weight

Symbolically

$$F_t = F_{t-1} + a\,(A_{t-1} - F_{t-1})$$

Where F_t = New forecast

F_{t-1} = Previous forecast

a = Smoothing constant ($0<a<1$)

A_{t-1} = Previous period's actual demand.

Marketing approach to demand measurement

In real world companies are more complex and require a great deal of information concerning the markets they operate in for forecasting demand of its product in the market. This information can be collected in a number of different ways.

Market surveys

It is the best known form of market research.This is not only used to forecast the level of demand for a product, but it may be used for a wide range of other purposes as well, including testing buyer's reaction to different product configuration and packaging, and identifying links between purchasing behaviour and other variables, like buyer's age, sex, social status and income. If the aim is to estimate the demand a sample of buyers are asked direct questions about their intentions to purchase the product within a specified future period. That information is used along with other evidence about the potential market to construct an estimate of the total volume of sales. The effectiveness of this technique depends upon a number of variables.

1) Number of potential buyers: If the number is very large only a small sample can be reached for the survey to be economical. Therefore if possible a truly representative sample is constructed and the results from the sample are extrapolated in order to reach a forecast for the market as a whole. Small sample is taken so that a very high proportion of potential buyers can be questioned.

2) Clarity of buyer's intention:If buyers themselves are vague about their own intentions they will be unable to provide useful information to the market researcher.

Other factors which will affect the cost-effectiveness of market surveys are:

- The cost of identifying and contacting buyers
- Buyers willingness to disclose their intentions
- Buyers propensity to carry out their intentions

The market surveys method is useful for industrial products, for consumer durables and for other products where buyers plan their purchase in advance. Market surveys are also useful for new products where there is no past data on sales, so that time series analysis or estimation is not possible.

Sales Force Opinion

If market surveys are inappropriate, an indirect method of forecasting buyer's intention is to survey sales force, asking them to provide estimates of the future volume of sales in their respective territories and sections. The rationale of this method is salesmen , being closest to the customer are likely to have the most intimate feel of the market i.e. customer reaction to the product of the form and their sales trend. The estimates of individual salesmen are consolidated to find the total sales estimate. They are then reviewed to eliminate the bias of optimism (over-estimate sales in order to secure greater advertising and promotion in their territories, or to justify their employment) and pessimism (under-estimate sales in order to be given low sales quotas which they would be able to exceed without effort) on the part of salesmen. These revised estimates are further examined in the light of factors like proposed changes in selling competition, changes in purchasing power, income distribution, employment and population etc. the final sales forecast would emerge after these factors have been taken into account.

Advantages:(1) The method is simple and does not involve use of statistical techniques. (2) As it involves input from salesmen who have detailed knowledge of different products, markets, distribution channels and individual customer, therefore they would be able to give more accurate forecast Also if sales force is directly involved in the construction of forecasts and the setting of sales quota they will have a better understanding of that process and will tend to exhibit greater commitment and motivation.

Disadvantages:(1)It is completely subjective as personal opinions can possibly influence the forecast.(2)method is useful for only short –term forecasting i.e. for a period of about an year.(3) salesmen may be unaware of the broader economic changes likely to have an impact on the future demand.

Expert Opinion

Third approach to demand forecasting is to ask experts in the field to provide their own estimation of future sales volume. Experts may include executives directly involved in the market, such as dealers, distributors and suppliers, or others whose major interest is in the forecast itself, such as stock brokers, industry analysts, officers of the trade associations or specialist marketing consultants. Various methods are used for the construction of such forecasts. One method could be to ask experts to independently provide a confidential estimate and the results could be averaged. The advantage of that approach is that there is no danger that the group of experts develop group thinking mentality where their independent judgment is influenced by their desire to be seen as a loyal and conforming member of a group. On the other hand if the estimates are produced independently the experts have no opportunity to weigh the opinions of the others or to take into account factors known to the others but not to themselves.

One approach which helps to pool in expert knowledge and avoid group thinking is **Delphi technique.** In this method each participant is asked independently to produce a forecast . Each of these forecasts with the reasoning behind it, is then presented as feedback to each of the participant, with anonymity being maintained so that none of the expert knows about origin of other forecasts. Each of the expert is then asked to revise his own forecast in the light of the others forecasts and reasoning, and this process is repeated until a consensus is reached. This may not always be possible if the experts disagree and will not allow their opinions to be shifted, but experience with the method suggests that the process of iteration does often lead to the convergence of the different forecasts around an agreed value.

Market testing

If a product is new or an established product is being sold in a new market or through new distribution channel, there would be no past data to analyse. Direct questioning of buyers will also be difficult as they will have only hypothetical information about the product's characteristics and neither the salesmen nor the experts will have any experience on which to base estimates of the likely demand. In this situation market testing could be the most appropriate technique to be used for collecting information. Kotler has identified a number of methods foe market testing which are as follows

Sales wave research *involves selecting a group of consumers, supplying them with the product free and then re-offering them the the product and/or competitors products at reduced prices a number of times. This allows the market researchers to measure the repeat purchase rate and to estimate the impact of different competing brands. Different group of customers may be given different packaging and different advertising concepts, in order to evaluate their different effect.*

Simulated store technique involves establishing a group of shoppers, showing them a number of advertisements, including those relating to the new product, and then giving them small amount of money which they may spend or keep. The amount of money spend on new product as well as competitors product are noted. The group of shoppers are brought together to discuss their immediate reactions to the product s and the reasons for their purchasing behaviou and follow up telephone interviews are carried out later to establish consumers more lasting responses.

Test marketing involves selling the product in a limited number of locations, while providing different marketing mixes or different packaging, advertising and promotional concepts in order to know their effectiveness. Test marketing can provide a realistic simulation of an actual product launch and may allow the company to identify any product fault but this method could be expensive and may not prove an accurate means of forecasting total sales volume. The sample markets chosen for testing may not be representative of the whole market and general economic conditions may vary between the test marketing and the actual product launch. Lastly test marketing reveals the company's intentions to competitors and they may well take counter measures, in which case the environment into which product is launched will be substantially different to that in which the test took place, making the results invalid.

There is no perfect solution to the problem of demand forecasting. The choice of technique depends upon the particular circumstances, the cost of acquiring better information and the value of investment put at risk. If the price of failure is low there is no point in spending substantial sums on improving demand forecasts. On the other hand if the cost of failure is high, spending on getting additional information will be worthwhile.

Questions

1. Enumerate the factors involved in demand forecasting. State the purpose of forecasting, both short-term and long-term.
2. Examine the 'Trend Projection' method and 'Collective Opinion' method of demand forecasting.
3. What are the factors that are considered while estimating a firm's sales? Enumerate the special difficulties in forecasting sales of consumers' durables.
4. Discuss briefly the various methods of forecasting demand and point out their limitations. What are the criteria of a good forecasting method?
5. Discuss critically the different methods of forecasting demand of established products.
6. Give the general approach to demand forecasting. What are the possible approaches to forecasting demand for new products?
7. Discuss the utility of demand forecasting. What are the criteria of a good forecasting method.
8. It is said that
   (i) Elasticity is higher at higher prices. Primarily it reflects the availability of substitutes.
   (ii) The demand for steel in late 1940s was highly inelastic because besides availability of close substitutes, steel was a small component of the value of many of the products of which it was a part. Today, of course, there are more substitutes for steel in many fields and steel in general has become very popular in several fields.

(iii) Time-use and use facilities characteristics have begun to complicate demand decisions of several firms.

9. Explain the significance of the above-mentioned statements and point out their relevance in forecasting demand in general of a consumer durable commodity like motorcycle.
10. Given the data on income elasticity of demand, how would you forecast, demand for certain products. Illustrate your answer with two examples.
11. Forecasting the demand for a new proudct poses special problems. How is it possible to overcome them?
12. "After all, in the final analysis, the best forecasting method is obviously the one which yields the highest percentage of correct predictions." Explain this statement by developing a set of criteria for evaluating a forecasting method for pressure cookers in Tamil Nadu.
13. How do demand forecasting methods for new products vary from those for established products?
14. You have been appointed in a market research organization and your assignment is to estimate the demand for packet tea. What factors would you like to consider while estimating the demand for packet tea in the next two years?

6

Market Structures

Introduction

Once a firm has established its objectives and identified the demand and cost conditions its facing, it can begin to consider how these objectives are to be achieved. This cannot be done without taking into consideration the structure of the industry in which the firm is operating, because that structure determines the relationship between a firm and its competitors. An important starting point for the development of a competitive strategy is a careful appraisal of the competitive structure of each industry in which the firm is involved. The competitive environment or the market structure in which an industry operates plays a decisive role in price and output decisions of a firm.

In the present chapter, we will classify the industry structure that is broadly called as market structure by the economists. A discussion will be done of the underlying principles in price-output decisions of a firm in various market structures followed by an assessment of each market form.

Need for Market Classification

A manager should be aware of the features and limitations of market types in which he operates for the following reasons:

1. The market in which a firm operates directly affects its pricing, marketing, production and investment behaviour. The market structure can help in understanding the behaviour pattern of the competitors.

2. The kind and degree of competition varies widely across market structures. Price competition tends to be blunted, where a few large firms dominate markets, as a result prices are high one result. Thus, the potential profits that a firm can earn and the prices consumers may pay can be expected to vary across different markets. It becomes necessary to understand how the variables of the process - price, product, and promotional activities increase firms' market share.

3. Market structure directly effects the role of government regulation towards the industry. In markets where competition is vigorous, government regulation is unnecessary and inappropriate. On the other hand, government regulation are needed to prevent the potential monopolisation of markets, prohibit anti-competitive practices by firms, and oversee the pricing, production and investment decisions of natural monopolies (such as utilities, television cable companies and the like).

Classification of Market Structures

Market structure refer to the number and size of buyers and sellers in the market for a good or service . Economists classify markets in four broad categories perfect competition, monopoly, monopolistic competition and oligopoly. Number of sellers, product differentiation, and entry and exit conditions are the major features that determine market structure.

In perfect competition, there are many sellers/firms in the market selling almost identical product. A firm cannot distinguish its product from those of other firms in the market. If a firm increases price the buyers will turn to other firms and buy product at the going price. The buyers have complete information about the price of the product. There is free entry and exit of firms. This means that in a perfectly competitive market, there are no legal or practical barriers to keep firms from entering or leaving the market.

In a monopoly market, there is a single seller due to which he has considerable control over the price. Public utilities like railways and water supply are such examples. This monopoly might be the result of government regulations, licence, scale economies or other factors. The product supplied is thus unique and hence, entry blocked. Monopolists also engage in advertising to increase total demand rather than capture sales.

Monopolist competition has features of perfect competition and monopoly. It is considered competitive because there are many sellers and it is relatively easy to enter in this market. But it is monopolistic because sellers try to differentiate their product as much as possible from their competitors. There is considerable emphasis on non price competition. They mainly compete on the basis of style, quality, product features or services. Many competitors focus on the market segments where they can meet customer needs in a better way and command a price premium.

Oligopoly markets have relatively few sellers who are large in size (in terms of market share, assets and number of employees). These firms may sell either standardised product (steel, aluminium etc) or differentiated ones (eg. Cars, motorcycles etc). Heavy capital investment tends to create practical barriers to entry, for example, it is expensive to build an auto plant or steel plant. Oligopolies rely heavily on non-price competition.

Division of these markets is quite flexible, for example any change in government policies and macro-economic environment may challenge the monopoly of a firm in the market, or a new break through technology may give monopoly powers to a monopolistic competitive firm.

Types of market structure	Number of independent sellers	Product differentiation	Part of economy where prevalent	Condition of entry
Perfect or pure competition	Large	Identical Products	A few agriculture commodities	Free or easy
Monopolistic competition	Large	Products are close substitutes	Retail trade, soap toothpaste etc.	Free or easy
Oligopoly	Few	Products may be homogeneous or close substitutes	Steel, aluminium, machinery, autos	Difficult
Monopoly	One	Single product without close substitutes	A few public utilities	Barred or impossible
Oligopsony	Few		Milk dairies	
Monopsony	One	Remote substitutes	Indian wagon industry	

Monopoly, monopolistic competition and oligopoly are often referred to as imperfect competition to distinguish from perfect competition. Market forms discussed above were defined in terms of sellers. However market structure can also be defined in terms of buyers of products or input. Monopsony refers to the market situation in which there is a single buyer of a good or input for which there is no close substitute. Monopsonistic competition comprises of smaller number of buyers competing against large number of sellers. Oligopsony comprises of few buyers competing against large number of sellers. Monopsony and oligopsony are common in input markets than in product markets. They sometimes exist in government purchases of large defence systems or in labour market dominated by one or few employers.

When a small number of buyers compete against a small number of sellers its said to be bilateral monopoly. When a small number of buyers compete against large number of sellers it is called a buyer's market, while under seller's market proportionately small number of sellers compete against large number of buyers. In buyer's market, buyers try to pull down prices as low as possible, where as in seller's market, sellers try to push up prices as high as possible.

Equilibrium Principles

One of the main decisions a firm has to make is about the optimal output level. A firm will always try to choose that output level which provides maximum output at a given price and given point of time. The two ways to approach the problem are given below.

Total Revenue and Total Cost Approach

A comparison of the total revenue and total cost schedules can explain whether the firm is earning profits or incurring losses. Fig. (a) shows that the profit of a perfectly competitive firm is maximum at output D, as the difference between TR and TC is maximum The total revenue (TR) curve is a straight line from origin as the demand curve is perfectly elastic under perfect competition.

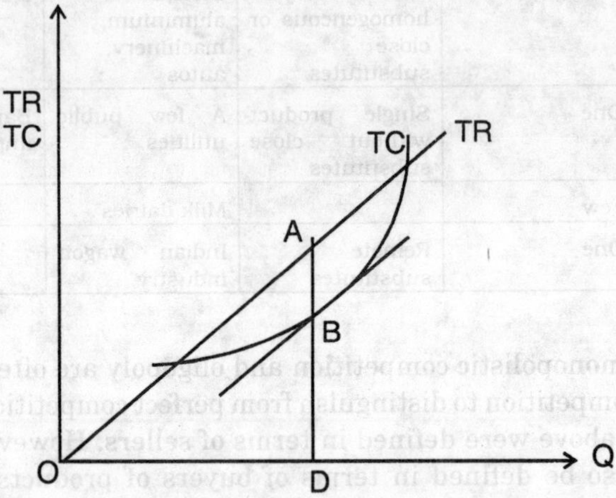

(a)

Fig : Equilibrium principle (a) & (b)

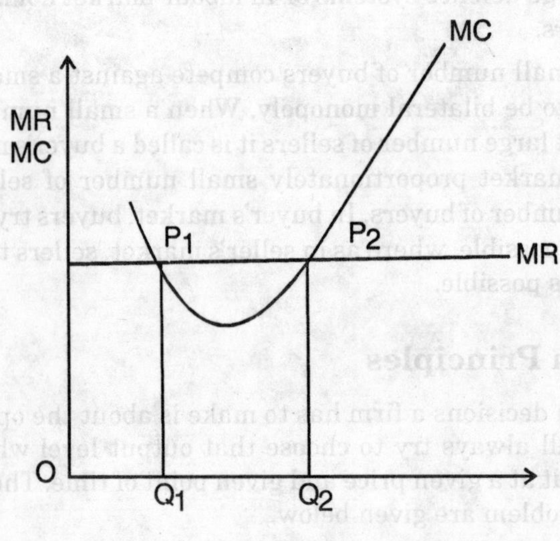

Marginal revenue and marginal cost approach

The relation between marginal revenue and marginal cost determines the optimal output that should be produced by the firm. The profit –maximising rule states that a firm should produce output where the additional revenue received from the last unit is equal to the additional cost of producing that unit i.e. MR=MC. In figure (b) the firm would increase output till point Q_2. The firm does not choose Point Q1 because the output is low and the marginal cost decreases with additional output. Therefore, at equilibrium point:

1. MC = MR and
2. The MC curve should be increasing i.e. it should intersect the MR curve from below.

It follows that the firm should increase output if MR > MC and reduce output if MR < MC. Both the above two approaches give same results.

Firm and Industry Equilibrium

Market/industry equilibrium is determined by the intersection of the industry demand and supply. The corresponding output and price is the equilibrium quantity and equilibrium price. Equilibrium of a firm differs from that of the industry under perfect competition as there are a large number of buyers and large sellers that establish the industry demand and supply as shown in figure below. The firm has to sell at the price set by industry demand and supply forces. Under monopoly, the industry equilibrium coincides with firm equilibrium, as there is a single seller in the market.

Perfect Competition

Perfect competition is an ideal form of market in which there is the greatest degree of competition.It should be noted that competition has different interpretations in economics and business. Businessman regards competition as a process of rivalry where firms try to gain advantage through pricing decisions, advertising, R and D, product quality and other means. In economics, however, when there is perfect competition, firms cannot engage in rivalries because they are price takers in the market.

Characteristics of Perfect Competition

The main features of perfect competition are discussed here. They are necessary for a firm to be a price taker.

1. The competitive market is composed of a large number of undifferentiated sellers and buyers, each of which is small in relation to the total market. As a result, each seller will accept the market price as it is, each buyer will also regard the price as determined by forces beyond his control. The firm in perfect competition is essentially a price taker.

2. Outputs of the firms in such a market are regarded as perfect substitutes for one another or are so perceived by the buyers. All firms produce a standard, homogenous and undifferentiated product.

3. Buyers have perfect information about cost, price, and quality of competing goods. Consumers will not pay a higher price than necessary for the product.

4. Entry and exit from an industry is assumed to be easy in a perfect competition. If a price is above cost, resulting in economic profit, resources (raw material, labour, capital) can be mobilised to create new firms or to expand the production capacity of the existing firm. If profits are below average, resources can be easily transferred from the industry and used to produce other products at higher profit rates. There are no patents or copyrights, and huge amount of capital are not necessary to enter the market. Established firms do not have any lasting cost advantage over entrants because of experience or size.

5. There is perfect mobility of resources. The workers and inputs can easily move from one job to another and can respond very quickly to monetary incentives.

Agriculture commodities like wheat vegetables etc fall under perfectly competitive market structure. Stock market is closest to perfect competition.

Short-run equilibrium in perfect competition

In the perfectly competitive situation, the price at which every firm must sell its output will be set by the market forces of supply and demand. Each individual firm be able to sell as much as it chooses at that price, but it will

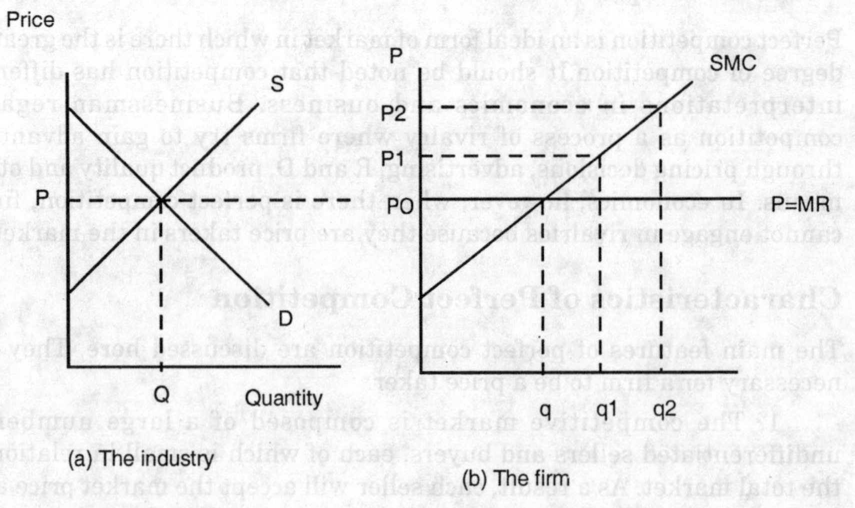

Fig: The firm and the industry in perfect competition

not be able to sell anything at all at a higher price, because its competitors are producing identical products selling them at the market price to consumers who are well-informed of the p' being asked by every firm.

Fig. shows the short-run situation for both an individual firm and for industry as a whole.

As the diagram shows, the forces of supply and demand determine a price of Pand a total industry output of Q. Each individual firm has a demand curve w' is a horizontal line PP, showing that it can sell any amount at the price P, but none at higher prices.Because the demand curve is horizontal the marginal revenue curve, which shows the additional revenue earned when one more unit of output is sold, is given by the same horizontal line. When the firm sells one more unit of output, the amount it receives for it is the price P, which is also the addition to revenue.
As each firm is a profit-maximiser it will produce the level of output given by q_0 in the diagram, which is the output at which the marginal revenue is just equal to marginal cost. If the firm were to produce more than qo then it would be producing units of output for which the marginal cost is more than the marginal revenue, which would reduce profit. On the other hand, if it produces less than q_0 then it is failing to produce some units of output for which the marginal revenue exceeds the marginal cost, which would add to profit.

As the industry is no more than the sum of the individual firms, it is clear that the industry's output Q must equal the sum of the outputs of the individual firms. This simple point also helps in understanqing the nature of the supply curve. It can be seen from the diagram for the firm that at price P the firm chooses to supply output q_0 because that is the ouput which yields most profit. If the price rose to P_1 the firm would choose to increase its output to q_1, and if the price rose further to P_2 the firm would increase output to q_2. The firm's marginal cost curve traces out the levels of output which the firm would choose to supply at each price. In other words, the marginal cost curve for the firm is the same thing as the firm's supply curve! The supply curve for the industry as a whole is simply the horizontal sum of the marginal cost curves for the individual firms.

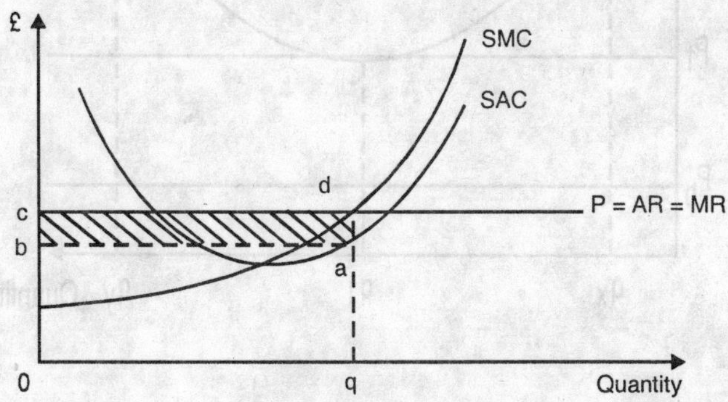

Figure: The perfectly competitive firm in short-run equilibrium

Fig above shows only the marginal cost curve for the individual firm, in order *to* be as clear as possible. However, a more complete picture requires the inclusion of the average cost curve, in order to examine the level of profits being made. This is shown in Fig below

In the diagram as shown, the individual firms are making 'economic profits' or 'supernormal profits', because the average cost of producing output q is less than the price P, set by the market. The amount of profit earned is shown by the shaded area abcd and consists of the profit margin bc multiplied by the number of units sold.

Equilibrium in the long run

Up to this point the analysis has been of short-run behaviour. Each firm has a given set of plant and equipment, involving in it some fixed costs. New firms cannot enter the industry because to do so would require them to set up new plants, which is not possible in the short run. In the long run, however, such profits would attract new firms into the industry. In that case, the additional competition would push the price downwards and eventually eliminate the profits being made. In terms of Fig. 9.1 above new entry will move the supply curve to the right as more firms set up and their marginal cost curves contribute to the supply curve.

In order to identify where the industry's price must settle in the long run, it is necessary to examine the long-run cost curves for the individual firms. Each firm must have the same long-run cost curve, because they all have access to the same technology and the same prices of inputs. Fig. below shows such a curve.

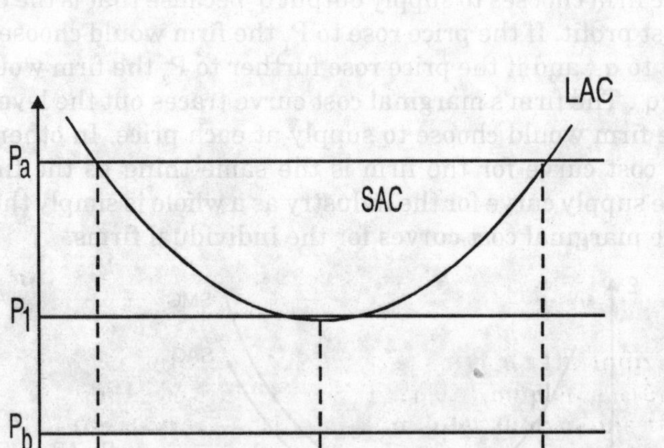

Fig: Long-run equilibrium for the firm in perfect competition

If the price were to settle at P_a, firms could continue to make supernormal profits by producing outputs anywhere between q_x and q_y. In that case, entry would continue to take place and the price would be pushed downwards. Clearly, P_a is too high to be the price at which the industry eventually settles. Similarly, P_b is too low to be the long-run equilibrium price, because if the price should fall to that level, no firm could make a profit at all, many would leave the industry and the price would rise.This argument makes it clear that in a perfectly competitive industry, the price must settle in the long run at P_L.

The long-run outcome of a perfectly competitive industry, then, is that the price is forced down to the level of the lowest possible average cost. Each firm uses the set of plant and equipment which gives least cost production and operates it at the most efficient level of output.

The working of a perfectly competitive industry is determined by its structure. The production of identical products by a large number of small firms, coupled with perfect knowledge on the part of consumers, ensures that each firm has a horizontal demand curve. Freedom of entry ensures that if supernormal profits are made in the short run they will be competed away in the long run by new entry. Provided economies of scale are limited, so that the industry contains a large number of small firms, all producing at the bottom point on their long-run cost curve, a long-run equilibrium, will be established and maintained until the external environment changes.

Perfect *competition* and 'rivalry'

In this type of market structure, the firm has very little opportunity to act for itself, and very few decisions to make. The price is set by the market, and the firm is a 'price-taker'. There is no reason to advertise because the firms are all producing exactly the same product and customers know them to be identical. The only decision the firm has to take in the short run is on the level of output. In the long run it has also to ensure that it has built the lowest cost plant, or it cannot survive. The firm is not even able to determine its own objectives because unless it makes maximum profit , it will make a loss and will cease to survive.

In perfect competition the industry is 'competitive' in the sense that its structure drives prices down to the level of lowest cost, not in the sense that firms are intense rivals for each other. Indeed, in such an industry there is no rivalry at all between individual firms because each firm is very small, being faced by anonymous market forces, rather than by identifiable rival firms. In perfect competition firms could not be said to have strategies. They simply take limited decisions under very powerful pressure from market forces.

Perfect Competition and Social Optimality

Perfect competition is often regarded as a socially optimal form of market structure, for a number of reasons. In the first place, every firm is forced by market pressures to build the least cost set of plant and equipment and to operate it at its optimal level of output, so that cost per unit is at the lowest possible level. Secondly, no supernormal profits can be earned, except in the short run. Thirdly, and most important from an economic point of view, price is equal to marginal cost. This is most important because price equal to marginal cost is the condition required for the maximisation of social welfare.

'Maximisation of social welfare' requires that the level of output produced is that , which gives the greatest 'net benefit to the economy'. Net benefit consists of the difference between the benefits consumers receive from having the commodity and the costs incurred in its production. If this apparently vague idea is to be given meaning, some method has to be found to measure the benefits received by consumers. This can be done quite simply if we accept three basic axioms about consumer behaviour. These are:

- consumers are rational
- consumers are self-interested
- each individual consumer is the only valid judge of his own welfare.

If these axioms are adopted then the benefit which a consumer receives from having different amounts of a commodity may be measured by the amount he is willing to pay for them. If a consumer is willing to pay a maximum of Rs100 for a pair of shoes and he is rational and self-interested, that Rs100 is a direct measure of the sacrifice he is prepared to make in return for the shoes and an indirect measure of the benefit he expects to get from having the shoes.

Once this idea has been established it becomes relatively easy to measure the bend to consumers from having different amounts of a commodity, because the demand curve shows how much individuals are prepared to pay for those different amout. For instance, if someone is willing to pay Rs150 for the first pair of shoes on the market. The total benefit from having one pair of shoes, then, is equal to Rs150. If the second pair of shoes will only be sold when the price falls to Rs130, and the third pair when the price has fallen to Rs110, then the total benefit of three pairs of shoes is equal to Rs150+Rs130+Rs110 =Rs390.

In general, the benefit to consumers from producing quantity Q of a commodity is given by the area under the demand curve at Q, as shown in Fig. 9.5(a).In a similar way, the costs of producing a commodity can be calculated by adding up the marginal costs of producing each successive unit, thereby measuring the costs of producing quantity Q by the area under the marginal cost curve, as shown in Fig 9.5(b).

Bringing the measure of the benefits and the costs together, in a simple form of cost/benefit analysis, it can be readily seen that the maximum net benefit is received at output Q_0 and price P. However, it has already been

noted that under perfect competition the marginal cost curve for the industry and the supply curve are the same. In other words, in perfect competition, the industry automatically produces the level of output which maximises social welfare.

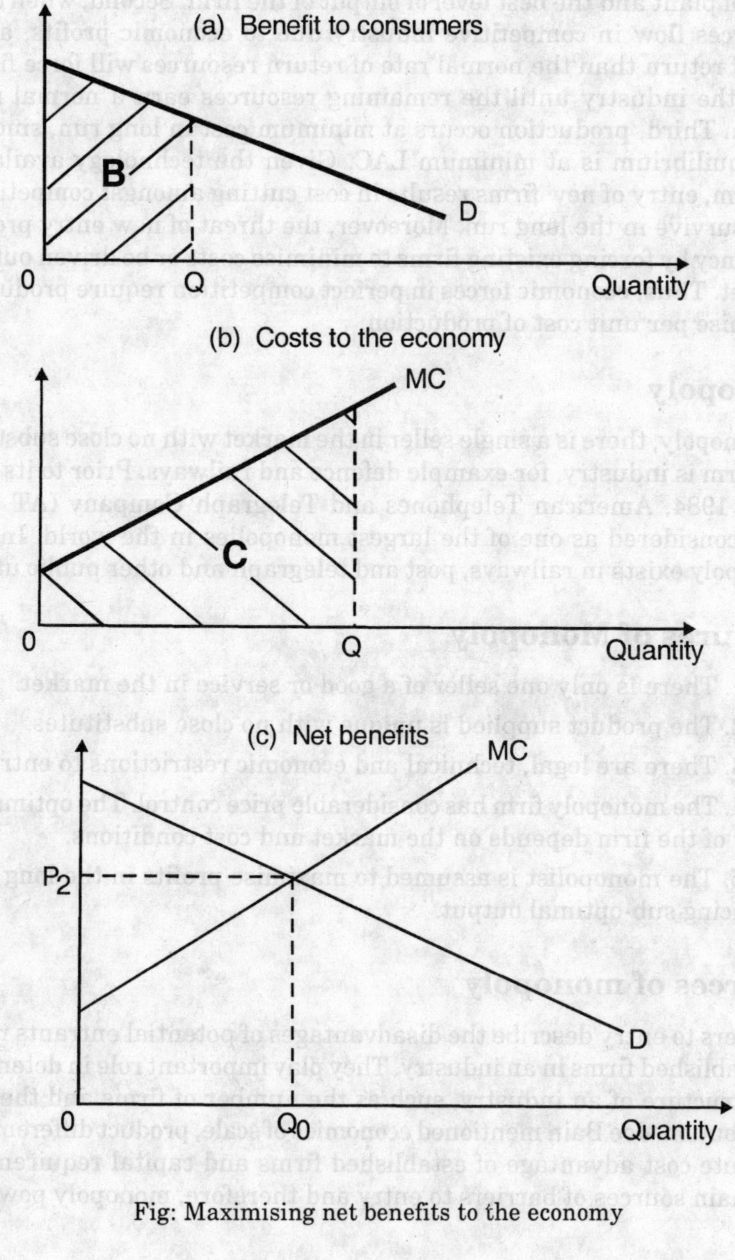

Fig: Maximising net benefits to the economy

Evaluation of Perfect Competition

Firms hardly observe long run equilibrium in real world as the market demand curve changes with a change in tastes, technology, and prices of inputs of production. Nevertheless, the long run analysis helps in explaining entry and exit reasons of firms. The analysis is a yardstick to assess how resources are allocated efficiently in the long run for three reasons. First, the tendency to move towards long run equilibrium leads to the optimal scale of plant and the best level of output of the firm. Second, when capital resources flow in competitive industry due to economic profits, a lower rate of return than the normal rate of return resources will force firms to leave the industry until the remaining resources earn a normal rate of return. Third, production occurs at minimum cost in long run, since long run equilibrium is at minimum LAC. Given the technology available to the firm, entry of new firms results in cost cutting amongst competitors so as to survive in the long run. Moreover, the threat of new entry promotes efficiency by forcing existing firms to minimise costs or be driven out of the market. Thus, economic forces in perfect competition require producers to minimise per unit cost of production.

Monopoly

In monopoly, there is a single seller in the market with no close substitutes. The firm is industry, for example defence and railways. Prior to its break-up in 1984, American Telephones and Telegraph Company (AT and T) were considered as one of the largest monopolies in the world. In India, monopoly exists in railways, post and telegraph and other public utilities.

Features of Monopoly

1. There is only one seller of a good or service in the market.
2. The product supplied is unique with no close substitutes.
3. There are legal, technical and economic restrictions to entry.
4. The monopoly firm has considerable price control. The optimal price policy of the firm depends on the market and cost conditions.
5. The monopolist is assumed to maximise profits in the long run by producing sub-optimal output.

Sources of monopoly

Barriers to entry describe the disadvantages of potential entrants relative to established firms in an industry. They play important role in determining the structure of an industry, such as the number of firms and the size of distribution. Joe Bain mentioned economies of scale, product differentiation, absolute cost advantage of established firms and capital requirement as the main sources of barriers to entry and therefore, monopoly power.

1. Economies of scale: Operation of scale economies over sufficiently large range of outputs leaves only one firm supplying the entire market. Such a firm is called a natural monopoly. The potential entrant would have to build a large plant in order to compete with such established firm. Figure depicts a large existing firm, producing output OQ_E. The firm will have lower average costs than a new firm attempting to enter the industry on a small scale and high cost such as AQ_N.

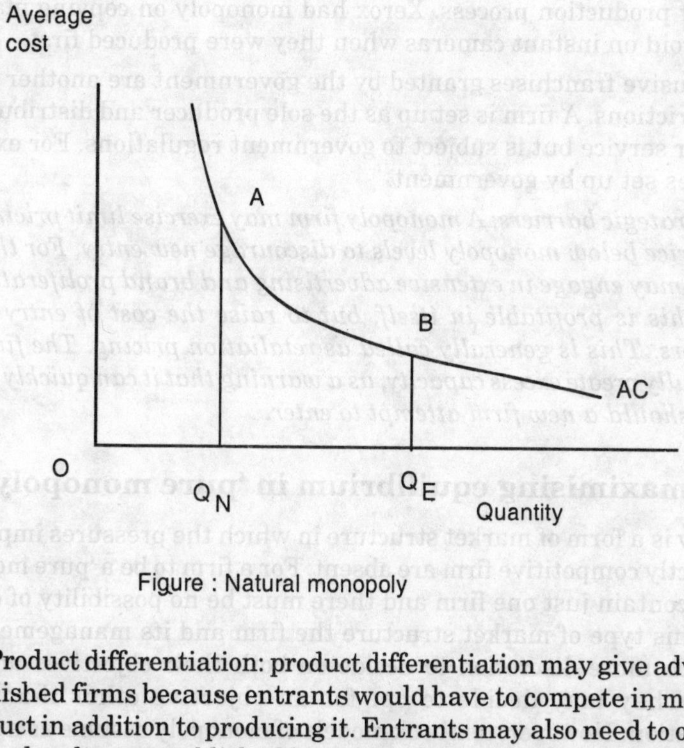

Figure : Natural monopoly

2. Product differentiation: product differentiation may give advantages to established firms because entrants would have to compete in marketing the product in addition to producing it. Entrants may also need to overcome consumer loyalty to established brands and this would increase costs and risks of entry. The new firm may be forced to sell the product at lower costs due to large advertisement budget.

3. Capital requirements: In some industries (oil refining, car manufacturing, defence etc) the capital requirements of production are huge. In others like chemicals, pharmaceuticals large investment in R&D is necessary. Entry becomes risky when large sunk costs of this kind are required.

4. Absolute cost advantage: established firms in the industry can obtain resources at a lower cost than potential entrants. This advantage occurs when established firms have access to important inputs, or unique assets, which allow them to produce at a lower cost than potential entrants. Under these conditions, established firms would be able to charge prices above their marginal costs and earn economic profits without attracting entry.

5. Control over inputs: Control over the entire supply of raw material like mineral deposits, oil supplies and even scientific talent can also lead to monopoly power. Till World War II, Alcoa, the Aluminium Company of America controlled supply of bauxite and, therefore, had monopoly in production of aluminium. Other examples of monopoly based on resource control are French Champagne, De Beers (diamonds) and OPEC (crude oil).

6. Legal restrictions: Patents held by existing firms make it virtually impossible for other firms to produce a comparable product or use a particular production process. Xerox had monopoly on copying machines and Polaroid on instant cameras when they were produced first.

Exclusive franchises granted by the government are another form of legal restrictions. A firm is set up as the sole producer and distributor of a product or service but is subject to government regulations. For example, post offices set up by government.

7. Strategic barriers: A monopoly firm may exercise limit pricing, that is, keep price below monopoly levels to discourage new entry. For the same reason, it may engage in extensive advertising and brand proliferation, not because this is profitable in itself, but to raise the cost of entry of new competitors. This is generally called as retaliation pricing. The firm may intentionally create excess capacity, as a warning that it can quickly expand capacity should a new firm attempt to enter.

Profit-maximising equilibrium in 'pure monopoly'

Monopoly is a form of market structure in which the pressures imposed on the perfectly competitive firm are absent. For a firm to be a 'pure monopoly' it has to contain just one firm and there must be no possibility of entry.

In this type of market structure the firm and its management have very much more discretion to decide on both their objectives and their actions. They may decide to opt for an objective other than profit-maximisation. However, textbook models of monopoly assume as a starting point that the aim of the monopolist, like the perfect competitor, is to make maximum profit.

For the pure monopoly, the analysis is relatively simple. Fig. 9.6 shows the diagram for a profit-maximising monopolist in the short run.

As there is only one firm in the industry, the demand curve for a monopolist is the same as the demand curve for the industry as a whole. It slopes downwards from left to right and, as a result, the marginal revenue curve lies below it. (This is because in monopoly the firm has to lower the price in order to sell more output, so the extra revenue received from selling one more unit is less than the price for that unit.)

The profit-maximising monopolist will produce output Q, where marginal cost equals marginal revenue, and must sell it at price P. Provided that cost and demand conditions are favourable, supernormal profits will

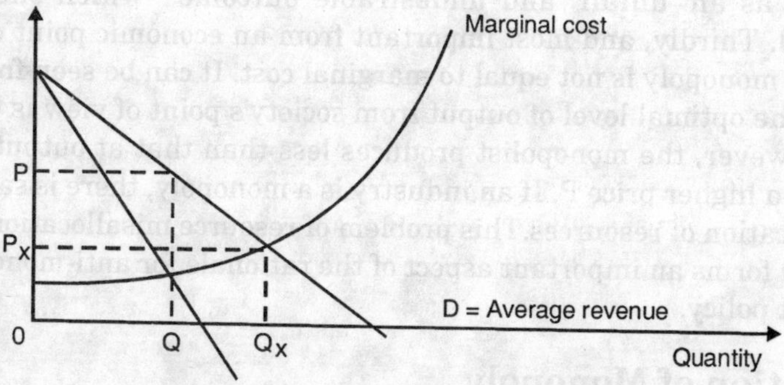

Fig. A profit-maximising monopolist

be made and the lack of competition from other firms or new entrants will mean that those profits can be maintained indefinitely .In the long run all the firm has to do is to consider whether there is a different set of plant and equipment which would allow it to make an even higher level of profit than that which it is making from its current capacity. If there is, then in the long run the monopolist will build that more profitable set of plant and equipment. If not, he will simply keep on replacing the current set of plant and equipment when it becomes worn out.

It is worth noting that a monopolist does not necessarily make supernormal profits.If a firm has a monopoly in a product which consumers do not want at all, or which is so expensive to produce that consumers are not willing to pay a price which is high enough to cover the cost, then it will not be able to make profits. What is important about monopoly is that if the firm is in a position to make profits those profits not be eroded away by competition.

A change in government policies or the market environment may attract new firms in the long run due to high rate of return. The demand curve of the monopolist will become more elastic and represent a smaller share of the total market sales and they have smaller effect on price. New entrants will capture some economic profit. The market structure may evolve into an oligopoly or monopolistic competition. If the monopoly position is a result of control over scarce resources, patents, unique managerial talent or a choice location, entry by other firms may be impossible and the firm will maintain monopoly position.

Monopoly and the misallocation of resources

Although a firm and its shareholders will find a monopoly position highly attractive the existence of monopoly is often regarded as socially undesirable, for a number of reasons. In the first place, the firm is not forced to set up the configuration of plant and equipment which has the lowest possible cost. In the second place earning monopoly profit is often regarded as an 'unfair' and undesirable outcome' which should be prevented. Thirdly, and most important from an economic point of view' price in a monopoly is not equal to marginal cost. It can be seen from Fig. 9.6 that the optimal level of output from society's point of view is Q_x, sold at P_x. However, the monopolist produces less than that at output Q and sells it at a higher price P. If an industry is a monopoly, there is said to be a misallocation of resources.This problem of resource misallocation under monopoly forms an important aspect of the rationale for anti-monopoly or anti-trust policy.

Evaluation of Monopoly

Mostly monopolist charges a high price by supplying less than desired in the market. The socially desirable output is when p = MC. The price (P) depicts the money that the society is willing to pay and marginal cost (MC) shows the cost incurred in the production of the last unit of the good. Downward sloping demand curve results in the price being higher than the MC (P > MC). Thus, it is often said that the monopoly price is higher than the competitive price. It is further stated that monopoly restricts consumer choice. The consumer has to purchase what is offered for sale in such a market situation, as there is a single seller of the good.

Despite these drawbacks, monopoly markets are regarded as a significant part of the economy as the monopolist is considered to invest in R&D due to supernormal profits earned by him. They also do not indulge in wasteful expenditure in the form of advertising, etc., that is essential in monopolistic competition and oligopoly.

Perfect Competition versus Monopoly

As there are large numbers of sellers under perfect competition thus, individual firms do not have any control over price. The firm is a price - taker as the forces of demand and supply establish market price. The firm has to decide about the output, it should produce at the going price. On the contrary, single firm is the sole producer of a good under monopoly. Thus, the firm is the industry. The industry supply curve is similar to the supply curve of the individual firm. Therefore, a monopolist is a price-maker.

The long run price under perfect competition is decreased lowest sustainable level, where economic profits are zero. As a result, a competitive market delivers maximum benefit to the consumers. On the other hand, monopolist sets a high price by restricting output below the competitive level. Comparisons between the two can be made graphically. In Fig. 7.7 equilibrium takes place where MR = MC. E_P and E_M are the equilibrium levels of a perfectly competitive market and monopoly respectively. P_P is the market price of a perfect competitor and P_M is the price set by the monopolist. The diagram shows that the perfectly competitive price is increased till it becomes equal to marginal cost, i.e., $P_P = MC$. But monopolist restricts output, therefore $P_M > MC$. For this reason, the price set by the monopolist is said to be higher than the socially desirable level. Hence competition is regarded to deliver output at a minimum price.

The monopoly output Q_M is lower than the competitive output of Q_P or the socially desirable output. Output produced in the competitive market (Q_P) corresponds to the minimum point of long run average cost (Q_P = min. LAC) while monopoly output is less (Q_M < min. LAC), i.e., lower than the optimal output. Thus, we have the following summary comparison of perfect competition and monopoly:

$$P_M > P_P$$

$$Q_M < Q_P$$

We also know that goods produced under competitive market are homogeneous but unique under monopoly. There are no entry barriers under perfect competition and exit is also easy. Due to less capital requirements, no product differentiation and absence of strategic and legal barriers, investors can enter perfectly competitive market with ease. On the other hand, presence of the aforementioned barriers under monopoly restricts entry and exit also becomes difficult.

Monopsony

Main characteristics of monopsony are

1. There is only one buyer of goods or services.
2. There is insignificant rivalry from buyers who offer remote substitutive outlets.
3. Buyer is in a position to determine the prices he pays for the goods or services he buys.

Monopsony is very rare in real business world. However example of Indian railways in relation to the wagon industry can be taken as a case approximating to monopsony. If for any reason workers are unable to move to other localities or other firms within the same area, their existing employer has a monopsony position over them.

The monopsonist must choose between paying higher wages that will enable him to attract more workers or limiting his working force to the smaller number of workers he can obtain at lower wages. This means that when he adds a man to his labour force, he adds to his costs not merely the wage of the new worker, but also the total of wage increases that must be paid to his old employees at the new rate. Thus in monopsonistic buying marginal expenditure of each input level exceeds average expenditure.

Monopolistic Competition

The central feature of monopolistic competition is product differentiation, which gives every firm some market power with respect to its product. For instance, shirts of Allen Solly are not exactly the same as that of Park Avenue, but they are not too dissimilar either. Product differentiation occurs to a greater or lesser degree in such markets where large numbers of sellers or firms supply a small part of market share. Firms sell goods with different attributes claimed to be superior to those of competitors. They also deliver varying levels of support and services to the customers. Advertising and marketing, aimed at creating product or brand name, reinforce product differences.

Competing firms producing similar products are often called a 'product group'. For instance' wrinkle free' shirts would be a typical product group within which there are no significant perceived differences among competitors. Similarly casual wears brands may form a product group.

Best examples of monopolistic competition are restaurants, grocery stores, florists hardware stores pharmacies etc. In these markets entry is easy and number of sellers is relatively large, however the firms within each of these markets differentiate themselves from competition on the basis of location, type of service etc. Product markets of soaps, vegetable oil, shampoo, toothpaste also falls under monopolist competition.

Features of monopolistic competition

The basic characteristic of a monopolistically competitive industry are as follows:

1. There are a large number of firms, each having small market share.

2. Every firm sells a differentiated product from its competitors and, therefore, it has some market power or monopoly advantage.

3. Each firm acts independently and does not consider reactions of rivals in its decisions.

4. There is free entry and exit of companies into and from the industry in the long run, which usually leads to lower market share and zero economic profit.

5. Emphasis is basically on non price competition, like product differentiation and advertising. Price competition helps the firm to operate on firm's demand curve, but price cuts can cause retaliation from competitors.

Equilibrum in monopolistic competition

A third form of market structure is known as 'monopolistic competition'. This type of industry resembles perfect competition in that it contains a large number of small firms and there is free entry to the industry in the long run. However, in monopolistic competition, there is some degree of product differentiation in that each firm produces a slightly different product, each of which is preferred to the others by some consumers. In this type of market structure each firm will have a downward-sloping demand curve, being a 'mini-monopolist' with respect to its own particular variant of the industry's product. The diagram which shows the firm's price and output in the short run will look exactly like Fig. 9.6, illustrating monopoly, with the qualification that there is no longer an industry demand curve.

In the short run, as in perfect competition, firms may make supernormal profits. However, if they do, new entrants will be attracted into the industry, each firm will lose some of its customers to the new entrants and eventually the supernormal profits will be competed away. Fig. 9.7 shows the position which firms in the industry will reach in the long run.

This result is sometimes known as the 'tangency solution', because the individual firm reaches a position where its demand curve is at a tangent to its long-run average

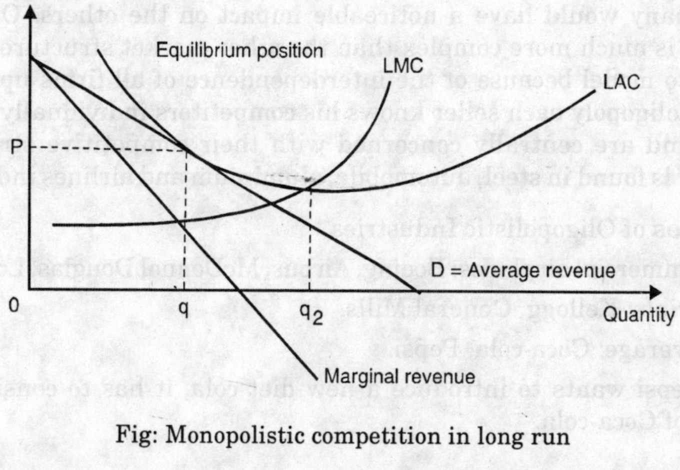

Fig: Monopolistic competition in long run

cost curve. The firm must find itself in this position because if the demand curve were any higher supernormal profits could be made and further entry would take place. On the other hand, if the curve were any lower losses would be made and firms would leave the industry, moving the remaining firms' demand curves upwards.

Monopolistic competition and the allocation of resources

Just as the outcome of perfect competition and monopoly can be evaluated from a social point of view, so it is possible to consider the outcome of monopolistic competition. In the long run, supernormal profits are not earned so that the charges of 'unfairness' does not arise. On the other hand, price does not equal marginal cost so that there is a misallocation of resources in that sense. Furthermore, as Fig above makes clear, each firm will not use the lowest cost set of plant and equipment.As the equilibrium is established where a sloping demand curve is tangential to the long run average cost curve, the equilibrium level of output is one where not all economies of scale have been exploited. If each firm set up the plant and equipment designed to produce level of output q_2 costs per unit would be considerably lower. A major effect of introducing product differentiation is to reduce efficiency as each firm fails to take the maximum advantage of economies of scale. This finding is sometimes referred to as the 'excess capacity theorem'. On the other hand it has to be remembered that consumers are able to choose from a wide variety of different product variations. If consumers value these differences there will be compensating gains.

Oligopoly

The term oligopoly refers to an industry in which there are only a few firms. The important characteristic of an oligopolistic industry is that the firms within it are interdependent on each other, such that the action of one company would have a noticeable impact on the others. Oligopoly situation is much more complex than the other market structures and is difficult to model because of the interdependence of all firms upon each other. In oligopoly each seller knows his competitors individually in each market and are centrally concerned with their competitive strategies. Oligopoly is found in steel, automobile, aluminium and airlines industries.

Examples of Oligopolistic Industries

Commercial airplanes: Boeing, Airbus, McDonnel Douglas, Lockheed.

Serials: Kellogg, General Mills.

Beverage: Coca-cola, Pepsi.

If Pepsi wants to introduce a new diet cola, it has to consider the reaction of Coca-cola.

Features of oligopoly are as follows

1. The industry has a few firms who are major suppliers in the market which gives each firm market power.

2. Oligopolies may vary with respect to the extent of product differentiation. At one extreme, the firm may all produce identical product (like steel, aluminium etc). At the other extreme they may produce highly differentiated products (like automobiles, airlines, cigarettes).

3. There is interdependence among firms. The smaller the number of firms, the more the interdependence.

4. At one extreme, entry to an oligopoly may be completely 'blocked' so that competition is only between existing firms. At the other extreme, entry may be completely free so that potential competition from new entrants is a key determinant of the existing firm's behaviour.

5. Non price competition exist in this market form as retaliation is less against advertising, promotional techniques, R &D and product improvement.

In oligopoly, its helpful for a firm to have knowledge of the rival's pricing policies, their market positions and the personal traits of the people who make their pricing decisions. The figure shows how the actions of rivals can affect the demand curve faced by oligopolists. If one firm reduces the price and other firms do not respond then the price cutter firm may increase the sales substantially, shown by the elastic demand curve, dd. A price decrease from P_1 to P_2 will result in movement along demand curve dd and increase sales from Q_1 to Q_2 as customers take advantage of the lower prices and leave other firms. However, if other firms in response to price cut also cut their prices to the same level, increase in sales will be less since other firms are selling at the same price, any additional sales must result from increased demand for the product. Thus, the effect of the price reduction is a movement down the relatively less elastic demand curve DD and the price reduction from P_1 to P_2 increases sales only to Q_3. Important differences between oligopoly and monopolistic competition.

1. Oligopoly exists because of significant entry barriers. e.g., economies of scale. Relatively few sellers dominate the industry. In monopolistic competition, entry of firms is easy, and a large number of firms compete each other.

2. In oligopoly, the product can be homogeneous of differentiated (cars, soaps, cigarettes). In monopolistic competition, products are differentiated.

3. In oligopoly, the actions of the firms are interdependent. In monopolistic competition, they are independent of each other.

4. In oligopoly, prices are relatively rigid; they do not change frequently, except when there are price wars or when there is collusive price fixing. In monopolistic competition, prices can change frequently.

Explicit collusion or cartelisation

One possible outcome of the recognisation by the firm of their interdependence upon each other is that they join together and behave as a monopolist. In that way they are able to make the maximum profit possible and avoid the cost of competing with each other. Price and quantity can be set as shown in the figure below

The formation of cartels as a strategy for firms to adopt is a usual outcome in oligopoly. The government of most industrial nations subscribe to the view that monopoly is harmful and have legislations, which make cartels illegal. Even if cartels are not made illegal there are a number of forces, which make establishment, and maintenance of cartels difficult. Firstly, A group of rivals who set to cartelise their industry have to agree on the price to be set in order to make maximum profit. Having taken this decision, the members of the cartel have to decide how much output can be sold at that price and to allocate production quotas for each member. If this is not done then cartel may produce more output than can be sold at the agreed price. Unsold output would pile up the stocks and would result in a pride decrease. The negotiation of quotas is a difficult issue because precise information about demand condition is rarely available so that the level of output which corresponds to profit –maximising price is not known with certainty. Once an estimate has been made of the total amount to be produced that total has to be divided amongst the member as quotas. This is a sensitive issue because the division of output determines the distribution of profit and it could be possible that certain members are unable to agree on quotas and the cartel collapses before it can be put into effect. Secondly, even if cartel is able to negotiate production quotas there continues to be a tendency for the cartel to collapse as a result of cheating or suspected cheating on part of members. Every member of a cartel has a very powerful incentive to cheat on others by charging a price which is a little below the agreed price, thereby attracting a very high level of demand. If one firm is suspected of cheating the others will follow suit by cutting their prices and cartel will collapse. However if all firms in a cartel are well informed about each other then cheating would be identified easily, the responses would be immediate, and the gain to cheating would be non –existent.

There are a number of variables, which will determine the likely success of a cartel, each of which affects the extent to which firms are well informed about each other.

1. The number of firms: If the number of firms in an industry is small, they will be able to monitor each other's activities at relatively low cost, thereby deterring cheating.

2. Product differentiation: If firms produce similar products they will be aware of their rival's cost and demand conditions, simply by being well informed about themselves thus deterring cheating. If there is a high degree of product differentiation, or if products are non –standardised, it will be difficult for firms to keep themselves in touch with the activities of others, and the differences between products will make it extremely difficult to set monopoly prices, taking into account the cost variations between different firm's brands.

3. Slow rate of technology progress: If technology change is rapid, the industry will face a much greater degree of uncertainty and instability than if companies are all using an established, mature set of techniques, which develops slowly. As a result, cartelisation becomes more difficult in conditions of rapid technological change.

4. Publication of prices: If prices are published, firms will find it easier to monitor each other's activities than if prices are kept confidential.

5. Trade Association: If there exist an active trade association in an industry, it can provide an effective channel of communication between firms, thereby assisting in the process of cartelisation. Trade associations may also be able to exert some degree of discipline over firms who do not conform by denying them access to the association's facilities.

In short run firms in a cartel are able to earn supernormal profits but in long run other forces explained below tend to break down the cartel's power.

1. Threat of new entry: If a cartel is successful in raising the price and increasing profits for its member this immediately creates an incentive for other firms to enter the industry. This need not matter if entry is 'blocked' but it is a rare phenomenon and cartels in most industries are subject to break down in the long run as a result of the cartel's success leading to new entry. It is possible that new entrants join the cartel but that would increase the number of firms and reduce the cartel's manageability. As long as cartel uses its power to earn supernormal profits there will be market forces working to break down the cartel.

2. Search for substitutes: If the price of the product produced by the cartel increases, this results in search for alternatives by users of the product. This provides an incentive for other firms to invent and produce such substitutes. While this may take some time its eventual effect will be to reduce the demand for the cartel's product and make it more elastic, thereby reducing the cartel's ability to charge high prices and make large profits.

The most important example of a cartel is the organisation of Petroleum Exporting Countries (OPEC), whose history provides a graphic illustration of the issues raised by cartels.

Price leadership and tacit collusion

Cartel is an example of explicit collusion, where the firms involved are parties to an agreement to reduce output and raise prices to the monopoly level, in order to make maximum joint profit. However in many countries its illegal to form cartels. As a result, firms develop unspoken or tacit collusion, these do not necessarily involve any form of conspiracy on part of firms involved, these simply arise due to the recognition of interdependence amongst rivals and of the costs, which may be involved if rivalry becomes too intense.

Price leadership is one of the most important form of tacit collusion. In this situation, one of the firm in the industry adopts the role of price leader, by setting a price which is followed by the others. If the firms are all producing identical products then the followers set the same price as the leader. If products are differentiated the followers use the leader's price as a benchmark and adjust their own prices upwards or downwards according to the different quality and cost of production of their particular product variants. In this way the firms in the industry can establish what is sometimes termed 'orderly' competition amongst themselves. In the language of the corporate strategies (Porter 1985) they behave as 'good competitors' for each other.

To establish a price leadership, the leader must have a powerful position in the industry, in order to be able to threat any firm which fails to act as a follower. The most obvious move would be to push the price down so far that the offending firm cannot survive. That implies that the price leader needs to be the lowest cost producer in the industry, and to have substantial market share and production capacity in order for the threat to be credible.

Price leadership may be either dominant or barometric. Dominant price leadership occurs when the leading firm is powerful enough to set a price which other firms will be forced to follow. Barometric price leadership occurs when the leading firm is followed merely because the price it sets reflects the market forces and the needs of the other firms in the industry.

Price leadership is evident in mature and stable industries producing highly standardised products such as steel, oil, cement or building materials. In some industries price leadership shifts among major firms but more commonly a single firm remains the price leader for long periods.

Advantages of price leadership situation

1. Small firms often lack sufficient insight into the principles of costing. They may safely assume that price set by market leader backed by efficient costing department would be correct.

2. It avoids the expense of production/cost studies and market surveys as a basis of estimating demand by follower firms.

3. Price leader tends to influence price towards stability as he usually anxious to avoid price wars. Therefore in periods of recession, the price leader will exert his power to stop rapid reduction in prices on the part of any firm. The more inelastic the demand for the product under question, the harder price leader will work to maintain prices.

4. Price leadership usually dampens the amplitude of cyclical fluctuations i.e. prices have not gone as high in boom periods or as low in depressions as they would have otherwise gone.

5. Price leadership considerably reduces the number of possible reactions to a price change and thus gives an element of certainty to the pricing aspects of market forecasting.

Kinky demand curve model

The analysis of oligopoly would be incomplete without reference to the kinky demand curve model. The starting point for this model is the assumption that firms in the industry have found some way of establishing a price (through collusion or price leadership) and each firm knows the level of output which it can sell at that price. Pest and Qest show this position in the diagram. While the firm in diagram knows the amount it can sell at the set price, the amount of output it can sell at higher or lower prices are less clear and depend upon the reaction of the firm's rivals. The firm can only make guesses as to the likely responses. If the firm raises its price, it guesses that its rival will not follow suit. As a result, price rise will imply the loss of a substantial proportion of the firm's customers, and the demand curve for prices above P_{est} will be highly elastic. On the other hand, if the firm lowers its price its guess with respect to its rival's reactions is that they will follow its example and also lower their prices. As a result the demand curve for price reductions is highly inelastic, as depicted in the diagram.

As a result of this analysis the demand curve has a kink as shown in the figure. The marginal revenue curve has even more pronounced discontinuity as shown in the figure. This follows directly from the behaviour from the behaviour of the demand. If the firm wishes to sell more than Q_{est} it has to lower the price, but if it does so then its rivals will also cut their prices so that a small increase in demand for the firm's product will require a proportionately large fall in price. As a result the additional revenue earned from an additional unit of output sold will be very small or even negative.

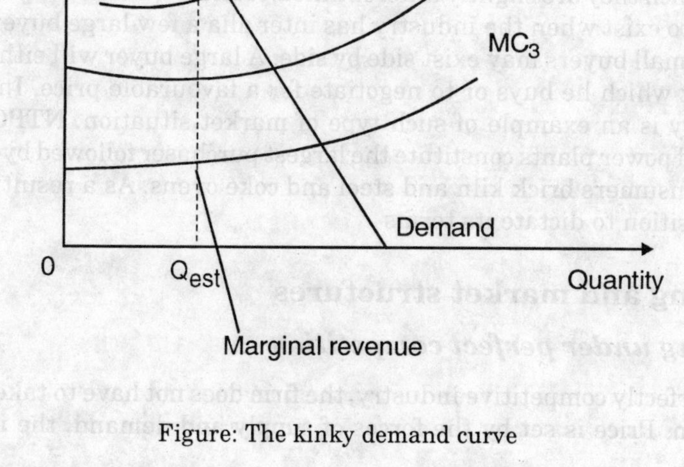

Figure: The kinky demand curve

If the oligopolist firm is a profit maximiser, it will operate at the point where marginal cost equals marginal revenue, which corresponds to output Q_{est}. The usefulness of this model is that the firm would continue choosing the same price and quantity, even if marginal costs vary quite substantially. In the example shown, marginal cost could rise as high as MC_2 , or as low as MC_3 without the firm choosing to change its price. Similar considerations apply to increase in demand. If the demand curve shifts to the right, the kink remaining at the same level of price, the firm will choose to increase its output, but the price chosen will remain the same for quite substantial changes in demand.

The kinky demand curve model does not provide a prediction about the level of price, which will be reached in an oligopoly situation. But it does predict that once a price has been established it will tend to be stable in the face of changing costs and demand conditions, within limits. In perfect competition, monopoly or monopolistic competition changes in cost or demand will lead to changes in price. However in oligopoly once a price has been established the firms are wary of disturbing the delicate equilibrium by changing prices, because if they do so, they might find rivals reacting adversely, to the detriment of their profitability.

Oligopsony

Main features of oligopsony are

1.Few buyers in a particular market

2.Size of each buyer is such that increase or decrease in his will considerably affect the price.

3.No single buyer can afford to ignore the reactions of his rivals to policies he might initiate eg. The offer of a higher price.

Examples of oligopsony are local labour market dominated by a firm, milk dairies etc.

Oligopsony may appear in markets in which the buyers are just alike or in which they are slightly differentiated. A situation similar to oligopsony is said to exist when the industry has inter alia a few large buyers though many small buyers may exist side by side. A large buyer will either set the price at which he buys or to negotiate for a favourable price. India's coal industry is an example of such type of market situation. NTPC and the thermal power plants constitute the largest purchaser followed by two other bulk consumers brick kiln and steel and coke ovens. As a result, NTPC is in a position to dictate its terms

Pricing and market structures

Pricing under perfect competition

In a perfectly competitive industry, the firm does not have to take a pricing decision. Price is set by the forces of supply and demand, the individual firm is too small to have any impact on that price, and firms are known as 'price-takers'. Each firm simply accepts the price which is set by the market and takes a decision on the level of output which maximises profit, given the market price. As each individual firm faces a demand curve which is infinitely elastic, profit- maximising behaviour on the part of each firm requires that price (which equals marginal revenue in this case) will be equal to marginal cost, at the profit-maximising level of output. If firms are able to make supernormal profits at the prevailing price then in the long-run entry will take place and the price will be forced down by market pressures until the supernormal profits are eliminated.

Pricing under monopoly

A monopolist is not a 'price-taker', but a 'price-maker', in the sense that the price which it sets is not pre-determined by external market forces. That is not to say that a monopolist has complete freedom with respect to price. In order to achieve maximum profit the optimal combination of price and quantity has to be chosen by selecting the level of output at which marginal cost equals marginal revenue and then adopting the market-clearing price for that level of output. This is illustrated in Fig below. In the figure , the profit-maximising level of output is Q and the profit-maximising price is P. A limit is set to the level of price by the buyers' ability to go without the industry's product, which in turn decides the elasticity of demand and the optimal price.

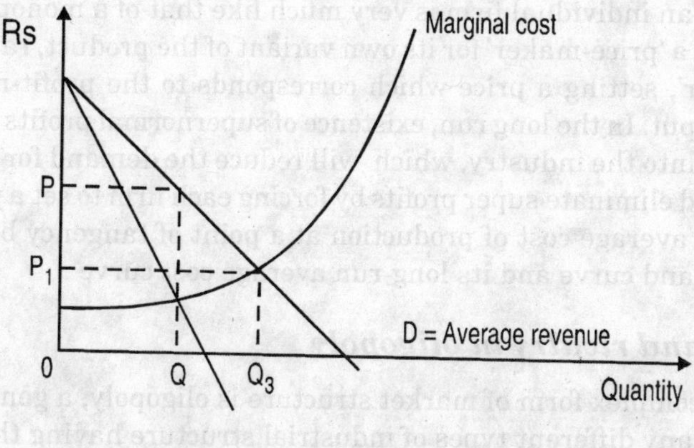

The textbook model of monopoly focuses attention on the short term, and by assumption the firm faces no threat of entry in the long term. As a result there are no long-term forces tending to eliminate any supernormal profits by forcing the price downwards. The only difference between the short run and the long run is that in the long run the firm can consider whether it has the most profitable set of plant and equipment, given the available technology and the demand curve facing it. If it does, then in the long run it will simply keep on replacing that set of plant and equipment.

Cost and demand conditions will remain as shown in Figure as will the profit-maximising price and output. On the other hand, if there is an alternative set of plant and equipment which would allow greater profits to be made, that set will be built in the long run and there will be a new profit-maximising level of output and price corresponding to the cost conditions associated with the new plant.

As the textbook model of monopoly involves a firm which is protected from entry by assumption there is no possibility that the threat of entry may be affected by the price set and the profits made. In that case simple profit-maximisation will take place and, no matter how large the resulting profits, new firms cannot establish a foothold in the industry. Such a situation may arise if entry to the industry is absolutely blockaded by legal restrictions or some other absolute barrier. However, in many other situations the barriers to entry are not absolute and a monopoly firm may to pay attention to the impact of its price and profits upon the behaviour of potential entrants. Earning maximum profit in the short run might encourage entry to take place in the long run and thereby erode the firm's monopoly position. The relationship between pricing and entry is considered further in the section on pricing and rivalry in oligopoly below.

Pricing in monopolistic competition

Monopolistic competition contains elements of both perfect competition and monopoly. Each firm has a downward sloping demand curve, arising from the production of differentiated products, so that in the short run the position of an individual firm is very much like that of a monopolist. Each business is a 'price-maker' for its own variant of the product, rather than a 'price-taker', setting a price which corresponds to the profit-maximising level of output. In the long run, existence of supernormal profits will attract new entry into the industry, which will reduce the demand for each firm's product and eliminate super profits by forcing each firm to set a price which is equal to average cost of production at a point of tangency between the firm's demand curve and its long-run average cost curve .

Pricing and rivalry in oligopoly

The most complex form of market structure is oligopoly, a generic term used for many different types of industrial structure having the common feature of consisting of just a few firms, each of which is interdependent upon the others.

The analysis suggested a number of possible outcomes of the oligopoly situation, each of which has implications for pricing. A simple integrated treatment for some of these can be provided, following Dorward (1987), by using a straightforward mathematical framework. The starting point is with the case where all firms produce identical products. In this case, the demand curve can be written:

$p = p(Q)$ where:

where p = price

Q = total output of all firms

$= q_i$

q_i = output of the i'th firm ,

The profit function for an individual firm is then given by:

$\$_i = p(Q)q_i - C_i\ (q_i)$

where:

$C_i(q)_i$ = total cost of q_i

cand the condition for profit-maximisation is:

$d\$ / dq_i = p+q_i.\ dp/dQ.\ dQ/dqi - dC_i/ cq_i = 0$

The most important term in this last equation is dQ/dq_i which illustrates the importance of the links between changes in the i'th firm's output and changes in the outputs of the other firms and the industry as a whole. If the i'th firm increases its output by one unit, and the other firms do not respond to that change, then clearly:

$dQ / dq_i = 0$

On the other hand , if the other firms respond to the unit increase in output by raising their own outputs by a units, then:

$dQ / dq_i = 1 + a$

The term a is a measure of rivals' reactions. As the individual firm can only conjecture about the reactions of its rivals a may also be described as a measure of conjectural variation, as perceived by that firm.

Just as the simple profit-maximising condition (MC = MR) can be rewritten to give:

$(P\text{-}MC) / P = 1/E_d$

The more complex Oligopoly version can be re-written to give:

$(P\text{-}MC_i) / P = (-)\ si\ (1+a)/E_d$

where

s_i = market share, firm i

a = conjectural variation

E_d= market elasticity.

Examination of this model shows that it encompasses both perfect competition (s_i and a both equal to zero) and monopoly (s_i equal to 1 and a equal to zero) as special cases.

In the oligopoly case, where a is non-zero, the firm's pricing behaviour depends upon the sign and size of the conjectural variation. If a is positive and large, indicating that other firms increase their output substantially when the firm under examination attempts to increase its own output (which implies lowering its price), then clearly demand for the individual firm's product will be very jnelastic and the corresponding margin between marginal cost and the optimal price will be large. In the opposite case, if rival firms were to respond to an increase in output by reducing their own output, demand for the firm in question would be highly elastic (a reduction in price would lead to a large increase in demand as other firms reduce their output) and the optimal price/marginal cost margin would be lower.

The model set out above illustrates the importance of rivals' reactions for the optimal price in conditions of oligopoly. It can also be linked back to the qualitative discussion of oligopoly in above section. In the case of collusion, for instance, if each firm conjectures that its partners in the joint monopoly will act in such a way as to maintain stable market shares then:

$$a = (1- si) / si$$

This reduces the equation given above to:

$$(P\text{-}MC_i) / P = (-)\ 1/E_d$$

which is exactly the same as in monopoly

In the case of the kinky demand curve model, a takes different values for price rises (output reductions) and price falls (output increases.) If the individual firm attempts to increase its output by lowering the price, the assumption is that its rivals will also lower price and increase output so that a is positive. If the firm raises its price, thereby lowering its output, the assumption is that rivals leave their price at the initial level and increase their output, so that a is negative. As a takes multiple values around the existing price level, this makes the solution indeterminate, which brings the analysis back to the basic objection to the kinky demand curve theory which is that it does not provide a prediction for the price level, but rather suggests that in oligopoly prices will tend to be stable.

Entry Barriers

If entry barriers are very high, the existing firms in the industry do not not to concern themselves unduly with the possibilities that high prices and profits may attract competitions from new entrants. On the other hand if entry barriers are low, entry may take place with ease whenever the incumbent firms in an industry make substantial profits. The determinants of the entry barriers may be considered in turn.

Economies of scale

If there are substantial economics of scale, a firm which is considering entering the industry must either build a large market share immediately, in order to achieve the scale required to keep costs down, or suffer higher cost then the incumbent firms. As a result, scale economics are an important source of entry barriers it is important to remember that such economies are not limited to production activities. There may be important scale effects in almost any business activities, including research and development, marketing and distribution.

Product differentiation and brand loyalty

If existing firms have successfully developed buyer loyalty to their products a new entrant may have to make expensive and risky investment in advertising and promotion in order to overcome that loyalty. If entry should fail, those investments become worthless.

Capital requirements

In some industries, very large amounts of capital have to be acquired if entry is to take place. While these may be available if capital markets work well, entry will often be regarded as a risky venture and investors will require high returns in order to persuade them to take that risk.

Switching costs for buyers

If customers have to face additional cost from switching from one supplier to another, they will be unwilling to change suppliers and it will be difficult for a new entrant to be successful, without a heavy investment to help customers overcome those switching costs.

Access to distribution channels

A new entrant must establish its own distribution channels, persuading wholesalers and retailers to stock and display its products along side, or in preference to the product of existing firms. If the incumbent firms have well established relationships with the distribution channels it may be difficult or expensive for a new entrant to gain access to them.

Absolute cost advantages

One of the most general sources of entry barriers is the existence of absolute cost advantages, whereby incumbent firms have lower costs than entrants. If there are such advantages, existing firms will always have the ability to cut their prices to a level at which new entrant cannot survive, which will provide a major disincentive to entry. The possible sources of absolute cost advantages include

i. Proprietary technology: If a firm has a product or a process which is protected by a patent, or by secrecy, new entrants will not be able to copy that product or process and will be at a disadvantage.

ii. Access to input: Existing firms may have access to inputs on favourable terms.

iii. Proprietary learning effects: As firms gain experience in an industry they are usually able to reduce their costs as the result of 'learning effects'.

If these effects are 'proprietary and a new firm can not acquire them simply by hiring executives from the existing firms, then an entrant will be at a disadvantage until it has had time to learn for itself, by which time the longer established firm s may have benefited from additional learning, staying one step ahead of the entrant.

iv. Favourable locations: for some activities there are only a limited number of suitable locations. If these are all occupied by existing firms, new entry will be extremely difficult.

Expected Retaliation

In many industries the reaction of the established firms to new entry is a key factor determining the entrant's success. If they are accommodating an entrant has a greater chance of success on the other hand, if they retaliate aggressively through price cutting or promotional campaigns, the entrant will only be able to survive if it has some very strong advantages to compete for it inexperience in the industry. As a result the threat of retaliation will in itself present an important barrier to entry.

Government Policies

In some industries, in some countries, government policies sets up barriers to entry. At the extremes these involves industrial licensing, where a firm has to have government permission before setting up in an industry. In other cases the barriers to entry established by government policies may be more subtle and are often unintended. For instance if a government imposes strict health and safety legislation on an industry this may increase the capital requirements needed to enter and thereby raise entry barriers. Patent law is also one such legislation which provides entry barrier.

Contestable markets

In recent years the term contestable markets has been used by Baumol, Panzer and Willig. A contestable market requires barriers to entry to be low, and a perfectly contestable market requires a total absence of barriers to entry. Barriers to entry for example being, special licences, patents, copyrights, high fixed costs, marketing barriers (legal and illegal) constructed by incumbent firms.A full exposition of 'contestable markets' lies beyond the scope of this text but it is possible to provide an outline.

The most important new concept is that of 'contestability'. A perfectly contestable market is one in which entry is free, exit is costless, existing firms and entrants compete on equal terms and potential entrants are not deterred from entering by the threat of retaliatory price-cutting by incumbents. In such a market it can be shown that the benefits associated with perfect competition will accrue, even if there are very few firms in the industry.

Clearly, the concept of a contestable market is related to the idea of entry barriers and such a market might simply be thought of as one where entry barriers are limited. However, the new theory also suggests that in many instances barriers to entry are less formidable than has previously been supposed. In particular, the analysis points to the importance of sunk costs as the major real deterrent to entry. (Sunk costs are those which cannot be eliminated, even by cessation of production.) If sunk costs are small, entrants will have little difficulty in competing with existing firms on equal terms and the threat of this competition will force incumbents to behave like perfect competitors. However, with some businesses the sunk costs are a large percentage of the business costs. Creating a brand name or corporate image can be hugely expensive. Advertising costs are often a significant part of a company's total costs for products such as cigarettes, perfume, soap powder and the like. Leaving the market means that all the money spent creating the brand may be lost – although even brand names can be sold. The costs of car production involve very high fixed costs in terms of machinery, design, staff training, advertising etc. so that sunk costs are high and this will discourage companies from entering the market unless they are planning to stay for the longer term. Thus a contestable market requires both low entry and exit barriers. But an established company does not have to leave the market entirely, it can leave part of the market. A high street multiple can close one shop in its chain in one town without closing the whole chain. A motor manufacturer might retreat from a country or a continent without closing down in the rest of the world.

Baumol (1982) provide a good example in a small airline market. If we consider the market for air travel between two towns where the number of people travelling is only enough to fill one aeroplane, we have an example of a 'natural monopoly'. It will always be cheaper for the route to be served by a single airline than for two or more to fly in competition. As a result the market will be monopolised, in the sense that there is only one supplier. However, that supplier will not be able to operate like a textbook monopolist. If aircraft can be rented, or if there is an active market for second-hand planes, then sunk costs are very limited. All an entrant need do, if the incumbent airline is creating a profitable opportunity by charging high fares, is to fly his aircraft on to the tarmac, undercut the incumbent and make a profit. If the incumbent then cuts his price the entrant can literally flyaway and either use the plane on another route or sell it (or cease renting it). The absence of sunk costs makes entry cheaply reversible and the threat or the reality of easy entry will discipline the incumbent 'monopolist'.

The contestable markets approach has a number of implications for competition policy. First, it shows that it is not appropriate to decide on whether to intervene in an industry by making reference to the degree of departure from the conditions of perfect competition. Second, it provides an alternative benchmark to the unattainable criterion of perfect competition, that of 'contestability'. When considering the structure and behaviour of an industry, the first step is to decide whether or not it constitutes a contestable market. If it does, government interference is not needed, even if the industry exhibits symptoms which have in the past been accepted as indicators of poor market performance, such as high concentration, price discrimination, mergers and vertical integration. On the other hand, if the industry is not contestable then intervention to make it so needs to be considered. First and foremost governments need to consider means by which entry to and exit from an industry can be made easier. In particular, policy needs to reduce the level of sunk costs, which form the major barrier to exit and the main impediment to contestability. Measures could include having sunk costs borne by government, which would then lease facilities to firms, or by mandating that sunk costs should be shared by a consortium. Alternatively, sunk costs might be reduced by tax advantages for rapid depreciation, for retooling, or for the reuse of old plant in new activities. Anything which improves the efficiency of the second-hand equipment markets would also be useful

Markets that have become more contestable in recent years

Internet Service Providers (including the entry of "free" ISP's - over 200 of these in September 1999

- Online Communications (including video conferencing; virtual reality games; publishing; home shopping; travel services; information services; databases)
- Home Banking and Financial Services
- Electricity and Gas Supply
- Parcel delivery
- Opticians
- Low cost domestic airlines
- Road Haulage Companies

In a contestable market there are **no structural barriers** to the entry of firms in the long-run. If existing businesses are enjoying high economic profits, there is an incentive for new firms to enter the industry. This increases market competition and dilutes monopoly profits for the incumbent firms.

Price and Quantity Determination in Duopoly

Cournot's solution

The French mathematical economist Cournot published his theory of duopoly in 1838. Although most of his models were crude and involved very unrealistic assumptions, his method of analysis has been useful for subsequent theoretical development in the area of oligopoly.

Assumptions:

1. There are two profit maximizing duopolists.
2. Both duopolists produce an identical product.
3. Both duopolists sell at identical prices
4. Duopolists act independently without collusion
5. Each duopolist assumes that the rival's output will remain unchanged.

The last assumption is very naive, because it implies that the duopolists do not learn from experience. But this assumption gives a deterministic solution to the problem.

In Cournot's example, two producers produce mineral water from two adjacent springs, produced at zero marginal cost.

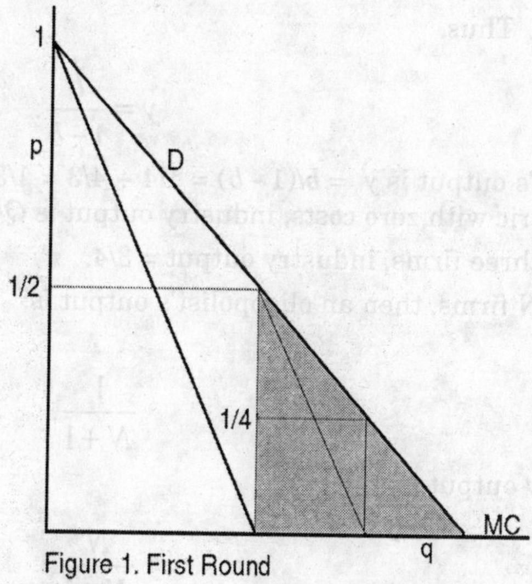

Figure 1. First Round

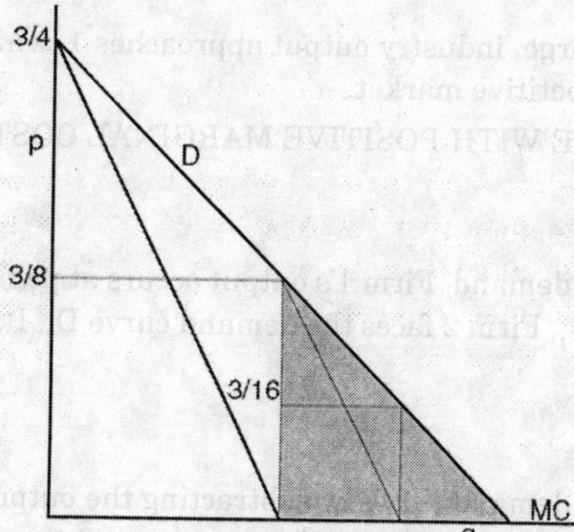

Figure 2. Second Round

Sequence of Outputs

Firm	1st round	2nd round	3rd round	4th round	...
I	½	-1/8	-1/32	-1/128	
II	1/4	+1/16	+1/64	+1/256	

I: 1/2 -1/8 -1/32 -1/128 - ...

II: 1/4 + 1/16 + 1/64 + 1/256 + ...

Equilibrium output of firm 2

$$y_2 = b + b^2 + b^3 + ...$$
$$by_2 = b^2 + b^3 + b^4 + ...$$

Then $y(1-b) = b$. Thus,

$$y = \frac{b}{1-b}.$$

Thus, firm 2's output is $y_2 = b/(1 - b) = 1/4 \div 4/3 = 1/3$. Since the two firms are symmetric with zero costs, industry output is $Q = 2/3$.

If there are three firms, industry output = 3/4.

If there are N firms, then an oligopolist's output is:

$$\frac{1}{N+1}.$$

The industry output is:

$$\frac{N}{N+1}.$$

If N is very large, industry output approaches 1, which is the output of a perfectly competitive market.

COURNOT'S CASE WITH POSITIVE MARGINAL COST

First Round:

D_1 = Firm 1's demand. Firm 1's output occurs at point A. Subtracting this output from D_1, Firm 2 faces the demand curve D_2. Its optimal output occurs at point B.

Second Round:

Firm 1 derives its demand curve by subtracting the output at point B and repeat the above process, and so and so on.

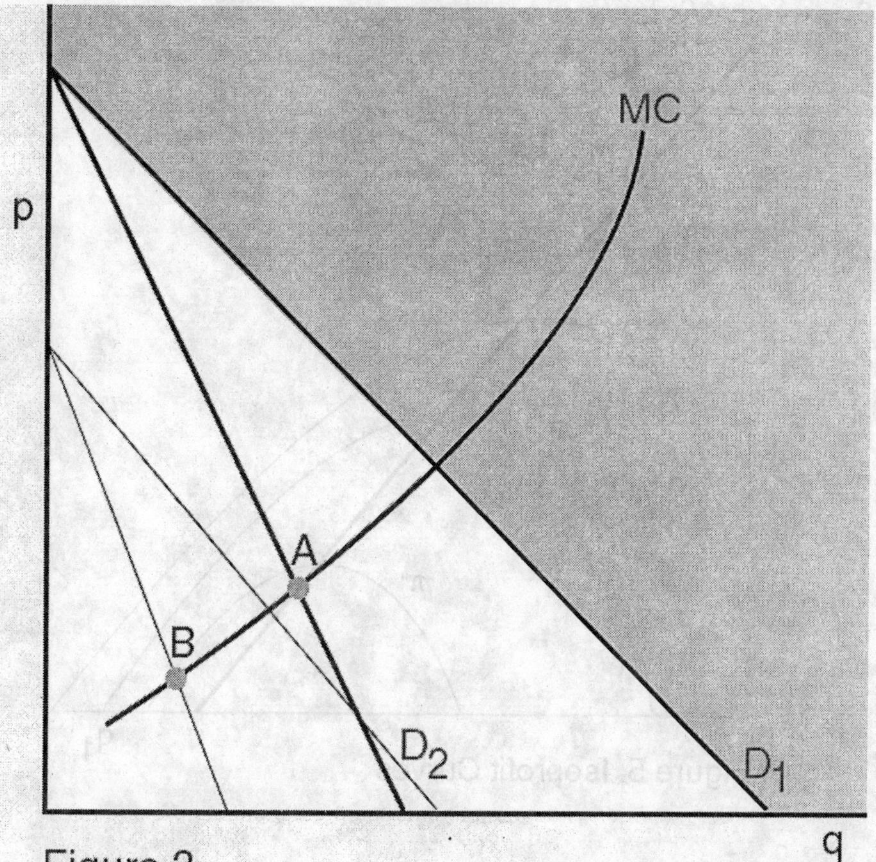

Figure 3

Reaction Function (Curve)

Reaction functions offer one way to examine oligopolistic interdependence. The simplest reaction function models are duopoly models but these models can be algebraically generalized to n-firm oligopolies from the simple two-firm model described here. The value of the two-firm model is that it is easy to describe graphically. Reaction Function is also called the best response function. For instance, R_1 is Firm 1's best response to Firm 2's output. Thus, it depends on its rival's output, and is written as $R_1(q_2)$. Similarly, the best response function of firm 2 depends on its rival's output, and hence is written as $R_2(q_1)$. Cournot equilibrium occurs at the intersection of the two reaction functions.

Derivation of Reaction Functions.
Cournot Equilibrium Is the intersection of two reaction curves.

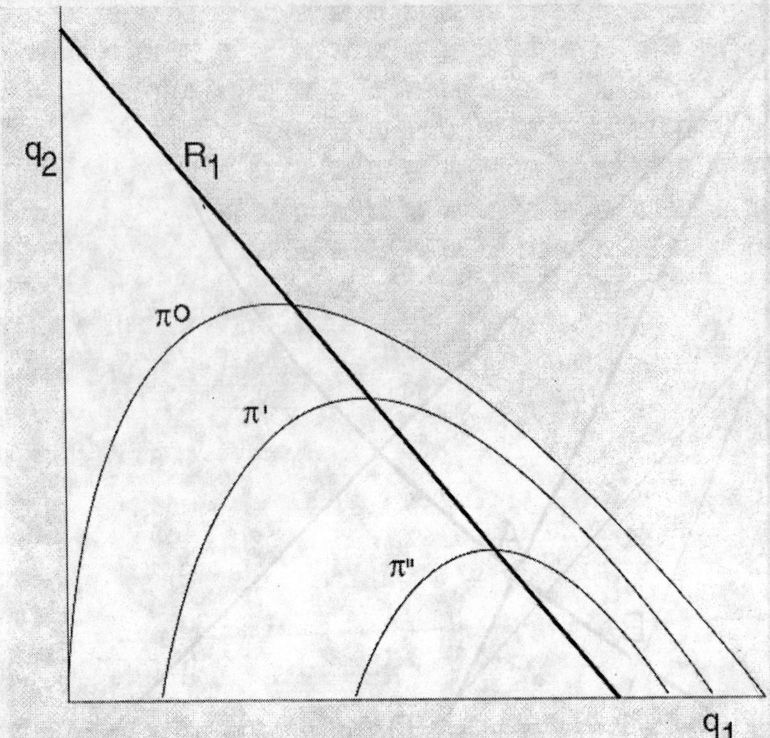

Figure 5. Isoprofit Curves

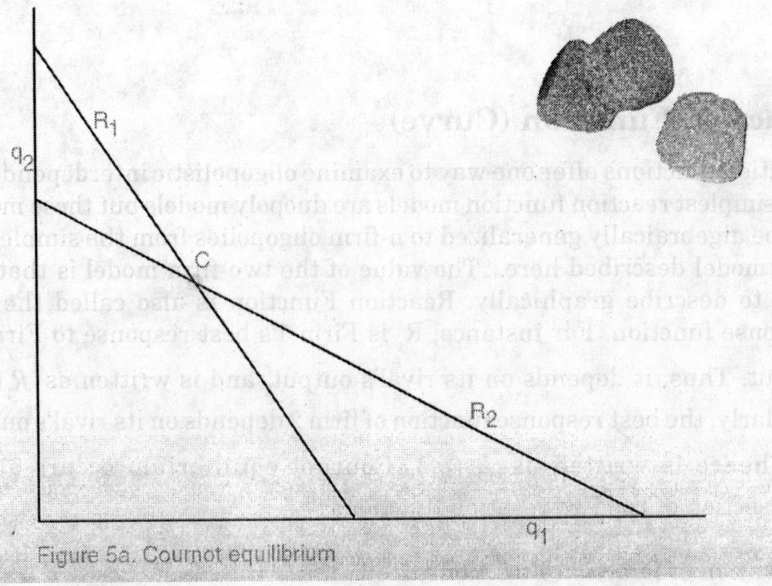

Figure 5a. Cournot equilibrium

Points to remember

A.Perfect Competition

- Many (small) firms, producing a homogeneous (identical) product, none of which having an impact on the price; each firm's product is non-distinguishable from other firms' product.
- Many buyers none of whom having any effect on the price.
- No barriers to entry and exit: in the long run firms can shut down and leave the industry or new firms can come into the industry freely.
- No interference in the market process: No price control or restrictions on production
- All firms have equal and complete access to the available inputs (input markets) and production technology; all firms have the same production and cost functions.
- All sellers and buyers have perfect information about the market conditions.
- Making above-normal profits by existing firms will result in new entries into the industry. Firms that have losses shut down and leave the industry in the long run.

How is the market price Determined?

- Market Supply: The (horizontal) sum of individual supply curves
- Market Demand: The (horizontal) sum of individual demand curves

B.Perfect Competition:Profit Maximization in the Short Run

- An individual firm takes the market price as given; the demand each individual firm faces is horizontal.
- MR = P: Demand
- Set the price equal to MC
- In the short- run the firm could have an economic profit

C. Adjustments in the Long Run

- If economic profits are present new firms will come into the industry
- The Market price will fall
- The profit shrinks
- Input prices may go up
- Firms try to stay profitable by taking advantage of economies of scale

- Firms adopt an optimal size
- Economic profits tend toward zero

D. Long-Run Equilibrium under Perfect Competition

- Many "optimal-size" firms, each producing at the minimum long run average cost and charging the market price where:

  P = MR= MC = SATC = LATC
- Allocative efficiency: MC = P
- Productive efficiency: MC= SATC = LATC
- Zero economic profit (normal profit) : P = ATC

E. Pure Monopoly

- A single firm producing a homogenous or differentiated (unique) good and facing the market demand.
- No substitutes
- No new entries allowed
- The monopoly is a price maker
- P>MR
- Possibility of a sustained economic profit

F. What circumstances lead to the formation of a monopoly?

- Extensive economies of scale: natural monopolies
- Exclusive patent rights
- Copy rights to intellectual properties
- Government franchises
- Exclusive access to a essential resource (input)
- Cartels A monopoly is a profit maximizer too!

G. The Dynamics of a Monopolistic Market

- As a profit maximizer a monopoly may try to take advantage of economies of scale
- A monopoly tends to try to protect its monopolistic position
- A monopoly may take advantage of technological advances
- A monopoly may face changes in demand
- A monopoly may try to promote its product to maintain demand

H. Monopolies and Profit Maximization

- A monopoly faces the industry demand curve
- To maximize profit: MR = MC

  $P = 80 - .0008Q$; $MR = 80 - .0016Q$

  $TC = 10{,}000 + .0092Q^2$; $MC = .0184\ Q$

  Set MR = MC → Q = 4000; P = 76.8

  Profit = 307,200 – 147,200 – 10,000 = 150,000
- Profit = (P- ATC). Q

Things Change

- Demand may go down
- Cost could increase
- In an attempt to keep the potential competitors out, the monopolist may lower its price to near its average cost
- Rent seeking: an attempt to maintain its monopolistic position by influencing the political processes-e.g., zoning laws
- Closer substitutes may emerge

I. The Case of Natural Monopolies

- A natural monopoly emerges out of competition among firms in an industry with extensive economies of scale; the downward-sloping segment of the LATC curve extends to or beyond the market capacity (or market demand).
- Smaller firms are gradually driven out by the larger (more efficient) firms.
- *The* surviving firm would become a (natural) monopoly.
- If unchecked, a natural monopoly behaves like a monopoly; it under-produces and overcharges.

J. Price Discrimination

- Segmenting the market into separate classifications or regions
- Assuming that each class of consumers have different demand, a monopoly can charge different prices in each market segment

  To price-discriminate
- The firm must identify consumer groups/classes with different downward-sloping demand curves
- The firm must be able to prevent consumers of one class from reselling its product to the consumers of another class; no intermarket redistribution of the product is allowed

K. Monopolistic Competition

- Many firms producing producing differentiated products
- Each firm would face a downward-sloping demand curve
- The 15-minute fame
- To maximize profit the firm set its estimated MR equal to its MC
- The firm may enjoy a short-run profit
- In the long run due to the emergence of substitutes the demand starts to shrink

L. Oligopolies

- A market with a few firms each large enough to have an effect on the price
- Interdependence among firms
- Each firm would try to guess its competitor's reaction to its pricing strategy
- Relative price stability
- Different Oligopoly models
- The Kinked Demand Curve Model

Questions

1. What are the main features of pure competition? How does a firm adjust its policies to a purely competitive situation?
2. "In a completely competitive market no one transaction can influence the price of a commodity." Do you agree with this statement?
3. 'The purely competitive entrepreneur provides a very effective service in helping to allocate resources consistently with consumers' preference and with the interest of resource owners." Elucidate.
4. Explain the possible effect of an increase in demand with a simultaneous decrease in supply on sales and price. Explain why the firm under perfect competition maximises profit or minimises loss by operating at the position where marginal cost and price are equal.
5. List the basic differences between the pure monopolist and the perfectly competitive firms. Explain with examples.
6. What basic assumptions do we make in order to determine the pure monopolist's equilibrium level of output?

7. How does the equilibrium of the firm under perfect competition differ from that of a monopolist?
8. Is it true that in the long run no super-normal profits are earned by a perfectly competitive firm?
9. Examine different types of competitive situations that may possibly be found in a market.
10. What is monopoly? State the factors which give rise to monopoly. Also distinguish between monopoly and monopsony.
11. Explain what price and output decisions are made by:
    (i) a firm buying competitively and selling monopolistically;
    (ii) a firm selling competitively and buying monopsonistically;
    (iii) a firm buying monopsonistically and selling monopolistically.

    Are these decisions consistent with the interest of consumers and resource-owners?
12. What is the difference between perfect competition and monopolistic competition? Show how price is determined under monopolistic competition.
13. Examine the relation between a monopolist's profits and elasticity of demand. Discuss the long-run considerations which affect the price policies of a monopolist.
14. Could long-range profits ever exist in a market of monopolistic competition? Why or why not?
15. Examine the efficiency of monopoly and competition in terms of price, output and costs. Should monopolies be controlled?
16. What is meant by monopolistic competition? How does a firm take its pricing and output decisions under it?
17. Define 'Oligopoly'. Explain how price and output decisions are taken under conditions of oligopoly.
18. Explain the meaning of price leadership. What are the conditions necessary for effective price leadership?
19. Explain what do you understand by monopolistic competition. How will price be determined under monopolistic competition when there is product differentiation?
20. How is the equilibrium of a firm determined *(a)* under competitive conditions, and *(b)* under monopolistic conditions?
21. Price is higher and the scale of output is smaller under monopolistic competition than under perfect competition. Explain with the help of necessary diagrams.
22. How should an oligopolist alter his prices or quantities in order to keep either his sales or prices constant?

23. "A monopolist aims at maximizing price rather than profits." Do you agree with this statement?

24. Examine the relation between a monopolist's profits and elasticity of demand.

    It is said:

    (i) that a firm in a perfectly competitive market cannot be a price maker it is only a price taker.

    (ii) prices set by oligopolistic firms like oil companies tend to be rigid, and

    (iii) in monopolistic competition since firms have a differentiated product, they price their product in the same manner as the monopoly firm does. Explain briefly the economic rationale behind the above-mentioned statements and point out clearly their policy implications.

25. "The kinked demand curve can explain both interdependence of firms and stickiness of prices under oligopoly." Comment.

7

Cost Analysis

Introduction

The cost analysis is important in the study of managerial economics because it provide a basis for two important decisions managers has to make (a) whether to produce or not (b) how much to produce. Under production analysis, we discussed about the input output relationship in terms of physical relationships. However, decisions about optimal output and optimal prices, require an understanding of relationship between output rate of the firm and costs. Managerial decisions with respect to quotation of prices, efficacy of a product line, change in volume of output, and use of excess capacity also depends on the cost analysis.

Cost Concepts

The kind of cost concept to be used in a situation faced by a firm depends upon the business decision to be made. An understanding of various cost concepts by the manager is essential for clear business thinking. Defining and distinguishing cost concepts are essential because i)cost estimates provided by financial accounting are not appropriate for all managerial uses ii)different business decisions need different kinds of costs.

Actual costs and Opportunity costs

Actual costs mean the actual expenditure incurred for producing a good or service. The actual cost is also called outlay cost or absolute cost. These costs are costs recorded in the account books. Example of actual costs are actual wages paid, cost of materials purchased, paid interest etc.

Opportunity cost is defined as the value of a resource in its next best use or it can be defined as revenue forgone by not making alternative use. Opportunity cost of a good or service is measured in terms of the revenue which could have been earned by employing that goods and services in some other alternative use. For example if an MBA student decides to have his own business instead of joining a job, the opportunity cost is the salary foregone which he could have earned in the job. Opportunity costs are incurred when budgetary resources are allocated to one department instead of the other. A firm cannot retain a hired input if it is paid a lower price for it than another firm. Opportunity cost includes the cost of inputs owned by the firm as well of those hired from outside. When a factor of production has no alternative use, its opportunity cost is zero. For example, if a firm receives an export order when its capacity is not fully utilised the opportunity cost of using the plant for export production will be nil. This is so because the unutilised capacity of the plant has no alternative use.

Explicit and Implicit Cost

Explicit costs are those costs which involve an actual payment made by a firm for use of an input owned or controlled by others. Explicit costs involve an actual payment to hire labour or purchase inputs required in production. They include the wages to hire labour, the interest on capital, rent on buildings and equipment and cost of raw material and semi finished goods. Implicit costs refer to the value of inputs owned and used by the firm in its production process. The amount, which a firm could earn by selling or hiring these inputs, is the implicit cost.

Sunk and Incremental Costs

Sunk costs are expenditures made in the past or that may be made in future as part of contractual agreement or previous decision. Examples of sunk costs are money already paid for machinery, equipment, inventory and future rental payments on a warehouse and contractual commitment to labour unions that must be paid as a long -term lease agreement. As sunk cost is one which is not affected by a change in the level or nature of business activity therefore, they are regarded as irrelevant for short run analysis. The most important example of sunk cost is the amortization of past expenses eg. depreciation. Sometimes they are also known as non-avoidable or non-escapable costs.

Incremental cost is the total additional cost due to change in level or nature of business activity. The change could be addition of a new product-line, change in distribution channels, adding a new machine, expansion into new markets etc. Thus the question of incremental costs arises when a change is contemplated in the existing business and not in the case of starting a new business. It helps in making short run decisions about profit maximising rates of output. Since incremental costs can be avoided by not bringing a change in the activity they are also called avoidable or escapable costs.

Historical Cost and Replacement Cost

The historical cost means the cost of plant at the price originally paid for it at the time of the purchase . Replacement cost means the price that would have to be paid currently for acquiring the same plant. Suppose, the price of a machine in 1990 was Rs 30,000 and the present cost is Rs 50,000. The original cost of Rs 30,000 is the historical cost and Rs 50,000 is the replacement cost. The balance sheets show assets at their historical costs. But due to variation in prices over time replacement costs are relevant for managerial decisions.

Fixed and Variable Costs

Total costs of a good or services could be divided into two components: fixed cost and variable costs. Fixed costs remain constant irrespective of a change in the volume of output, upto a certain level of plant capacity. They are incurred even when output is nil. On the other hand variable costs vary in direct proportion to changes in output. The distinction between fixed cost and variable costs is important in forecasting the effect of short run changes in volume of output, costs and profits.

Short Run and Long Run Costs

Short run costs are the costs incurred on the variable inputs in the short run when plant and capital equipments remain the same.They vary with the variation in output within a given plant capacity. Long run costs are the costs which vary with output when all input factors including plant and equipment vary. They are costs across all possible capacities. Knowledge of short run costs is useful for pricing and output decisions and long run costs provide information for planning the growth and investment policies of the firm.

Private and Social Costs

Private costs relate to costs incurred by the firm as a production unit. While social costs are the costs borne by the society though generated by productive activity of the firm. The cost incurred by expansion of output is private cost but pollution, traffic congestion, and accidental hazards are external to the firm, thus known as social costs. Development of dams, rose garden, amusement parks and the like are benefits to the society by the productive activity of the firm. Taxes and subsidies are private costs to be borne solely by the firm.

Shutdown and Abandonment Costs

Shutdown costs are those costs which would be incurred in the event of suspension of the plant operation and which could be saved if production continues. Eg of shurdown costs are sheltering of plant and equipment, layoff expenses etc. Additional expenses like re-employment of workers would be incurred when operations restart. Abandonment costs are the cost of retiring a fixed asset like plant from use. Permanent cessation of production raises the problem of disposal of assets.

Shutdown and abandonment costs become important when firm is faced with the decision of either continuing the existing plant or closing the plant altogether.

Separable and Common Costs

Costs that can be attributed to a product, a department, or a process are the separable costs and the rest are common costs. For example, in a multi product firm, raw material can be separated product wise. But the managerial cost is a common cost. The distinction between the two is also called as direct and indirect cost respectively.

Inventory Costs

Inventories are the stocks held by a firm. Costs incurred to hold inventories are known as inventory costs they comprise capital tied up in the inventory, the carrying costs and the ordering costs of inventories. Carrying costs are the costs of holding materials in the stores. They include the cost of storage space, bins, protection of assets, interest on blocked funds, insurance, and costs of spoilage/ obsolescence. Ordering costs comprise the costs of placing orders, inspection, checking and handling of goods, the cost of floating tenders, etc. The inventory costs are minimised when the carrying costs and ordering costs are balanced and the resulting order quantity is called the economic order quantity / economic lot size. Holding of inventories gives rise to capital costs. Capital cost primarily is the opportunity cost of capital used up in form of raw materials, intermediate goods and finished goods.

Information Costs

Globalisation of economic activity has led to intenationalisation of production and consumption. The manager must be aware of the latest developments in the industry in which he operates so as to make better decisions. He may have to make inventory capacity decisions, modify product line, customise products to local tastes, and so on. With the advent of information economy creation of value is increasingly based on knowledge and. communications rather than on natural resources and physical labour as in the past. For instance, computer-aided design (CAD) and computer-aided manufacturing (CAM) has increased producers' ability to produce several products for different markets. Spread of computer networks and IT speed up delivery of goods, decrease inventory, cuts wastes and generally increases productivity. Thus, in the present Age of Information, a manager has to incur costs

- to acquire an information source that can help in forecasting, or
- acquire information that influences forecasts.

The decision maker should acquire the additional source or information only if its expected value (in making better decisions) exceeds its costs.

Determinants of cost

Several factors may influence the cost of a firm. Table below briefly describes the major determinants of costs.

Determinant	Description
1. Prices of input factors	Input prices and the amount of inputs influence the total cost of a product
2. Technology	Better techniques and innovations decrease cost
3. Size of the plant	Initial fixed costs is high and variable cost are low in a big size plant
4. Law of returns	Cost increase with decreasing returns and decreases with increasing returns
5. Productivity of factors of production	Cost decreases with input efficiency/ productivity.
6. Capacity utilisation	Per unit cost of output is low with large level of capacity utilisation
7. Lot size	With manufacturing of bigger lot size the total cost and the per unit cost decreases
8. Production cycle	Production by breaks and disruptions is costly
9. Breadth of product range	Processing of different goods can share inputs, distribution and promotion can also be done jointly.

Cost- Output Relationship

To price intelligently. management should know how costs change with a change in production. Cost functions gives the relationship between the cost and the output rate They show the minimum costs of producing various levels of output on the assumption that the firm uses the optimal or least cost combination to produce each level of output

The study of cost-output relationship has two aspects I) cost-output relationship in short and ii) cost output relationship in long run. The short run is the period in which fixed equipments (machinery, building etc.) and the size of the organisation can not be changed. If any a firm has to increase its output in short run, it can do it within the range permitted by the existing fixed factors of production. The long run is a period in which there is sufficient time to alter the equipment (machinery, building, land etc.) and the size of the organisation. Thus in the long run output can be increased without the limitation of fixed factors of production as they can be changed.

Cost output relationship in short run

In economic theory , cost output relationship in short run can be studied in terms of (1) average fixed cost, (2) average variable cost and (3)average total cost as follows:

1.Average fixed cost and output: The relationship between output and fixed cost is applicable for all kinds of business. The greater the output, the lower is the fixed cost per unit, i.e. the average fixed cost because the total fixed costs do not change with a change in output. Average fixed cost falls continuously as output increases. The fixed total fixed cost remains same and the average fixed cost falls because certain factors are indivisible i.e .if a smaller quantity is to be produced then factor can not be used in smaller quantity it has to be used as a whole. Average fixed cost (AFC) is the ratio of total fixed cost to the output (Q) produced by the firm.

$$\mathbf{AFC = TFC / Q}$$

The AFC declines continuously with increase in output since the TFC is spread over as additional units of output produced in the short run. For this reason the AVC curve is a rectangular hyperbola.

Average total cost (ATC or AC) measures the total economic costs of production per unit produced in short run. It includes the opportunity cost of capital employed, that is, the normal risk -adjusted rate of return on capital. Therefore, a firm operating at its AC earns zero economic profit. Economic profits are a signal for entry and exit from the industry. The ATC represents a benchmark curve in the short run for predicting whether entry or exit will occur.

AC in the short run consists of average variable cost (AVC) and average fixed cost (AFC).

ATC or AC = AVC + AFC

We are aware that fixed costs of production do not vary with level of output and are fixed in the short run. Therefore, the AC (fixed cost per unit produced) decreases as the quantity produced increases (AVC decreases). Thus, the typical AC curve is U- shaped representing decreasing costs per unit initially as more units are produced but reaching a minimum and then rising as output rises per period.

2.Average Variable cost and output: The Average variable cost (AVC) is the variable cost per unit of output produced. It can be derived from the TVC as:

$$AVC = \frac{TVC}{Q}$$

Average variable cost will first fall and then rise as output increases. This is because of the fact that as we add more units of variable factors in a fixed plant, the efficiency of the inputs first increases and then decreases. In fact, the variable factors tend to produce somewhat more efficiency near a firm's optimum output than at very low levels of output. Once the optimum capacity is reached, any increase in output will increase average variable cost quite sharply. The A VC decreases initially and eventually rises because of diminishing returns to variable input. If the firms' production is nil, these costs will not be incurred. They are affected by the per unit cost of each variable input in production (for example, hourly wage rates of workers), the productivity of inputs and the production technology available to the firm. Suppose, labour is the only variable input in production then TVC per output level (Q) equals wage rate (w) multiplied by the number of labourers used. Thus,

$$AVC = \frac{TVC}{Q} = \frac{wL}{Q} = \frac{w}{Q/L} = \frac{w}{AP_L}$$

The AVC is important for short run decisions when the price received for producing output is so low that the firm may choose not to produce. A firm will shutdown when it cannot earn revenues sufficient to pay its AVC. The firm has no choice regarding fixed cost in short run since these must be paid whether or not the firm shuts down. Therefore, fixed costs have no effect on firms' short run decisions. For a perfectly competitive firm, shutdown point occurs where MC = AVC (i.e., where AVC is minimum). At any price below this point revenues earned from operations will fail to cover the cost of operations. The firm will generate losses if it operates and it should shutdown.

3. Average total cost and output: Average total costs will first decline and then rise upwards. Turning point in the case of average cost would come a little later than in the case of average variable cost. As can be seen , average fixed cost continues to fall with an increase in output while average variable cost first decline and then rises. As long as average variable cost declines the average total cost will also decline. But after a point, the average variable cost will rise. Here if the rise in variable cost is less than the drop in fixed cost, the average total cost will still continue to decline. It is only when the rise in average variable cost is more than the drop in average fixed cost that the average total cost will show a rise.

The least cost-output level is the level where the average total cost is the minimum and not the average variable cost. In fact, at the least cost-output level, the average variable cost will be more than its minimum. The least cost-output level is also called the optimum output level. It may not be the maximum output level. A firm may decide to produce more than its cost-output level.

Total Cost Functions

Total fixed costs (TFC) are the total costs per period of time incurred by the firm for the fixed inputs. They include:

Interest payment on borrowed capital,Contractual rent, Depreciation of machinery and building, and Salaries of administrative staff and/or salaries fixed by contract. These costs have to be incurred despite negligible output by the firm. In the example, the firm has to incur TFC of Rs 60 even though output is zero, in order to remain in business. At zero output, the TC of the firm is equal to fixed costs.

The costs incurred for variable inputs are the total variable costs (TVC). They include: Payment for raw materials, Fuel and power used, Depreciation by use of plant and equipment, Wages for direct labour and/ or temporary employees, and Excise taxes.Running expenses like routine maintenance and ordinary repairs are also included in variable expenses. The TVC increases with the increase in output of the firm, since a larger output requires more variable inputs.Total cost (TC) is the sum of TFC and TVC. The TC curve is parallel to the TVC due to fixed costs in the short run.

Marginal cost is the addition to the total cost resulting from the addition to the last unit of output. It can be derived from the change in TVC or TC, per unit change in output. Thus MC does not depend on TFC. It should be noted that MC is always plotted halfway between the various levels of output.

A firm's decision to produce a certain level of output is influenced by its marginal cost. The 'U' shape of MC can be attributed to the law of variable proportions.

This can be proved as follows:

$$MC = \frac{\Delta TC}{\Delta Q} = \frac{\Delta TVC}{\Delta Q} = \frac{\Delta(wL)}{\Delta Q} = \frac{w(DL)}{\Delta Q} = \frac{w}{\Delta Q/\Delta L} = \frac{w}{MP_L}$$

Short-run cost curve

In the short run, the level of capital is fixed, so that costs are not arrived at by calculating the cost minimising ratio of capital to labour as in the isocost/ isoquant analysis. Returns to scale are also irrelevant as scale can only be varied in the long run. The level of cost in the short run is determined by the total cost associated with the combinations of capital and labour given by the line k*B in the figure. The determining factors to cost here are the spreding of the fixed costs across a large number of units of output, on the one hand, and the principle of diminishing returns on the other. Fixed costs per unit fall as the level of output rises, but variable costs per unit tend to rise beyond a certain point. The total and average short run cost curves implied in this analysis are shown in the figure (a) and (b) below .

As the figure shows, fixed cost is constant, at an amount equal to K*r (the cost of using K* units of capital), yielding a downward sloping curve for average fixed cost (AFC). Variable cost increases with a slope that first decreases (indicating decreasing marginal cost) and then increases (indicating increasing marginal cost) giving an average variable cost (AVC) curve which falls and then rises. The combination of fixed and variable costs yields an average total cost curve (ATC) which is u-shaped and which is intersected by the marginal cost curve (MC) at its lowest point.

The short run curves are derived from the short run production curves given the factor prices They depict variations in cost over output for plant of a given capacity The short run costs may exceed the long run costs for this reason

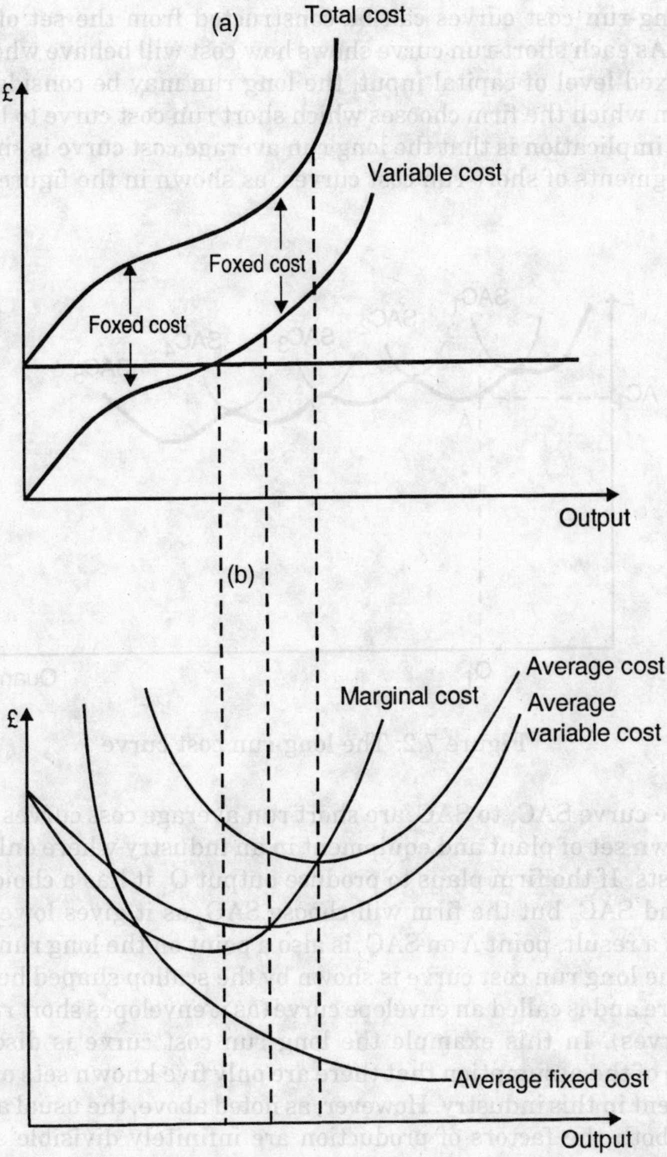

Figure 7.1: Costs in short run

Long Run Cost Functions

In the long run firm is free to choose whichever combination of inputs it expects to be most profitable, and in long run firm is mainly concerned with investment decisions. The behaviour of costs in this period depends fundamentally upon the extent to which there are economies of scale attained from the construction of larger sets of plant and equipment.

Long-run cost curves can be constructed from the set of short-run curves. As each short-run curve shows how cost will behave when the firm has a fixed level of capital input, the long run may be considered as the period in which the firm chooses which short run cost curve to locate itself on. The implication is that the long run average cost curve is simply made up of segments of short-run cost curves, as shown in the figure.

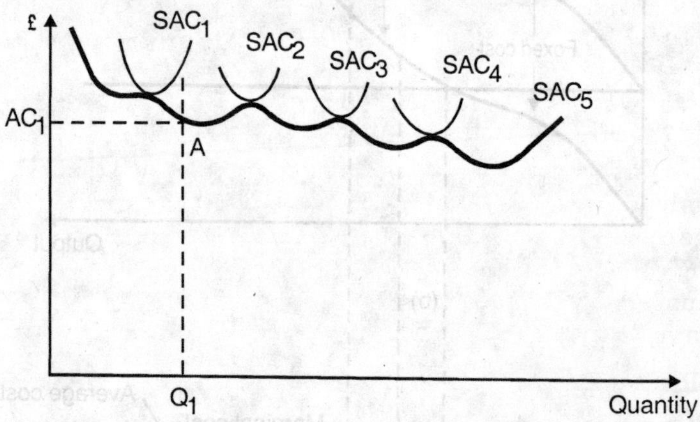

Figure 7.2: The long-run cost curve

The curve SAC_1 to SAC_5 are short run average cost curves for each of the known set of plant and equipment in an industry where only five such sets exists. If the firm plans to produce output Q_1 it has a choice between SAC_1 and SAC_2 but the firm will choose SAC_2 as it gives lower costs per unit. As a result, point A on SAC_2 is also a point on the long run cost curve LAC. The long run cost curve is shown by the scallop shaped heavy line in the figure and is called an envelope curve (as it envelopes short run average cost curves). In this example the long run cost curve is discontinuous because of the assumption that there are only five known sets of plant and equipment in this industry. However, as noted above, the usual assumption is that both the factors of production are infinitely divisible so that the amount of capital used could be augmented by very small amounts, giving an almost infinite number of different sets of plant and equipment. In that case there will be an infinite number of short-run cost curves and the long-run cost curve will become smooth and continuous almost U- shaped.

Most of the firms will have a number of plant sizes to choose from, and there is a short run average cost curve (SRAC) corresponding to each. Some of the short run average cost curves for these plants are shown in figure below

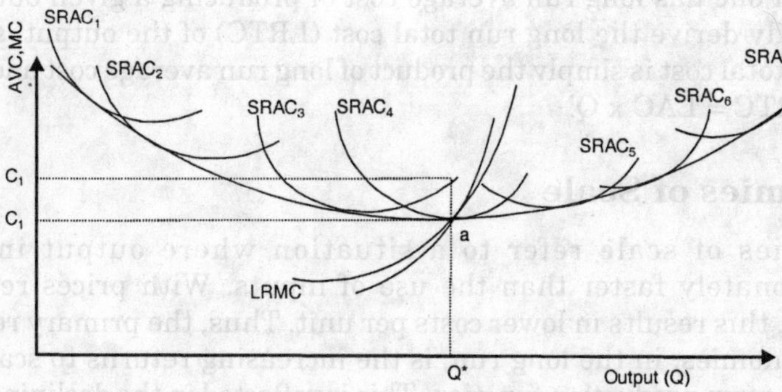

Fig 7.3: Short-run and long-run average cost and marginal cost curves

Only one point of each short run cost curve will lie on the long run average cost curve (LAC). Corresponding to the long run average cost curve is a long run marginal cost curve (LRMC), which is intersecting LAC at its minimum point a, which is also the minimum point of the short run average cost curve $SRAC_4$. At point a :

SRAC = SRMC when LAC = LRMC

here SRMC = short run marginal cost.

The long run cost curve shows the least per unit cost at any output produced after the firm has made adjustments in its plant size. Thus it also serves as a long run planning mechanism for the firm. For example, suppose the firm is operating on short run average cost curve $SRAC_3$ as shown in figure above and the firm is producing an output Q*. By using $SRAC_3$ we can find that C_2 is the firm's average cost. Clearly if projectios of future demand indicate that the firm could expect to continue selling Q* units per period at the market price, profit could be increased significantly by increasing the scale of the plant to the size associated with short run average cost curve $SRAC_4$. With this plant size , average cost for an output rate of Q* would be C_2 and the firm's profit per unit would increase by $C_2 - C_1$. Thus, total profit would increase by $(C_2 - C_1) \times Q^*$.

The U-shaped of the LAC curve reflects the laws of returns to scale. According to these laws, the cost per unit of production decreases as plant size increases due to the economies of scale, which the larger plant sizes make possible. But the economies of scale exist only up to a certain size of plant, known as the optimum plant size where all possible economies of scale are fully exploited. Beyond the optimum plant size, diseconomies of scale arise due to managerial inefficiencies. As plant size increases beyond a limit, the control, the feedback of information at different levels and decision making process becomes less efficient. This makes the LAC curve turn upwards. There are increasing returns to scale up to Q* and decreasing returns to scale beyond Q*. Therefore, the point Q* is the point of optimum output. If one has long run average cost of producing a given output, one can readily derive the long run total cost (LRTC) of the output, since the long run total cost is simply the product of long run average cost and output. Thus, LRTC = LAC x Q.

Economies of Scale

Economies of scale refer to a situation where output increases proportionately faster than the use of inputs. With prices remaining constant, this results in lower costs per unit. Thus, the primary reason for scale economies, in the long run, is the increasing returns to scale in the firm's long run production function. This is reflected in the declining portion of the LAC. While under decreasing returns to scale, output increases at a proportionately slower rate than the increase in inputs. With input prices constant, this leads to higher costs per unit. The rising portion of LAC depicts this change. The lowest point on the LAC curve occurs at the output level at which the forces for increasing returns to scale are just balanced by the forces of decreasing to scale.

Economies of scale arise because of technological and financial reasons, also referred as economies at plant level and firm level respectively .Scale economies at the plant level arise because of increase in the scale of operations. Greater division and specialisation of labour can take place with more specialised and productive machinery. Each worker is assigned task in accordance to his skill and qualification. This division of labour leads to specialisation in a task due to repetitive work, which increases his proficiency. As Prof. Marshall has stated 'learning by doing' saves time lost in moving from one activity to another

It has been observed that per unit costs decline with large plant size. Certain plants and equipments are indivisible in smaller units/ sizes, like tractors and computers. Small firms cannot employ such sophisticated machines and are, therefore unable to earn benefits of updated technology. Thus, by increasing scale, the firm may be able to use new production methods that are not feasible in smaller outputs. It is also regarded that a machine that costs twice as much as smaller one will typically produce more output i.e., its productivity/.price is more. Large firms need fewer supervisors and spare parts and smaller inventories per unit of output as the scale of operation increases.

At the firm level the economies of scale arise due to financial reasons. Due to bulk purchases large firms receive quantity discounts for raw materials and components that result in lower average cost. The cost of capital per unit of output is often found to vary inversely with the size of firm. Large firms are able to raise funds in the capital markets at lower costs than smaller firms. Large firms usually sell bonds and stocks more favourably and receive bank loans at lower interest rates than smaller firms.

Large firms are able to secure quantity discounts even in securing space and time in various advertising media. They can afford to initiate promotional schemes to increase sales. Besides, the promotional cost is spread out, which decreases the burden per unit of output on larger firms, than smaller ones. For instance, a 30 - second television advertisement represents the same fixed cost to a large fast food chain and a small chain alike. But this expense comprises a much lower cost "per" dish for the large chain. The same can be said about innovations. Large firms are in a better position to carry out R and D and thereby adopt latest methods of production and sales, and material procurement, than their small counterparts. Large firms enjoy benefits of top calibre management personnel.

Diseconomies of scale

Virtually every industry is subject to some degree of economies of scale. It is almost impossible to think of any activity which can be carried out as cheaply at the minimum conceivable scale as at a larger one. It is also indisputable that in some industries, including automobile companies and chemical companies, the cost reduction due to large scales of output are substantial indeed. What is much more difficult to determine is whether or not firms face diseconomies of scale once their level of output expands beyond a certain size.

If only technological factors are considered then there is little reason to suppose that diseconomies of scale exists. There may come a level of output beyond which no further economies can be had, in which case the long-run cost curve will become flat, but none of the forces which lead to economies of scale are likely to work in reverse at very high level of output. If diseconomies of scale do exist they are due to *managerial* factors rather than technological factors. As firm produces a higher level of output it also becomes a larger organisation. As the size of the firm increases, firms' planning and coordinating activities become difficult. Additional bureaucratic layers separate managers from the market and their customers. If the consumers' preferences change rapidly or if rivals introduce a new product, larger firms may be disadvantaged by their lack of flexibility and\slow adjustment to market. An interesting example has been the reorganisation of IBM. In early years of computer industry, there were no independent suppliers of computer chips and peripherals. Computer manufacturers had to be vertically produce those inputs. But as the industry grew, so did independent suppliers who could specialise in product components efficiently. As this occurred, change in technology, and factor costs decreased the minimum efficient scale for computer manufacturing. Even though IBM's separate divisions were as efficient as their competitors, the internal pricing and cost information did not reflect the efficiency. The organisation had to be restructured so that divisions could operate as separate companies to be closer to the market.

Per unit transportation costs rise as a firm increases the production capacity. These involve delivery of goods, handling expenses, insurance and security expenses, and inventory costs. Thus, managerial inefficiencies and transportation costs more than offset the fall in per unit costs due to economies of scale.

Till now we discussed factors that give rise to internal economies and diseconomies of scale, which are a result of expansion of the firm. External economies may arise due to the expansion of the industry as a whole. Provision of training facilities and skill formation, improved transportation and communication facilities, and lateral and vertical integration may result in a reduction in per unit costs of industry as a whole. Excessive expansion may give rise to external diseconomies, like environmental pollution.

LAC Curves and Empirical Studies

Many studies have been conducted to investigate the shape of long run average cost curve. One general finding is that for most goods and services, there are significant economies of scale at low levels of output, followed by a wide region of constant returns at higher levels. In short, for many industries, the long run average cost curve tends to be L-shaped as shown by figure (a). This case is usually found under natural monopoly and includes many local utilities, local telephone service, and cable television. It is observed that in these industries, economies of scale outstrip diseconomies of scale as a firm expands leading to no net economies or diseconomies rather efficient scale. Minimum efficient scale (MES) is defined as the lowest level of output at which long run average cost is minimum.

Minimum efficient scale is helpful in determining the number of firms a particular market can support. For instance, in the production of sulphuric acid (a standard chemical), the MES for the plant is about 4 per cent of total US consumption. The average cost disadvantage of producing one-half of MES is only one per cent. The implication is clear that there is ample room in the market for as many as 25 (1/ .04) firms.

In some other cases it has been observed that there is no MES because LAC declines continuously as shown in fig above . The LAC falls monotonically as output expands because economies of scale outweigh the diseconomies of scale at all levels of output. However , the rate of fall in LAC declines as output expands. Therefore, the LAC is convex from below.

Economies of scope

Economies of scope may be defined as the reduction of a firm's per unit cost by producing two or more goods jointly rather than separately. The reduction in per unit cost is due to the joint use of input or production facilities, joint marketing programs, or possibly the cost savings of a common administration. For example chicken and egg, mutton and wool are joint products. The formula for scope economies(SC) is:

$$SC = \frac{C(Q_1) + C(Q_2) - C(Q_1,Q_2)}{C(Q_1 + Q_2)}$$

Where $C(Q_1)$,$C(Q_2)$ represents cost of producing output Q1 and Q2 respectively and C(Q1,Q2) the joint cost of producing both outputs (Q_1 + Q_2).

For example a firm produces 15000 Tv sets and 5000 DVD players per year at the cost of 10 crores, and another firm produces 15000 TV sets only at cost of 11.5 crores and if it produces 5000 DVDs only then the cost would be 0.75 crores. Thus we can see the cost of producing both TV and DVD is less than the cost of producing each separately. Therefore there are economies of scope

$$SC = \frac{11.50 + 0.75 - 10.00}{10} = 0.22$$

which implies there is 22 percent saving of cost if joint production is done.

Product diversification within the given scale of plant results in economies of scope which decreases cost of production. Firms often find that per unit costs are lower when two or more products are produced. Excess capacity of the firm can be used to produce additional products with little or no increase in total costs. An airline that carries passengers also contracts to carry cargo so that it could utilise unused cargo space in the flight.

Learning by experience and transfer of know how is another important source of economies of scope. Soft drink companies produce many types of carbonated drinks, fruit juices, sparkling waters, and the like. Presumably, experience of producing beverages gives cost advantages in producing related drinks also same distribution channels can be used jointly for other drinks also.

Scope economies can be demand related. Firms can also take benefit of their unique skills or comparative advantage in marketing to develop products that are complementary with the firm's existing products. For example, Proctor and Gamble sells numerous cleaning products. Some of these products are complementary (like detergent bleach and fabric softeners), whereas other products are specialised substitutes.

An important source of economies of scope is the latest sophisticated hi tech machines and computer-aided manufacturing systems which can quickly switch from one product to another, allowing the production of many products and designs, all using similar inputs.

Other 'cost-drivers'

The analyses presented above have suggested that costs are determined by three factors, First, in the short run, there is the level of capacity utilisation. Secondly, in the long run, there are economies of scale. Thirdly, there is the degree of X-efficiency, which determines whether firms are on their cost curves or above them.

These three cost drivers are the ones which are given the most extensive treatment in economic analysis. However, as Porter (1985) points out, there area number of other cost drivers which will also have an influence on the level of costs. Each of these merits a brief examination.

Learning effects may mean that in many activities costs decline as the activity is repeated an increasing number of times. As workers and management become more familiar with a production process or a particular product there will be cost reductions to be had from improvements in plant layout, design modifications, improved scheduling and tailoring of raw materials purchased to the process and product. The end result of such learning effects may be that costs reduce with the total volume of production to date, as well as with the scale and rate of output.

Costs may also be determined by **linkages** and **interrelationships** between different activities carried out within the firm, or between the firm and its customers or suppliers. One such example is what economists have called economies of scope, which occur when the firm can produce a number of products together more cheaply than it could produce them independently. Such economies will tend to occur when the processing of different goods can share inputs, or where distribution and promotion can take place jointly. In this case, the breadth of the product range as well as the other factors discussed above will determine costs.

Linkages and interrelationships are not restricted to those which lead to economies of scope. There may be cost reductions to be had by co-ordinating other activities taking place within the firm, like advertising and direct sales, or production and maintenance. There may be gains to be had by increasing **the degree of vertical integration** within the firm, moving closer to the final customer (forward vertical integration) or to sources of supply (backwards vertical integration). Alternatively some of these gains could be had by co-operation with suppliers and distribution channels, rather than by undertaking these activities within the firm. Porter cites the example, for instance, of a confectioner arranging with his supplier to have chocolate delivered in bulk as liquid, rather than in solid blocks, thereby reducing costs for both the confectioner and the supplier.

Costs will also be affected by **timing** within the business cycle or timing with respect to other firms' actions. The purchase of major items of capital equipment may be heavily influenced by the level of demand and capacity utilisation in the supplying industries, where highly advantageous deals may be had if suppliers are suffering from a lack of orders and over-capacity. There may be **first-mover advantages** to be had by being the first to undertake an activity, especially if there are substantial learning effects, which a first-mover will begin to gain from before late-comers. On the other hand, in some situations there may be **late-mover advantages**, as in situations where the technology is developing very rapidly and first-movers may have invested heavily in technology which has become out-dated.

Costs may also be affected by **geographical location** when factor prices, tax regimes and government incentives vary from place to place, and by **institutional factors** like unionisation, tariffs and local content rules.

Finally, it should be noted that costs will also depend upon a very wide range of the firm's **discretionary policies**, like the nature and design of the product being produced, the level of service provided to customers, delivery dates achieved, the form of distribution, the nature of the technology and raw materials produced and the full package of human resources policies adopted on pay, training, incentive schemes and employee benefits.

A business which hopes to be successful will need to think very carefully about which cost drivers are the most important in its own particular case in order to concentrate its efforts on keeping cost as low as possible, commensurate with implementing its overall company strategy.

Cost Function

Cost function depicts the relationship between cost and determinants. It can be expressed in form of an equation as:

$$\mathbf{C = f(Q, F, P)}$$

The total cost (C) is a function of total output (Q), factor productivity (F), and prices of inputs (P). There is a direct relation between total cost and output. The total cost increases with an increase in output as inputs have to be made payments. Output plays a significant role in cost as it is variable and under the control of the firm.

Apart from this, the amount of change in total cost varies from one firm to another, though all firms may experience an increase (decrease) in cost from an increase (increase) in output but the change in total cost may differ.

Factor productivity and cost have an inverse relation An improvement in factor productivity, other things remaining constant, decreases the amount of inputs and, therefore, results in a fall in costs Factor productivity or efficiency depends on level of technology Modem and efficient technology, better managerial skills, good working condition and a congenial industrial environment (absence of strikes and lockouts) improve factor productivity . Increase in prices of factor inputs, other factors remaining constant increases cost of production

Forms of Cost Fnctions

There are three functional forms of cost functions that are popular. The choice of a function depends on statistical data available.

Linear Cost Function

Suppose a firm is producing goods with fixed costs' a' which must be met irrespective of the quantity of output produced. In order to produce Q units of the good, it must buy a proportional amount of raw material, labour and other necessary inputs, the cost of which is the variable amount bQ. Then the total cost of production for the firm is the linear equation

$$TC = a + bQ$$

Figure below shows a linear cost function .The average or unit cost function can be obtained by dividing the total cost function by output That is,

$$ATC = TC / Q = (a / Q) + b$$

The shape of average or unit cost function is shown in fig.(b). At zero output level the total cost comprises total fixed cost that includes depreciation, insurance, and property taxes. In case of a linear function, average variable cost equals b (=ATC -a/Q), and marginal cost also equals b.

Quadratic Cost Function

Quadratic cost function has been widely used in empirical studies. It is written as:

$$\mathbf{TC = a + bQ + cQ^2}$$

The implications of this equation are:

i) When Q=0, TC = a. In other words, total cost equals fixed cost when output is zero.

ii) The equation is quadratic therefore it has only one bend as against linear total cost function which has no bends. The number of bends is always one less than the highest exponent of X.

iii) Also average total cost, average fixed cost, average variable cost and marginal cost can be derived as

$$ATC = \frac{a}{Q} + b + cQ$$

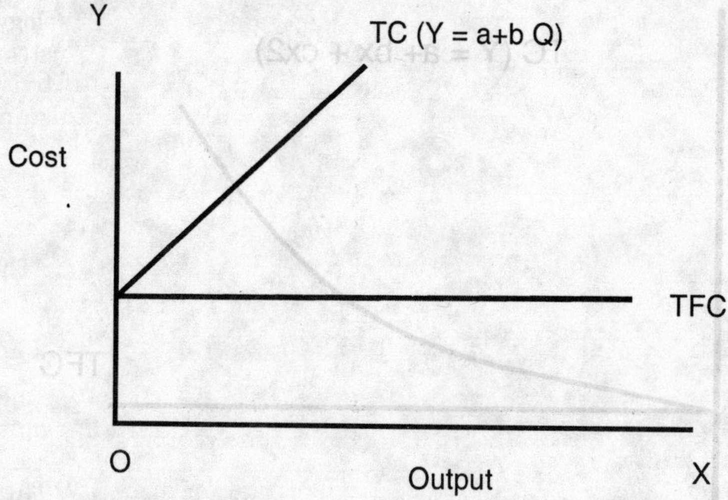

Fig 7.4 Linear cost function

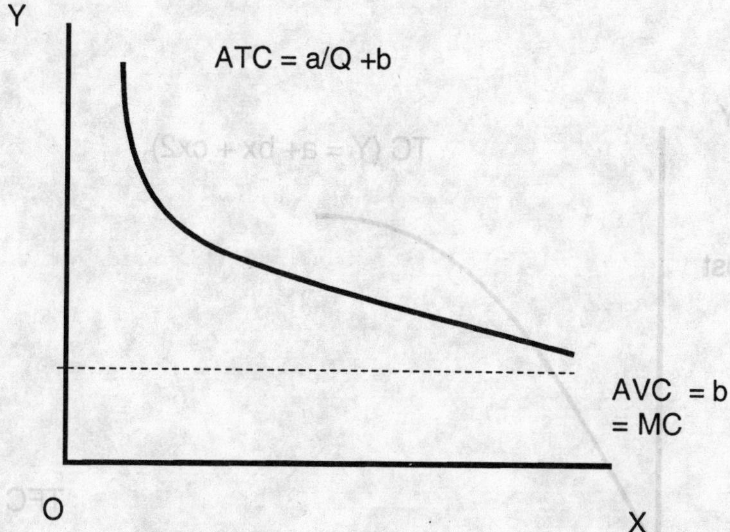

Figure 7.5

where AFC = a/Q,

AVC = b + cQ and

MC = dTC/dQ = b + 2cQ.

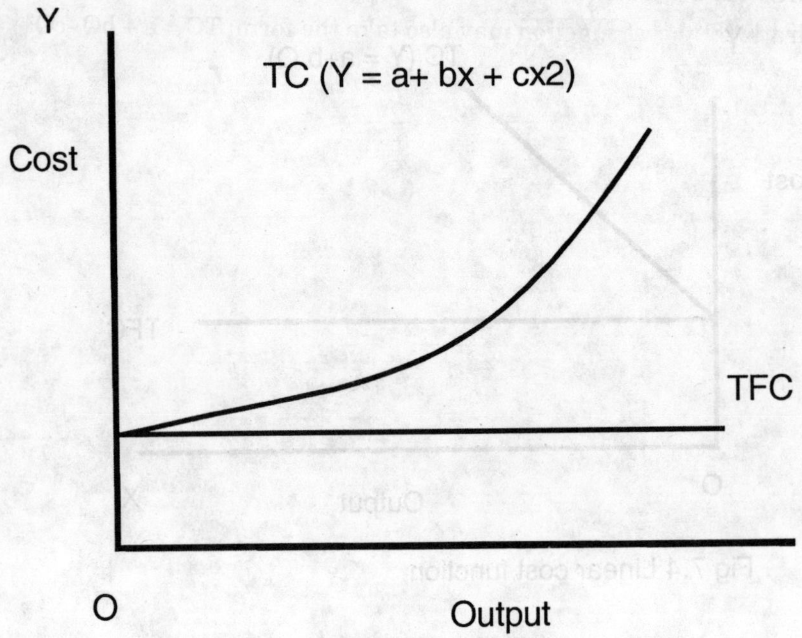

Fig. 7.6 Quadratic cost function

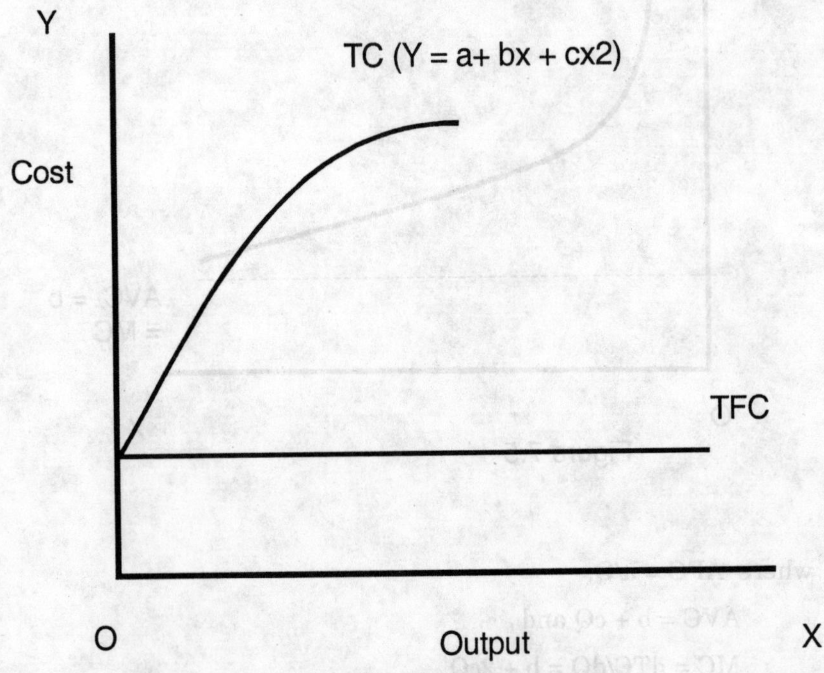

Fig. 7.6 Quadratic cost function

iv) MC= AVC = b when X=0.

The quadratic total cost function may also take the form: $TC = a + bQ - cQ^2$

Quadratic total cost functions have shape similar to TC curves as depicted in diagram below. The curve represents increasing returns or decreasing costs, as the total cost curve rises at a decreasing rate. The quadratic total cost function may also take the form: $TC = a + bQ + -cQ^2$.

Cubic Total Cost Function

A cubic cost function is written as

$$TC = a + bQ - cQ^2 + dQ^3$$

The total cost function of a cubic form shall have two bends as it combines both increasing and decreasing returns of productivity, as shown in figure.

Increasing returns occur at all levels to the left of the vertical dashed line showed if fig. as the total cost rises at a decreasing rate. On the right

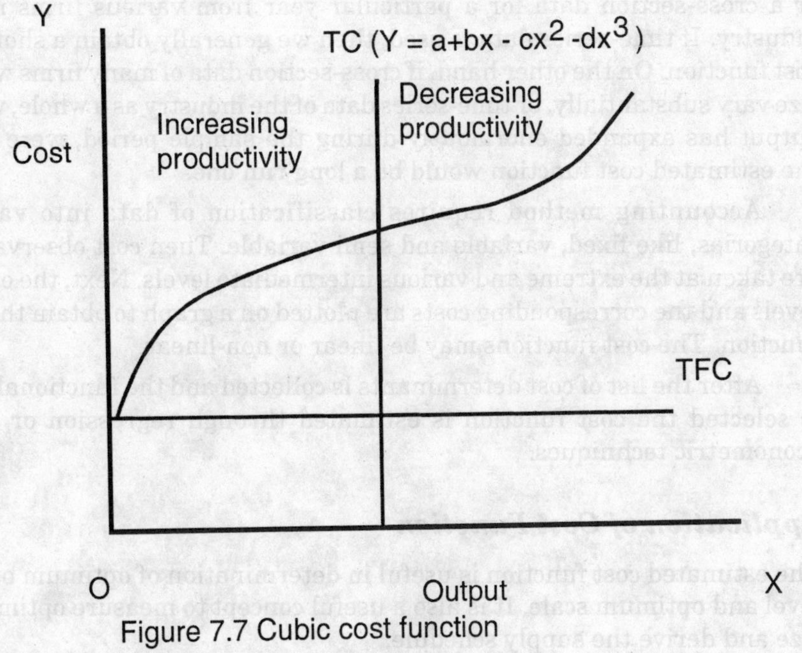

Figure 7.7 Cubic cost function

hand side of dashed line, total cost is rising at an increasing rate denoting diminishing returns. Cubic cost function is not much used as its not much improvement over the less complicated quadratic function.

Estimation of Cost Function

There are three main approaches to measure the actual cost output relation for a particular firm or a group of firms, namely

a) Engineering method
b) Statistical method
c) Accounting method

Physical relationships of a particular product expressed in the production function are taken into account to estimate a production function under engineering method. Optimum input combination for producing any given quantity of output is estimated from the production "function and input prices. The cost curve is then formulated by multiplying each input in the obtained least cost combination by its price and then ldding to develop the cost function. This method is useful when historical data is not available. But the method requires knowledge of production technology and factor prices.

Under statistical method, statistical techniques are applied on historical data on cost and its determinants. The data could be a time-series data for a particular firm in the industry or of all firms in the industry or a cross-section data for a particular year from various firms in the industry. If time-series data is used, then we generally obtain a short run cost function. On the other hand, if cross-section data of many firms whose, size vary substantially, or time-series data of the industry as a whole, whose output has expanded enormously during the sample period, were used, the estimated cost function would be a long run one.

Accounting method requires classification of data into various categories, like fixed, variable and semi variable. Then cost observations are taken at the extreme and various intermediate levels. Next, the output levels and the corresponding costs are plotted on a graph to obtain the cost function. The cost functions may be linear or non-linear.

After the list of cost determinants is collected and the functional form is selected the cost function is estimated through regression or other econometric techniques.

Application of Cost Function

The estimated cost function is useful in determination of optimum output level and optimum scale. It is also a useful concept to measure optimal lot size and derive the supply schedule.

Determining Optimum output: The average cost is minimum at the optimum output level or where the average cost is equal to marginal cost (AC = MC). For example optimum output level is to be estimated for the following cost function.

$$TC = 128 + 6Q + 2Q^2$$

$$\text{Then } AC = \frac{TC}{Q} = \frac{128}{Q} + 6 + 2Q \quad \text{and } MC = \frac{dC}{dQ} = 6 + 4Q$$

$$\text{Therefore } \frac{d(AC)}{DQ} = \frac{(-128 + 2)}{Q^2} = 0 \quad \text{Hence } Q = 8$$

Therefore Q = 8 which is the optimum output level for the short run. Note that it is a short run case as TFC = 128.

Optimum scale: The optimum scale is given by the value of plant size (K) at which the total cost is least. The two conditions for optimum scale are:

Necessary condition $\partial C / K = O$

Sufficient condition: $\partial^2 C / \partial K^2 > 0$

Break-even analysis

The most common use of linear cost function is in break even analysis, it shows how to identify the level of output and sales volume at which the firm 'breaks even' with revenues being sufficient enough to cover all the costs. There are three ways to calculate break-even point namely

1. The graphical method
2. The equation method
3. The contribution margin method

In graphical method, the horizontal axis depicts the level of output and the vertical axis shows revenues and costs. Total revenues are shown by a straight line, showing the revenues which will be earned at different levels

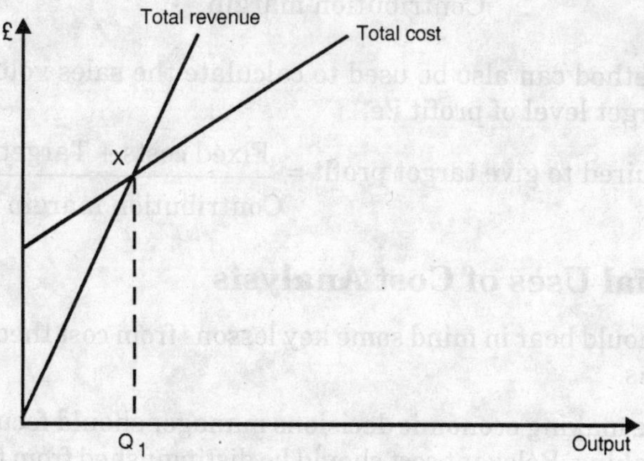

Figure:break-even analysis

of output if the same price is charged. Total costs are also shown by a straight line. For each level of output profits or losses are indicated by the vertical distance between the total revenue function and total cost function, which is zero at the break-even point X at Q_1 level of output.

Break-even analysis of this kind can be used to calculate the level of sales which must be achieved in order to avoid losses, or to calculate the margin of safety which exists between the break-even point and the firm's actual or expected level of sales. Margin of safety is defined as:

Margin of safety = Actual sales revenue – Break-even sales revenue.

And Margin of safety ratio = margin of safety / actual sales

Same results may be arrived at with the help of equation method , which begins by noting:

Profit = Sales revenue – variable costs – Fixed costs

where

Sales revenue = Price x Volume

Variable cost = variable cost per unit x volume

Fixed cost = a constant

And break-even volume is where profit = 0

Thus,

$$\text{Break-even volume} = \frac{\text{Fixed cost}}{\text{Price} - \text{Variable cost per unit}}$$

The expression on the bottom of right hand side of the above equation represents 'contribution per unit of output' or 'contribution margin'. The contribution margin approach to break even analysis simply consist of rewriting the above equation of break even volume in the following form

$$\text{Break -even volume} = \frac{\text{Fixed cost}}{\text{Contribution margin}}$$

This method can also be used to calculate the sales volume required to have a target level of profit i.e.

$$\text{Volume required to give target profit} = \frac{\text{Fixed costs + Target profit}}{\text{Contribution margin}}$$

Managerial Uses of Cost Analysis

Managers should bear in mind some key lessons from cost theory in making cost decisions.

1. While making economic decisions manager should focus on relevant cost while making. Relevant cost should be distinguished from the irrelevant cost.

2. One should recognise the possibility of diminishing returns in short run production process, and be aware that this will cause the marginal cost to increase as output increases. It is often assumed that the production of additional units of output of a product will cost the same extra amount. However, the additional profit from the sale of additional units may begin to decline, if marginal cost begins to rise even though the firm is able to sell more at the same price.

3.The economies of scale and the economies of scope may enable a firm to reduce its unit cost of production as it increases its entire scale of operation. It should be considered whether the w1it costs of production decrease as a firm increases the size of a particular site (like sales branch office, manufacturing facilities, and warehouses) or its scale of operation for the entire firm.

4. Increase in the entire scale of operation does not automatically lead to reduction in per unit cost. This may be due to firstly insufficient demand for the product to enable the firm to take advantage of larger scale of operation. At lower levels of demand, it is beneficial to operate at a lower level of capacity at less than maximum efficiency. Secondly, increase in scale of operation may lead to an increase in unit costs. This is so because of diseconomies of scale resulting mainly from managerial diseconomies (eg large bureaucracy and disproportionate increase in staff positions).

Questions

1. Distinguish between absolute or outlay costs and alternative or Opportunity costs.
2. What is the difference between direct and indirect costs?
3. Explain the nature of the distinction between Incremental costs and sunk costs.
4. State briefly the basic differences between sunk, shutdown and abandonment costs. Give examples.
5. Distinguish between:

   (a) Urgent and postponable costs,

   (b) Escapable and inescapable costs,

   (c) Past and future costs,

   (d) Out-of-pocket and book costs,

   (e) Controllable and non-controllable costs, and

   (f) Fixed and variable costs.
6. "All direct costs are variable and all indirect costs are fixed." Do you agree?

7. Point out whether marginal costs are most closely related to fixed costs or variable costs or total costs. State reasons for your answer.
8. Explain the concept of opportunity cost. Calculate total cost and marginal cost from the following data:

Units of output	Fixed costs (Rs)	Variable cost (Rs)
0	350	0
1	350	150
2	350	200
3	350	350

9. *(a)* Is Incremental cost the same as marginal cost? Explain.
   (b) From the following data. find out Total Variable Cost, Average Total Cost, Average Variable Cost and Marginal Cost:

Units of output	Total cost
0	150
50	240
100	285
150	360

10. A firm has the demand function, 22- 0.5Q – P = 0 and the average cost function AC = 1/3 Q^2 – 8.5 Q + 50 + 90/Q. Find the level of output, which maximises (a) total revenue and (b) total profit.
11. Discuss the various concepts of costs which are relevant from the stand point of production, planning and control.
12. "As fixed costs are unaffected by a change in the volume of operations they are always irrelevant to any managerial decision short of the decision to discontinue operations altogether." Discuss.
13. Discuss briefly different cost concepts relevant to managerial decisions of planning and control.
14. Explain briefly the managerial uses of estimated cost function.
15. A company manufactures agricultural equipments and distributes them in several adjoining States. The company is faced with shrinking demand and has limited cash funds to use. The management is faced with the question whether or not to expand distribution into three more States for this purpose and how much the expansion would cost. Show which costs are to be taken into account in the above problem and how will these help the management in its decisions.
16. Discuss the various cost concepts relevant for decision-making at the firm level. Do you feel that 'break-even analysis' could be a useful tool to Indian managers?

17. Explain. "A competitive producer must look to average variable cost in determining whether or not to produce in the short run, to marginal cost in deciding upon the best volume of production and to average total cost to calculate his profits or losses." Explain why a firm might produce at a loss in the short run rather than close down.
18. Distinguish between fixed and variable costs. Why can this distinction be made in the short run? Classify the following as fixed or variable costs: advertising expenditure, interest on company issued debentures, payments for raw materials, depreciation charges and executive salaries.
19. Explain clearly the relation of cost to output.
20. Explain why both long-run and short run average cost curves first fall, then rise.
21. Explain the cost-output relationship in the short run. How does the economic view differ from the accounting view? What empirical evidence is available in this regard? .
22. Examine the relationship between; *(a)* Average fixed cost and output, *(b)* Average variable cost and output, and (c) Average total cost and output in the short run. How are the short-run cost curves derived?
23. Why is it useful for a business to classify its expenses as variable and non-variable? What are the main difficulties in making this classification?
24. State the salient features of LAC curve and discuss its usefulness in managerial decision-making. Why is it known as planning. curve?
25. Explain how the long-run envelope cost curve is defined as the lower frontier of all short-run cost curves. Illustrate with *(a)* the cases of a few plant sizes, and *(b)the* case of infinitely continuous plant sizes.
26. "The long run average cost curve, though U-shaped, will be flatter and less pronounced than the short.run average cost curve," Explain it with the help of a diagram.
27. 'Knowledge of short-run cost is for pricing and output decisions while the long-run costs provide useful information for planning the growth and investment policies of the firm." Explain.
28. What is the break-even point? Given fixed expenses at Rs. 7860, selling price as Rs. 5 and variable cost as Rs. 3, calculate break-even point in terms of physical units of a car spare part.
29. Explain the term "Break-even Analysis" and discuss its usefulness. Calculate the break-even point from the following data:

    Sales: 550 units.

Sales Receipt:	Rs. 28,875
Total Fixed Costs:	Rs. 18,000
Total Variable Costs:	Rs. 11,000.

30. Explain the nature of break-even analysis. Given the following total *cost* and total revenue functions. find:
    (i) Break-even point.
    (ii) Profit at output 50.

    Total cost = 110 + 5x

    Total revenue = 10x

    where x is the quantity sold or purchased.
31. "The objective of the break -even chart is to indicate what happens to total costs and total revenues as output and sales change from one level to another." Explain this statement by drawing a break-even chart and discuss its significance.
32. What do you understand by contribution analysis? How does it help in managerial decision-making? Discuss the managerial uses of break-even analysis as a tool for profit planning.What are its limitations"?
33. How Can management use the information relating to the break-even point? What are the principal limitations of the break-even calculation?
34. What is break-even point. What are its uses? If the variable costs of A Ltd. are75 per cent of its Sales and the fixed costs are Rs. 5.000, find out the BEP for the company.
35. (i) Explain the concept of the break-even point With the help of a profit-volume graph or otherwise.
    (ii) From the following particulars compute the break-even point in terms of (i) physical units. (iz) rupee sales value, and (iii) percentage of operating capacity:

Variable cost per unit	Rs 16
Annual fixed expenses	Rs 48,000
Selling Price per unit	Rs 20
Annual capacity	15,000 units

    What should be the selling price per unit if the break-even paint Is brought down to 10,000 units?
36. "Economies of scale maybe either external or internal: they may be technical, managerial, financial or risk-bearing." Elucidate.
37. The long-run average cost curve is L-shaped. Does this mean that the economies of scale do not exist?
38. Explain the role played by economies of scale in determining the minimum efficient size of firm. Are there any advantages to be gained from going beyond this size?
39. Discuss the various economies of scale, Do they result in monopolies?
40. What are the advantages and limitations of large-scale production?

8

Production Analysis

Introduction

A manager is faced with a choice problem of 'how to produce?' He has to make a decision about the combination of fixed and variable quantities that should be employed to produce a good most efficiently. That is, he has to decide about the input combination. This requires, firstly the engineering or technological information on production possibilities (the production function) and, secondly economic data on prices of inputs and output (cost analysis). In this chapter we will discuss the operating efficiency, i.e., the relation between physical input and output.

Production and Production Function

Production in economics refers to the process by which man utilises or converts the resources provided by nature into goods to satisfy human wants. In other words, **production** is an economic activity that transforms inputs or resources into output of goods and services, thus creating or adding utility. Utility is the want satisfying power of a good or service. Production process involves the transformation of inputs (land, labour, capital, raw material, entrepreneurship etc) into outputs (goods or services). In a production process manager has to take four types of decisions:

1. Whether to produce or not?
2. How much output to produce?
3. What input combinations to use?
4. What type of technology to use?

Production function is simply a mathematical statement of the relationship between inputs and outputs. It shows the maximum output which can be obtained from a given combination of inputs. It expresses the technological relationship between inputs and outputs of a product. In its simplest and most general form the production function (when there are only two inputs capital and labour) is usually written as follows:

$Q = f(K, L)$

where Q = level of output
K = quantity of capital input
L = quantity of labour input

This function defines the maximum rate of output (Q) obtainable for a given rate of capital and labour input. In general form it could be written as

Q = f (x1, x2,……..xn)

where x1,x2,....xn are the quantities of various inputs

There are various more specific functional forms which could be taken by the production function, but one of the most useful and best known is the Cobb- Douglas production function, which is written as:

$Q = AK^aL^b$

where A = a constant

a,b = positive fractions

the production function is assumed to have a number of properties. Firstly, both K and L are assumed to be infinitely divisible and independently variable and the function is continuous, so that output increases smoothly as either the capital, labour or both are increased. If the level of one input, capital for instance, is kept constant and the level of the other input i.e. labour is changed, the rate at which output changes is called the marginal product of labour. In accordance with the principle of diminishing returns it is assumed that as more and more of one factor of production is combined with fixed quantities of another then a point is reached where marginal product begins to decline as shown in figure 8.1.

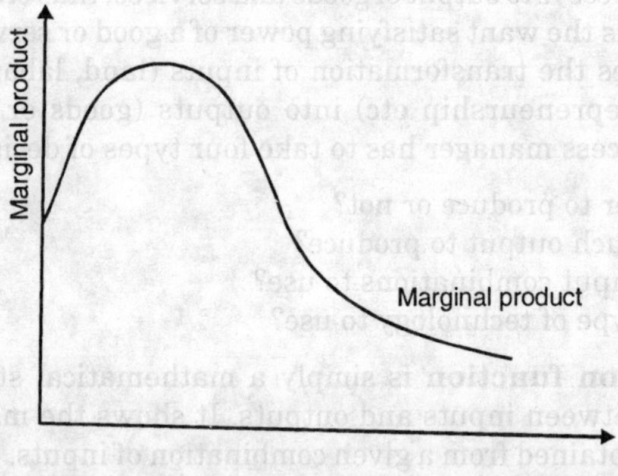

Fig. 8.1 The marginal product of a factor of production

Economic Efficiency and Technical Efficiency:

The production function incorporates the technically efficient method of production — the latest technological processes are used. When economists use production functions they assume that the maximum level of output is obtained from any given combination of inputs; that is, they assume that production is technically efficient.

When producers are faced with input prices, the problem is not technical but economic efficiency: how to produce a given amount of output at the lowest possible cost. To be economically efficient, a producer must determine the combination of inputs that solves this problem. What then is technical inefficiency? If, for example, an alternative process can produce the same amount of output using less of one or more inputs and the same amounts of all others, then the first process is technically inefficient.

If, however, the second process uses less of some inputs but more of others, the economically efficient method of producing a given level of output depends on the prices of the inputs. One might cost less but actually be less technically efficient.

Let us take an example to differentiate between technical efficiency and economic efficiency. Suppose a garment manufacturing company is producing cotton readymade garments and it was found that twelve percent of the fabric is wasted in the production process. An engineer suggested that the wastage of cloth could be eliminated by modifying the present production process. To this an economist suggested that if the cost of wasted cloth is less than that of modifying production process then it might not be economically efficient to modify the production process.

Classifying Inputs

All inputs can be divided into two categories:

1. Fixed: a fixed input is one that is required in the production process. The amount of the fixed input employed is constant over a given period of time regardless of the quantity of output produced. These include plant, equipments of the firm etc.

2. Variable Input: one whose quantity employed in the production process is varied, depending on the desired quantity of output to be produced. These include raw material etc.

Whether or not an input is fixed or variable depends upon the time period involved. The longer the length of time period under consideration, the more likely it is that the input will be variable and not fixed. Economist finds it convenient to distinguish between long run and short run. The short run is defined to be that period of time when some of the firm's inputs (i.e. plant and equipment which are generally difficult to change) are fixed. In contrast, the long run is that period over which all the firm's inputs are variable. In other words, the firm has the flexibility to adjust or change its environment. There is no universal rule for distinguishing between the short and long run, rather the dividing line must be drawn on a case- by-case basis. For an oil refinery, the short run might be any period less than 5 years (the length of time it takes to build a new refinery). For a fast food chain, 6 months (the time it takes to obtain approvals and construct a new restaurant) may be the dividing line between the short and long run.

Total Product: The total output that results from employing a specific quantity of resources in a production system.

Marginal Product: the incremental change in total output that can be produced by the use of one more unit of the variable input in the production process.

-or-

The change in output associated with a unit change in one input factor, holding other inputs constant.

ΔQ change brought about by a change in
ΔX units of the variable input
Y remains fixed

$$MPx = \frac{\Delta Q}{\Delta X}$$ -or, in continuous terms:

$$MPx = \frac{\partial Q}{\partial X}$$

Average Product: The ratio to total output to the amount of the variable input used in producing the output.

$$APx = \frac{Q}{X}$$

Production Elasticity: The percentage change in output resulting from a given percentage change in the amount of the variable input X employed in the production process with Y remaining constant.

-or-

The percentage change in output associated with a 1 (one) percent change in all inputs.

$$= \frac{\%\Delta Q}{\%\Delta X} = \frac{\Delta Q/Q}{\Delta X/X}$$

Rearranging Terms $$E_X = \frac{\Delta Q/\Delta X}{Q/X} = \boxed{\frac{MPx}{APx}}$$

Production function with one variable input

In economics, the production function with one variable input is illustrated with well known Law of variable Proportions, it is also called law of diminishing marginal returns. Law of variable proportion shows the input-output relationship or production function with one factor variable while other factors of production are kept constant.

Law of Diminishing Marginal Returns:

The use of increasing amounts of a variable factor in a production process beyond some point, given the amount of all other production factors remains unchanged, will eventually result in diminishing marginal returns in total output. In other words, the law of diminishing returns states that as additional units of variable input are combined with a fixed input, the additional output (i.e., MP) initially increases at an increasing rate, then diminishing rate, eventually leading to a decline in the total product. This observation is easily verified by reviewing the slope of the marginal product curve in the figure below. As the number of units of the variable input increases, other inputs held constant, there exists a point beyond which the marginal product of the variable input declines.

The concepts of total and marginal product and the law of diminishing returns to a factor are important in identifying efficient as opposed to inefficient input combinations.

The Three Stages of Production

The total, marginal and average product curves in figure shows the law of variable production and figure also shows three stages of production associated with law of variable production. The total product curve is divided into three stages of production as given below:

Stage I

1. It is the segment from the origin to point X_2
2. At the point X_2 the marginal product of X equals its average product.
3. X_2 is the point at which the average product is maximised
4. in this stage production function is characterised first by increasing marginal returns to the variable factor from origin to point X_1 and then from point X_1 to X_2 marginal returns are diminishing.

Stage II

It lies in the range from X_2 to X_3 i.e it begins where the average product of the variable factor is maximised and continues to the point at which total product is maximised and marginal product is zero. This stage is characterised by diminishing returns to the variable input over its entire range. Total product is increasing in this stage, but at a continuously decreasing rate.

Stage III

The area beyond X_3 is stage III, where the total product curve starts decreasing. In this range the marginal product of the variable factor is negative.

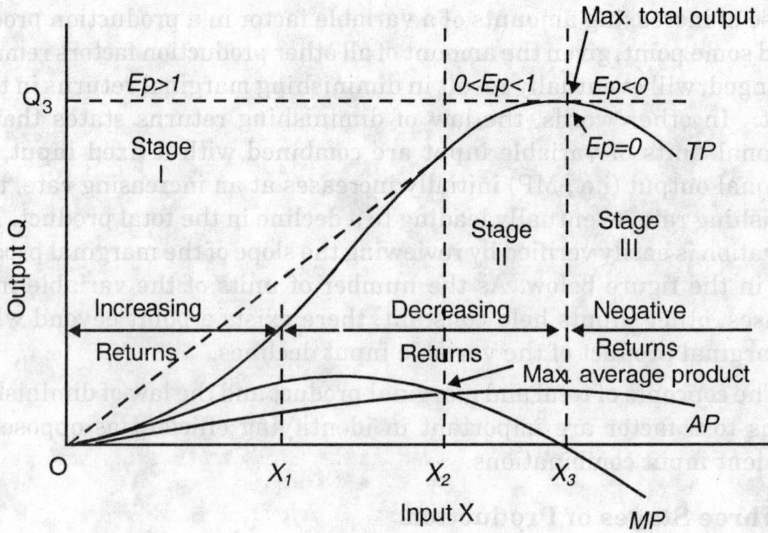

Figure 8.2: Three stages of production associated with Law of Variable Proportions

A rational firm is considered to operate only in the stage II. The fixed factor is utilised properly in this stage. In the stage I, the firm will be grossly underutilising its fixed capacity. Stage III is irrational because the firm will be using more of the variable input to produce less output.

Three things should be noted about the law. First, this is an empirical law and is therefore, a generalisation about the nature of production process and cannot be proven theoretically. Secondly, it is assumed that technology remains fixed. The law cannot predict the effect of an additional unit of input when technology is allowed to change. Third, it is assumed that there is at least one input whose quantity is being held constant. The law does not apply to cases where there are increases in all inputs

Applied to management, Friedman argues that the law of variable proportion requires firms to produce by using inputs in such proportions that there are diminishing returns to each input in production. It helps the firm in making decisions about the quantity of production and the ratio of variable input to fixed input.

Production function with two variable inputs

To understand a production function with two variable inputs, it is necessary to first understand what is an isoquant (also known as iso-product curve,equi-product curve or a production indifference curve). An isoquant is a curve connecting all combinations of inputs which give the same level of output, when combined efficiently. The isoquants are smooth curves,

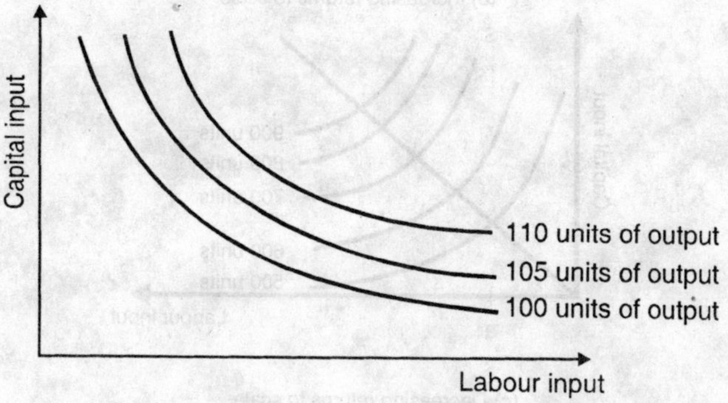

Figure 8.3: Isoquants

reflecting the assumption that there are continuous possibilities for substitution between one factor of production and another. They are convex to the origin or concave upwards and their slope shows the rate at which one factor has to be substituted for another in order to maintain a constant level of output. This is known as the marginal rate of technical substitution. For every level of output there is an isoquant and no two isoquants cross each other.

If a set of isoquants were drawn for equal increments of output, the distances between the isoquants would reflect the returns to scale in tht production function as shown in the figure. In figure a) isoquants are evenly spaced showing constant returns to scale. In figure b) isoquants are closer together as the distance from the origin increases, showing that there are increasing returns to scale, and in (c) they are further apart indicating decreasing returns to scale.

(a) Constant returns to scale

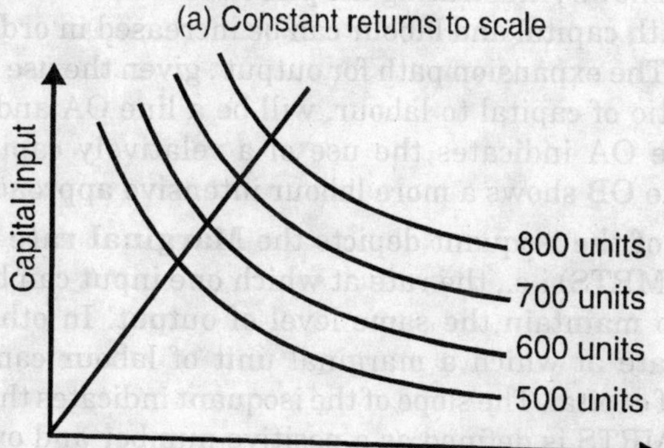

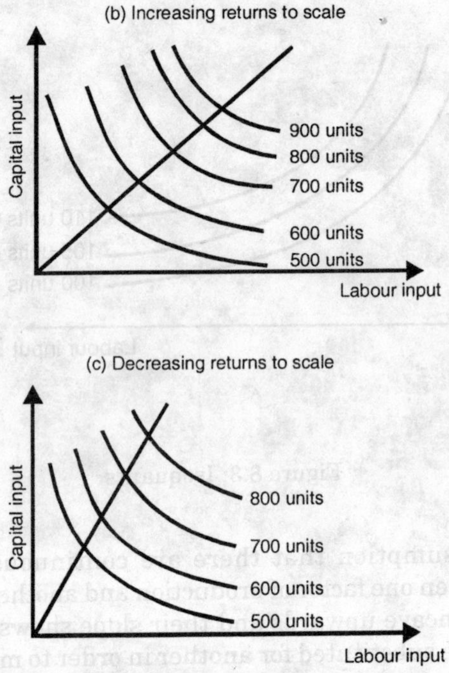

Figure 8.4: Isoquants and scale economies

Isoquant may be used to depict the way in which a firm can increase its output in the long run and the short run. In the short run, there are some fixed factors of production, represented by the capital input, and output can only be increased by using more of the variable factor which is labour. In figure below , the level of capital input is fixed at K^1 ,the short run expansion path is shown by K^1B. For equal increments in output, shown by the isoquants, increasingly large increments of labour input are required, as the diagram shows , illustrating the principle of diminishing returns. In the long run, both capital and labour can be increased in order to raise the level of output. The expansion path for output , given the use of a technique with a fixed ratio of capital to labour, will be a line OA and OB from the origin. The line OA indicates the use of a relatively capital- intensive technique, while OB shows a more labour intensive approach.

The slope of the isoquant depicts the **Marginal rate of technical substitution** (MRTS) i.e., the rate at which one input can be substituted for the other to maintain the same level of output. In other words, the MRTS is the rate at which a marginal unit of labour can substitute a marginal unit of capital. The slope of the isoquant indicates this rate (MRTS = $| dK/ dL |$). MRTS is defined as a positive number and over a relevant range of production MRTS diminishes. There is a simple relationship

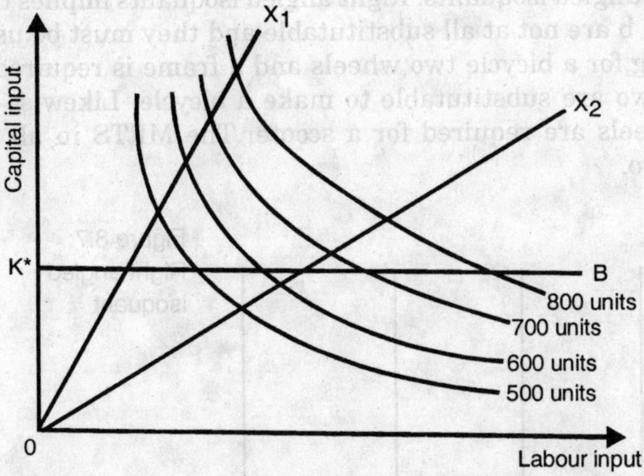

Figure 8.5: Expansion paths

between MRTS of labour for capital and the marginal product MP_K and MP_L of capital and labour respectively. In an isoquant as the level of output remains same, if ΔL units of labour are substituted for ΔK units of capital, the increase in output due to ΔL units of labour should match the decrease in output doe to a decrease of ΔK units of capital. In other words

$\Delta L \,.\, MP_L = \Delta K.\, MP_K$

which implies $MRTS_{L\ for\ K} = MP_L / MP_K$

Types of Isoquants are

1.Linear isoquants: In these the inputs a and b are perfect substitutes. Linear isoquants are straight lines with constant slope or MRTS.eg natural gas and fuel oil are perfect substitutes in energy production process.

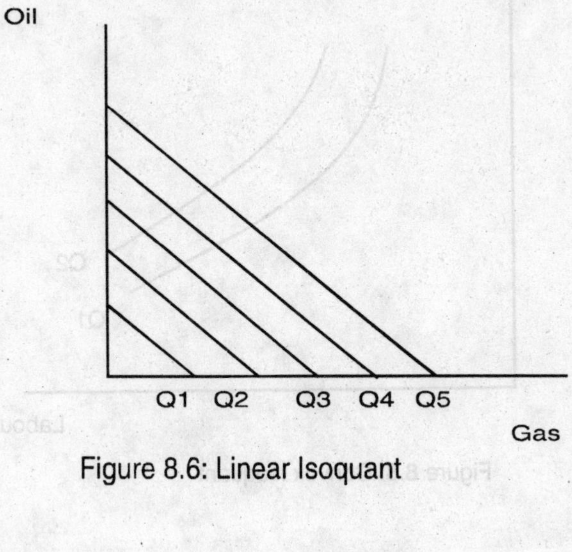

Figure 8.6: Linear Isoquant

2.Right angled isoquants: Right angled isoquants implies that the two inputs a and b are not at all substitutable and they must be used in fixed proportion.eg.for a bicycle two wheels and a frame is required and in no way these two are substitutable to make a bicycle. Likewise one chasis and two wheels are required for a scooter.The MRTS in all such cases would be zero.

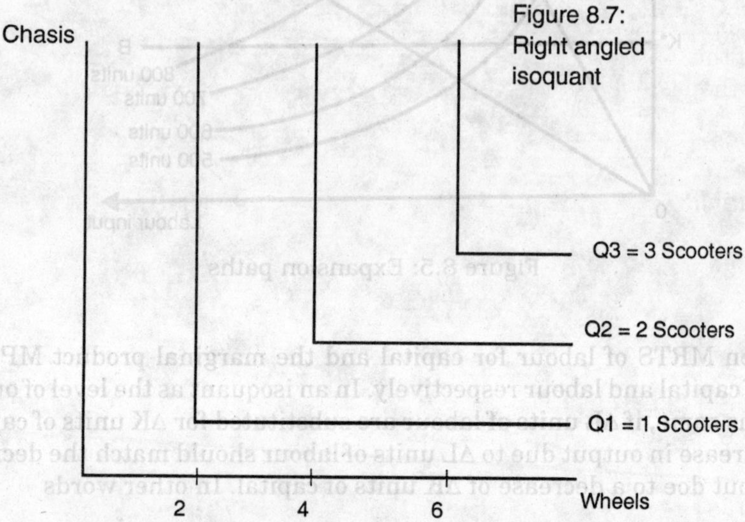

Figure 8.7: Right angled isoquant

3.Convex isoquants: these are the most common isoquants. Inputs are imperfect substitutes in this case and rate at which input a can be given up in return for one unit of input b keeping the output constant diminishes as the amount of input b increases.

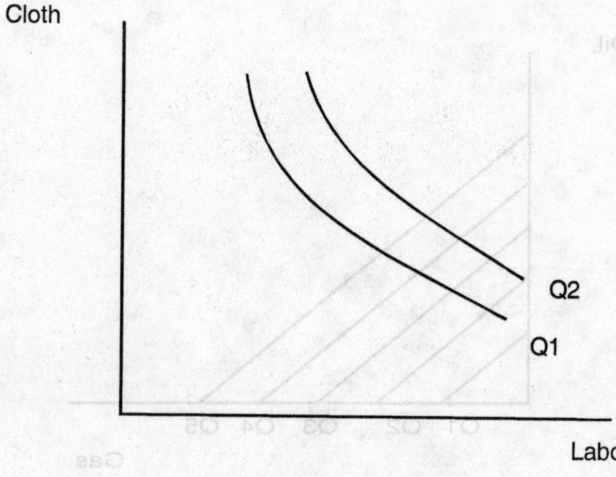

Figure 8.8: Convex Isoquant

Cost minimising choice of technique

Isoquants provide a graphical means by which the cost minimising technique of production can be found. If the unit cost of labour is w and the unit cost of capital is r then the total cost is given by the equation

TC = wL + r K

where L = units of labour used

K = units of capital used

If the cost minimising method of producing Q* units of output is to be found theproblem can be stated as:

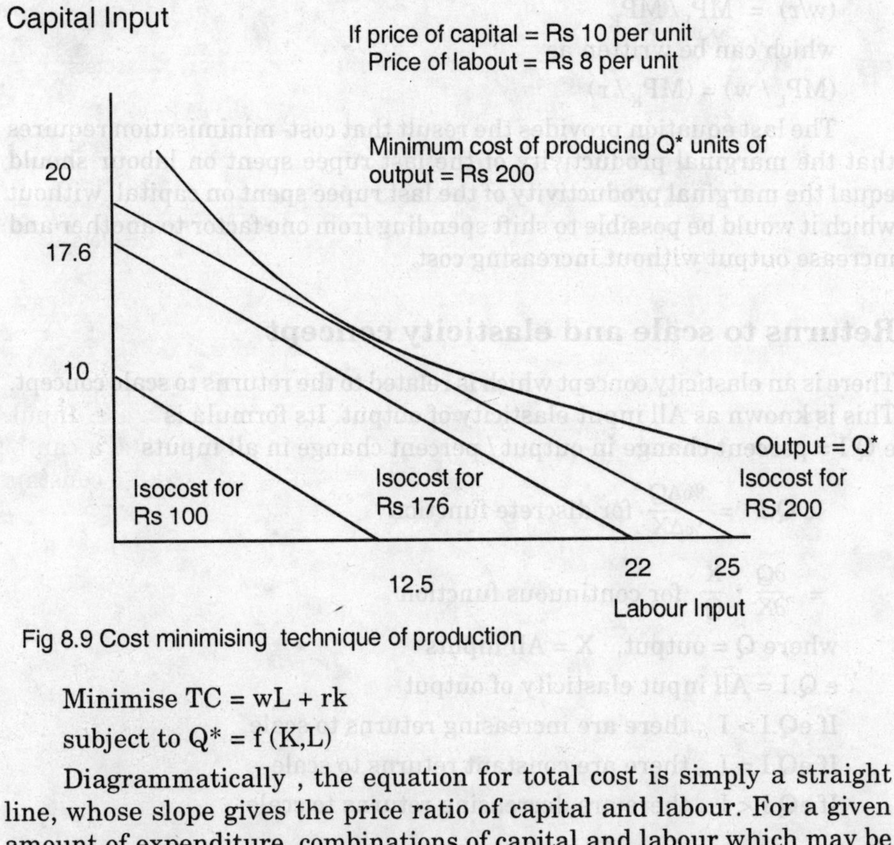

Fig 8.9 Cost minimising technique of production

Minimise TC = wL + rk

subject to Q* = f (K,L)

Diagrammatically , the equation for total cost is simply a straight line, whose slope gives the price ratio of capital and labour. For a given amount of expenditure, combinations of capital and labour which may be purchased are given by a straight line known as **isocost** line. Higher levels of spending are shown by isocost line which are further away from the origin as shown in the figure. If level of output Q* is to be produced at a minimum cost, it is necessary to find the lowest cost at which the firm can purchase a combination of capital and labour which is sufficient to produce output Q*.This combination is shown in figure by the point where an isocost line is tangent to isoquant for output Q*.

The cost minimising technique of production depends upon the relative prices of capital and labour. If labour is expensive, the isocost lines will be relatively steep and the chosen production technique will be capital intensive. If the labour is cheap, the isocost lines will be relatively flat and the cost minimising technique will be relatively labour intensive.

The condition for optimality is that the slope of the isocost line should be equal to the slope of the isoquant. It can be seen from the diagram that the slope of the isocost line is equal to the ratio of the factor price (w / r). The slope of the isoquant is equal to the marginal rate of substitution which is in turn equal to the ratio of the marginal product of substitution which is in turn equal to the ratio of the marginal product of labour to the marginal product of capital. The equilibrium condition can be written as:

$(w/r) = MP_L / MP_K$

which can be written as

$(MP_L / w) = (MP_K / r)$

The last equation provides the result that cost- minimisation requires that the marginal productivity of the last rupee spent on labour should equal the marginal productivity of the last rupee spent on capital, without which it would be possible to shift spending from one factor to another and increase output without increasing cost.

Returns to scale and elasticity concept

There is an elasticity concept which is related to the returns to scale concept. This is known as All input elasticity of output. Its formula is

e Q.I = percent change in output / percent change in all inputs

$$e\,Q.I = \frac{\%\Delta Q}{\%\Delta X} \text{ for discrete function}$$

$$= \frac{\partial Q}{\partial X} \cdot \frac{X}{Q} \text{ for continuous function}$$

where Q = output, X = All inputs

e Q.I = All input elasticity of output

If eQ.I > I , there are increasing returns to scale

If eQ.I = I , there are constant returns to scale

If eQ.I < I , there are decreasing returns to scale

Returns to scale

Returns to scaledescribe what happen to the rate of outpur when each input rate is increased by the same proportion. If output increases by more than an increase in inputs (i.e. by more than 10%) then the situation is that of increasing returns to scale. If output increases by less than the increase in inputs, then it is a case of decreasing returns to scale. If output increases by exactly the same proportion as inputs it's the case of constant returns of scale.

The returns to scale concept is important in the theory of production. If an industry is characterised by increasing returns to scale then there will be a tendency for expanding the size of the firm, and thus the whole industry will be dominated by large firms. For decreasing returns to scale the opposite would be true. In case of industry characterised by constant returns to scale, firms of all sizes would survive equally well.

Determining the optimal Use of the Variable input

With one of the inputs (Y) fixed in the short run, the producer must determine the optimal quantity of the variable input (X) to employ in the production process.

This is a study of Marginal Revenue Product (MRP) and Marginal Factor Cost (MFC). That is, this is a study about the role of revenue and cost in the production system.

MRP

The conversion from physical to economic relations is accomplished by multiplying the MP of input factors by the MR resulting from the sale of goods or services produced to obtain a quantity known as the *Marginal Revenue Product* of input:

Def: the amount that an additional unit of the variable input adds to total revenue, -or-

MRP is the economic value of a marginal unit of a particular input factor when used in the production of a specific product.

$$MRP = \frac{\Delta TR}{\Delta X}$$

where DTR is the change in total revenue associated with the given change (DX) in the variable input.

MRPx is equal to the marginal product of X (MPx) times the marginal revenue (MRQ) resulting form the increase in output obtained:

$$MRP = MP_X \bullet MR_Q$$

Example

Units	TP	MP	MR at Rs.5
1	3	3	15
2	7	4	20
3	10	3	15
4	12	2	10
5	13	1	5

If the addition of one more laborer to a work force would result in the production of two incremental units of a product than can be sold for Rs.5, the MP of labor is 2, and its MRP is Rs.10 (2 x Rs.5).

Marginal Factor Cost

Def: MFC is the amount that an additional unit of the variable input adds to total cost

$$MFC = \frac{\Delta TC}{\Delta X}$$

Optimal Input Level

Given the marginal revenue product and marginal factor cost, we can compute the optimal amount of the variable input to use in the production process.

Recall that prior discussions on optimality and marginal analysis suggest that an economic activity should be expanded as long as the marginal benefits exceed the marginal costs. The optimal point occurs at the point where the marginal benefits are equal to the marginal costs.

$$MRP = MFC_X$$

Single Input System

Profit maximization requires production at a level such that marginal revenue equals marginal cost. Because the <u>only</u> variable in the system is input L, the marginal cost of production is:

$$MC = \frac{\Delta TC}{\Delta output}$$

$$MC \ \frac{P_L}{MP_L}$$

Since marginal revenue must equal marginal cost at the profit-maximizing level, MR_Q can be substituted for MC_Q

$$MR_Q \ \frac{P_L}{MP_L}$$

solving for PL yields:

$$P_L = MR_Q \times MP_L$$

-or-

$$P_L = MRP_L$$

The profit maximizing firm will always employ an input up to the point where its marginal revenue product equals its cost.

NOTE: if $MRP_L > P_L$ the expand labor usage.
if $MRP_L < P_L$ the cutback labor usage.

Measurement of production function

There are a number of mathematical functions employed in the measurement of production function but only four types are widely used in applied research. These are

Linear function

Linear function can take the form

Total product : $Q = a + bX$

From this function, equation of average product will bw

$Q / X = a/ X + b$

The equation for the marginal product will be:

"Y/ "X = b

Power function

A power function expresses output Q, as a function of input X in the form:

$Q = aX^b$

Some important properties of such power functions are

i) The exponents are the elasticities of production. Thus, in the above function, the exponent b represents elasticity of production.

ii) The equation is linear in the logarithms i.e.

$\log Q = \log a + b \log X$

when the power function is expressed in logarithmic form as above, the coefficient b represents the elasticity of production.

iii) if one input is increased while all others are held constant, marginal product will decline.

Quadratic production function

The production function may be quadratic of the form:

$Q = a + bX - cX^2$

Where the dependent variable, Q, represents total output and the independent variable,X, denotes input. The small letters are parameters, there probable values are determined by a statistical analysis of data.

The special properties of the quadratic production function are

i) The minus sign in the last term denotes diminishing marginal returns

ii) The equation allows for decreasing marginal product but not for both increasing and decreasing marginal products.

iii) The equation never allows for an increasing marginal product.

iv) The elasticity of production is not constant at all points along the curve as in a power function, but declines with input magnitude.

v) When X = 0, Q = a. This means that there is some output even when no variable input is applied.

vi) The quadratic equation has only one bend as compared with a linear equation which has no bends.

Cubic production function

The cubic production function takes the following form:

$$Q = a + bX + cX^2 - dX^3$$

Important properties of a cubic production function are:

i) it allows for both increasing and decreasing marginal productivity.

ii) The elasticity of production varies at each point along the curve.

iii) Marginal productivity decreases at an increasing rate in the later stages.

Estimation of Production Functions

One of the more common approaches utilizes the Cobb Douglas production function method.

$$Q = \alpha L^{\beta 1} K^{\beta 2}$$

1. Both inputs are required to create output.
2. MRTS will diminish as required by production theory

Logarithmic Specification

$$Ln\, Q = Ln\, \alpha + \beta_1 Ln L + \beta_2 Ln K$$

Elasticity of Production

$$E_L = \frac{MP_L}{AP_L}$$

where;

$$MP_L = \alpha^{\beta 1} L^{\beta 1^{-1}} K^{\beta 2} \text{ and,}$$

$$AP_L = \frac{\alpha L^{\beta 1} K^{\beta 2}}{L} = \alpha L^{\beta 1} \text{-} 1 K^{\beta 2}$$

thus:

$$E_L = \frac{\alpha \beta 1 L^{\beta 1^{-1}} K^{\beta 2}}{\alpha L^{\beta 1^{-1}} K^{\beta 2}} = \beta^1$$

The Exponents - Returns to Scale

1. Increasing: $\beta 1 + \beta 2 > 1$
2. Constant: $\beta 1 + \beta 2 = 1$
3. Decreasing: $\beta 1 + \beta 2 < 1$

Example

$Q = 1.01\ ^{0.75} K^{0.25}$

Q was an index of physical volume of manufacturing; L was an index of the average number of employed wage earners only (that is, salaried employees, officials, and working proprietors were excluded); and K was an index of the value of plants, buildings, tools and machinery reduced to dollars of constant purchasing power.The sum of the exponents were restricted to one (constant returns to scale).

Later Studies by Cobb and Douglas

$Q = .84\ L^{0.63}\ K^{0.30}$

A one (1) percent increase in labor input results in about a 2/3 percent increase in output, and a one (1) percent increase in capital input results in approximately a 1/3 percent increase in output.

The sum of the exponents is slightly less than one (1). Seems to indicate the presence of decreasing returns to scale, however, the sum is not significantly different from 1.0; hence, it really confirms constant returns to scale.

A Three Variable Model

$Q = \alpha L_p^{\beta_1} L_n^{\beta_2} K^{\beta_3}$

Q is the value added by production plants over 18 industries

L_n is non-production work-years

L_p is production work-hours

K is gross book values of depreciable and depletable assets

Empirical Estimation of Production Functions

To be useful to the manager, production functions must be estimated and constructed based on actual data gathered by the firm. Statistical techniques are applied on historical data of input and output to estimate empirical production functions. Three types of statistical approaches available to form a production function are discussed here.

Time-series data

Time series data concerning the amount of various inputs used in various periods in the past and the amount produced in each period can be used to estimate the production function For example, data can be obtained about the amount of labour, capital and raw materials used in the steel industry each year from 1991 to 2000. On the basis of these estimates and the total output of the steel industry, relationship between amounts of the inputs and the resulting output can be estimated by regression technique

Cross-section data

Cross-section data regarding the amount of various inputs used and the output produced in various firms or sectors of the industry at a given time C3Q be collected to form a production function. For example, data can be obtained regarding the amount of labour, capital, and raw materials used in various firms in the steel industry in 2000. On the basis of this data and information of output of each firm in 2000, regression techniques can be applied to estimate the relationship between the amount of inputs and the resulting output.

Similarly, by observing production in the automobiles industry, a number of questions can be answered: What is the effect on output of expanding labour force (for instance, adding extra shifts)? Does the industry exhibit economies of scale, and if so over what range of output? (That is will a 40 per cent increase in plant scale deliver more than 40 per cent increase in output?)

Engineering data

A manager can use technical information supplied by the engineer or the agricultural scientist. This information is usually based on experience or from day-to-day working of similar production processes. For this reason, the estimated production function is only as accurate as past production experience on which it is based.

Regardless of which approach is used, the data may not always represent technically efficient combinations of input and output. For example, because of errors or constraints, the amount of inputs used in steel industry in 2000 may not have been the minimum requirement to produce the output produced by the steel industry in that year. Since the production function theoretically includes only efficient combinations, a case of this sort should be *excluded, if the result* requires correct estimation of future, however, such cases are not always excluded, as a result the estimates have some error.

Managerial use of Production Functions

Though production functions may seem to be highly abstract and unrealistic, in fact, they are both logical and useful. If the price of a factor of production declines whereas that of another goes up, the former is likely to substitute the latter. The usefulness of the production function can be explained with the help of an example. Dairy economists, for instance. are interested in minimising the cost of feeding cows in milk production. Taking a cow as a single firm, and grain and roughage as input~. i, the question arises: What proportion of grain and roughage would be economical in feeding the cow? In the past, there has been some tendency to prescribe a fixed ratio.

but economic analysis suggests that the optimal ratio depends on the input prices. For Instance, if we draw isoquants relating various quantities of grain and roughage to various levels of milk output and then superimpose isocost lines on the isoquant diagram. the optimum-the point of largest output for a given outlay or of minimum outlay for a given output-would depend on the prices of the factors of production, and It would change as these prices change. The dairy farmer can use such analysis for Increasing the return from his expenditure on feeds.

Production functions thus are not just theoretical and useless device. On the other hand, they can be used as aids in decision-making because they can give guideline in two directions: a) how to obtain the maximum output from a given set of inputs; and b) how to obtain a given output from the minimum aggregation of inputs. Of course, in more complex problems, with larger numbers of inputs and outputs, the mathematics of optimisation becomes complicated. But recently. the development of linear programming has made it possible to handle these complex problems. The use of complex production functions in managerial decision-making is going to be further facilitated with the development of electronic computers.

Points to remember

The Theory of Production

A. Production theory forms the foundation for the theory of supply. Managerial decision making involves four types of production decisions:

1. Whether to produce or to shut down
2. How much output to produce
3. What input combination to use
4. What type of technology to use

B. Production involves transformation of inputs such as capital, equipment, labor and land into output - goods and services

In this production process, the manager is concerned with efficiency in the use of the inputs

- technical vs. economical efficiency

C. Two Concepts of Efficiency

Economic efficiency:

- occurs when the cost of producing a given output is as low as possible

Technological efficiency:

- Occurs when it is not possible to increase output without increasing inputs

The objective of efficiency will provide us with some basic rules about the manner in which firmsshould utilize inputs to produce goods and services

D.Basic production theory is simply an application of the constrained optimization: the firm attempts either to minimize the cost of producing a given level of output

or

to maximize the output attainable with a given level of cost.

Both optimization problems leads to same rule for the allocation of inputs and choice of technology

E.Production Function

A production functionis a table or a mathematical equation showing the maximum amount of output that can be produced from any specified set of inputs, given the existing technology

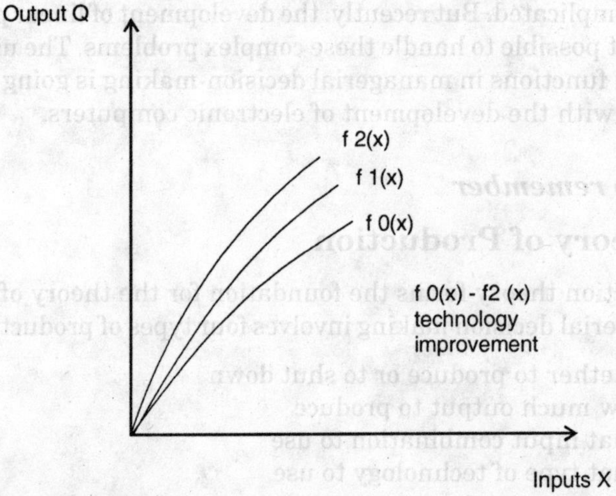

Production Function

Q = f(X1, X2,…, Xk)

where

Q = output

X1,…,Xk = inputs

For our current analysis, let's reduce the inputs to two, capital (K) and labor (L):

Q = f(L, K)

All of these outputs are assumed to be technically efficient.

But which one is economically efficient?

- That is the question facing the Decision Maker

F.Short-Run and Long-Run Production

In the short run some inputs are fixed and some variable

- e.g. the firm may be able to vary the amount of labor, but cannot change capital
- in the short run we can talk about factor productivity

In the long run all inputs become variable

- e.g. the long run is the period in which a firm can adjust allinputs to changed conditions
- in the long run we can talk about returns to scale

G. Relationship Between Total, Average, and Marginal Product: Short-Run Analysis

- Total Product (TP) = total quantity of output
- Average Product (AP) = total product/total input
- Marginal Product (MP) = change in quantity when one additional unit of input used

H.The Marginal Product of Labor

The marginal product of labour is the increase in output obtained by adding 1 unit of labor but holding constant the

inputs of all other factors

Marginal Product of L:

MPL = $\Delta Q/\Delta L$ (holding K constant)

$= \partial Q/\partial L$

Average Product of L:

APL = Q/L (holding K constant)

I.Law of Diminishing Returns

(Diminishing Marginal Product)

Holding all factors constant except one, the law of diminishing returns says that: beyond some value of the variable input, further increases in the variable input lead to steadily decreasing marginal product of that input

e.g. trying to increase labour input without also increasing capital will bring diminishing returns

J.Three Stages of Production

Stage i : Fixed input grossly underutilized;specialization and teamwork cause AP to increase when additional X is used

Stage ii:Specialization and teamwork continue to result in greater output when additional X is used;

fixed input being properly utilized

Stage iii:Fixed input capacity is reached; additional X causes output to fall

K. Optimal Decision Rule:

A profit maximizing firm operating in perfectly competitive output and input markets will be using optimal amount of

an input at the point at which the monetary value of the input's marginal product is equal to the additional cost of using that input (L) - in other words, when MRP = MLC

L. Production in the Long-Run

- All inputs are now considered to be variable (both L and K in our case)
- How to determine the optimal combination of inputs?

To illustrate this case we will use production isoquants.

An isoquantis a curve showing all possible combinations of inputs physically capable of producing a given fixed level of output.

M. Substituting inputs

Substituting Inputs

From above we can see that there exists some degree of substitutability between inputs.

Different degrees of substitution:

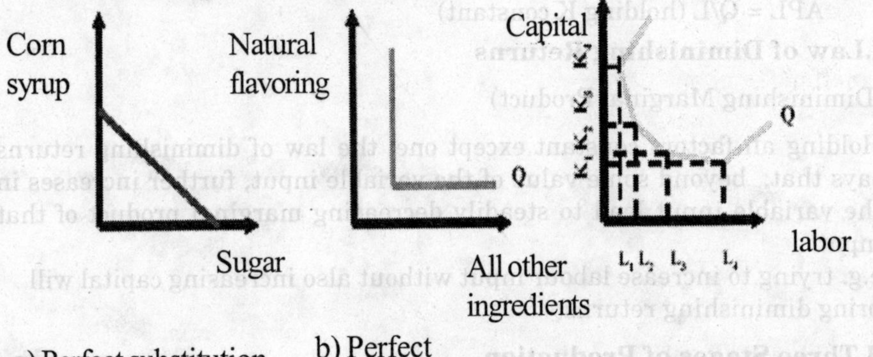

a) Perfect substitution b) Perfect Complementarity c) Imperfect substitution

a) In case the two inputs are imperfectly substitutable, the optimal combination of inputs depends on the degree of substitutability and on the relative prices of the inputs

b)The degree of imperfection is measured with marginal rate of technical substitution (MRTS):

MRTS = ΔL/ΔK

M.Optimal Levels of Inputs

The earlier rule, MRP =MLC, can be generalized:

• a firm in competitive markets should use each input up to the point where Pi = MRPi

where

Pi = price of input i

MRPi = marginal revenue product of input i

A profit maximizing firm will always try to operate at the point where the extra revenue received from the sale of the last unit of output produced is just equal to the additional cost of producing this output.

This is same as MR = MC

N. Returns to Scale

To explain how much the output will increase we will use the concept of returns to scale

Often we can assume that firms experience constant returns to scale:

• for example doubling the size of a factory along with a doubling of workforce and machinery should lead to a doubling of output

• Why could a greater (or smaller) than proportional increase occur?

Reasons for Increasing Returns to Scale:

• Division of labor

• Indivisibility

• Geometrical reasons

Decreasing returns to scale can result from certain managerial inefficiencies:

• problems in communication

• increased bureaucracy

O. Measurement of Returns to Scale

• 1.Coefficient of output elasticity

EQ= percentage change in Q / percentage change in all inputs

So if, EQ>1, increasing returns

EQ=1, constant returns

EQ<1, decreasing returns

- **2.Multiplying the coefficients of the production function:**

If original production function is

$Q = f(X,Y)$

and if the resulting equation after the multiplication of inputs by k is

$hQ = f(kX, kY)$

where h presents the magnitude of increase in production

Then, if

$h>k$, increasing returns

$h=k$, constant returns

$h<k$, decreasing returns

Questions

1. **Define a production function. Explain and illustrate isoquants and isocost curves.**
2. **Explain the nature and managerial uses of production function.**
3. **How is a least-cost combination arrivedat with the help of iso-product and iso-cost curves? Explain the significance of the tangential points.**
4. **"A firm buys inputs in quantities determined by the production function and the prices of the inputs." .Discuss.**
5. **Discuss the equilibrium of the firm with the technique of isoquants.**
6. **Distinguish between production function and cost function. How would you develop the production function? What are its uses?**
7. **A firm has the production function X= LK (X = output, L= Labour, K= capital); Labour and capital price are Rs 8 and Rs 10 per unit; and it desired to produce 32 units of output. What is the least cost combination of labour and capital?**
8. **Consider the production function $Q= 86\ L^{0.61}\ K^{0.39}$**

   (i) Find the marginal products of labour and capital

   (ii) Find the marginal rate of technical substitutions.
9. **A firm has the following short-run total cost function:**

   $C= Q^3 - 9Q^2 + 300\ Q + 25$

   (a) Derive the average variable cost (AVC) function and show that when AVC is at minimum , marginal cost (MC) = AVC.

   (b) Derive the average Total Cost (ATC) function and check that where Q= 5 ATC is at minimum and MC = ATC.

10. For each of the following situations, determine whether the manager is concerned with a short-run or a long – run production decision. Explain briefly for each case

    (1) A petroleum drilling supervisor on an off shore drilling platform decides to add an extra six hour shift each day in order to keep the drill rig running 24 hours per day

    (2) The director (Projects) of off-shore petroleum drilling operations at the Mumbai High chooses to deploy three more off-shore drilling platforms in the Mumbai High.

    (3) A manufacturing engineer plans the production schedule for the month.

    After studying a demographic report on future increases in birth rates, a hospital administrator decides to add a new pediatric wing to hospital.

9

Supply Analysis

Introduction

The supply of a good or service means the amount of that good or service which producers are able and willing to offer for sale at a given price. Supply is related to scarcity i .e only scarce goods have a supply price. The supply function is a statement of the relation between the quantity supplied and all factors affecting the quantity. The supply function can be written as:

$$Qx = f(Px, P_R, P_c, P_L, P_i, T, G, N, W)$$

Where:

Qx	=	Quantity Demanded
Px	=	Price of Product x
P_R	=	Price of other products related in productin
P_c	=	Price of Capital
P_L	=	Price of Labor
P_i	=	Interest cost
T	=	Technology / Innovation
G	=	Government Policy
N	=	Number of People in the Economy
W	=	Weather Conditions, strikes and other short run forces.

Supply curve

Each point on the supply curve gives the price- quantity supplied combinations of the firm. Supply curve shows the minimum price that firm is ready to take for different quantities of the goods or services. Slope of supply curve is positive i.e as the price of the commodity increases its quantity supplied also increases. In contrast to demand curve , the supply curve slopes downwards from right to left. Industry supply curve can also be derived from supply curves of individual firms (by adding the amount supplied by each seller at different prices so as to get industry supply at different prices).

Law of supply states that as the price of a commodity rises, its supply increases and as price falls, its supply declines with the condition that other things remaining the same. The reasons for quantity offered for sales directly varying with price are:

Price increase would give more profits as a result producers would offer more quantities for sale.

In the long run due to greater profits new producers may enter the market leading to an increase in output.

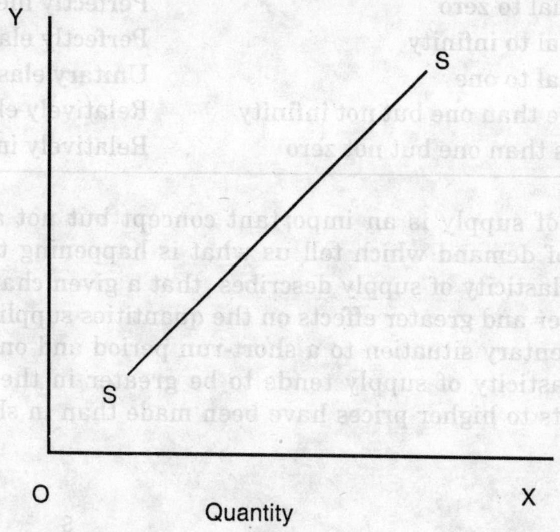

Figure 9.1: Supply Curve

Limitations of law of supply

1. When the price of a commodity rises seller expects the prices to rise more in future, as a result supply decreases as seller may withhold supplies so as to sell later and earn more profits. Likewise, when the prices falls the supplier will sell more fearing that prices may fall further giving him less profits.

2. Law of supply does not apply to agricultural commodities as their production can not be increased instantaneously as prices increase.

3. The change in technology can bring about a change in quantity supplied even if prices of the commodity does not change.

Elasticity of Supply

It is defined as the degree of responsiveness of supply to a change in price. Its formula is:

$$e_s = \frac{\text{Proportionate change in quantity supplied}}{\text{Proportionate change in price}} = \frac{\Delta Q/Q}{\Delta P/P}$$

The different types of supply elasticities are given in table below

When elasticity of supply is	It is known to be
1) Equal to zero	Perfectly inelastic supply
2)Equal to infinity	Perfectly elastic supply
3)Equal to one	Unitary elastic supply
4)More than one but not infinity	Relatively elastic supply
5)Less than one but not zero	Relatively inelastic supply

Elasticity of supply is an important concept but not as important as elasticity of demand which tell us what is happening to total revenue. However elasticity of supply describes that a given change in price will have greater and greater effects on the quantities supplied as one moves from momentary situation to a short-run period and on to the long-run period. Elasticity of supply tends to be greater in the long run when adjustments to higher prices have been made than in shorter periods of time.

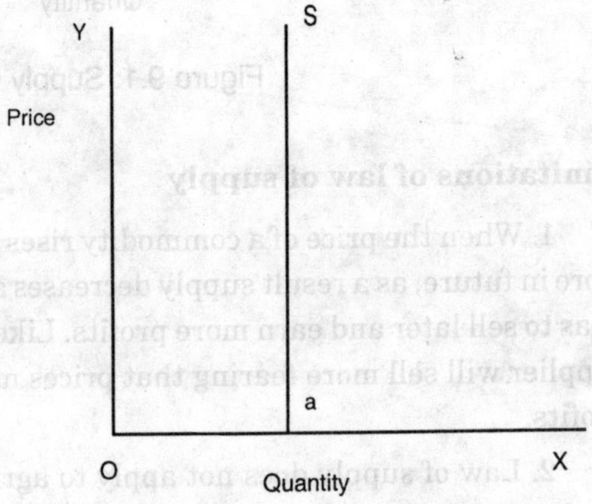

Fig: 9.2: A supply curve of zero elasticity

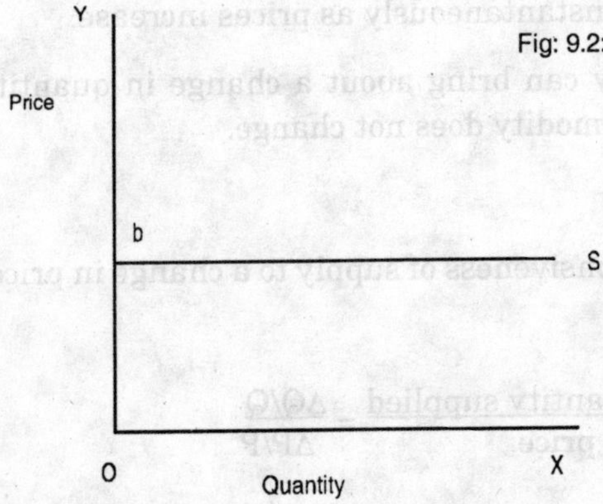

Figure : 9.3: A supply curve of infinite elasticity

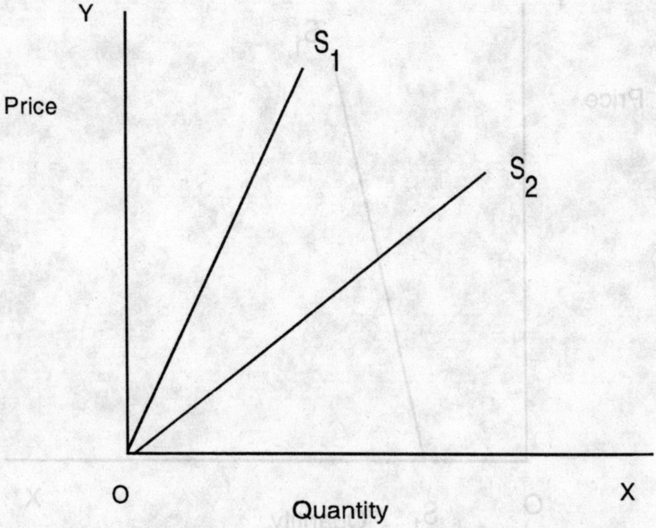

Figure 9.4: Supply curve of unit elasticity

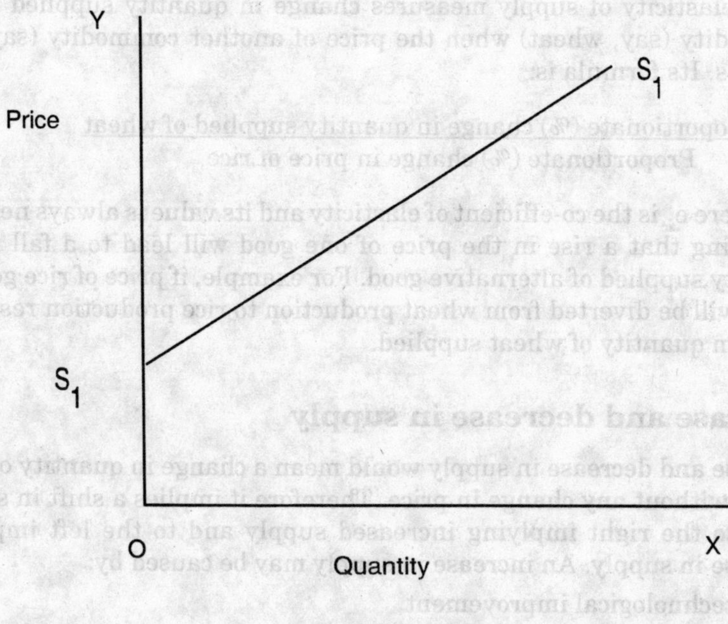

Figure 9.4: Supply curve of unit elasticity

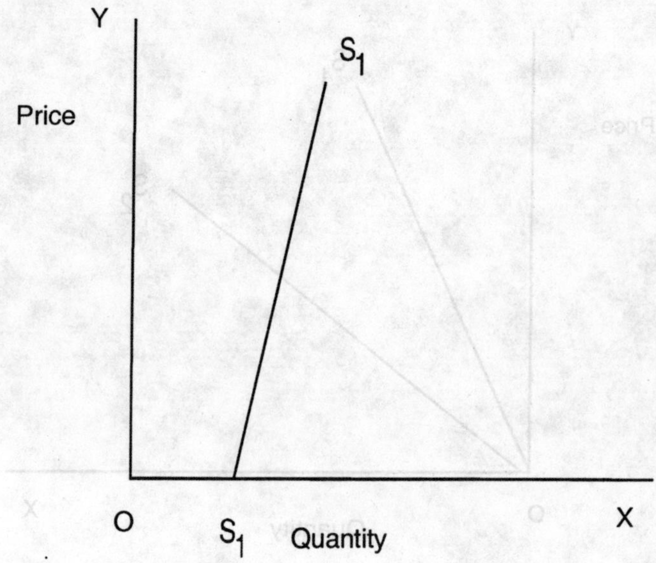

Figure 9.6: Relatively inelastic supply curve

Cross elasticity of supply

Cross elasticity of supply measures change in quantity supplied of one commodity (say, wheat) when the price of another commodity (say rice) changes. Its formula is:

$$e_{sc} = \frac{\text{Proportionate (\%) change in quantity supplied of wheat}}{\text{Proportionate (\%) change in price of rice}}$$

Here e_{sc} is the co-efficient of elasticity and its value is always negative indicating that a rise in the price of one good will lead to a fall in the quantity supplied of alternative good. For example, if price of rice goes up , land will be diverted from wheat production to rice production resulting in fall in quantity of wheat supplied.

Increase and decrease in supply

Increase and decrease in supply would mean a change in quantity offered to sale without any change in price. Therefore it implies a shift in supply curve to the right implying increased supply and to the left implying decrease in supply. An increase in supply may be caused by:

1.technological improvement
2.decrease in price of other commodities
3.decrease in the prices of factors of production used in manufacturing of the concerned product/commodity.

A decrease in supply involving reluctance on the part of seller to sell as much as before at each price may be due to

1.Increase in prices of other commodities
2.Increase in the prices of factors of production.

In the figure below SS is the supply curve before the change S'S' shows a decrease in supply because at the same price PM less quantityOM' is offered for sale. S"S" shows an increase in supply because at the same price PM more is offered for sale.

Increase in quantity supplied is different from increase in supply. Increase in supply means entire supply curve has shifted to right whereas increase in quantity supplied means more of commodity is being offered at a higher price, supply curve is same in this case.

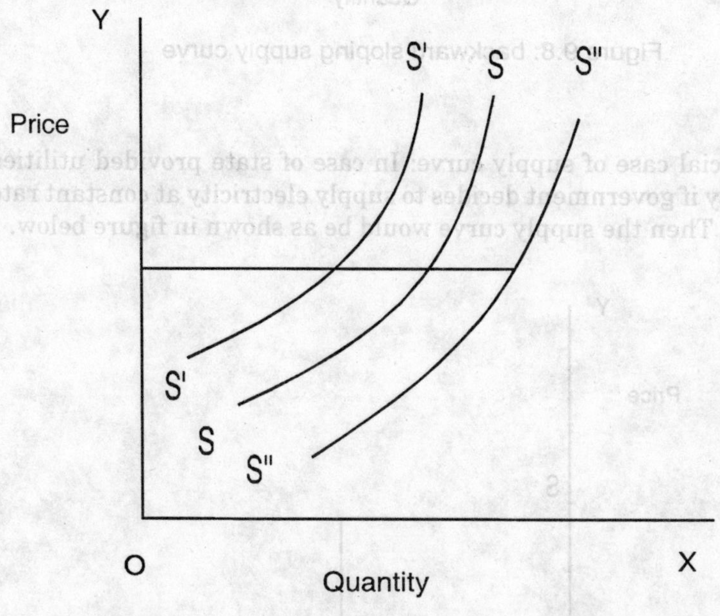

Figure 9.7: Increase and decrease in supply

Backward sloping supply curve: Generally, the law of supply states that more quantity is supplied at higher prices. But in some cases beyond a point less is offered at higher prices, the supply curve therefore begins sloping backwards towards left as shown in the figure. Example for this can be supply of labour, rising wages induce more work but after a point, leisure is preferred to labour and hence higher wages induce workers to work less.

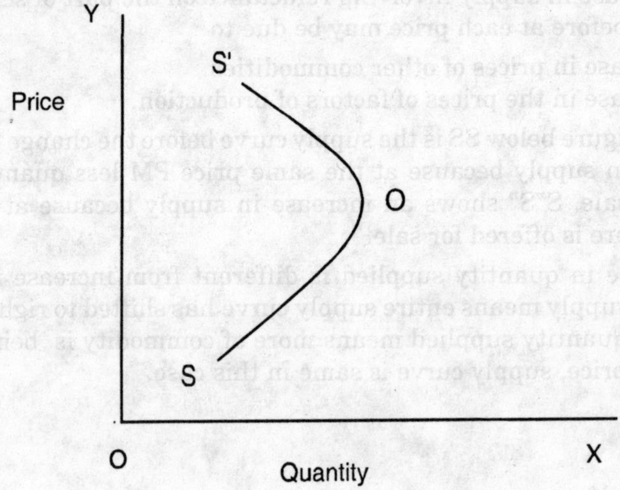

Figure 9.8: backward sloping supply curve

Special case of supply curve: In case of state provided utilities like electricity if government decides to supply electricity at constant rate and no more. Then the supply curve would be as shown in figure below.

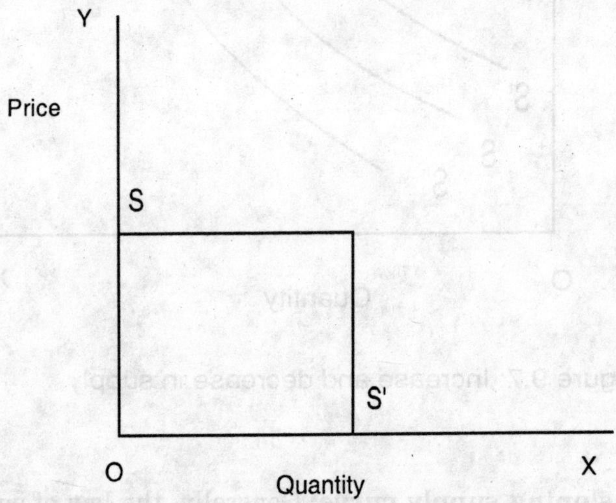

Figure 9.9: A special supply curve

Joint supply and composite supply: When production of one good would automatically result in production of other or when two or more goods are supplied together its called joint supply eg. Hides and bones, wheat and husk, wool, mutton and hide etc. When various supply a single commodity

sources its called composite supply. For example energy can be supplied by electricity, gas, oil.

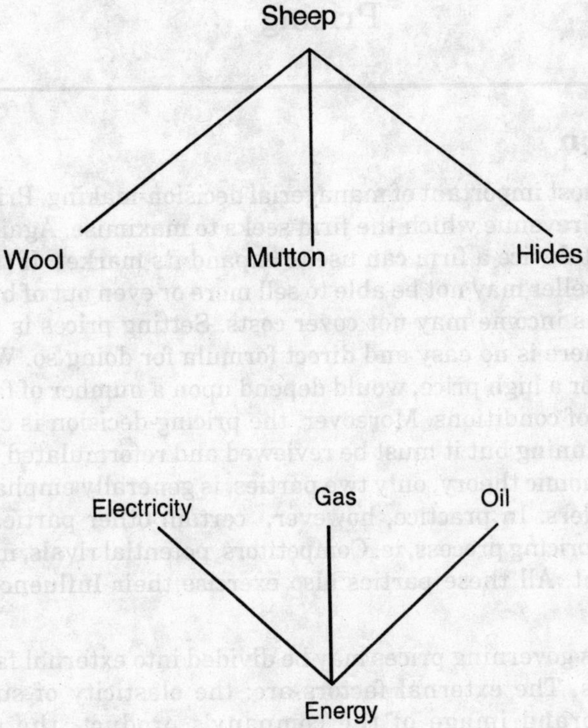

Figure 9.10 : Joint supply and composite supply

Questions

1. **State the law of supply. Show how industry supply curve is obtained from firm's cost curve.**
2. **Define elasticity of supply. How does it differ from change in supply?**

10

Pricing

Introduction

Pricing is the most important of managerial decision-making. Price, in fact, is the source of revenue which the firm seeks to maximise. Again, it is the most important device a firm can use to expand its market. If the price is set too high, a seller may not be able to sell more or even out of business. If it is too low, his income may not cover costs. Setting prices is a complex problem and there is no easy and direct formula for doing so. Whether to set a low price or a high price, would depend upon a number of factors and a wide variety of conditions. Moreover. the pricing decision is critical not only in the beginning but it must be reviewed and reformulated from time to time. In economic theory, only two parties, is generally emphasised, i.e. buyers and sellers. In practice, however, certain other parties are also involved in the pricing process, ie. Competitors, potential rivals, middlemen and government. All these parties also exercise their Influence in price determination.

The factors governing prices may be divided into external factors and internal factors. The external factors are: the elasticity of supply and demand, the brand image of the company's product, the extent of competition in the market, the trend of the market, the purchasing power of the buyers, and the government policy towards prices. The internal factors are: (1) the costs. and (2) the management policy towards the gross margin and the sales turnover. In addition, the basic characteristics of the product, the stage of the product on the product life cycle, the use pattern and turnaround rate of the product and extent of distinctiveness of the product and extent of product differentiation practised by the firm, are also among the internal factors.

Certain general considerations which must be kept in view while formulating the price policy are :

1. *Objective of the firm*: The firms objective effect the pricing decision in significant way. The broadest of these is survival, or assured continued existence. On a more specific level, objectives relate to rate of growth, market share, maintenance of control or ownership and finally profit. Very often companies fix a target rate of profit. Whether the company will be able to achieve the target rate of profit will depend upon the forces of competition. The various objectives may not always be compatible and hence the need for their reconciliation. A pricing policy should never be established without taking into consideration its impact on the other policies and practices of the firm.

2. *Market structure of the industry*: An effective solution of the pricing problems requires an understanding of the competitive environment. In perfect competition, sellers have no pricing problems because they have no pricing discretion. Price policy has practical significance only where there is considerable degree of imperfection in competition. Thus, we are concerned only with competitive structures where there is some room for managerial price discretion.Under the present competitive conditions, it is more important for the firm to offer the product which best satisfies the wants and desires of the consumers than the one which sells at the lowest possible price. As a result, pricing policy should be governed more by the relative than by the absolute height of prices.

3. *Product and Promotional Policies*: A firm must consider pricing together with its product and promotional policies. Thus, before making a price change, the firm must be sure that the price is at fault and not its sales promotion programme, the quality of the product, or some other element.

4. *Price Sensitivity*: Businessmen often tend to exaggerate the importance of price sensitivity and ignore the many identifiable factors at work which tend to minimise it. The various factors which may generate insensitivity to price changes are variability in consumer behaviour, variation in the effectiveness of marketing effort, nature of the product, importance of service after sales, the existence of highly differentiated products difficult to compare and multiple dimensions of product quality.

5. *Routinization of Pricing* : Pricing in practice is often routinized though its extent may differ from company to company and product to product. For example, the management may prefer to depend on suggested prices, mechanical formulae or price followership. The degree of routinization, however, depends on the following factors:

(i) Number of Pricing Decisions:A firm which may have to take thousands of pricing products, none of which provides a substantial proportion of sales, will find that the costs of separate analyses on each product are too high. It would, therefore, find it economical to adopt relatively mechanical routines for pricing.

(ii) Speed Required by Pricing Decisions: Mechanical formulae, such as a pre-determined mark-up on full cost, have the advantage of speed though flexibility and adaptability to special conditions is thereby lost.

(iii) Quality of Available Information: If the data on demand and costs are highly conjectural, the best the firm may be able to do is to rely on some mechanical formula such cost plus.

(iv) Competitive Market:If a firm is selling its product in a highly competitive market, it will have little scope for pricing discretion. This will pave the way for routinized pricing.

6. *Effect of government policies on price determination*: The Government acting on behalf of the public seeks to prevent the abuse of monopolistic power and collusion among businessmen. There is a complex body of laws and even more confusing series of judicial decisions. Very often, the Government elects to control certain prices. Collective bargaining and strikes by the labour unions attempt to raise wages. The entry of the Government into the pricing process, in alliance with farmer and labour interests, tends to inject politics in price determination .

Pricing is not an exact science. There is no cut short and reliable formula of determining the right price for a product. Every pricing situation is unique. The pricing decision should result from the balancing of a number of considerations, in fact pricing is a matter of judgement. But the judgement should be based on sound principles and the correct information possible. Pricing is a process of trial and error and no matter how logical the price may seem to be, if its not able to attract sufficient number of customers, it is a wrong price.

Objectives of Pricing Policy

Pricing decisions are usually considered a part of the general strategy for achieving a broadly defined goal of the firm. While setting the price, the firm may have the following objectives:

1. Maximisation of profits for the entire product line. As Kotler has pointed out. firms set a price which would enhance the sale of the entire product line rather than yield a profit on one product only.

2. Promotion of the long-range welfare of the firm; *e.g* discouraging the entry of competitors.

3. Adaptation of prices to fit the diverse competitive situations faced by different products.

4. Flexibility to vary prices to meet changes in economic conditions affecting the various consumer industries.

5. Stabilization of *prices* and *margin.*

Price in the simple economic model of firm

The basic rules for optimal pricing

The simple model of the profit maximising firm, is one in which price and quantity are the only decision variables. The nature of product is given, there is assumed to be no spending on promotion or advertising, and no attention is given to the question of distribution channels. In this model, the rule for profit maximisation is , the firm should produce the level of output such that marginal cost = marginal revenue (the first order condition) and the slope of the marginal cost curve is greater than the slope of the marginal revenue curve (the second order condition). The price which should be charged is then derived from the profit maximising quantity, being the price at which that quantity can be sold.A formula for price can be derived from first order condition as:

$$(P - MC)/ P = 1/E_d$$

where:

P=price

MC= marginal cost

E_d = elasticity of demand

The above formula makes clear, the margin between price and marginal cost is essentially a function of elasticity of demand. If demand is infinitely elastic, being equal to infinity, the profit maximising price will be equal to marginal cost. As demand is less and less elastic, so the margin between price and marginal cost will be larger. Another specification of the basic model which can be used to shed light on the profit maximising price involves restating the cost conditions in terms of an average cost function, giving:

Total cost = AC (q) .q

Where: AC = average cost

q= output

In this case, the basic profit maximising equation is as follows:

Profit = Total revenue – total cost

= P(q).q – AC(q).q

The first order condition for profit maximisation can be written as

Price = AC + q. dAC/ dq –dP / dq

This approach has the apparent advantage of expressing the price in terms of average cost plus a margin, which corresponds with much of the evidence on business practice. On the other hand, if it is viewed as a decision rule for managers, it suffers from the same disadvantage as the previous formulation. It cannot be applied until the profit maximising level of output is known, along with the values of dAC/dq and dP/dq at that level of output

Pricing of Multiple Products

In a multi-product corporation, production decisions relating to one product may affect the manufacturing or marketing costs of other related products. The product may be interrelated or independent. For example, Pringles and Tide of p and G are independent while Pantene and Head and Shoulders are interrelated. In case of independent products, demand and cost of one product is not influenced by that of the other. Each product will be produced where MR = MC. However, pricing of related products requires that demand inter-dependencies should be taken into account.

Products with Interdependent Demand

Related products can be complementary or substitutes. Personal computer and keyboard are complements but two different sizes of PC's of different firms are substitutes. The effect of a change in the price of one product on the demand of the other has to be taken into account. Profit maximisation requires that the output levels and prices of various products produced by the firm be determined jointly.

Suppose a firm produces and sells two products, X and Y, its total revenue (i.e., sales) can be represented as

$$TR = TR_x = TR_y$$

where TR_x and TR_y is the revenue from product X and Y, respectively. The marginal revenue (MR) of each product is

$$MRx = dTRx/dQx + d\,Try/dQx$$

$$MRy = d\,Try/dQy + dTRx\,/dQy;$$

dTRx/dQx represents a change in revenue for good X resulting from a unit increase in sales of X While d TRy / dQx reflects a change in revenue from the sale of good Y, caused by a one unit increase in sales of good X {the demand interdependency) Similar interpretation can be made for the second equation If the two goods are complements, this effect will be positive, since an increase in the quantity sold of one product will increase the total revenue from the other product On the other hand, if products X and Yare substitutes, this effect will be negative, since an increase in the quantity sold of one product will reduce the total revenue from the other product Thus, proper attention should be given to demand inter relationships among the products a firm sells, If two goods are complements profit maximisation requires greater role of output for product X In fact, output of X should be increased until

$$dTRx/\,dQx + d\,Try/\,dQx = MCx$$

where MCx is the additional cost incurred by the firm in producing an additional unit of product X Similarly, for goods that are substitutes, it can be easily shown that ignoring demand interdependency will cause too many units of output to be produced

Pricing Strategies

Pricing of joint products

Products are often interrelated in production as well, for example some products are produce in fixed ratio like production of beef and hides in the slaughter house. When goods are produced in fixed proportion, they are regareded as the product package. Thus one hide and two sides of beef might be a bundle in the case of the cost of production between the two goods.

To determinant optimal price and output of each such product, the marginal revenue of the out bundle should be compared with its marginal cost of product.

If the total MR i.e is sum of marginal revenue from each product package is > then marginal cost, the n the output should be increase, thus, output should be increased until marginal cost equal the sum of the marginal revenues obtain from the selling an additional unit of product package.

Price Discrimination

In the monopoly case, firm may find it both feasible and profitable to sell the same product at different prices in different markets, thereby practising price discrimination. However the sale of the same product at different prices is not in itself sufficient to show that price discrimination is taking place, because the differences in prices could be due to differences in costs involved in servicing the different markets. If buyers in distant markets are charged higher prices this could be because of higher transportation costs and not due to the reason that price discrimination is being practised. True price discrimination involves charging different net prices in different markets, the net price being the actual price corrected to cost differences.

A firm can engage in price discrimination, when following conditions are fulfilled.

1. The firm must have some control over the supply of the product or service. In a perfectly competition market the seller has no control over price, therefore, he cannot practise price discrimination. Mainly price discrimination exists in monopoly as seller have total control over supply also buyers have no choice but to buy from him as there are no close substitutes

2. The different segments of buyers are separable at moderate cost and are unable to sell the product from one market to another.

3. The different markets/buyers should have different price elasticity of demand. This may be due to difference in income levels, tastes or availability of products..

The extent to which a seller can separate the market and discriminate between buyers, gives rise to three types of price discrimination.

First Degree Discrimination

First degree price discrimination is possible when every buyer of the firm's product can be charged a different price. In this case there is a separate market for each unit of output sold so that the seller can extract the maximum amount which each buyer is willing to pay for each unit sold. This form of discrimination is feasible in case of legal, medical, personal or financial services as the product is customised and sold to individual buyers It is assumed that the firm is aware of each consumer's demand curve for the commodity and fixes the price accordingly. For example a lawyer or doctor may charge different fees based on the income of the clients and patients respectively.

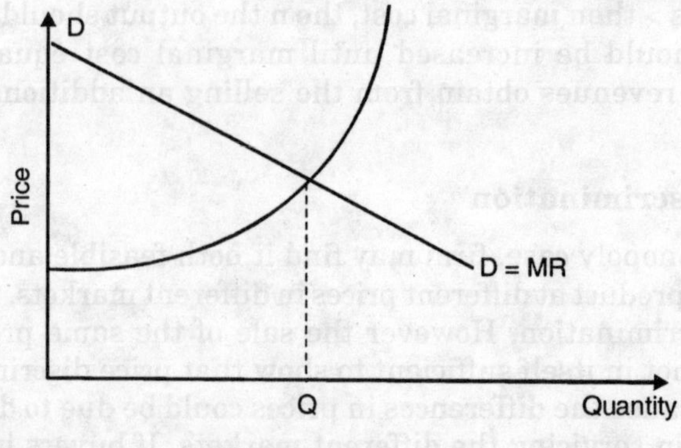

First degree price discrimination

Figure 10.1

In the figure curve MC indicates the firm's marginal cost curve. The curve DD gives the firm's demand curve. If first degree price discrimination is possible then the buyer of each unit will be forced to pay the maximum price he is willing to pay for that unit, so that the demand curve will also indicate the firm's marginal revenue. A profit maximisation firm will produce the Q level of output, and will charge different price for each unit of output.

Second Degree Price discrimination

The second degree price discrimination is based on the volume of consumer purchases . Other form of second degree price discrimination is two –tier tariff i.e. prices where customer first pay a flat fee for access and then a separate fee for usage This is common in many clubs, amusement parks etc. Second degree price discrimination is also called multipart pricing as it is a block or step type of pricing, in which the first set of units is sold at one price, a second set at another price etc.

Third Degree Discrimination

In third degree price discrimination the total market is divided into a number of sub-markets/market segment, each containing a number of buyers, who will be charged same price set for that sub-market.

Segmentation of markets can be done in many ways such as geographical location, by age, by social status and other demographical differences of consumer. For example in cinema hall, ticket prices varies according to audience preferences for different seating location in the hall.

For goods which can not be stored at reasonable cost, segmentation through timing may be possible. In case of electricity , journeys and telephone calls, it is not possible to purchase the good for onr time period and then use it at another. As a result, suppliers will be able to charge different prices at different times without arbitrage taking place. If elasticities of demand differ at different times it will be profitable as well as feasible to introduce price discrimination in the form of peak and off peak pricing.

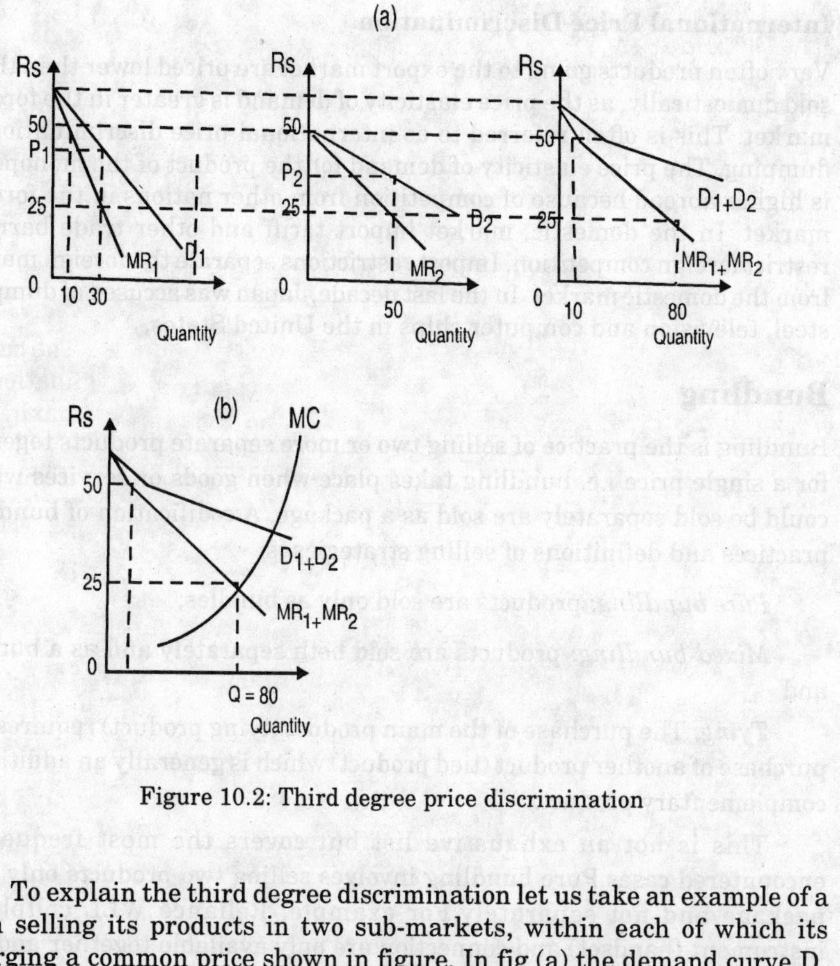

Figure 10.2: Third degree price discrimination

To explain the third degree discrimination let us take an example of a firm selling its products in two sub-markets, within each of which its charging a common price shown in figure. In fig (a) the demand curve D_1 indicates demand in the first sub-market and D_2 demand in second sub-market. Each has its own marginal revenue curve shown by MR_1 and MR_2. If the two markets are aggregated to give the overall demand and marginal revenue of the firm the result is given by lines $D = D_1 + D_2$ and $MR = MR_1 + MR_2$. In figure (b) marginal cost curve of the firm is also added to the diagram, which shows that the profit maximising level of total output is Q. The distribution of this total output across the two sub-markets can be seen by taking into consideration that in each sub-market profit is maximised when marginal revenue equals the marginal cost of supplying in that market. It is assumed here that the marginal cost of supplying the same unit to either market is the same, this implies that for profit maximisation in each market $MR_1 = MR_2 = MC$. As marginal cost at profit maximising total output is 25 which is equal to MR_1 at level of output 30 and MR_2 at level of output 50, which are the levels of outputs sold in each sub-market. The prices to be charged in each market would be P_1 from first market and P_2 from second market as can be seen in the diagram.

International Price Discrimination

Very often products going to the export market are priced lower than those sold domestically, as the price elasticity of demand is greater in the foreign market. This is often referred to as international price discrimination or dumping. The price elasticity of demand for the product of the monopolist is higher abroad because of competition from other nations in the foreign market. In the domestic, market import tariff and other trade barriers restrict foreign competition. Import restrictions separate the foreign market from the domestic market. In the last decade, Japan was accused of dumping steel, television and computer chips in the United States.

Bundling

Bundling is the practice of selling two or more separate products together for a single price i.e. bundling takes place when goods or services which could be sold separately are sold as a package. A codification of bundling practices and definitions of selling strategies is:

Pure bundling: products are sold only as bundles;

Mixed-bundling: products are sold both separately and as a bundle; and

Tying: The purchase of the main product (tying product) requires the purchase of another product (tied product) which is generally an additional complementary product.

This is not an exhaustive list but covers the most frequently encountered cases.Pure bundling involves selling two products only as a package and not separately.For example, Reliance WLL cellphone instrument (handset) and connection are only available together and not available separately. Microsoft's bundle of Windows and Internet Explorer could be considered a pure bundle. Also Cable TV Channels are an example of pure bundling. In India, the prospective CAS(Conditional Access System) also has similar channel packages where some of the channels can't be purchased separately like Zee TV, would only be available with other, Zee Channels.

Mixed Bundling involves selling products separately as well as a bundle.McDonald's Value Meals and Microsoft Office are examples of Mixed Bundling. In a recently introduced offer, The Times of India and The Nav

Bharat Times can be purchased together for weekdays for a price much less than if purchased seprarately. This is also an example of mixed bundling. In most cases mixed bundling provides price savings for consumers.

Tying involves purchase of the main product (tying product) along with purchase of another product (tied product) which is generally an additional complementary product. A well known example is that used by IBM in 1930s wherein if you purchased IBM tabulating machines agreed to purchase IBM punchcards. As a result, IBM was trying to extend its monopoly from one market to another. But it had to abandon this practice of it in 1936 due to antitrust cases. Today when you buy a Mach3 razor, you must buy the tied product i.e. the cartridge that fits into the Mach3 razor.

Financial bundling has become widespread. It has been suggested that manufacturers such as GE, General Motors and Lucent grow ever more involved in providing finance, so "manufacturing is becoming the loss-leader of the profit chain for many companies." In other words, give away the product; make money on the lending that is bundled with it. In India too, a number of automobile companies are providing finance and bundling the automobile with financing.

Bundling can be good for consumers. It can reduce "search costs" (the bundled goods are in the same place), as well as the producer's distribution costs. There are lower "transaction costs" (because a single purchase is cheaper to carry out than multiple ones). And the producer may be a more efficient bundler than the customer: few of us choose, after all, to buy the individual parts of a computer to assemble them ourselves.

In perfectly competitive market s, bundling should be done if its more efficient to than selling the products separately. Where there is less than perfect competition, that is , most markets- economic models suggest that bundling sometimes benefits consumers and sometimes producers. When firms have a measure of market "1 power, they can engage in price discrimination, charging different prices to different customers. Bundling can play a part in price discrimination, as different bundles of goods and prices may appeal to different customers. In a celebrated case that caught much media attention, Microsoft was accused of anti-competitive conduct in 'bundling' Internet Explorer and Windows as a pure bundle. Microsoft claimed they are not a bundle at all, rather a single product incapable of being broken into parts. It is of course difficult to settle such arguments and these go beyond the economic domain to the judicial domain, and are settled in courts. But the interesting aspect is that the company does not consider its product (Windows and Internet Explorer) as being capable of being broken into parts.

Two-Part Tariffs

When the buyers have to pay a fee for the right to purchase their product and then to pay a regular price per unit of the product i.e the fee for privilege of service plus prices for services consumed is called a two- part tariff. For example, local telephone companies charge a monthly base fee and then charge additional fees based on message units. Cable Tv operators also practice two part tarrif.. Theme parks such as Disney World usually employ such a pricing scheme to increase their profits. To see how the scheme works, suppose you operate a theme park and have a local monopoly. Figure below shows the demand for rides at your theme park by any given tourist, along with the marginal revenue and marginal cost of the rides. If you charge a single monopoly price, your rides will be priced at $6 each and each tourist will consume four rides per visit, spending $24.Now let's see if a bit more can be extracted from each tourist. Given the demand curve drawn, each tourist would be willing to pay more than $24 to enter your theme park and take four rides. If you know the demand curve for rides, you know that the typical tourist is enjoying a consumer surplus of$8, corresponding to the area *of* triangle ABC in the graph (area ABC=1/2*4*4). Therefore, if you charge an entry fee *of* $8 in addition to $6 per ride, you can add $8 per tourist to your profit. Given the demand curve of a typical tourist, you can add still more to your revenue from each tourist if you eliminate the price per ride and just charge an admission fee equal to consumer surplus at zero price per ride. For example, if the price per ride were zero, a tourist would go on 10 rides per visit and you would get revenue of$50 per tourist -0.5($10)(10)-instead of the $32 you would get from the two-part pricing scheme. But be careful. With more rides your marginal costs will increase, and thus your profit might not increase. Also, if you extract the entire consumer surplus with a single entry fee, you increase the tourists' cost per visit, so the total number of admissions will fall.

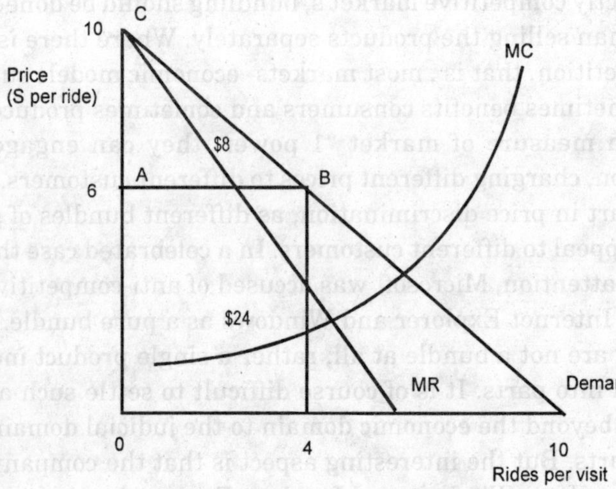

Fig: demand for rides

Two-part tariff is often a good way to increase profit by extracting some, but not all, of the consumer surplus from a monopolist's clients, A two-part tariff is often a good way to increase profit by extracting some, but not all, of the consumer surplus from a monopolist's clients. Monopolists usually experiment with various two-part tariff pricing schemes before hitting on the one that gives them maximum profit.

When Esselworld opened in December 1989, it was the first amusement park of its kind in Mumbai and so had no precedent to go by. As the objective was to sell the concept to as many people as possible, it avoided charging a composite fee, for a stiff entrance fee would keep families away. Instead, it selected what seemed the most sensible approach: pay-as-you-go. It charged and entrance fee ofRs. 5 for children and Rs. 10 for adults. And the individual rides were priced between Rs. 2 and Rs. 15.In February 1990, however, Esselworld jettisoned the split pricing strategy and switched over to composite pricing. Under the new tariff structure children were charged a fee of Rs. 80, while adults had to pay Rs 100. There were no charges levied on the rides. What prompted the switch? According to their vice-president they found difficult to implement the pay-as-you-go strategy because of logistical problems.

Transfer Pricing

The prices discussed so far are those which the firm sets for its customers. However, in an era of large multi-divisional firms prices may also need to be set for transactions that take place between one part of the firm and another. These are known as transfer prices.

If a firm wants each of its divisions to behave autonomously, choosing its own level of output and maximising its own profit, and yet still achieve maximum profits for the firm as a whole, then the concept of transfer pricing becomes important. Pricing problem arises because if one unit provides intermediate good to the other, the revenue of the unit will depend on the price charged. A high price will increase profits of the unit at the earlier stage of production, whereas a low price will make later stage production more profitable. While an incorrect price can affect the total profit earned by the firm. There are a number of cases which need to be considered in transfer pricing.

Transfer pricing in the absence of an external market

Take the first case of a firm which has two divisions, manufacturing and distribution. The manufacturing division produces an intermediate good which is sold to the distribution division, and for which there is no external market. In this case the amount which the manufacturing division chooses to produce and sell internally must be equal to the amount sold externally by the distribution division, and that amount must equal profit-maximising level of output for the firm as a whole. The analysis can be seen graphically in the figure given below.

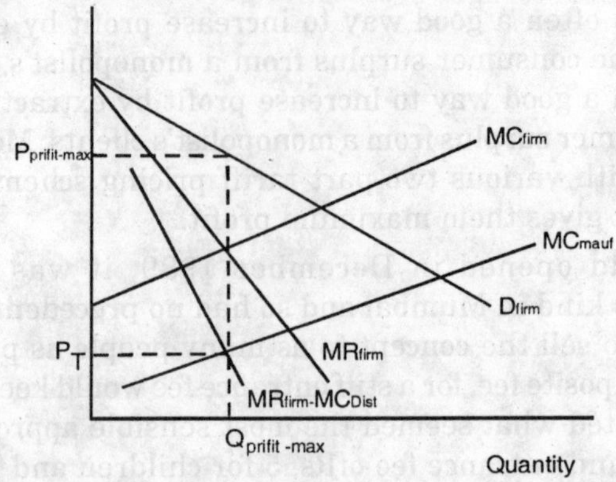

Figure 10.3: Transfer pricing in the absence of an external

In the figure the marginal revenue and marginal cost for the firm as a whole are represented by MR_{firm} and $MC_{f.irm}$ The profit maximising level of output is given by Q and the price to be set for external sales is $P_{profit\text{-}max}$. As the firm is composed of two divisions manufacturing and distribution, it is necessary to identify the cost and revenue conditions of each of those divisions. For the distribution division, revenue conditions are given by the revenue conditions for the firm as a whole. Its costs are given by the costs of distribution division plus the cost of purchasing the intermediate product from the manufacturing division. For manufacturing division, costs are equal to the costs of manufacturing and revenues are given by the transfer price at which it sells to the distribution division, multiplied by the number of units which yield it maximum profit.

The transfer price can be calculated by first considering the net marginal revenue curve for the distribution division, depicted in diagram by (MR_{firm} - MC_{dist}). This is arrived at by taking the marginal revenue to the firm as a whole and subtracting the marginal cost of distribution. For each marginal unit this gives the net marginal contribution to the distribution division, before taking account of the cost of purchasing units from the manufacturing division. The next step is to find out the marginal cost of manufacturing, which is equal to the difference between the marginal cost to the firm as a whole and the marginal cost of distribution, given in the diagram as MC_{manuf} . As shown in the diagram MC_{manuf} must intersect the net marginal revenue for distribution curve at the profit maximising level of output. This is so because at that output level:

$$Mc_{firm} = MR_{firm}$$

And subtracting MC_d form both sides we get

$$MC_{firm} - MC_{dist} = MC_{manuf} = MR_{firm} - Mc_{dist}$$

Now if the manufacturing division is to choose to supply Q level of output, the transfer price will have to be set at P_T. That price represents the marginal revenue for the manufacturing division, which will maximise its own profit by equating that to its own marginal cost, at level of output Q.

Similarly the distribution division will choose to purchase quantity Q from the manufacturing division because, in order to make maximum profit it will wish to distribute every unit of output for which the net marginal contribution, given by ($MR_{firm} - MC_{dist}$) exceeds the cost of purchasing the unit from manufacturing. In other words, the curve ($MR_{firm} - MC_{dist}$) is essentially the distribution division's demand curve.

To summarise the analysis, if there is no external market for the intermediate product, the optimal transfer price is equal to the marginal cost of manufacturing the intermediate product, at the level of output which maximises the firm's overall profit. If management of the whole firm sets the transfer price at this it can then simply order each division to maximise its own profit and the result will be consistent with profit maximisation for the firm as a whole. Alternatively, instead of actually setting that price, the management could provide the divisions with information about each other's situation which would lead to that price being arrived at without intervention from central management. If the distribution division is informed of the manufacturing division's marginal cost curve and told that this represents the supply function which determines the amount which manufacturing will supply to distribution at each price, distribution will choose to offer the transfer price P_T, which will induce manufacturing to produce just the correct amount. Similarly central management could provide the manufacturing division with information on the distribution division's net marginal contribution curve and ask it to treat that as its own marginal revenue curve when deciding how to supply.

Transfer pricing in the presence of perfect market for intermediate product

Second case to be considered is where the intermediate product may be bought or sold in a perfect market. In this case , the quantities supplied by the manufacturing division need not be equal to the quantities required by distribution division and the analysis can be explained with the figure below.

The starting point lies in the demand and marginal revenue curves for the final product, shown by the sloping curve market D_{final} and MR_{final}, and the horizontal demand curve for the intermediate product, shown by D_{inter}, which also represents the marginal revenue for the intermediate, indicated by MR_{inter}. The analysis also requires information on the marginal cost of producing the intermediate product, MC_{inter}, and the marginal contribution made by units of the final product, before making payment for the transferred intermediate product. This curve is shown by ($MR_{final} - MC_{final}$).

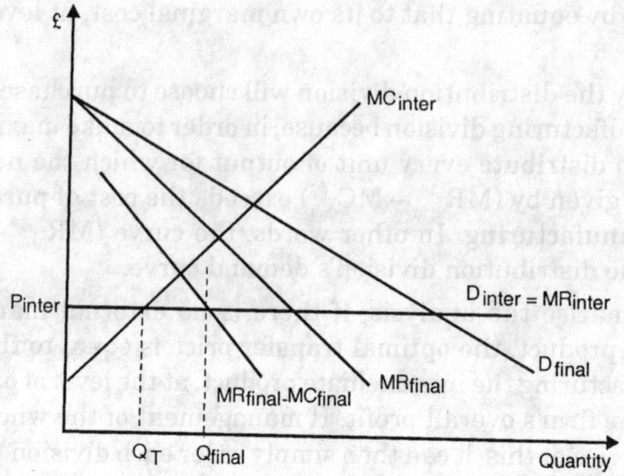

Figure 10.4: Transfer pricing with a perfectly competitive external market for the intermediate

For the department producing the intermediate product, profits will be maximised at level of output Q_T, where the marginal cost of producing the intermediate product is equal to its marginal revenue. However, for the department selling the final good profits are maximised at level of output Q_{final} where the marginal cost of purchasing the intermediate product is just equal to the marginal contribution earned by units of the final product. As figure shows, the division selling the final product requires more of the intermediate product than will be produced within the firm. However, it poses no difficulty as the difference can be made up by purchases on the open market. If the firm itself were to supply all of the intermediate product needed profits would fall as the cost of supplying the additional units of the intermediate product beyond Q_T is higher than the cost of purchasing them in the open market. Similar considerations apply if the division producing the intermediate product should wish to produce more than is required by the final product division. In that case the excess internal supply would simply be sold in the open market.

Complex Issues in Transfer Pricing

The cases discussed above in transfer pricing are simple cases, in real business world more complicated cases arises such as :

1. There may be an external market for the intermediate, but it may be imperfect.

2. There may be differences in the cost and the degree of risk associated with transactions carried out internally and those carried out between independent firms.

3. There may be many different divisions competing for the use of the intermediate product and finally there may be interdependencies between the cost and the demand for the intermediate and the final product.

If all of these complicating factors occur together it becomes extremely difficult even in theory to identify the appropriate transfer price. As firms rarely have the kind of cost and demand information which would be required to calculate optimal transfer prices in such situations it is hardle surprising that the evidence of transfer pricing in practice suggest that external market prices are used where ever possible, and where there is no external market for intermediate most firms use some form of simple cost plus formula for the setting of such prices. This latter pratice can lead to inefficiencies in the supplying division which is able to pass excessive costs on to down stream users, unless some form of standard cost is used in calculation, rather than costs actually incurred.

Various pricing methods

Cost Plus Pricing

Most firms use cost plus pricing or full cost pricing or average cost pricing technique as its simple to use. This can be an optimal pricing policy where prices are set to cover all direct costs plus a percentage mark-up for profit contribution. It applies only for market structures where companies have some market power and are, therefore, able to set prices for their products. There are various forms of cost plus pricing, the typical form involves following two steps.

Step1. The firm estimates the cost per unit of output of the product. The cost per unit is the variable production and marketing cost per unit of output plus the average overhead cost.

$AC = AVC + AFC$

$AVC = TVC/Q$

$AFC = TFC/Q$

Since this cost generally varies with output, the firm must base this computation on some assumed level. Usually, firms use for this purpose some percentage of capacity, generally between two-thirds and three-quarters.

Step2. A mark-up or profit margin is added to the estimated average cost. This mark- up is generally in form of a percentage and includes certain costs that provide a return to firm's investment. It is determined by demand elasticities and competition. Mark-ups are lower where demand is more elastic and competition intense. The mark-up can be expressed as follows:

$$\text{Mark-up} = \frac{\text{Price -Cost}}{\text{Cost}}$$

Where price -cost is profit margin. Suppose the cost of a paperback book is Rs 4 and its price is Rs 6.

Markup =(6-4) /4 = 0.50

or 50 per cent. If we solve the equation of mark-up for price we get,

Price = AC (1 + mark-up)

Thus the price of the paperback book is,

Price = 4 (1 + .50) = Rs 6

Some firms set a target -return figure, that they hope to earn, which determines

the mark-up. If Rs X is the total profit, the mark-up over cost on each unit of output will be X/Q. Thus under target rate of return pricing, price is set equal to

P = AVC + AFC + X/Q

Evaluation of Cost -Plus Pricing

Cost plus pricing may contribute to price stability and it is simple and easy to use. It provides justification for price changes. Despite these merits, it is criticised for not taking demand conditions into account. It is also criticised for relying on historical or accounting data instead of incremental or opportunity costs.

If applied properly, cost plus pricing may result in firms corning close to maximum profits. Though it appears to be inconsistent with profit maximisation as it does not takes elasticity of demand or marginal costs explicitly. As one may ask in the example, why 50 per cent mark-up was taken. Why not 25 per cent or 150 per cent? Though average cost is a basis of price determination, it is close approximation of marginal cost decision making. The mark-up is determined by price elasticity of demand for the book. To understand why this is true, recall that

$MR = P[l+1/e_p]$

Since profit is maximised when MR = MC, we can rewrite the equation as

$MC = P[l+1/e_p]$

Further under certain conditions MC = AC. Thus the equation is rewritten as

$AC = P[1+1/e_p]$

or $AC = P[(e_p + 1)/e_p]$

By rearranging the equation we get

$P = AC[e_p / (e_p + 1)]$

Under conditions of cost plus pricing

P = AC (1 + mark-up)

If we compare the previous two equations

$(1 + \text{mark-up}) = ep / (e_p + 1)]$

The equation clearly shows that, a firm's maximum profit depends on the products' price elasticity of demand. The optimal mark-up goes up as the price elasticity of demand for the product goes down. If the quantity demanded of a product is not very sensitive to its price, a high price can be set to make maximum profits. Table 10.1 shows the relationship between optimal mark-up and price elasticity of demand.

Price elasticity of demand	Optimal percentage markup of MC
1.2	500
1.4	250
1.8	125
2.5	67
5.0	25
10.0	11
20.0	5
50.0	2

Table 10.1: Optimal Price Mark-up and Price Elasticity of Demand

Incremental / Marginal Cost Pricing

Correct pricing and output decisions require incremental analysis. That is, a firm should change the price of a product, introduce a new product, accept new orders, and so on if the incremental revenue exceeds incremental costs. Incremental/marginal/direct cost pricing implies that price of a product is based on incremental cost of production.

When excess capacity exists in the short run, overhead or fixed costs are irrelevant in determining whether or not a firm should undertake a particular course of action. Since fixed or overhead costs have already been covered, any action on the part of the firm that increases revenues more than costs leads to an increase in total profits of the firm and should be undertaken. Long run effects should be considered if the firm anticipates the demand to increase in future if it decides to introduce a new product or lower prices of existing product in the short run to use idle capacity.

In case firm is operating at full capacity, then a lower price to increase sales or introduce a new product will increase all costs, including those for plant and equipment. Full cost and incremental cost pricing in such a case result in same results. Thus, a product can be produced profitably if its price exceeds incremental costs of supplying the product.

Unlike the full cost pricing that is based on average cost, incremental cost pricing considers only variable cost. The two differ on grounds of fixed cost. In a competitive situation, a firm will shut down in the short run only when the price is below the AVC, while in the long run the firm tries to cover its total average cost. That is AC = AVC + AFC, which is equal to fully distributed costs. If the firm considers incremental cost, it will not shut down in the short run.

Other approaches to pricing

Besides cost plus pricing approach there are a number of other approaches which managerial economists have identified. A brief outline of these approaches is given below:

Target return pricing: in this approach a firm's objective is to obtain a target rate of return on its capital employed.In order to link the target rate of return and the price a firm first calculates the total profit required, which is given by the formula:

Required profit = rK

where:

r = target rate of return

K = capital employed

The margin to be charged over unit cost can be arrived at by dividing the total profit required by the expected, or budgeted ,level of output, to give:

$$m = rK / Q^b$$

where:

m = the margin

Q^b = budgeted level of output

Firms use this approach do so because they wish to take a long-run view of pricing and because they wish to prevent short-run cyclical influences from leading to erratic price change. As a result it can be shown to be inconsistent with short-run profit maximisation. It is of not much assistance in maximising long-run profits because the target rate of return which is aimed for and used in the pricing calculation is usually accounting rate of return, not a true economic rate which would reflect the time-value of money.

Going rate pricing: It is also called market-determined or competition-oriented pricing. In its simplest form this is the type of pricing policy which is imposed by market forces on firms operating in a perfectly competitive industry. Each firm is obliged to charge the same price as the others, or lose all its customers. In more complex situations a firm may not simply set exactly the same price as its competitors, but may use their prices as a benchmark against which it adjusts its own price to take account of differences between them. For instance , a firm which is producing a high cost/ high quality variant of the product will set its price above that of the competitor, while a firm aiming for cost leadership may set a lower price. A firm attempting to enter a new market may set its price lower than that of rivals in order to overcome existing brand loyalties and build a large enough volume of sales to allow economies of scale and capacity utilisation to be achieved.

Competition oriented pricing takes proper account of rival's prices and their impact on the demand conditions facing the individual firm then it potentially offers a means of earning maximum profit. In real practice whether this happens or not depends upon the firm's ability to judge the appropriate differences between its own price and that of the competition. In the case of perfect competition this judgement is simple as the differences must be zero. In other market conditions it may be more difficult, especially in oligopoly where a firm's rivals will react to its price setting. One situation where this problem may be resolved is that of price leadership. If one firm in an oligopolistic industry acts as a price leader, followers may respond by setting the same price, or one which has been adjusted in a way which is mutually understood by all, so that the rivals know how each other will react, thereby creating an orderly form of competition.

Sealed bid pricing: This type of pricing is commonly associated with government purchases of large quantities of goods or services, or with major construction projects, the purchaser advertise the specifications which it wishes to meet and invites potential suppliers to submit the prices at which they are prepared to supply to that specification. Bids are made in confidence i.e sealed bids in order to avoid collusion and the firm which offers to meet the specification at the lowest price is awarded the contract, provided the purchaser is satisfied that the supplier will be able to deliver on time and to a satisfactory quality. As this method is totally competition base, there is a risk of collusion among the bidders. In such a case, the buyers may have to pay very high price if sellers collude. Conversely, the sellers may receive very low price if buyers collude.

Information for pricing decisions

A lot of information and authentic data relating to the product and its substitutes, and the relevant markets is required by a firm for scientific pricing decision. The nature of detailed information may vary from product to product, market to market, and firm to firm. At the firms level the information could be taken from past records of firm regarding costs incurred and revenue earned etc. Other important sources of information are economic advisors offices, economic periodicals and dailies like economic times, business standard, financial express etc, data published by finance ministry and various organisations like FICCI, etc. The most general kind of information and data needed for facilitating correct pricing decisions are :

Product information: a) Production cost details, b)Duties like excise duties, cess etc, c)Product guarantees and after sales requirements, d) floor price and ceiling price regulations, e)packing requirements, f) percentage incidence of defective /rejected pieces of the product.

Market information: a) prevalent market prices, b) price of substitutes, c) prices of competitors, d) consumption patterns, e) production statistics, f) consumer preference, brand loyalty etc., g) sales promotion costs, h) channels of distribution and the margins allowed to the various intermediaries.

Information regarding firm: a) production capacity of the firm-installed and utilised, b) the market share of the firm- total and regional.

Pricing and the product life cycle

The standard analysis of pricing take into consideration the demand for a product, volumes that can be sold depending upon consumer behaviour. Unless any of these factors change demand is assumed to be constant, so that time itself has no influence upon the level of demand for a product. However, marketing analysts frequently find it useful to introduce the concept of the product life cycle into the discussion of pricing and marketing strategies.

The product life cycle (PLC) hypothesis consists essentially of the assertion that products have different lives and that in course of those lives they pass through a series of distinct stages (shown in figure).

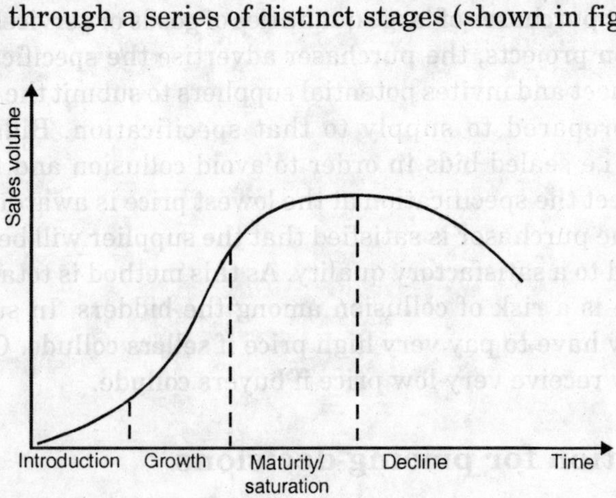

The product life cycle

Fig:10.5

The first stage in the PLC is the introductory period when potential buyers are hardly aware of the product. At this stage in the product's life sales volume is low and demand is price inelastic. The marketing department is likely to concentrate its effort on promotion of the new product, rather than on pricing it, but at this stage a substantial margin should be charged over marginal cost, if the aim is to make maximum profit.

The second stage of PLC is the growth phase, when buyers become more aware of the product and sales grow rapidly. As competitors will also have had sufficient time to enter market, demand will have become more price elastic, implying that the optimal price involves a smaller margin over costs.

The third stage is that of maturity and saturation when the growth of sales slows down, eventually to zero. Customers are well informed about the product and experienced in its use and competitors are well versed in the production of substitutes, leading to an increase in the elasticity of demand, and a further reduction in optimal margin between price and marginal cost.

The fourth and final stage is that of decline, arising from changes in buyer's tastes and requirements, increasing competition, or technological progress. In this phase, sales volume declines, competition amongst incumbent firms is fierce and demand is highly price elastic, leading to very narrow margins between cost and price.

It is possible to identify a relatively simple relationship between the different stages of the PLC and the optimal level of price, the two being linked by the gradually increasing elasticity of demand over time. However, both the theoretical rationale and the practical usefulness of the product life cycle concept are the subject of debate.

While the development of a product through various stages of the cycle is usually presented as an inevitable result of forces beyond the control of the firm it is clear that some factors, like the extent of buyer awareness or the entry of competing forms into the market, are at least partly dependent upon the firm's own actions, such as its spending on promotion and its decision on whether or not to set entry forestalling prices. It may be possible, therefore, for a firm to alter the development of the product cycle through its own actions, thereby rendering valueless any prescriptions based upon the inevitability of the transition from one phase to another.

At the practical level, there are a range of problems. The form and timing of the PLC may vary widely with the level of aggregation at which it is applied, so that the life cycle of a broad product category will generally be much longer than that of a product form or an individual brand. There is a real danger that if managers have been persuaded of the existence of the product cycle they may act on that belief in ways which reduce the firm's profits and simultaneously confirm the manager's mistaken confidence in the usefulness of the PLC as a forecasting tool. For instance, if sales of a product have been growing for sometime, believers in the PLC hypothesis will be expecting a slowdown in sales as maturity is reached, at which point they will reduce the level of promotion and advertising for the product, and probably reduce its price, on the grounds that these are the appropriate actions for a product which is in maturity and is about to decline. However, these actions in themselves may lead to fulfilment of the prediction. Price cutting may stimulate retaliation from competitors and the reduction in promotion will erode buyer loyalty and alter buyer's perception of the product. As a result, a product which might have yielded healthy profits for a number of years goes into decline, not as a consequence of real changes in environment but because the decision makers had an inappropriate faith in the product life cycle hypothesis.

Pricing New Products

There are two basic strategies for pricing new products given by Dean (1950). The first approach is known as Skimming strategy. In this case the firm sets an initially high price for the product, deliberately selling it to a relatively selected group of users who are prepared to pay a high price. As the product moves through its life cycle and imitations take place, price can be gradually reduced as demand becomes more elastic until the margin between price and cost is much lower. The second strategy is known as penetration strategy. This involves setting a low price at the outset, in order to build a relatively large market quickly.

Skimming is recommended when there are sufficient buyers prepared to pay a high price, when demand is price inelastic, when a high price will not attract rapid entry, and when the cost penalty for operating at relatively low volume is small. Penetration is recommended when demand is price elastic, when new firms can enter quickly if attracted by high price and when there are cost advantages to be had by operating at high volumes of output.

Questions:

1. Discuss the role of costs in pricing.
2. How does consumer behaviour affect pricing policies?
3. What are the principal pricing problems of a manufacturer? How does consumer behaviour affect pricing policies?
4. Critically examine price as a weapon of competition.
5. What would be your pricing strategy (i) if you are able to reach economies of scale, (ii) there is a fall in the price of your major raw materials?

6. What is the utility of the cost-plus pricing for public sector units?
7. What are the advantages and limitations of marginal pricing?
8. What methods do businessmen employ in setting prices?
9. Would you prefer-a low penetration price to a high initial price for a new product?
10. Discuss the price policies to be adopted in the *(a)* pioneering stage, and *(b)*maturity stage of a product.
11. Your firm has introduced a new product in the market which has never been marketed before. As a marketing manager, you have to advise on the price strategy to be followed and you are assumed to be aware of Product Life Cycle and also to be maximising long-run profits and not immediate profits. Your exclusive patent on the product expires in three years and technology matures and small firms can enter in seven years from the date product is launched.
    (a) How will you formulate your pricing strategy?
    (b) Suppose the demand is expected to be 20,000 units in the fourth year and by the end of third year your firm expects to produce 12,000 units in three equal-sized plants operating at minimum efficient scale of production. Will the pricing strategy change? Give reasons for your answer.
12. What is meant by 'price discrimination'? What are its objectives? Is price discrimination anti-social?
13. Distinguish between various- degrees of differential pricing. What conditions are needed for effective differential pricing?
14. Explain the effects of government intervention in price fixation. What steps necessary to make this intervention effective?
15. How does a company determine the prices of its products? Examine in the connection the validity of the theory that long-period price is equal to cost.
16. "Pricing decisions are constrained by product policy decisions and considerations of corporate planning." Comment on the above statements by giving real world examples.
17. "A rise in demand raises both equilibrium price and quantity, a fall in demand lowers both. A rise in supply raises equilibrium quantity but lowers equilibrium price; a fall in supply lowers equilibrium quantity but raises equilibrium price. Explain
18. Examine the weaknesses of the traditional theory of pricing from the point of view of an individual firm.

11

Capital Budgeting and Investment Decisions

Introduction

Capital budgeting is a required managerial tool. One duty of a financial manager is to choose investments with satisfactory cash flows and rates of return. Therefore, a financial manager must be able to decide whether an investment is worth undertaking and be able to choose intelligently between two or more alternatives. To do this, a sound procedure to evaluate, compare, and select projects is needed. This procedure is called **capital budgeting**.

Capital is a Limited Resource

In the form of either debt or equity, capital is a very limited resource. There is a limit to the volume of credit that the banking system can create in the economy. Commercial banks and other lending institutions have limited deposits from which they can lend money to individuals, corporations, and governments. In addition, reserve Bank of India, requires each bank to maintain part of its deposits as reserves. Having limited resources to lend, lending institutions are selective in extending loans to their customers. But even if a bank were to extend unlimited loans to a company, the management of that company would need to consider the impact that increasing loans would have on the overall cost of financing.

In reality, any firm has limited borrowing resources that should be allocated among the best investment alternatives. One might argue that a company can issue an almost unlimited amount of common stock to raise capital. Increasing the number of shares of company stock, however, will serve only to distribute the same amount of equity among a greater number of shareholders. In other words, as the number of shares of a company increases, the company ownership of the individual stockholder may proportionally decrease.

The argument that capital is a limited resource is true of any form of capital, whether debt or equity (short-term or long-term, common stock) or retained earnings, accounts payable or notes payable, and so on. Even the best-known firm in an industry or a community can increase its borrowing up to a certain limit. Once this point has been reached, the firm will either be denied more credit or be charged a higher interest rate, making borrowing a less desirable way to raise capital.

Faced with limited sources of capital, management should carefully decide whether a particular project is economically acceptable. In the case of more than one project, management must identify the projects that will contribute most to profits and, consequently, to the value (or wealth) of the firm. This, in essence, is the basis of capital budgeting.

Definition: Capital budgeting refers to the investment decisions of current finances most efficiently in long-term productive activities with expectations of flow of benefits over a long period of time. Also it could be said that, capital budgeting is investment decision-making as to whether a project is worth undertaking. Capital budgeting is basically concerned with the justification of capital expenditures.

Current expenditures are short-term and are completely written off in the same year that expenses occur. Capital expenditures are long-term and are amortized over a period of years .

The decision of "where to invest" is significant because of several reasons

1. Funds available to a firm are limited.
2. There are a variety of options to invest the available funds.
3. Investment decisions have long-term impact on the investor and the society.
4. Long-term capital decisions are mostly irreversible.

Types of Capital Projects

Capital projects are those that are expected to generate returns for more than an year. Capital budgeting is the process of planning capital projects, raising funds and efficiently allocating resources to those capital projects. In general, firms classify investment projects into following categories:

1. Replacement: Investments to replace existing equipment that is worn out in the production process with more efficient equipment. Here one has to match the costs with the expected increase in earnings, i.e. savings resulting from lower operating and/ or profit from additional volume.

2. Expansion : Shall we build or buy a new plant or factory ? Investments to expand production facilities in response to increased demand for the firm's traditional products in traditional or existing markets. In case of expansion decision one has to estimate both the costs which will be incurred and the receipts which will be earned , if the investment is done. Net cash flow of the asset or the project which is equal to the receipts from the sale of output of the asset minus all the costs (except depreciation on the asset) incurred in producing that output, has to be estimated for each year of the asset's life and then compared with the amount to be invested.

3.Choice of equipment: Which of the several proposed equipments shall be purchased for a given purpose say for production process of a new product? The criterion for making choice should be which equipment will give the largest return on investment to the firm. Here as the receipts from sale of the product will be the same whichever equipment is used, they do not enter the problem of choice.

4.Buy or lease: Should we buy or lease the desired building or equipment? If the asset is acquired on lease or rented, then a series of annual or quarterly or monthly rental payments are made. If the asset is purchased there will be a large initial outlay, but no further payments . Here the question arises which course of action will be better to follow? The criterion would be whether or not the investment required to purchase the asset will earn an adequate return as compared with leasing.

Basic Steps of Capital Budgeting

1. Estimate the cash flows
2. Assess the riskiness of the cash flows.
3. Determine the appropriate discount rate.
4. Find the PV of the expected cash flows.
5. Accept the project if PV of inflows > costs. IRR > Hurdle Rate and/ or payback < policy

Definitions:

Independent versus mutually exclusive projects.
Normal versus nonnormal projects.

Basic Data

	Expected Net Cash Flow	
Year	**Project L**	**Project S**
0	(Rs 100)	(Rs 100)
1	10	70
2	60	50
3	80	20

Evaluation Techniques

A. ***Payback period***

B. Net present value (NPV)

C. Internal rate of return (IRR)

D. Modified internal rate of return (MIRR)

E. Profitability index

Payback Period

Payback period = Expected number of years required to recover a project's cost.

	Project L	
	Expected Net Cash Flow	
Year	**Project L**	**Project S**
0	(Rs 100)	(Rs 100)
1	10	(90)
2	60	(30)
3	80	50

$\text{Payback}_L = 2 + \text{Rs}30/\text{Rs}80$ years

= 2.4 years.

$\text{Payback}_S = 1.6$ years.

Weaknesses of Payback:

1. Ignores the time value of money. This weakness is eliminated with the discounted payback method.
2. Ignores cash flows occurring after the payback period.

Net Present Value

$$NPV = \sum_{t=0}^{n} \frac{CF_t}{(1+k)^t}$$

Project L:

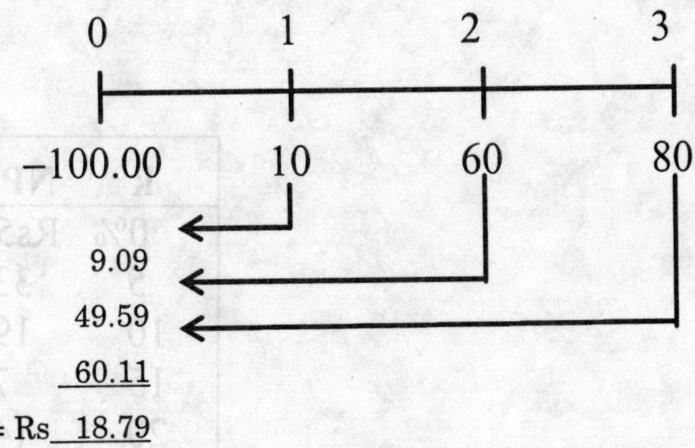

$NPV_L = \text{Rs}\ 18.79$

$NPV_S = \text{Rs}19.98$

If the projects are independent, accept both.

If the projects are mutually exclusive, accept Project S since $NPV_S > NPV_L$.

Note: NPV declines as k increases, and NPV rises as k decreases.

Internal Rate of Return

$$IRR: \sum_{t=0}^{n} \frac{CF_t}{(1+IRR)^t} = \$0 = NPV$$

Project L:

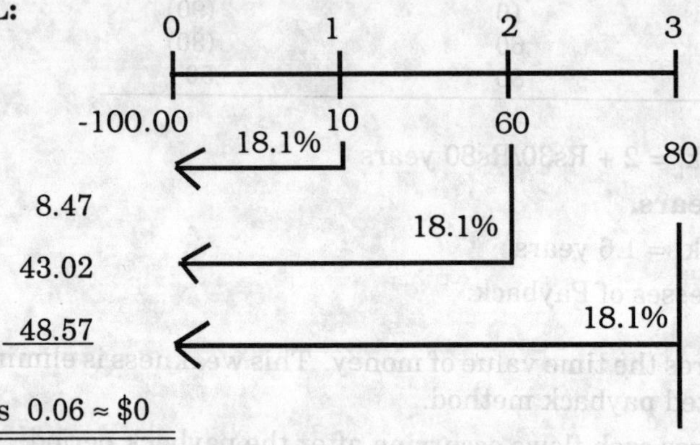

$IRR_L = 18.1\%$

$IRR_S = 23.6\%$

If the projects are independent, accept both because IRR > k.

If the projects are mutually exclusive, accept Project S since $IRR_S > IRR_L$.

Note: IRR is independent of the cost of capital.

k	NPV_L	NPV_S
0%	Rs50	Rs40
5	33	29
10	19	20
15	7	12
20	(4)	5

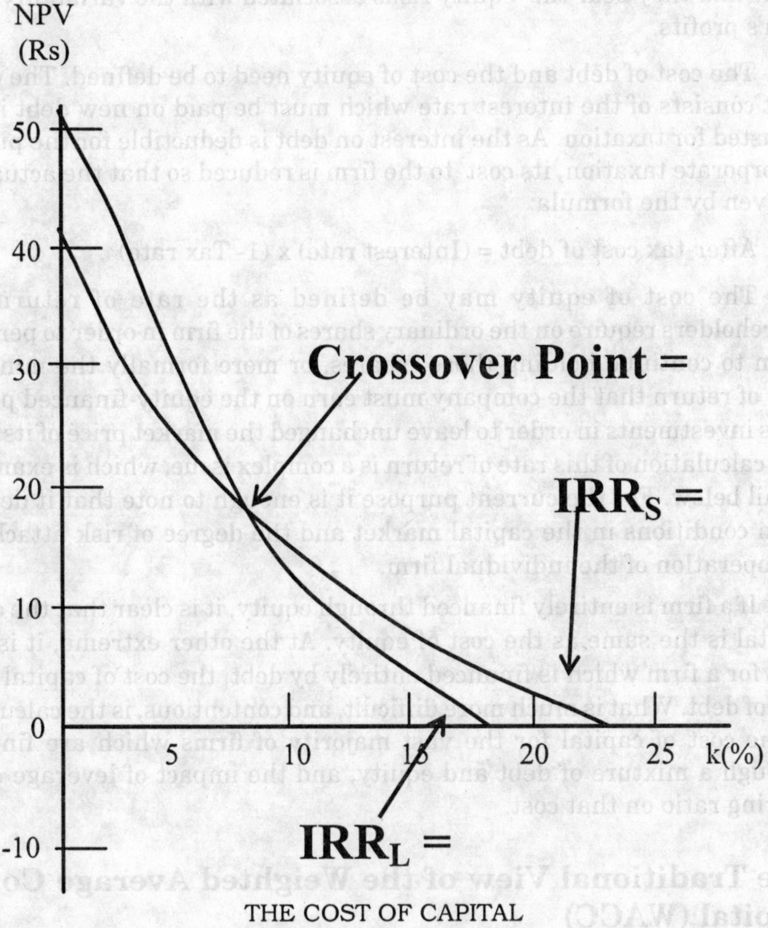

The Weighted Average Cost of Capital

A firm may raise the funds for investment projects in a number of ways, including loans, debentures, retained earnings, and equity issues. Each of these may take a variety of forms in detail and each is subject to different accounting, legal and tax procedures, which render a detailed and comprehensive discussion impossibly complex. For simplicity, just two different types of capital will be considered. The first is **debt** and the second is **equity**.

The key characteristics of debt are that those who hold it have first call on any operating profits earned by the firm and they bear the risk of default. The key characteristics of equity are that its holders are the owners of the firm, they are the beneficiaries of any increase in the firm's value, they have the right to any profits made after interest payments have been made and they bear the equity risks associated with the variability of the firm's profits.

The cost of debt and the cost of equity need to be defined. The cost of debt consists of the interest rate which must be paid on new debt issues, adjusted for taxation. As the interest on debt is deductible for the purpose of corporate taxation, its cost to the firm is reduced so that the actual cost is given by the formula:

After-tax cost of debt = (Interest rate) x (1- Tax rate)

The cost of equity may be defined as the rate of return that shareholders require on the ordinary shares of the firm in order to persuade them to continue holding those shares, or more formally the minimum rate of return that the company must earn on the equity-financed portion of its investments in order to leave unchanged the market price of its stock. The calculation of this rate of return is a complex issue, which is examined. detail below. For the current purpose it is enough to note that it depends upon conditions in the capital market and the degree of risk attached to the operation of the individual firm.

If a firm is entirely financed through equity, it is clear that the cost of capital is the same as the cost of equity. At the other extreme, it is clear that for a firm which is financed entirely by debt, the cost of capital is the cost of debt. What is much more difficult, and contentious, is the calculation of the cost of capital for the vast majority of firms which are financed through a mixture of debt and equity, and the impact of leverage or the gearing ratio on that cost.

The Traditional View of the Weighted Average Cost of Capital (WACC)

The starting point for the debate is to be fbund in the 'traditional' view of the issue which states that the cost of capital is given by a weighted average of the cost of equity and the cost of debt, as given by the formula for the weighted average cost of capital (WACC):

WACC = (After-tax cost of debt x Proportion of debt financing) + (Cost of equity x Proportion of equity financing)

Both the cost of debt and the cost of equity are held to vary with the gearing ratio, as shown in Fig. 11.1 below, which also shows the WACC.

As the figure shows, the cost of debt is held to be lower than the cost of equity, whatever the gearing ratio, because the holders of debt have the first call on the firm's profits. They are therefore exposed to less risk and will accept a lower level of return. As the gearing ratio increases, the cost of debt increases because the higher the level of debt, the higher the probability that the firm's profits are insufficient to service the debt and make repayments when due. At higher levels of gearing, the holders of debt are exposed to greater risk and therefore require a higher rate of return.

Similar considerations apply to the cost of equity. It begins at a higher level than the cost of debt because equity-holders bear a greater degree of risk, and it rises with the gearing ratio because a higher level of debt increases the risk to equity holders as well as to debt holders. The cost of debt and the cost of equity curves are therefore as shown in Fig. 11.1. The WACC which corresponds to these curves is U-shaped, as shown, because as the gearing ratio rises from a low level, the increasing proportion of cheaper debt lowers the average until it reaches the minimum point, after which the increasing risk attached to greater proportions of debt raise the WACC.

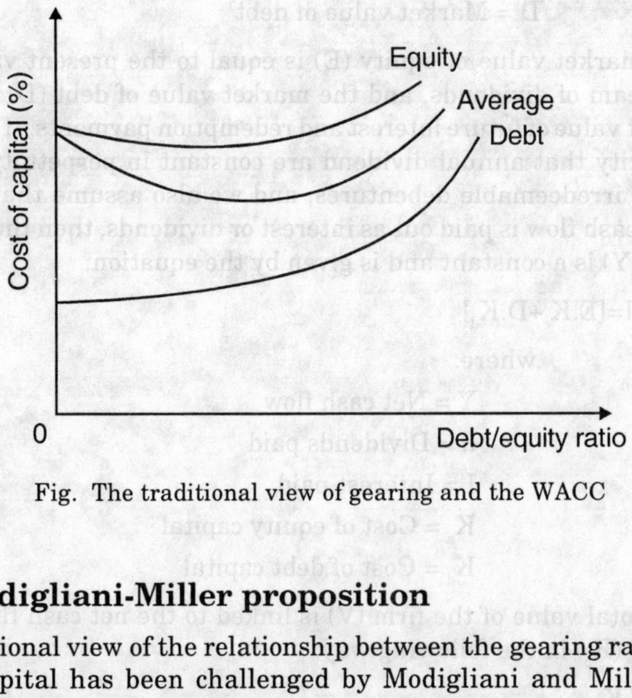

Fig. The traditional view of gearing and the WACC

The Modigliani-Miller proposition

The traditional view of the relationship between the gearing ratio and the cost of capital has been challenged by Modigliani and Miller (M-M). According to M-M, the cost of capital is not affected by the gearing ratio, as it is constant and equal to the cost of equity in a firm which has no debt.

The starting point for the M-M proposition lies in a very rigorous set of assumptions. These are:

- There are no taxes
- The capital market is efficient and competitive
- There are no transactions costs, .There are no costs associated with bankruptcy
- Shareholders can borrow on the same terms as corporations
- The cost of debt is constant, whatever the level of gearing.

If these assumptions hold, the total market value of two firms which are identical except for their levels of gearing must be the same, and their WACCs must be same. If they were not, investors could improve their position by 'arbitrage', sell the shares of one and buying shares in the other, which would alter the relative prices of shares until the WACCs become equal. The level of gearing is therefore irrelevant to the WACC and the value of the firm.This very striking proposition requires further explanation if it is to be fully understood. The total market value of a firm is given by the following equation:

$V = D+E$ where:

V = Total market value

E = Market value of equity

D = Market value of debt

The market value of equity (E) is equal to the present value of the future stream of dividends, and the market value of debt (D) is equal to the present value of future interest and redemption payments. If we assume for simplicity that annual dividend are constant in perpetuity and debt consists of irredeemable debentures, and we also assume that all of the firm's net cash flow is paid out as interest or dividends, then the firm's net cash flow (Y) is a constant and is given by the equation:

$$Y=d+I=[E.K_e+D.K_d]$$

where:

Y = Net cash flow

d = Dividends paid

I = Interest paid

K_e = Cost of equity capital

K_d = Cost of debt capital

The total value of the firm (V) is linked to the net cash flow (Y) and the WACC (K_o) in the following way:

$$V=Y / K_o$$

If we now take two firms which have the same net cash flows and the same level of business risk, it is possible to show that they must have the same WACC and the same market value, even if they have different levels of gearing. If the assumptions made by M-M are valid, the WACC is independent of the gearing ratio and is equal to the cost of equity in an ungeared firm. The relationship between the cost of debt, the cost of equity and the WACC is as given in Fig. 11.2, The WACC is constant, the cost of debt is constant and the cost of equity increasa in a linear fashion with the gearing ratio.

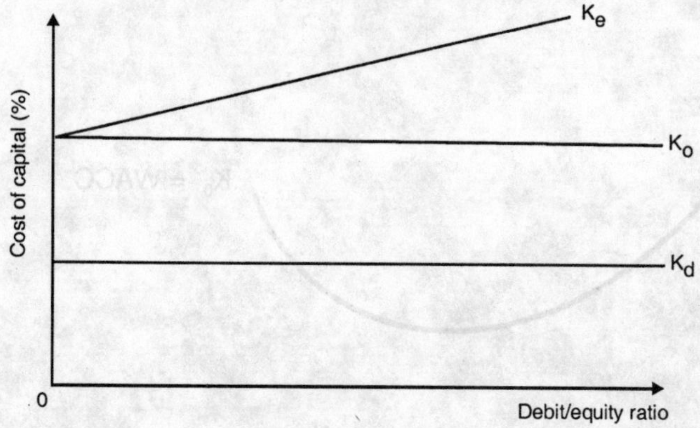

Fig. 11.2 The M-M view of gearing and the WACC

While the M -M proposition provides a rigorous approach to the cost of capital, and illustrates the weaknesses of the traditional approach, its assumptions are extremely restrictive and the conclusions change if they are relaxed. The existence of transactions costs will affect the process of reaching equilibrium, although exactly how is not clear. If individuals and corporations cannot borrow at the same cost and risk, then 'home-made' gearing cannot provide a perfect substitute for corporate gearing, and the arbitrage process will be impeded. If there are costs associated with bankruptcy then the higher probability of bankruptcy which is associated with a higher gearing ratio will mean that investors require a higher rate of return from more highly geared firms.

Perhaps the most important issue of all in practice concerns the M -M assumption that there are no corporate taxes, which is clearly unrealistic. If the existence of taxation is recognised, and the interest on debt is tax deductible, then a higher level of gearing allows the firm to increase its net cash flows. The market value of the firm increases as gearing increases, and the WACC declines. As a result a firm seeking to maximise its total market value would have a capital structure consisting of 99.99 per cent debt and the minimum possible amount of equity. This is an uncomfortable result in many ways because while it is clearly more realistic to assume that taxes are present, the conclusion drawn as a result, is not one which matches firms' real-world behaviour where very high gearing ratios are rarely observed. As a result, the debate remains unresolved. Perhaps the most satisfactory, though tentative, conclusion is that the combined effects of bankruptcy costs and taxation lead to a W ACC curve as shown in Fig.

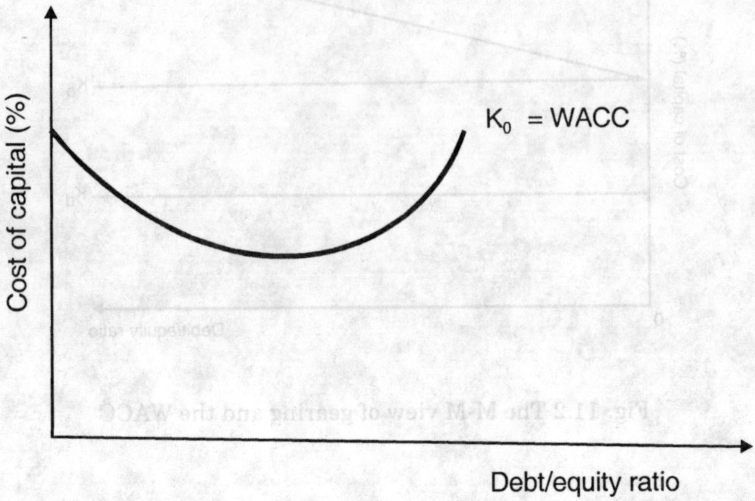

Fig: WACC and gearing in the presence of taxes and bankruptcy costs

As the figure shows, at low levels of gearing, WACC declines with higher gearing, due to the advantages of tax relief on debt interest. However, beyond some point these advantages begin to be offset by the bankruptcy costs associated with higher gearing. At very high levels of gearing, the bankruptcy effect is more powerful than the tax effect and the WACC begins to rise. If this conclusion is valid, capital structure does have an effect upon the WACC and the M -M proposition no longer holds.

The Cost of Equity Capital I: the Dividend Valuation Approach

It has been noted above that the cost of equity capital (K_e) is the rate of return which the firm must earn on its equity in order to leave the market price of its stock unchanged. The estimation of that rate may be approached in two different ways based upon the **dividend valuation model** or the **capital** asset **pricing** model, each of which merit brief consideration.

The dividend valuation approach to the cost of equity capital is based upon the relationship between dividends, market price and the expected return on an investment As the market price of a firm's equity (E) is equal to the present value of the dividend it earns (d), discounted by the required rate of return (K_e), the value of a firm which produces an annual flow of dividends which is constant (i.e. 'd' is the value of perpetuity) is given by the equation:

$E = d / K_e$ which can be rearranged to give $K_e = d / E$

This is a very simple method to use for the estimation of the cost of equity and is restricted to the case where dividends are constant over time. A more sophisticated version may be developed for the case where **dividend growth** is constant over time, rather than the **dividend** level. If 'd_1,' is the dividend payable at the end of the first year, and 'g' is the growth rate of dividends, the market value of equity is given by :

$$E = d_1 / (1- K_e) + d_1(1 + g) / (1- K_e)^2 + d_1(1+g)^2 / (1- K_e)^2 + ... + d_1(1+g)^n / (1- K_e)^n$$

Simple algebraic manipulation of this equation allows it to be rearranged as:

$E = d_1 / (K_e - g)$ *or*

$K_e = d_1/E + g$

In order to make use of this formula, some estimate has to be made of the dividend growth rate 'g'. The simplest approach is to extrapolate the past rate of growth adjusted in the light of any additional information which is available, or more sophisticated forecasting techniques might be preferred. Whichever method of estimation is chosen, the basic approach remains the same, using the present value of the expected future stream of dividends to establish the relationship between dividends, market price and the expected rate of return.

The cost of equity II: the capital asset pricing model

The dividend valuation approach makes no explicit reference to the degree of risk attached to the ownership of equity, being based entirely upon the future flow of benefits which it is expected to generate. An alternative approach, which places the valuation of risk at the heart of the analysis, is known as the capital asset pricing model (CAPM). This has its basis in a relatively complex body of financial analysis, known as portfolio theory, which lies outside the scope of this text. Nevertheless, it is possible to outline the basic principles involved, leaving a fuller treatment to the financial management textbooks.

The starting point for a brief overview of the CAPM is to note that the required return on a risky security may be divided into two components. The first is the return which could be earned on a riskless security and the second is a premium in compensation for the risk involved. (It is generally assumed that investors are risk- averse to some degree, and not risk-lovers.)

The risk-free return depends upon general conditions in financial markets and may be reasonably approximated by the return on Government bonds. The premium for risk which is to be applied for an individual firm is calculated by measuring the variability of the return on the firm's stock, and comparing it with the variability of the 'market portfolio' of stocks, which reflects the variability of the stock market as a whole. This is encapsulated in a measure known as the 'beta co-efficient' for the individual stock. If the shares of a firm have a 'beta' which is greater than one, investing in those shares is more risky than investing in the stock market as a whole. If the beta is less than one, the shares are less risky than the market as a whole, and if beta equals one investing in the share bears exactly the same risk as investing in the market as a whole. The expected return on a security is then given by the following equation:

$$K_e = R_F + b[K_M - R_F]$$

where:

R_F = the return on a risk-free security

b = the 'beta' for the individual security

K_M = the return on the market portfolio of shares, representing the market as a whole

As the equation shows, if the security has a beta of one, the expected return will be the same as that for the market as a whole. If beta is larger than one, the return will be higher, if beta is less than one it will be lower, reflecting the lower level of risk associated with the individual security being assessed.

Clearly, the calculation of beta is of central importance to the application of the *CAPM.* It may be defined as the co-variance between the returns on a security and the returns to the market as a whole, divided by the variance of the returns to the market. Investment advisory services publish estimates of 'beta' for most stocks, which allow the CAPM to be used to calculate cost of equity for the stock of most major companies.

Whether or not the CAPM is an entirely effective means of estimating the cost of equity capital remains a matter for debate and for empirical testing which is extremely difficult. All of the returns referred to in the model are expected returns which are not directly observable and may not be well approximated by historical returns. The market portfolio, whose returns and variability are central to the analysis is very difficult to construct but should in principle contain every asset a' investors, including human capital, personal money and jewellery, and a whole range of assets which are non-marketable and whose returns cannot be directly observed. The empirical tests which have been carried out suggest that the CAPM has some predictive value, but have also tended to find that low beta stocks earn more than the CAPM would predict, while high beta stocks earn less. Factors other than beta, like price/earnings ratios and firm size also seem to have an influence on the rate of return, which reduces the usefulness of the CAPM equation which relies entirely upon beta as the determining variable.

Techniques for appraisal of investments / appraisal of profitability

For evaluation of projects , we need to know some basic data about the alternative proposals like the initial investment, the economic life, the scrap value, if any, the annual earnings and the cash flow. For objective evaluation, we also consider a)the timing of the proceeds over the economic life of the investment proposal b) the duration of proceeds, i.e. number of years the project is capable of generating proceeds. The various methods of appraising the relative profitability of the alternative investment projects are:

1.Pay-back method
2.Accounting rate of return
3.Internal rate of return
4.Net present value index method.

The pay back method and the accounting method are considered as traditional methods of investment appraisal as they are very commonly used. The Discounted cash flow method or the internal rate of return and the net present value index method are the modern techniques as the development and the use of discounting methods are relatively new.

For explaining all the methods of appraising profitability of alternative investment projects we would take the following example of five alternative proposals given in table below

Table: Basic data about alternative proposals.

ProposalsI	nitial investment` (in Rs)	Annual cash flow (in Rs)	Life in years
1	60000	12000	15
2	80000	22500	20
3	2150	1500	3
4	20500	4000	10

The relavant cost of capital is 10 percent.

Pay back method

This is a thumb rule method to decide about the desirability of the project. The pay back period is the length of time required for the initial investment to be recouped out of the annual cash flow produced by the investment. This method gives only the number of years it will take to recover the initial investment and does not measure the rate of return. The formula is:

Pay back period = Initial investment / Annual cash flow

If the cash flow is not uniform over the years, then we calculate cumulative cash flow. When cumulative cash flow is equal to the initial investment , we get the pay back period.The pay back period for various projects of our example would be

Proposal 1	60,000 / 12,000	= 5 years
Proposal 2	80,000 / 22,500	= 3.5 years
Proposal 3	2,150 / 1,500	= 1.4 years
Proposal 4	20,500 / 4,000	= 5.1 years

The pay back method is widely used in practice because it is seen as a means of avoiding risk and ensuring that firms maintain adequate liquidity. This method emphasizes quick cash return flow. This method is specially useful in industries subject to rapid technological advances, where the plant becomes obsolete before the end of its physical life. In period of tight money when funds are difficult to get, a quick pay back project may be preferred to one which may yield a higher rate of return, yet commit funds for a longer period of time i.e. this method favours a short term project against a long term one.

Limitation of pay back method

1. It ignores the time value of money. The returns to an investment are simply added together year by year until they equal the initial investment, at which point the pay back period is established. As a result an amount of money which accrues in year one of a project carries exactly the same weight as the same amount of money accruing in year three, provided that the cut off point for acceptance of a project is three years or more. However, this ignores the fact that money accruing in year one could be invested with interest for two years and be worth more than the original amount by year three.

2. It ignores any returns which accrue after the payback period, which is itself chosen arbitrarily. For example, if two projects have identical payback periods of three years, but one of them yields very substantial profits in year four and the other yields nothing, the technique will not discriminate between them.

3. The pattern of returns within the payback period is ignored. Hence, a project which yields very rapid returns within the first two years of a five year payback period will be rated in exactly the same way as a project which pays back nothing until a full repayment in the fifth year.

Accounting Rate of Return

This method essentially consists of estimating the net profits accruing to a project over its life, calculating an average profit per year, and then expressing that profit as a percentage of the initial outlay, to give an estimate of rate of return. Projects are then accepted if the rate of return calculated exceeds the firm's minimum requirement and projects are ranked by their rate of return.It is also called financial statement method. In this method capital employed and related income are determined following the principles and practices employed in accounting. The formula for calculating the rate of return is:

(Estimated net profits / capital employed) x 100

Some firms compute this rate of return on the initial amount invested others on the average amount invested over the life of the project. The average investment may be calculated in this manner (Initial investment + scrap value) / 2. Average investment assumes regular periodic recovery of capital over the life of the project and to that extent is more realistic. Applying the formula to our example of five alternative proposals we get rate of returns as shown in table below. But for calculating the rate of return under the accounting method , we must know the net profit. Therefore we would subtract depreciation from the annual cash flow to get net profit.

Table: Rate of return under accounting method.

Proposals	Initial investment (in Rs.)	Annual cash flow (in Rs)	Life in years	Annual depreciation	Net profits	Rate of return *
1	60,000	12,000	15	4,000	8,000	26.67
2	80,000	22,500	20	4,000	18,500	46.25
3	2,150	1,500	3	717	783	72.83
4	20,500	4,000	10	2050	1950	19.02

* Based on average investment, assuming scrap value as zero.

The rate of return on initial investment will be half of the return on average investment.

Limitations of accounting method

1.It does not take into account time value of money

2. The expected profit is not likely to be same every year. The use of profit in a typical year or of the average profit per year is likely to be misleading because both ignore the year or year profits.

3.Earning life of the project is not taken into account.

Internal Rate of Return

This method is based on the fact that amount of money received today is more valuable than the same amount received after a year . The reason for this lies in the fact that the money received today can be invested to earn a certain amount of interest. The process of adjusting the face value of future cash flows to their present value by means of an imputed interest rate is called discounting. This imputed interest rate will be the rate of return. In general , the present value of a sum of money 'X' which does not accrue until 'n' periods into the future is given by the formula:

Present value = $X / (1 + r)^n$

The amount X is said to be discounted 'n' times at interest rate 'r'

The rate of return calculation that takes into consideration the time value of money is called the discounted cash flow method. The discounted rate of return is that interest rate, on applying it to a series of future cash flows, brings the sum of their present values to the same level as the original investment. The rate of interest can be calculated with the help of the arithmetic formula or from the present value tables. There can be two possibilities i) the annual cash flowis uniformover the years ii) annual cash flow is irregular over unequal over the years

When the cash flow is uniform

First we will calculate the P ratio with the following formula:

$$\text{P ratio} = \frac{\text{Initial investment}}{\text{Annual cash flow}}$$

Then in the Present Value Table showing the Present Value of an annuity of Re. 1 (Table No.2), read against the number of years of the asset's useful life up to the interest rate column in which the computed P ratio is located. It is unlikely that the exact P ratio will appear in the Table, but an approximation is sufficient for most business

purposes. This rate will be the expected rate of return. Let us apply the formula to our example:

Proposal No.	P Ratio	Expected rate of return
1	5	Between 15 and 20 % (18.97%)
2	3.5	Between 25 and 30% (28.65%)
3	1.4	Over 40% (52.5%)
4	5.1	Between 15and20% (15.46%)

*We have expressed here 'over 40 per cent' because the relevant table does not cover an Interest rate of more than 40 per cent. .

An example as to how to arrive at the rate of interest may be given here. For proposal number 1, the life is 15 years. Reading against 15 years, to locate the P Ratio, we find that the required P Ratio of 5.00 lies between 15 per cent (5.9638) and 20 per cent (4.7509). The rate can be interpolated but it would be nearer 20 than 15.

The interpolation will be done by the following formula:

$r = r_2 - [(v - v_2) / (v_1 - v_2)] . (r_2 - r_1)$

Or

$r = r_1 + [(v_1 - v)/(v_1 - v_2)] . (r_2 - r_1)$

where r = rate of return to be determined by interpolation.

r_1 = lower rate of return,

r_2= higher rate of return.

v_1= the P ratio at the lower rate of return,

v_2 = the P ratio at the higher rate of return,

v = theP ratio for which r is to be interpolated.

Applying the formula, we get

r = 20 - [(5 -4.7509)/ (5.9638- 4.7509)]_x (20 -15) = 18.97

The figures in brackets shown against the various proposals in the table above give interpolated rates of return.

For long-life projects, with constant cash flows. the pay-back reciprocal provides a close approximation of the rate of return calculated by the discounted cash flow method.. Taking proposal No. I, the reciprocal of the pay-back period is 1/5 which comes to 20 per cent meaning thereby that the approximate rate of return on this project is 20 per cent. This is very near the rate we calculated above.

When the Cash Flows are Unequal

Let us assume that an investment of Rs. 15,500 which has a useful life of 5 years (with no scrap value) has the following cash inflows: 1st year Rs.3.000, 2nd year Rs. 4,000 , 3rd year Rs. 6,000 , 4th year Rs. 5,000 , 5th year Rs. 4,000.

We have to calculate the rate of return through a trial-and-error approach. Accordingly, we must start by guessing at a rate of interest which will discount the future cash flows so that the total of the present values of all cash inflows proves to be equal to the initial investment. The rate which so equates the two figures is the sought-for rate of return. Very often, several guesses will have to be made before we are able to arrive at the desired rate. Let us begin with an interest rate of 15 per cent. In this case. we have to consult Table 1 which shows the present value of Re. 1 received or paid in a steady stream throughout a particular year. The present value of all cash flows comes to Rs.15.109 (*i.e..* less than 15.500). This means that the rate of interest must be less *than* 15 *per cent.* (The higher the rate of interest, the lower is the present value. So also, the further in the future the amount payable is, the less the present value of that amount). Let us now try with an interest rate of 14 per cent. It will be seen that the present value of all cash flows comes to Rs. 15,474 which is approximately equal to our investment. Thus we can say that the rate of return is slightly lower than 14 per cent.

Year	Annual cash flow	Present value factor 15%	Present value
1	3000	0.9286	2785.8
2	4000	0.7993	3197.2
3	6000	0.6879	4127.4
4	5000	0.5921	2960.5
5	4000	0.5096	2038.4
			15,109.3

Year	Annual cash flow	Present value factor 15%	Present value
1	3000	0.9332	2799.6
2	4000	0.8112	3244.9
3	6000	0.7053	4231.8
4	5000	0.6131	3065.5
5	4000	0.5330	2132.0
			15,473.7

The merits of the internal rate of return method are:

(i) It considers the time value of money.

(ii) It considers the cash flows over the entire life of the project.

(iii) The calculation of the cost of capital is not a pre-condition for the use of this method. Iii spite of its merits. the method has one basic limitation. It is difficult to understand and use in practice as its computation is complicated.

Net Present Value Index Method

The net present value of an investment proposal is the difference between the total of present values of the estimated annual cash flows over the life of the project and the initial investment of the project. If the net present value is positive, *i.e.*, the present value of the inflows exceeds the initial investment, the investment is profitable. If the net present value is negative, investment is unprofitable. The investment proposal that simply breaks even will have a net present value of zero. The annual cash flows are discounted to find out the present value with an interest rate which is equal to the average cost of capital of the company or the lending rate, whichever is higher.

The simple basis of the net present value method is that it recognises that the cash a firm gets out of a project should be greater than the cash put in plus the interest that could have been earned by investing the money elsewhere.

When there are a number of proposals under consideration, we can compute the present value of cash flows of all the proposals under consideration. We can then calculate the net present value index (NPVI) of each proposal by the following method:

Net Present value index = Total Present Value of all Cash Flows / Initial investment

I"

The higher the index, the more profitable the project is. We can then rank the various proposals according to their net present value index.If the projects have a salvage value, we can find out the present value of the scrap value at the same rate of interest and add it to the total present value of all cash flows.

The net present value index method has all the merits of the internal rate of return method and both of them duly recognize the time value of money. However, under the former, we have to find out the desired rate of return by the process of trial and error which is very tedious. The latter avoids the problem by assuming the interest rate equivalent to the cost of capital for finding out the present values of the cash flows. Thus, the net present value index method has the advantage of simplicity and involves discounting of the cash flows only once.

Evaluation of Appraisal Methods

Having discussed the various methods of appraising the profitability of alternative investment projects, we may now attempt a comparative evaluation or these methods. The accounting or the financial statement method is of doubtful utility as it ignores the time value of money. Both the internal rate of return and the net present value index method do consider the time value of money and are, therefore, basically acceptable. or these two methods, we consider the net present value index method better because of its simplicity. It is also superior in situations involving unequal lives or unusual cash flow patterns.3 However, we suggest that the *net present value index method should* be *supplemented by the pay-back method.* The basic reason for this is that other things being equal, the investment that pays itself back quickest is the best. The question of quick pay-back assumes special significance in the case of firms with poor liquidity, when capital funds are either in scarce supply or there is an apprehension that future availability of funds will not be adequate to finance expected future projects of greater profitability. Pay-back period may also become-important when the risk of obsolescence is high. A shorter pay-back period is also a factor in cases where the future cash flows are relatively uncertain.

It may be added that the methods we have discussed above, apply to the projects that offer themselves between the two extremes of (1) being absolutely necessary and unpostponable so that they have to be accepted, and (2) being absolutely unprofitable so that they have to be rejected in any case.

Advantages and disadvantages of IRR AND NPV

A number of surveys have shown that, in practice, the IRR method is more popular than the NPV approach. The reason may be that the IRR is straightforward, but it uses cash flows and recognizes the time value of money, like the NPV. In other words, while the IRR method is easy and understandable, it does not have the drawbacks of the ARR and the payback period, both of which ignore the time value of money.

The main problem with the IRR method is that it often gives unrealistic rates of return. Suppose the cutoff rate is 11% and the IRR is calculated as 40%. Does this mean that the management should immediately accept the project because its IRR is 40%. The answer is no! An IRR of 40% assumes that a firm has the opportunity to reinvest future cash flows at 40%. If past experience and the economy indicate that 40% is an unrealistic rate for future reinvestments, an IRR of 40% is suspect. Simply speaking, an IRR of 40% is too good to be true! So unless the calculated IRR is a reasonable rate for reinvestment of future cash flows, it should not be used as a yardstick to accept or reject a project.

Another problem with the IRR method is that it may give different rates of return. Suppose there are two discount rates (two IRRs) that make the present value equal to the initial investment. In this case, which rate should be used for comparison with the cutoff rate? The purpose of this question is no' to resolve the cases where there are different IRRs. The purpose is to let you know that the IRR method, despite its popularity in the business world, entails more problems than a practitioner may think.

Why the NPV and IRR Sometimes Select Different Projects

When comparing two projects, the use of the NPV and the IRR methods may give different results. A project selected according to the NPV may be rejected if the IRR method is used.

Suppose there are two alternative projects, X and Y. The initial investment in each project is $2,500. Project X will provide annual cash flows of $500 for the next 10 years. Project Y has annual cash flows of $100, $200, $300, $400, $500, $600, $700, $800, $900, and $1,000 in the same period. Using the trial and error method explained before, you find that the IRR of Project X is 17% and the IRR of Project Y is around 13%. If you use the IRR, Project X should be preferred because its IRR is 4% more than the IRR of Project Y. But what happens to your decision if the NPV method is used? The answer is that the decision will change depending on the discount rate you use. For instance, at a 5% discount rate, Project Y has a higher NPV than X does. But at a discount rate of 8%, Project X is preferred because of a higher NPV.

The purpose of this numerical example is to illustrate an important distinction: The use of the IRR always leads to the selection of the same project, whereas project selection using the NPV method depends on the discount rate chosen.

Project Size and Life

There are reasons why the NPV and the IRR are sometimes in conflict: the size and life of the project being studied are the most common ones. A 10-year project with an initial investment of Rs.1000,000 can hardly be compared with a small 3-year project costing Rs100,000. Actually, the large project could be thought of as ten small projects. So if you insist on using the IRR and the NPV methods to compare a big, long-term project with a small, short-term project, don't be surprised if you get different selection results.

Different Cash Flows

Furthermore, even two projects of the same length may have different patterns of cash flow. The cash flow of one project may continuously increase over time, while the cash flows of the other project may increase, decrease, stop, or become negative. These two projects have completely different forms of cash flow, and if the discount rate is changed when using the NPV approach, the result will probably be different orders of ranking. For example, at 10% the NPV of Project A may be higher than that of Project B. As soon as you change the discount rate to 15%, Project B may be more attractive.

When Are the NPV and IRR Reliable?

Generally speaking, you can use and rely on both the NPV and the IRR if two conditions are met. First, if projects are compared using the NPV, a discount rate that fairly reflects the risk of each project should be chosen. There is no problem if two projects are discounted at two different rates because one project is riskier than the other. Remember that the result of the NPV is as reliable as the discount rate that is chosen. If the discount rate is unrealistic, the decision to accept or reject the project is baseless and unreliable. Second, if the IRR method is used, the project must not be accepted only because its IRR is very high. Management must ask whether such an impressive IRR is possible to maintain. In other words, management should look into past records, and existing and future business, to see whether an opportunity to reinvest cash flows at such a high IRR really exists. If the firm is convinced that such an IRR is realistic, the project is acceptable. Otherwise, the project must be reevaluated by the NPV method, using a more realistic discount rate.

Modified IRR (MIRR)

The MIRR is similar to the IRR, but is theoretically superior in that it overcomes two weaknesses of the IRR. The MIRR correctly assumes reinvestment at the project's cost of capital and avoids the problem of multiple IRRs. However, please note that the MIRR is not used as widely as the IRR in practice.

There are 3 basic steps of the MIRR:

(1) Estimate all cash flows as in IRR.

(2) Calculate the future value of all cash inflows at the last year of the project's life.

(3) Determine the discount rate that causes the future value of all cash inflows determined in step 2, to be equal to the firm's investment at time zero. This discount rate is know as the MIRR.

Project L:

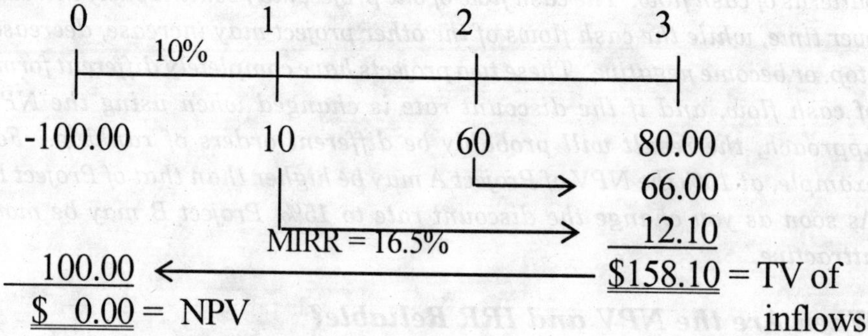

PV outflows = $100

TV inflows = $158.10.

$MIRR_S = 16.9\%.$

$$PVcosts = \frac{TV}{(1 + MIRR)^n}$$

MIRR is better than IRR because

1. MIRR correctly assumes reinvestment at project's cost of capital.
2. MIRR avoids the problem of multiple IRRs.

Profitability Index (PI)

The *profitability index,* or PI, method compares the present value of future cash inflows with the initial investment on a relative basis. Therefore, the PI is the ratio of the present value of cash flows (PVCF) to the initial investment of the project.

$$PI = \frac{PVCF}{\text{Initial investment}}$$

In this method, a project with a PI greater than 1 is accepted, but a project is rejected when its PI is less than 1. Note that the PI method is closely related to the NPV approach. In fact, if the net present value of a project is positive, the PI will be greater than 1. On the other hand, if the net present value is negative, the project will have a PI of less than 1. The same conclusion is reached, therefore, whether the net present value or the PI is used. In other words, if the present value of cash flows exceeds the initial investment, there is a positive net present value and a PI greater than 1, indicating that the project is acceptable.

PI is also know as a benefit/cash ratio.

Project L

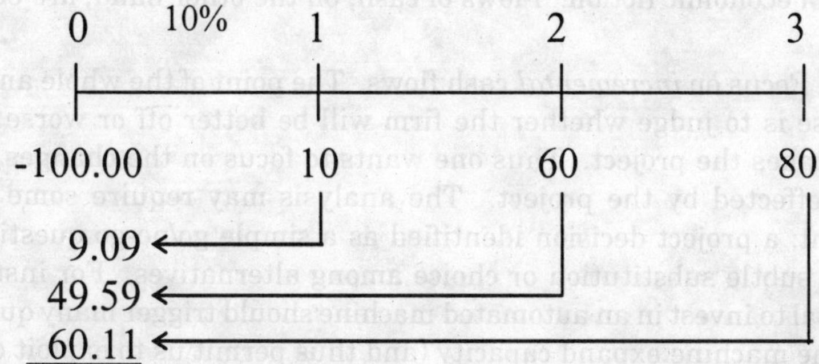

PV_1 9.09

PV_2 49.59

PV_3 60.11

118.79

$$PI = \frac{\text{PV of cash flows}}{\text{initial coast}}$$

$$= \frac{118.79}{100} = 1.10$$

Accept project if PI > 1.
Reject if PI < 1.0

Equivalent Annual Annuity

What do you do when project lives vary significantly? An easy and intuitively appealing approach is to compare the "equivalent annual annuity" among all the projects. The equivalent annuity is the level annual payment across a project's specific life that has a present value equal to that of another cash-flow stream. Projects of equal size but different life can be ranked directly by their equivalent annuity. This approach is also known as equivalent annual cost, equivalent annual cash flow, or simply equivalent annuity approach. The equivalent annual annuity is solved for by this equation:

Equivalent Annuity = PV(Cash Flows) / (present value factor of n-year annuity)

Project Decision Analysis

Making Go/on-go Project Decision

Virtually all general managers face capital-budgeting decisions in the course of their careers. The most common of these is the simple "yes" versus "no" choice about a capital investment. The following are some general guidelines to orient the decision maker in these situations.

1. Focus on cash flows, not profits. One wants to get as close as possible to the economic reality of the project. Accounting profits contain many kinds of economic fiction. Flows of cash, on the other hand, are economic facts.

2. Focus on *incremental* cash flows. The point of the whole analytical exercise is to judge whether the firm will be better off or worse off if it undertakes the project. Thus one wants to focus on the changes in cash flows effected by the project. The analysis may require some careful thought: a project decision identified as a simple go/no-go question may hide a subtle substitution or choice among alternatives. For instance, a proposal to invest in an automated machine should trigger many questions: Will the machine expand capacity (and thus permit us to exploit demand beyond our current limits)? Will the machine reduce costs (at the current level of demand) and thus permit us to operate more efficiently than before we had the machine? Will the machine create other benefits (e.g., higher quality, more operational flexibility)? The key economic question asked of project proposals should be, "How will things change (i.e., be better or worse) if we undertake the project?"

3. Account for time. Time is money. We prefer to receive cash sooner rather than later. Use NPV as the technique to summarize the quantitative attractiveness of the project. Quite simply, NPV can be interpreted as the amount by which the market value of the firm's equity will change as a result of undertaking the project.

4. Account for risk. Not all projects present the same level or risk. One wants to be compensated with a higher return for taking more risk. The way to control for variations in risk from project to project is to use a discount rate to value a flow of cash that is consistent with the risk of that flow.

These 4 precepts summarize a great amount of economic theory that has stood the test of time. Organizations using these precepts make better investment decisions than organizations that do not use these precepts.

The Process of Project Evaluation

1. Carefully estimate expected future cash flows.

2. Select a discount rate consistent with the risk of those future cash flows.

3. Compute a "base-case" NPV.

4. Identify risks and uncertainties. Run a sensitivity analysis.

Identify "key value drivers".
Identify break-even assumptions.
Estimate scenario values.
Bound the range of value.

5. Identify qualitative issues.

Flexibility

Quality

Know-how

Learning

6. Decide

Other Considerations

We have so far discussed that the projects should be ranked according to their profitability and the various methods for finding out the relative profitability. However, in actual business, managerial decisions about investment proposals may not always be made according to their relative profitability. There are a number of other considerations which have to be taken into account besides profitability. Some of these considerations are discussed below:

Urgency of the Project

In some cases, the firm may have no choice but to make the investment Irrespective of its rate of return, *i.e.,* a roof blown by the cyclone should be replaced at once. Here the main point to be considered is the cost of not doing so, *Le.,* the damage to merchandise and equipment which is imminent if the roof is not Immediately replaced. In other words, some investments are postponable; others are not. Thus what is uppermost among other considerations is the urgency of the project.

Likewise, if according to government requirements, a housing colony has got to be added, the construction of houses would be compulsory. The only decision then would be about the type of houses and the cost involved. An investment that is required to comply with anti-pollution legislation is another example.

Type of Investment

A firm would accept a lower return on a cost reduction programme (with relatively certain results) as against a project with a higher but uncertain return.

Type of Decision Being Made

The management may decide to make a *tactical* decision to provide funds to a division which is making a low return to preserve its earning power and maintain its existing market share. This may be unavoidable till the firm makes a strategic decision to leave the industry.

Intangible Factors

Very often, intangible factors assume importance such as the effect of a course of action on company's prestige and image or on the employees' morale. These factors cannot be ignored and some projects may have to be accepted whether they are profitable or not. But if the final choice is made on account of intangible factors, the management must realise the cost thereof.

Overall Profitability

If we strictly follow the rate of return criterion, we may be persuaded to choose a smaller investment proposal with a higher rate of return over a large investment proposal with a lower rate of return. This decision would be sound only if the funds left after undertaking the smaller investment can be employed to yield a satisfactory profit but if by undertaking the smaller investment, the company finds that it has to undertake some projects of rather low profitability (because the available funds are inadequate to be invested in a more profitable project), the decision may prove to be an unsound one. So what we have to see is that the total funds are employed in a way that the overall profitability is the highest. In fact, it would be appropriate for the management to ensure that some large proposals with smaller but adequate rate of return are not rejected when opportunities do not exist for fuller utilization of the funds available with the company. It may be worthwhile to say that if in management's judgement, the expected rates of return on all alternative proposals are very low, management should consider: (1) postponing all capital expenditures until a later time when prospects may appear better; or (2) using the valuable funds for dividends to shareholders so that they may put them to more profitable use elsewhere.

Degree of Certainty About Cash Flow

As the cash flows from various projects occur in future after the total investment has been made, they are always susceptible to a degree of uncertainty in being realised as anticipated. And longer the period involved, the more uncertain are the chances of realizing the expected cash flow. The degree of uncertainty in relation to the estimated cash flows is an important consideration to be kept in view. Hence, projects with relatively assured cash flows even with lower rates of return are to be preferred to projects with uncertain cash flows despite high rates of return.

Government's Industrial Policy

While appraising projects in India, it might be necessary to take into account the industrial policy of the Government as reflected by the Industries (Development and Regulation) Act, Monopolies and Restrictive Trade Practices Act, Foreign Exchange Regulation Act, etc. and various tax incentives for development of backward areas and priority industries as also availability of various industrial inputs.

F**uture Disposable Value of the Assets/Project at Year Ends2**

In the present context of liberalization wherein a lot of mergers, takeovers and acquisitions take place, merely relying on the cash flows alone for taking a decision regarding the financial commitment may not be quite prudent. A few years ago, it was almost unthinkable that a promoter would leave a project in the middle to sell off the same to some one else; it was a kind of permanent marriage and divorces were seldom thought of. In those days, it was alright to consider only usual techniques for evaluating the project for its financial performance. When the contingencies of takeover, selling and merger take place, the project appraising mechanism should take into account the possible value of the project at the end of each year during the life time of the project, so that it would a1so serve as a decision making tool instead of merely depending on the classical tools, which are still very useful techniques.

Therefore, in addition to applying the usual techniques, the project appraisal may also use another technique namely, estimating the *future disposable value of the assets / project* at the end of each year so that the financing institutions are guided properly

Capital Rationing

Capital is a scarce resource and has a cost. Therefore, an essential factor in appraising investment opportunities is that the return on investment must be more than the cost of capital. Thus the basic approach is that only those investments should be considered for acceptance which yield a rate of return in excess of the cost of capital. In other words, the cost of capital sets the minimum rate that the investment must promise to return. In effect, it is a measure to determine the cut-off point in capital budgeting.

Moreover, the basic aim of capital budgeting is to maximise the firm's long-run profit potential. Specifically, the firm must select the most profitable projects for investment. There may be a variety of alternative investment opportunities. Again, the prospective return on these opportunities differs from each other. Thus, management must select those investment proposals which are most profitable. It is not enough to identify investment opportunities as profitable. In addition, they must be ranked according to their relative profitability. This is necessary because the capital required for all these opportunities exceeds the available supply of capital.

Thus not all profitable investment opportunities may be accepted because of the scarce supply of capital. There are a number of reasons why situations of capital rationing may arise:

(a) Non-availability of finance due to the policies of the Government of India and the Reserve Bank of India.

(b) Projects being considered as too risky by the financial institutions leading to their refusal to accommodate the firm.

(c) The already existing heavy indebtedness of the firm leading to refusal of the , financial institutions to provide funds for otherwise worthwhile projects,

(d) The reluctance of the managemt to obtain external finance to avoid , dilution of ownership and control.

Capital rationing exist whenever enterprises cannot, or choose not to, accept all value-creating investment projects because of following reasons a)Banks and investors say "NO" b)Managerial conservatism. However a thorough analysis is required and decision maker must consider sets of projects, or "bundles", rather than individual projects. The goal should be to identify the value-maximizing bundle of projects. Capital rationing constraints heightens the influence of nonfinancial considerations, such as following:

- Competition among alternative strategies
- Corporate politics
- Bargaining games and psychology

Some remedies which could make budget rationing less dangerous or threatening are as follows:

- Relax and eliminate the budget constraint.
- Manage the process rather than the outcomes.
- Develop a corporate culture committed to value creation.

To conclude, capital budgeting consists of (1) determining the cost of capital, (2) determining the rate of return on different investment proposals under consideration, and (3) ranking them on the basis of profitability, The expected return on the various projects has to be compared with the cost of capital to determine which projects to drop and which ones to select as the best investment among the profitable ones.

Questions

1. Define capital budgeting and give examples of capital budgeting problems. Examine the need for capital budgeting.
2. What is meant by cost of capital? Explain how it is calculated.
3. Examine the various yardsticks for evaluating the profitability of project proposals, pointing out their suitability and limitation.
4. Compare Internal Rate of Return and Accountant's Rate of Return as methods of capital expenditure analysis.
5. Discuss some of the principal problems involved in an attempt to rank several alternative investment proposals in order of their profitability.
6. Explain the 'Pay-back period' of appraising capital expenditure projects. What are its limitations and under what circumstances is the use of this method appropriate?
7. How do you calculate the cost of debt capital?
8. Which would you prefer-Internal Rate of Return Method or the Net Present Value Index Method-for appraising project proposals and why?

12

Business Strategy and Game Theory

Introduction

Business strategy derives optimal managerial decisions when other firms (or persons) possibly change their behaviour in response to your behaviour. In earlier chapters we learned that demand for a firm's product depends on what competitors charge. But the competitor's price was held fixed. We did not consider that if we change our price, competitors will likely match our price change. In order to really assess the value of, say, cutting prices, we need to consider what other will do in response to our actions. A critical calculation that is often overlooked in business situations is how other firms will react. Business strategy determines optimal managerial decision when other firms and persons change behaviour in response to your decisions.

Framework: Two Person Games

Here we suppose only one other player, but the other player could be another firm, person or industry.

Payoff Matrix

The pay off matrix lists all rewards that each player gets as a function of decisions made by all players. Consider " a price war" game. Firm A (you) and firm B are the dominant firms in the industry because of anti trust laws, you are forbidden from colluding with B to raise prices or even from discussing prices. You know that if you cut prices and firm B does not , you can take the majority of the market share and make a large profit, say $ 6 million, while firm B loses $ 1 million. The reverse is also true, If firm B cuts prices and you do not , then the firm B gains market share and makes $ 4 million and firm A makes $ I million. However, if both firms cut prices, profit are zero for both firms. Finally if both firms do not cut prices, the market is split between the two firms, but the relatively high prices allows each firm to make a profit of $ 3 million.

Notice that the first number is always the payoff of the firm listed on the left (rows) where as the second number is the pay off of the firm listed on top (columns).

		Firm B	
		Hold prices	Cut prices
Firm A	Hold prices	3,3	1,4
	Cut prices	6,-1	0,0

Dominant Strategy

If your best action is independent of what the other player does, then the decision is easy.

Def inition1: A Dominant strategy is an action that is at least as good as all other actions regardless what thc opposing player chooses.

Let us look at the above game. Suppose Firm B elects to hold prices. Then it is in the best interest of firm A to cut prices and steal firm B's customers (since $ 6 million is greater than $ 3 million). However, if firm B elects to cut prices then it is in the best interest of firm A to hold prices. Firm A will loose most customers but make $1 million on remaining customers (if firm A cuts prices, Firm A makes nothing). Thus firm A does not have a dominant strategy; the optimal decision depends on what firm B does. However, Firm B does have a dominant strategy. If firm A holds prices, Firm B should cut prices and steal business away from firm A . If firm A cuts prices, then Firm B does better by cutting prices, splitting the market and making no profit is better than loosing $1 million. So the dominant strategy of cutting prices generate the highest possible profits for firm B regardless of the actions of firm A.

Nash Equilibrium

We need a way to compute the optimal strategy where no dominant strategy exists for at least one of the players. The trick is to predict the behaviour of the other firm. In the above example, firm A might predict that firm B will cut prices. After all, cutting prices is the dominant strategy for firm B, regardless of what firm A does. Once firm A predicts what firm B will do, then firm A needs to compute the optimal strategy. Given that firm B will cut prices, firmA should hold prices. Now the last step is to check if our prediction is accurate; if firm A holds prices then firm b will certainly do better by cutting prices, so our prediction that firm B will cut prices is correct. Therefore the optimal strategy for firm A is to hold prices and the optimal strategy for firm B is to cut prices. Together, these strategies are what we expect to see in equilibrium.

Let's see if cutting prices can be an optimal strategy. Suppose firm A cuts prices, then firm B responds by cutting prices. But then it is no longer optimal for firm A to cut prices; Firm A does better by holding prices. So cutting prices is not an equilibrium strategy for firm A, since they will regret their decision if firm B acts in an optimal way.

Definition **2 A nash equilibrium is a set of strategies such that each player accurately believes that he/ she is acting optimally given the strategy of the other players.**

The Nash equilibrium is conditional on what other player do . By assuming the other player will act optimally and accurately predict what you are doing, you can predict what the other player will do.

Let's get some insight into what is happening. Firm A, perhaps a dominant firm with loyal customers, has certain advantages. Firm A does as well as firm b when both firm use the same strategy . However, when firm A is undercut by B, firm A makes more profits than firm b would in the reverse case. This actually works against firmA, however. Firm B knows that firm A will not match B's price cut, since firm A does better by ignoring firm B and just making money from its loyal customers. Therefore, firm B can make inroads into firm A's business by offering goods at low prices. Firm A is then forced into one of the worst possible outcomes. One would think that firmA, a big firm, could threaten to cut prices and try to intimidate B into holding prices. But such a threat is not credible.

Let's try another example

		Firm B	
		Hold prices	Cut prices
Firm A	Hold prices	3,3	1,4
	Cut prices	5,0	0,0

Here we have slightly altered the payoffs that occur when firm A cuts prices and when firm B holds prices. The previous Nash equilibrium continues to hold: If firm B predicts firm A holds, then firm B does at least as good by cutting, in which case firm A should hold. So firm A holds and firm B cuts continues to be an equilibrium. Now suppose firm B predicts firm A cuts, then firm B does at least as well by holding, in which case firm A should cut. Therefore the set of strategies firm A cuts and firm B holds is also Nash equilibrium. Often more than one Nash equilibrium exists, in which case the behaviour gets harder to predict, Consider the "coordination" game of which side of the road to drive on.

	Car B	
Car A	B's Left Side	B's Right Side
A's Left Side	10,10	-5,-5
A's Right Side	-5,-5	10,10

If both drivers drive on the opposite sides of the road, it is disaster for both players. But it does not matter if both players drive on their right or left. Therefore, two nash equilibrium exist, and we should be able to observe that in some countries people drive on the left and in other countries on the right.

Some Simple Games

Anti-coordination Games: to Compete or not?

Suppose firms need to decide which markets to target. ATT and Sprint can target cell phones or conventional land lines via advertising and investing in towers and satellites in the case of cell phones, or conventional cables in the case of land lines. If both firms invest in the same business , competition will be fierce and each company will price close to marginal cost, which is low relative to the highest fixed costs of the towers and cables. However, if each focuses on a different market, both will make money by charging more:

	Sprint	
ATT	Call Phones	Land Lines
Cell Phones	0,0	2,5
Land Lines	2,5	0,0

So two Nash Equilibria exist , one with ATT specializing in land lines and Sprint cell phones and vice versa. Notice that whoever gets the cell phone business is better off since the cell business makes profits equal to 5. This can make the outcome somewhat uneasy: both firms, deciding together, may choose cell phones and then hope the other firm chooses land lines. Or if the game is not perfectly simultaneously, both firms may rush into the cell phone business in the hopes that competitors will be deterred from doing so.

Coordination games

Clearly if the firms sell complementary goods, such as cameras and film developing centers, the incentives are to locate together.

C Mixed coordination and anti-coordination

Lets try a tougher one of store location

		Target			
		Uptown	Center City	East Side	West Side
	Uptown	30,40	50,95	55,95	55,120
Macy	Center City	115,40	100,100	130,85	120,95
	East Side	125,45	95,65	60,40	115,120
	West Side	105,50	75,75	95,95	35,55

Both firms would like to locate in the relatively wealthy center city, due to the high incomes (and the ease of shopping while at center city for work). In addition, if both stores locate together, they could possibly draw larger crowds by establishing the area as a place to shop. Macy is a more upscale place, however, and does better than target in the high income areas (such as the east side). Target has low prices and does better than Macy's in the low income areas, but still does better in the high income area than the low income area.So the Nash Equilibria is for both stores to compete; the extra income of center city outweighs the losses from competing.

Let's try another one. Let's suppose Dave, Deana and Jack are brokers trying to pick the latest hot stock. The stock may go up or down, no one really knows. If an advisor picks correctly , they are rewarded with more business. If advisors are incorrect, they lose business. Further, if an advisor recommends buy whilethe others recommend sell and the stock goes up , the advisor gets a lot of new business. But suppose the reverse is worse, if the advisor recommends buy when everyone else is recommending sell and the stock goes goes down, the advisor loses a lot of business. Here are the payoffs:

Pick any two players, say Jack and Deana. If Dave predicts Jack and Deana pick buy, then Dave is better off picking buy. Similarly, if Jack and Dave pick buy, Deana should recommend buy. Similarly, if Deana and Dave pick buy, jack should pick buy. The same

is true for sell. So two nash Equilibria exist, one where all players pick buy and the other where all players pick sell. A rule I use in life: when asking an opinion of someone, never let them know what others have said.

Advantages of coordinating or not coordinating.

Jack Pick's Buy

		Dave	
		Buy	**Sell**
Deana	**Buy**	**5,5,5**	**6,4,6**
	Sell	**4,6,6**	**6,6,4**

Jack Pick's Sell

		Dave	
		Buy	**Sell**
Deana	**Buy**	**6,6,4**	**4,6,6**
	Sell	**6,4,6**	**5,5,5**

Coordinate by locating near competitors to draw shoppers to the area.

Coordinate by locating near competitors if demand (even with two competitors) in the area is better than other areas.

Coordinate if differentiating your product and being wrong about customer preferences yields more losses than the gains from being right about customer preferences

Coordinate only if incumbant firms will not react forcefully to your entry.

Prisoners Dilemmas

Suppose a symmetric version of the price war game:

		Firm B	
		Hold prices	**Cut prices**
Firm A	**Hold prices**	**3,3**	**0,5**
	Cut prices	**5,0**	**1,1**

So here a unique Nash Equilibrium exists where both firms cut prices (a price war ensues0. Notice a peculiar feature of this game. We can think of the "social optimum" as the set of strategies that benefits all players (with, say, equal weight) the most. So the upper left corner has a social benefit (SB) to the two firms (obviously not to the consumers) of SB= 3+3 = 6. Similarly

		Firm B	
		Hold prices	Cut prices
Firm A	Hold prices	$SB = 6$	$SB = 5$
	Cut prices	$SB = 5$	$SB = 1$

So the Nash Equilibrium is the worst possible outcome for the two firms! In fact, if firms could only collude on prices, they would surely agree to both hold prices high. The prisoners dilemma is the basis for antitrust rules prohibiting collusion or discussion of prices, the market keeps intact the incentive to cut prices (benefiting consumers).

Cartels and cheating

Of course, in reality, prisoner's dilemmas are not always fully non-cooperative (meaning each player moves simultaneously without knowledge of the other's move). Some degree of information sharing about prices is always possible , and firms can sometimes agree to form a cartel and not cut prices. However, the incentive to cheat on such an agreement is vary strong. If you know the other firm is sticking to the agreement and keeping prices high, you have a strong incentive to cut prices.

Mixed Strategies

Some games have no Nash equilibrium. When each player has an interest in disguising their actions, it is often optimal to choose a random or mixed strategy.

A Using mixed strategies to prevent opponents from reacting

Consider the " Blue light special sale". The seller wants to get rid of excess inventory. But if the seller announces a sale on a specific date , then all customers would shop on that date only , including those who would have bought the product at the high price . what would be ideal is if non price sensitive customers did not change their behaviour in response to when the sale was.

		Customer	
		Shop today	Shop tomorrow
Firm	Sale today	5,10	8,4
	Sale Tomorrow	10,5	4,8

The customer (let say this customer woulsd buy at full price0 is better off shopping on the day when the sale is. The firm is better off if this customer comes on a day when there is no sale. No nash equilibrium exists in this game. Suppose the firm predicts customers will shop today.Then the firm chooses to have the sale tomorrow. But then after announcing the sale , customers will shop tomorrow so customer shopping today is not a nash equilibrium. Similarly if the firm predicts shopper will shop tomorrow and announces a sale for today then customer react by shopping today and the firm regrets the decision to have a sale today. But an equilibrium exist in which the customers and firms make random decisions. Suppose the firm offers a sale today with probabilities q. Then the customer who shops today gets 10 with probability q and 5 with probability 1-q for a total of 10q+ 5 (1-q)

The payoff for shopping tomorrow is 4q + 8 (1-q). The seller wishes to equalize the two payoffs. If they are different , the shopper will always shop when the sale is m ore likely, which is not good for the seller. So we have :

$10q + 5(1-q) = 4q + 8(1-q)$ .. (1)

$9q = 3$

$q = 1/3$ .. (2)

So having a sale one third of the time today and two third of the time tomorrow is the best firm can do.Similarly the customer does not want to give away to the firm which day they will be shopping so they also randomize. Let p be the probability that a consumer shops today. The payoff to the firm of a sale today is then 5p + 8(1-q) and the payoff of a sale tomorrow is 10p +4 (1-p). Equalizing these two equations gives:

$5p + 8(1-p) = 10p + 4(1-p)$ ..(3)

$p = 4/9$ .. (4)

Any other probabilities and the firm can have the sale when consumer are less likely to come , which is detrimental to the interests of consumers. So the mixed strategy Nash equilibrium is to shop today with probability 4/9 and to have a sale today with probability 1/3.

Using mixed strategies to avoid coordination

Consider two firms, Macy and TJ Maxx. Macy is a high priced retailer that carries a variety of nice clothes in all sizes (and thus higher inventory costs and higher prices) and TJ Maxx is a retailer who charges low prices, but carries whatever surplus nice clothes manufacturers happen to have,

		Customer B	
		Shop TJ Maxx	Shop Macys
Customer A	Shop TJ Maxx	5,5	10,7
	Shop Macys	7,10	4,4

usually in odd sizes. Customers can shop at Macy, putting up with high prices but knowing they will find what they want, or they can go to TJ Maxx, paying lower prices if TJ Maxx happens to have what they want, Further, the more customers go to TJ Maxx, the more likely they are to be out of something. So the payoffs are:

Here two Nash equilibria exist , corresponding to the customers shopping at different stores. If B predicts A will shop at Macys, the B should not shop at crowded macys, where prices are high and the large crowd means macys may be out of stock, but instead shop at the low price (a nd not crowded) TJ Maxx. But then A will shop at Macys and we have a Nash equilibrium. The game is symmetric, so A shops at TJ Maxx and B shops at Macys is also an equilibrium.

Dynamic games

Two versions of games played over time exist

A Finite repeat game

In most cases, firms play the above games against each other repeatedly. For example the price war game is played repeatedly . In the

		Firm B	
		Hold prices	Cut prices
Firm A	Hold prices	3,3	0,5
	Cut prices	5,0	1,1

one shot game, if one firm cuts prices, the firm wins market share at the expense of the firm that holds prices, without any negative consequences. In reality, the game is repeated, so the firm which may cut prices has to consider possible retaliation in the next period by the firm holding prices constant. Let's see if this alters the equilibrium strategies. Recall the payoff matrix is:

The way to solve games is via backward induction: start with the last period and work backwards. Let's suppose the price war game is repeated 3 times. Start with period 3. This is always equal to the one shot game. The Nash equilibrium is for both players to cut prices. Each firm need not fear retaliation next period because the game is over. Now look at period 2. Each player knows both firms will cut prices in period 3. Thus, we can add one to the payoffs of each player, regardless of their actions. Thus period 3 is irrelevant for period 2: there is no hope that if you hold prices the other firm will do the same next period, because you already know the other firm will cut prices in period 3. Therefore, the nash equilibrium is again to cut prices for both firms in period 2 . And so on. Thus the Nash equilibrium in the repeated game is identical: always cut prices. The payoffs are equal to 1+1+1= 3 for both players.

Infinitely repeated games

If the game never ends, the backward induction argument breaks down. There is no final period in which you know the other firm will cut prices. Also games in which the end point is unknown are equivalent to infinitely repeated games. The calculations of infinitely games is too complex to discuss here, so we can discuss the optimal strategy.

Definition3 A Tit for Tat strategy is to hold prices in the first period, and then in subsequent periods play the move your opponent played the period before.

Tit for tat says if your opponent cuts prices, you should retaliate next period by cutting prices. If your opponent does not cut prices, you should cooperate and hold prices high next period. A famous result is that tit for tat is a Nash equilibrium in the infinitely repeated game if firms care enough about the future. Suppose you know your opponent will play tit for tat, and you do not discount the future. Then you have the opportunity to get $ 5 million immediately cutting prices. But then your opponent will cut prices next period, and indeed every period thereafter (forcing you to get $1 million each period), until you hold prices while your opponent continues to cut prices. So you must get zero in order to persuade your opponent to hold again. The sum of these two is 5 + 0 = 5 which is less than 3 + 3 = 6 you would get by simply continuing to hold prices, knowing that your opponent will cooperate as long as you do. However if you do not care much about the future, it may be optimal to grab the high profits today, and then hold prices high later to persuade your opponent to begin cooperating again.

In general , tit for tat predicts that we will observe long periods of mutual cooperation or long periods of mutual retaliation. In practice tit for tat can easily breakdown into a price war. If both players play tit fot tat, if one firm , even by mistake, perceives the other as cutting prices, it will trigger a price war from which there is no escape.Tit for tat is known as ' forgiving " strategy. You will allow those that have cheated you the chance to return to your good graces if they prove themselves. Other strategies , are less forgiving and work if firms care less about the future.

Sequential games

Extensive form

It is easiest to represent sequential games in extensive form, that is as a decision tree. Consider the anti-coordination game where one player now moves first. Compaq, the first mover, can either expand capacity in the PC market or not expand capacity. Then HP has the same choice. As in the

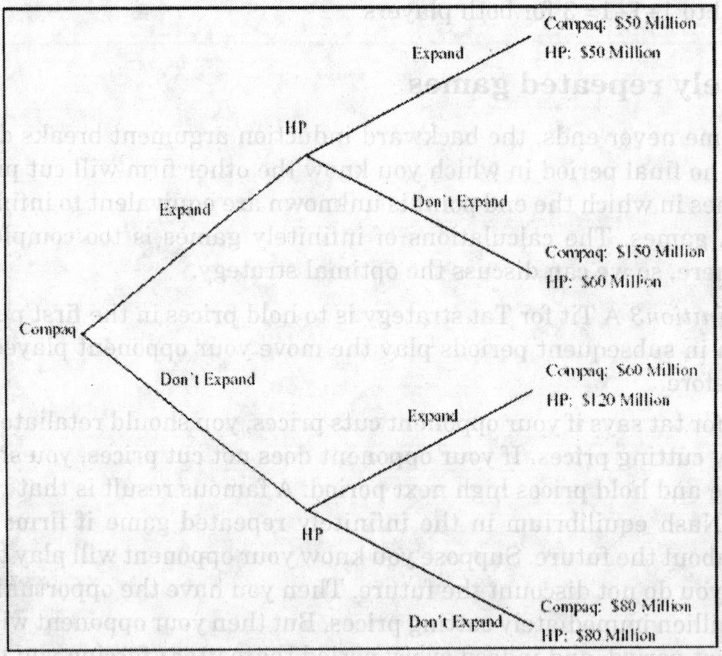

anti-coordination game, if both firms expand in the PC market, the competition will be fierce and profits will be low for both firms. If one firm expands and the other firm does not, profits will be high for the firm that expands. The firm that does not enter makes more money than the case where both expand into PC market, but less than if the firm entered and the other firm did not.

To solve this problem we again work backwards. If Compaq expands, HP does better by ceding Compaq the market and focusing business

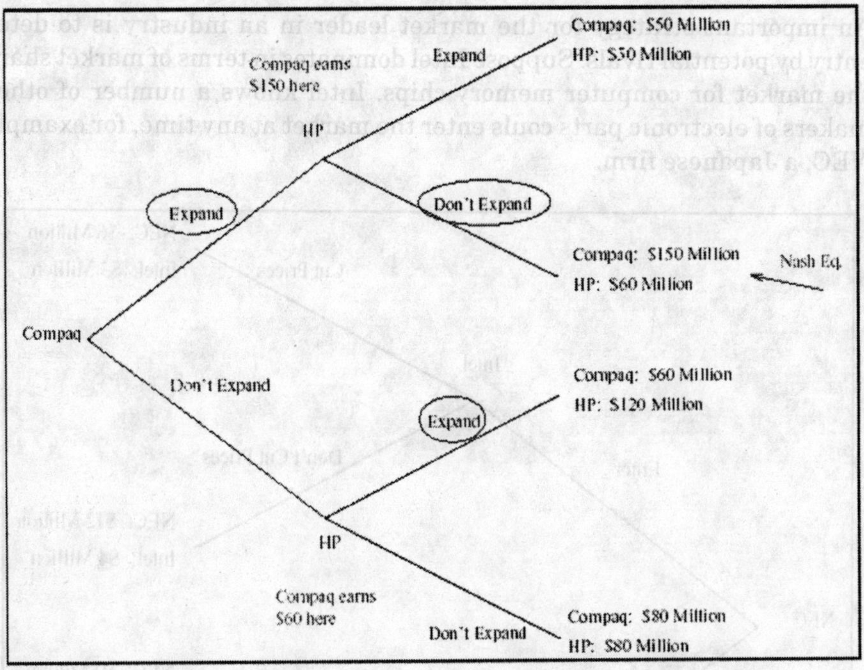

elsewhere (say on printers). If Compaq does not expand , HP does better by expanding into the PC business. Knowing this , Compaq can either expnd, knowing HP will not expand , and make $150 million, or not expand, knowing HP will expand, and make $60 million. Thus Compaq will expand. The equilibrium, which we will call sub-game perfect , is for Compaq to expand and HP not to expand. Compaq makes $150 million and HP makes $50 million.

Recall the problem of the simultaneous game that two Nash equilibria existed and both players preferred different equilibria, is solved in the sequential game. The first mover gets an advantage and gets the better Nash equilibrium of the simultaneous game.

Definition 4 First Mover advantage: Advantage to the first mover in sequential games when the simultaneous game has multiple Nash equilibria.

Notice also HP is powerless to threaten Compaq with retaliation if Compaq expands into the PC market. Compaq knows that such threat is not credible.

Definition 5 A sub game perfect equilibrium requires each sub tree to be a Nash equilibrium.

We see in this example that sub-game perfect equilibria are more stringent than Nash equilibria (only one equilibrium exists, not two)

Entry and Exit games

An important strategy for the market leader in an industry is to deter entry by potential rivals. Suppose Intel dominates in terms of market share the market for computer memory chips. Intel knows a number of other makers of electronic parts couls enter the market at any time, for example NEC, a Japanese firm.

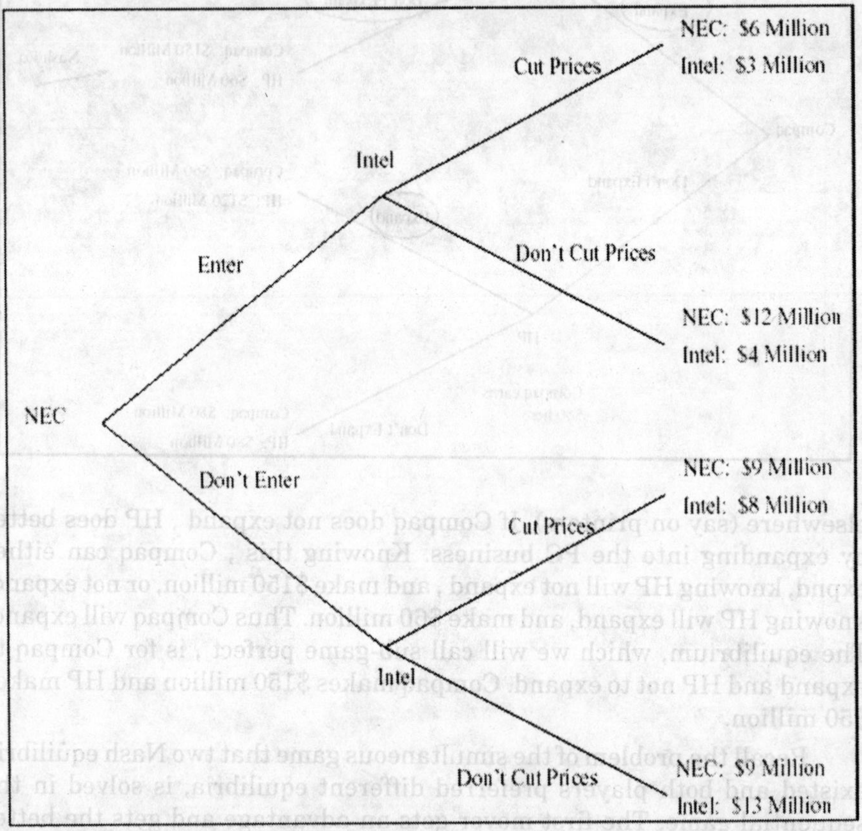

NEC moves first, by deciding whether or not to enter. Then Intel decides whether to respond by cutting prices and expanding output, or ignoring NEC and sharing the market. We solve the problem by backward induction. First, if NEC enters, then an ensuing price war would mean that Intel's profits are lower than if it instead kept prices high, making money from the most loyal customers, while ceding some of the market to NEC. If NEC does not enter, than Intel od course does much better holding prices high. So NEC has the choice of entering, knowing that Intel will not cut prices or not entering. Thus NEC enters.

Intel can threaten to cut prices, but NEC knows the threat is not credible and enters. Sub game perfection requires threats to be credible while the Nash equilibrium does not. To see this , suppose NEC predicts

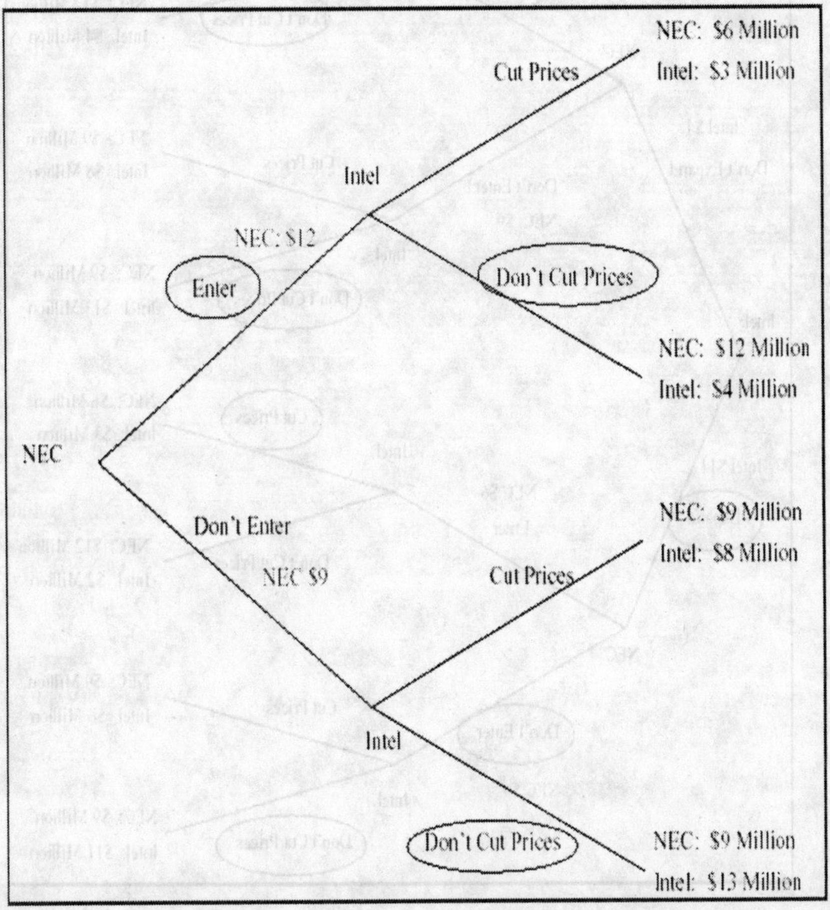

intel will cut prices if NEC enters. Then NECshould not enter. Then Nash equilibria requires us to check whether or not our prediction is correct. But in this case the prediction does not matter, because NEC has decided not to enter. So we can say the prediction is correct.

Next suppose we add another move for Intel. Intel can add capacity or not add capacity before NEC decides whether or not to enter. If Intel adds capacity, then Intel can efficiently produce a large volume of chips in NEC enters. However, the expansion results in $2 million of extra fixed costs if the factory is not used. The payoff matrix then changes as shown below, and NEC decides not to enter. Building capacity is one way to make threats more credible and deter entry. Building excess capacity is of course costly , however.

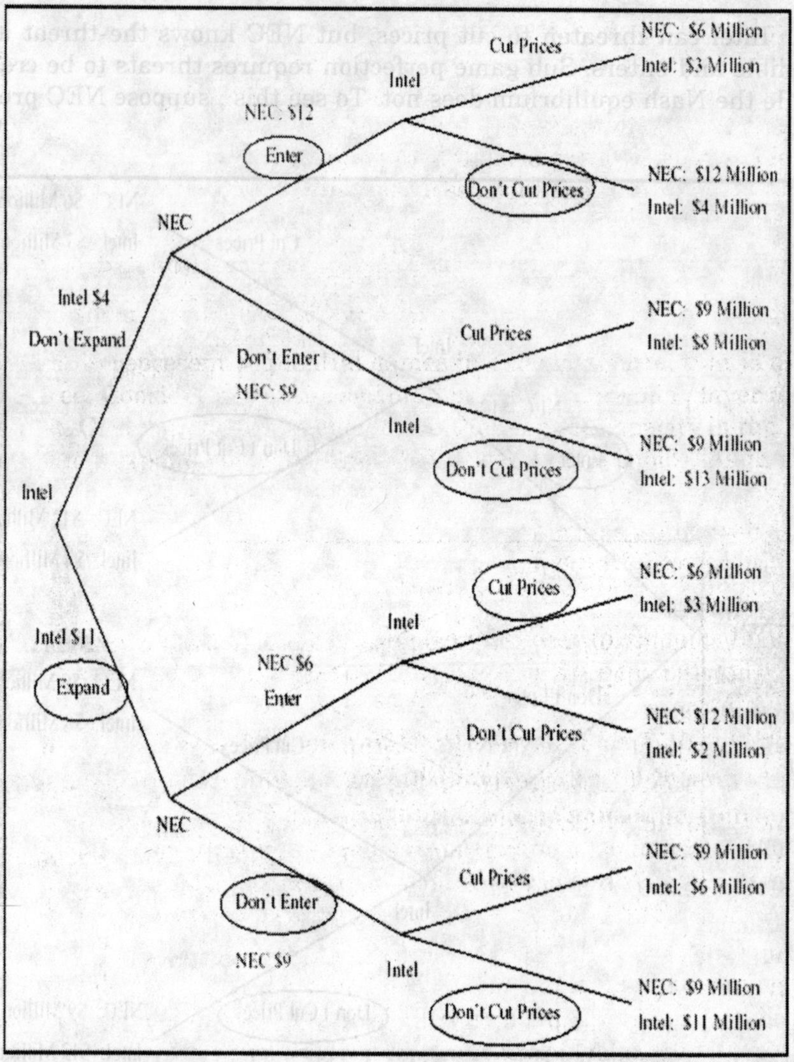

Examples of entry deterrence

1. Du Pont in 1979 invests $ 0.33 billion in titanium dioxide plants to deter rivals with older plants from updating to newer, more competitive plants. The government for anti-trust violations later sued Du Pont.

2. Wallmart's strategy is to build large stores in smaller towns first in order to deter others form building similar stores, since each town can support at most one store.

13

Economic Forecasting for Business

Introduction

Businessmen must plan ahead. Every business decision is based on some assumption about the future, whether right or wrong, implicit or explicit. And as business plans and decisions have to be based either directly or indirectly on the outlook of the national economy. economic projections or forecasts are increasingly becoming a vital part of managerial decision-making.

Economic forecasting consists of making forecasts of general business or economic activity such as movements of national income, aggregate industrial production or employment, and total exports or imports. Economic forecasting may be distinguished from business forecasting which relates more directly to the activity of the particular firm and comprises short and long-term forecasts of sales and price forecasts for raw materials and equipment. However. the distinction between economic forecasting and business forecasting is not always clear-cut. For example. from the viewpoint of a firm which is one of many such firms in an industry, a sales forecast for the entire industry would be somewhere between a forecast of general business activity and of activity pertaining to the firms.

Why are Accurate Economic Forecasts Possible?

Though future is uncertain, there are several factors, which explain why a fairly accurate forecast of general business activity is possible:

1.The current economic situation contains many clues to the future; economic events are not entirely capricious and haphazard but are caused largely by ascertainable factors. Hence a detailed examination of the current economic situation provides significant clues to what will take place in times ahead.

2. Many of the future economic developments result from the commitments, which have already been made in the past. The comrnitments are often publicly known. *e.g.,* in case of government appropriations, plans of government industrial projects, unfilled orders of government departments or undertaking, etc.

3. Many business developments are part of a process, which takes time. Once forces have been set in motion. the process conforms to a fairly stable pattern. Hence, the process having begun, the forecaster can project about future with reasonable, accuracy. For example, increases in sales after a while result in increased business inventories; and increases in the number of hours worked tend to be followed by an increase in the number

of workers employed in manufacturing. Also, when inventories become excessive. a fairly regular and predictable process of inventory liquidation begins.

Predicting Firm's Sales

The most important single use of an economic forecast is to have a reasonable basis for predicting the firm's sales volume. A firm's sales forecasts must rest upon economic forecasts for the simple reason that almost every firm's sales are affected by the state of general business. It is true that sales of certain firms might have risen during depression: or conversely, sales of others might have declined during prosperity. But almost invariably, the rise in sales would have been larger in the former case and the fall in sales steeper in the latter, had the general business condition not been changing. Moreover, because every firm's decisions about production, raw material purchases, plant expansion, sales quotas, borrowing, etc. hinge on its sales forecast, an economic forecast can be said to have its greatest signal value as the basis of sales forecast.

As such, the economic forecast is the necessary first step in predicting a firm's sales. The next step is a forecast of the industry's total sales. Based on these, a firm can estimate its own sales, say, by a projection of its market share. Different industries vary in their sensitivity to changes in general business conditions and in the speed with which they are affected by such changes. Hence, it is also necessary to determine the turning and amplitude of changes in its own industry's activity in relation to changes in general business conditions.

Again, the economic forecast contains a prediction of several segments of the economy. For example, it will give an estimate of gross national product, consumer spending. wholesale and retail prices, employment, interest rates, exports and the like. In practice, the business firms may be far more concerned with certain segments of the economic forecast than with others. For example, sellers of consumer goods will be affected much more by changes in consumer expenditure and savings than by changes in government expenditure. In other words, in building a sales forecast for one's own firm or industry, one finds certain segments of an economic forecast more relevant than others.

Other Uses

Besides facilitating a sales forecast, an economic forecast has several uses for an average business firm:

Labour

An economic forecast may tell about the severity of competition for labour and the likely pressure on wages. Hence it is specially useful to those entrusted with labour negotiations. training and recruitment. Often workers have to be trained before they are useful to a firm.

Raw Materials

An economic forecast also suggests the likely intensity of competition for raw materials which may be in short supply. Hence a knowledge of general business outlook will indicate when to place orders for raw materials and how much inventory to hold.

Finance

The economic forecast also indicates the response it will get in borrowing from banks or public and the likely rates of interest it will have to pay. As such. it may considerably help in planning the timing of a capital expansion programme.

Inventory and Investment

A forecast of price movements can be used with great advantage as a basis of inventory and investment policy. Normally. an expected price increase will make it advantageous to build up stocks in advance of the price rise. provided carrying costs are not excessive.

Plant Expansion or Contraction Plans

These plans have to be based on a long-term forecast of the demand for the firm's output. Hence, a forecast should cover the period during which fixed capital equipment is normally amortized.

Methods of Economic Forecasting

Four Important methods of economic forecasting may be distinguished: (I) Trend Projection. (2) Leading Indices. (3) Diffusion Index and (4) Econometric Models. The methods which involve the use of indicators. *e.g.*, leading indices and diffusion index are known as barometric techniques.

Trend Projection

A common method of economic forecasting is simply to construct a graph showing the actual movement of a series and then to project (extrapolate) the apparent trend of the data into the future. The projection is usually a straight line, but it can be curvilinear as well. This method is not based on any particular theory as to what causes the variable to change but merely assumes that whatever forces contributed to change in the recent past will continue to have the same effect

However. trend projectors are often able to show a high percentage of forecasts which are correct in direction at least But the method has the serious defect of missing all of the sudden downturns or upturns and these are just the changes which It Is most important to predict correctly. Despite this. trend projection may be the only available method when the variable under consideration is affected by a large number of factors, the separate influence of which cannot be readily measured because of lack of data or time for other reasons.

Leading Indices

This approach to forecasting stems from the empirical work done at the National Bureau of Economic Research, U.S.A. The 'Leading Indices' also known as 'Leading indicators' refer to certain sensitive series, which tend to turn upward or downward in anticipation of other series. The value of such indicators, if reliable. is obvious. If one knows a series, which would reliably lead, say commodity price indices, it would not be difficult to purchase raw materials in advance, if prices are expected to rise.

Certain important leading indices are:

1. New orders for durable goods.
2. Residential building contracts,
3. Commercial and industrial building contracts,
4. Number of new incorporations, and
5. Wholesale prices of basic commodities.

New orders placed with manufacturers, building contractors and new registered companies clearly have 'leading' characteristics. They are an early reflection of the demand for products, raw materials, labour and loans and capital.

As pointed out earlier, the main limitation of a trend projection as a forecasting technique is its failure to predict the vital upturns and downturns. It is only in respect of these turns, however, that significant modifications of inventory policy, capital budgeting, and the like, are required. Hence the importance of 'Leading Indices..

A significant limitation of the leading indices is that they often point in different directions at the same time. so that until their movements become substantial in magnitude and similar in direction, it is difficult to know where they are leading to. Also, in practice, the data may be available with a time-lag . Again, the leading indicators do not always lead by the same length of time. Further, the leading indicators give no indication of the magnitude or duration of the predicted rise or fall in economic activity .Finally a leading series which shows a short lead may be a good forecasting tool but may not be of much use for economic or business policy. Nevertheless, a downturn of some of these indicators after a consistent rise might at least warn the business that a general turn is possibly round the corner and may be a signal for action in anticipation of lower prices and reduced business activity.

Diffusion Index

A diffusion index is an indicator of the extensiveness of an expansion or contraction. A set of leading indicators usually contains conflicting signals. Hence the need for summarizing their net indication. The National Bureau of Economic Research, U.S.A., has developed such a method called the Diffusion Index.

The diffusion index is the percentage of members of a set of series that is moving upward. It ranges from zero (when all are moving downward) to 100 (when all series are moving upward). The number of indicators in a group that are rising at a given time are counted and the percentage of these indicators in the total group of indicators is computed. This percentage is called the Diffusion Index because it is believed to show how widely diffused the economic movements are. A larger concentration of rising indicators signifies movement in the upward direction and conversely, the lower concentration indicates the downturn in economic activity. For example, if during an expansionary period, the diffusion index for all leading indicators stands near 90 for several months but then begins to fall, it warns the forecaster that some of the leading series are beginning to turn downward. A general decline in economic activity may be forthcoming. Often the 50, per cent mark is used as a guide so that where more than 50 per cent of the leading Indicators are rising, one can predict an upturn in aggregate business activity.

The diffusion index can be used with advantage in business forecasting. The peaks and troughs of the index precede the peaks and troughs of general business activity. The utility of the diffusion index, however, depends upon the choice of indicators and the reliability of these indicators as forerunners of business movements. It is nevertheless a simple and quick device of economic forecasting.

Econometric Models

Econometric combines economics. statistics and mathematics. Breaking the word 'nto its two parts, 'econo' and .'metric", it is obvious that its subject-matter deals with the science of economic measurement. And this is precisely what econometrics does; it explains past economic activity by deriving mathematical equations that will express the most probable inter-relationship between a set of economic variables. The economic variables may include disposable income, inventories, government revenues and expenditure, foreign trade and so on. By combining the relevant variables, each in a separate series covering a past period of time, into what seems to be the best mathematical arrangement, econometricians proceed to predict the future course of one or more of these variables on the basis of established relationship. The "best mathematical arrangement" is thus an econometric model which takes the form of an equation or a system of equations that seems best to describe the past set of relationships according to economic theory and statistical analysis. Econometric models follow in the tradition of Keynesian theory .The first econometric model has been due to Tinbergen.

Econometric models are used to forecast not only the aggregate economy, but also specific economic series of importance to business. For example, models have been constructed to forecast the sales of capital goods, of consumer durables, of construction materials, and so on.

Experience shows that econometric models built for a country's economy have not proved so fruitful for prediction as was expected because of the manifold variables involved and the complex inter-relationship between them. However, recent advances in programming econometric models on computers offer hope that they may prove effective in forecasting economic activity .

Selecting a Forecast

Several guidelines may be indicated with a view to choose among available forecasts and use them effectively:

I. Prefer forecasts which are explicit about what is expected and in the reasoning underlying the forecast, against those which are categorical and declaratory.

2. Disregard forecasts which lack qualifiers. Future is uncertain and if the forecaster does not explain the assumption on which his predictions rest, his analysis may be shallow and it will be difficult to interpret his forecasts if conditions change.

3. Examine the records of the reliability of various forecasts made in the past. Such an examination should thoroughly see why the forecasts proved right or wrong; one should specially beware of the forecasters who have been right but for wrong reasons.

4. Use several different forecasts which have good records of reliability. The selected forecasts should be such as to have been prepared by forecasters having different biases, and by employing different techniques of construction.

5. Reject a forecast if the forecaster has injected himself too strongly as an individual into his forecast.

Evaluating Forecasts

For evaluating forecasts. it is important to bear in mind the following considerations:

I. It is necessary that the forecasts must be verifiable. For instance a forecast that the price of TISCO share win increase, can never be proved false because the prediction does not tell when the event forecast is supposed to occur.

2. While evaluating forecasts, it is again important to know whether economic or business policies were or were not altered as a result of the forecast itself. Sometimes a forecast may prove wrong because of the accuracy of the forecast. For example. a correct forecast of a coming recession might appear to be incorrect if prompt and adequate governmental measures, fiscal as well as monetary taken in the light of the forecast, prevented its occurrence. Hence the need for caution in evaluating a forecast.

3. It is also important to recognize that at times, a forecast can be true because decision-makers accept the forecast as probable and adjust their policies so that they are consistent with the forecast. Thus, if rising prices were predicted, business policy would require a 'buy now' policy causing an increase in prices.

4. It is also necessary to realize that a forecaster cannot possibly predict 'acts of God' or events of political nature.

Price forecasting

A business firm is constantly faced with the risk of a substantial change in the prices of its raw material as well as its product. The price change could be due to general economic fluctuatons but at times the prices of certain commodities might change even during comparative stability of the general price level and the economy.

The price risk can be shifted to professional risk takers by a firm but only to a limited level. Hedging against price changes is feasible for few important industrial products. Therefore it becomes necessary for the buyers sellers and all other financially interested parties in commodity markets to make a forecast. An analysis of the price movements of a commodity over a period of time will reveal certain typical fluctuations. In addition certain typical relationships of the price of commodity concerned with other business and economic factors can also be identified. These fluctuations and relationships are helpful in price forecasting and are discussed below:

a) Seasonal price variation: are common in case of agricultural commodities and food products. Such variations would take place in a market having seasonal change in either supply or demand without a corresponding change in the other of these two determinants. Seasonal variation in production, storage on large scale being uneconomical, with a comparatively constant demand is more often to be found than seasonal variations in demand with a comparatively constant supply. Prices of manufactured good doesn't have mush seasonal variations as their supply can easily be adjusted to change in demand. In some cases however manufactured goods will show a seasonal fluctuation due to marked seasonal fluctuation in the prices of its raw material. In some commodities like potato and hides the seasonal price fluctuation is not due to variations in supply and demand conditions but it is due to change in the quality of products available in different seasons.

b) Cyclic price fluctuations : Prices of all commodities show price fluctuation during business cycles. However prices of individual commodities are affected in different ways and to different extent by variations in business cycles. Some commodities would have wide fluctuations while some would have narrow fluctuation, this information is useful for forecasting prices for a commodity. The general business conditions influence the commodity prices through changes in demand and supply relationships in the market for each individual commodity.

c) Time relationship: Sometimes a time relationship between the fluctuations in the price of a commodity and certain other economic series could be found. For example, by comparing the price fluctuations of individual commodities with the fluctuation in the average price lavel, it could be observed that some commodities are early movers at cyclical turning points while others are late movers. In price forecasting for a commodity its useful to find out whether it's an early or late mover during cyclical fluctuations and to give special attention to those economic series which are particularly sensitive to pending developments.

d) Cob-web cycles : These occur on the account of the cumulative effect of the false price expectations of large number of independent producers. When farmers expect higher prices in future, they plan to produce more also new ones start producing. As a result the aggregated output when the final date arrives, is so large that prices fall. When prices fall, all the producers plan to produce less because they have suffered lassoe on account of non materialization of their expected prices. This decision results in smaller output thus creating shortage, hence raising prices, which , in turn again induces farmers for larger production plans. The alternate contraction and expansion of output create cyclic fluctuations of cob-web type in the prices of individual farm commodities. The length of the period of the cycle is generally two production periods or a bit longer.

In agriculture, the formation of the cob-web is influenced by following factors:

i) Agricultural production is biological by nature and seasonal. Hence once it has commenced, its difficult to make any changes afterwards. Also as production takes a definite lengh of time, it cannot be increased suddenly to any noticeable extent.

ii) Farm entrepreneurs are mostly small-scale operators, lack general aggregative view and wrongly believe that prevailing prices will hold on in future .

The cob-web cycles can take three forms namely

a) Explosive or divergent cycle: it's the one in which successive variations in production and prices keep on magnifying themselves

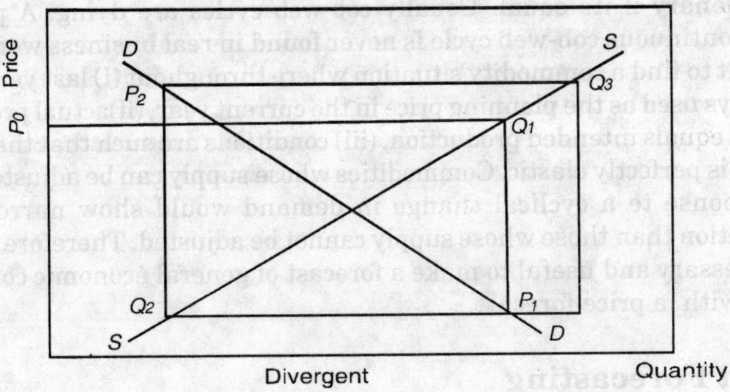

Fig. 1

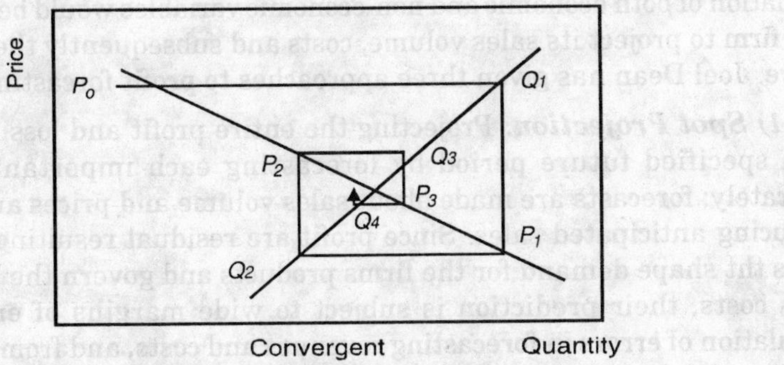

Fig. 2

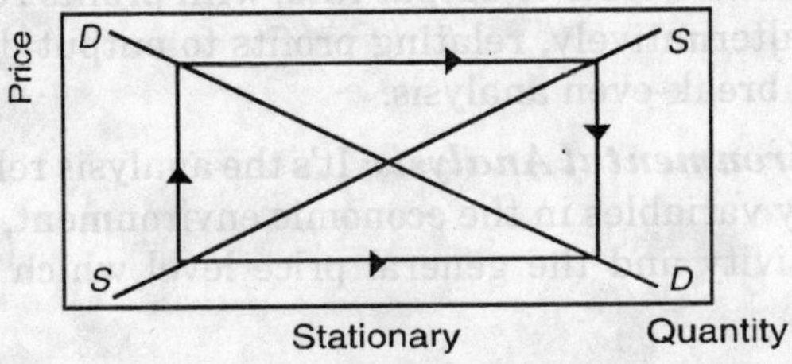

b) Dying or convergent cycle: is the one in which successive variations in production and prices keep on declining.

c) Stationary cycle is the one in which the successive variations keep constant.

Thus, if price elasticity of production is more than that of demand, the movement is dying; If less, the movement is explosive; and movement is stationary if its equal. Usually cob-web cycles are dying. A perfectly neat, continuous cob-web cycle is never found in real business world i.e its difficult to find a commodity situation where throughout (i) last year's price is always used as the planning price in the current year, (ii)actual production always equals intended production, (iii) conditions are such that the market supply is perfectly elastic. Commodities whose supply can be adjusted easily in response to a cyclical change in demand would show narrow price fluctuation than those whose supply cannot be adjusted. Therefore it would be necessary and useful to make a forecast of general economic conditions along with a price forecast.

Profit Forecasting

Projection of future earnings taking into consideration all the factors affecting (costing policies, depreciation policy, firm's pricing policies etc) business profit size is called profit forecasting. A thorough study including estimation of both economic and non-economic variables would be necessary for a firm to project its sales volume, costs and subsequently the profits in future. Joel Dean has given three approaches to profit forcasting:

1) Spot Projection: Projecting the entire profit and loss statement for a specified future period by forecasting each important element separately: forecasts are made about sales volume and prices and costs of producing anticipated sales. Since profit are residual resulting from the forces tht shape demand for the firms products and govern the behaviour of its costs, their prediction is subject to wide margins of error, from cumulation of errors in forecasting revenues and costs, and from the inter-relation of the various components of income statement.

2) Break-even analysis: Analysis identifying functional relations of both revenues and costs to output rate, with profits related to output as a residual:or alternatively, relating profits to output directly by the usual data used in break-even analysis.

3) Environmental Analysis: It's the analysis relating the company's profits to key variables in the economic environment, such as the general business activity and the general price level which are external to the company.

Factors that control profits tend to move in regular and related patterns; rate of output, wages, prices,material costs and efficiency are all inter-related by their connection with the mational markets, and by their interactions in aggregate business activity. Theories of business cycles are based on the hypotheseis that the national values of production, employment, wages and prices show systematic patterns of behaviour as business activity fluctuates.

These patterns of confluence raise the possibility that the profits of a company can be forcasted directly by finding a relation to key variables in the economy that either control or combine the movement of a number of direct forces that are reflected in the profit and loss statement. The problem is to find a direct functional relationship between profit earned by company and the national activity that shows statistical significance.

In practice, these three approaches are not necessarily mutually exclusive, instead they can be used jointly for obtaining maximum information. In projecting the profit and loss statement, functional relations of cost to output and to its other determinants can be used. Similarly direct measurement of impact of outside economic forces upon the company's profit can be make spot guessing easy and can also increase the accuracy of break-even analysis.

Questions

1. Why is economic forecasting necessary? What are the various methods of forecasting ?
2. Why is profit and price forecasting necessary for a firm ,illustrate with example. Explain the methods of price and profit forecasting

14

Some Concepts

Multi Product Firm and Pricing

Introduction

A1though economics texts at elementary and inter- mediate levels tend to focus on the single-product firm, in practice most firms produce more than one product. The reasons for this can usually be traced to either technologica1 or organizational economies. If firm is producing products which- bear 1ittle relationship to one another, and whose production processes may be large1y independent. In such cases, where products are genuinely independent of each other on both the demand side and the production side, the problem of pricing and marketing products is no different from that of the sing1e-product firm. However, in practice, most firms produce a product line in which the individual products are either substitutes (often strong substitutes) or complements.

EXAMPLE Most car manufacturers offer not on1y a range of models (substitutes), but also a range of variations for any given model type (close substitutes). That is, these products will feature positive cross-price elasticities (increasing one car's price will increases sales of the other models). They also manufacture spare parts for the cars they offer to the public. Spares are typically complements, having negative cross-price elasticity(increasing the price of spares decreases **the** demand for the associated car).

It follows that most of the products sold by the firm will be demand-interdependent. Furthermore, there is the possibility that there are cost interdependencies too. These arise when the marginal cost of manufacturing one product is affected not only by its own output level, but also by the output of the other products produced by the firm. This typically happens when products utilize common production processes, common inputs, common inventory, etc.

These interdependencies imply, theoretically at least, that it is no longer possible to determine the profit-maximizing price of each product in isolation. Pricing of the whole range of the firm's products needs to be undertaken simultaneously, in a system- wide solution. In practice most firms use ad hoc rules of thumb (often simple mark-up pricing rules) which take little account of the interdependencies discussed here. However, some firms do practise the sophisticated multi- product analysis of the type in which interdependency is taken into consideration. Large fitms and public utilities blessed with fairly stable demand functions are most likely to fall into this category, since the approach does rely on the statistical estimation of demand functions. Thus electricity, gas, telecoms, and posts are more amenable to this type of analysis.

Why Multi-Product Firms?

Essentially, products are likely to be produced within a single organizational structure if it is more profitable to do so than to produce the goods separately. The issue of what determines the internal structure and external boundaries of the firm can be stated as demand-related, cost-related, or financial.

Demand-Related Reasons for Multi-Product Firms

The argument here is that drawing products under the umbrella of a single firm may help to facilitate

price discrimination, to create barriers to entry, and to leverage monopoly power.

(a) Price Discrimination: A firm with monopoly power could improve its profitability by designing a non-linear pricing schedule by which it sells its product. Typically, this involves quantity discounts. Firms routinely apply this type of pricing when they bundle products. Thus, a car manufacturer will typically offer a model with a wide range of specifications, such that a higher-specification model is cheaper than the cost of buying a lower-specification model and buying separately the additional specification. If we imagine separate firms providing each item of specification, each with a monopoly over its item, and ask what the benefits is of putting these firms together in a single unit, the answer is that, if there are no cost-side savings, the gain can only be in organizational economies. That is, the pricing of different commodity bundles is something, which is likelv to be better co-ordinated and controlled within a single firm than by a larger number of firms. Whilst it is possible in principle for individual firms to negotiate and co-ordinate their pricing policies to achieve the same outcome, this is likely to be difficult and costly relative to that of internalising the problem, making it into a multi-product firm pricing problem.

(b) Barriers to Entry and Monopoly Leveraging It is also sometimes possible through what is termed monopoly leveraging, to exploit monopoly power in one market either to prevent others being able to enter, or to achieve a dominant position in another market. This is perhaps most likely to occur in markets where there, is a degree of lock-in to the monopoly product.

EXAMPLE Microsoft was indicted in the US for anti-competitive practices . The US Justice Department (and 20 US states) charged in their anti-trust lawsuits against Microsoft that (amongst other anti-competitive practices) Microsoft forced PC manufacturers to install its Internet browser softwa.re (Microsoft Explorer) as a condition of obtaining licences for the Windows 95 operating system.

The point behind Microsoft's behaviour is that its Internet browser is not a superior product to those of the competition -but, because Microsoft has a stranglehold over the market for operating systems, it is able to leverage a significant market share for that product.

Does such leveraging benefit the firm? A simple argument that it does can be given, based upon the s dominant-firm model. The idea is that the dominant firm (here Microsoft, selling its Internet browser) sets the market price, and other firms, acting as a competitive fringe, match this price. If so, then the dominant firm faces a is residual demand curve, and sets price such that the marginal revenue from this residual demand curve is equal to the marginal cost of production. The price set is then matched by the other manufacturers. The point is that the dominant firm leads the market, and in particular, is able to set a price above its marginal production cost (and a price above that which would result if no firm had a dominant position). The dominant firm gains additional profit from the market. Thus tying products together may be beneficial for the multi-product firm -in that tying may earn greater profit than if the products were produced separately.

Of course, in principle, separate firms can also tie their products too, and such practices are not uncommon

EXAMPLE Microsoft also entered into anti- competitive agreements with the largest online services, such as America Online, as well as with Internet providers. In return for promoting these services on Windows, these companies agreed not to promote Netscape's browser software- Netscape being an Internet browser competitor to Microsoft Explorer.

Inter-firm collusive agreements of this type are typically illegal and so are subject to government intervention (as in the above examples). It is some what more difficult for the state to track such processes if they occur within a firm, so this suggests a further rationale, alongside the usual organizational economies, for the multi-product firm.

Cost-Related Reasons for Multi-Product Firms

The cost-based rationale for the multi product firm is based on the concept of economies of scope. In general, economies of scope arise because input resources have the characteristics of a public good. A public input is one in which the use of the input does not deplete its availability for other uses. Thus many can use a database, once set up,; use by one individual does not deplete it in any significant way (although there may be access congestion, of course). Shared facilities often give rise to this type of effect; production of one item often creates spare capacity which can be utilized for the production of other items more cheaply than if they are produced in a stand-alone mode. Thus, once capacity for day- time electricity demand is installed, it is available for the provision of night-time electricity. Whilst it may be possible in principle to offer to sell the use of spare capacity to other producers, there are usually organizational economies for multi-product firms in bringing these products in-house. Of course there are many famous cases where there are natural economies of scope associated with production, such as beef and hides, mutton and sheep, wheat and straw, and the refining of oil into a multiplicity of products. It is clearly cheaper to produce these jointly rather than separately (in these cases, single-product production would simply throwaway a nearly finished additional product). Multi-product production thus tends to facilitate a fuller asset (capacity) utilization over time by reducing indivisibilities or lumpiness in the production process. For example, when a product's demand is seasonal, it pays the firm to try to find other products which can utilize the capacity at other times.

It is useful to distinguish technological or plant economies of scope from overall firm economies of scope. Technological economies of scope are those associated with the production process itself (as in the hides and beef example) whilst firm economies of scope include these, but additionally involve organizational economies of scope. Organizational economies of scope are common as very little addition in overhead are required in order to add a new product to the product range

Financial Reasons for Multi-Product Firm

It is sometimes argued that, by diversification and producing a wider range of products, the firm spreads its risks, particularly if the products are not close substitutes and therefore less likely to be affected by the same environmental factors and market movements. Basic finance theory suggests this argument is fallacious, on the grounds that diversification of this type does not add value to the company. This is because shareholders are already diversified, so they get no further advantage from the firm itself diversifying (they can, relatively cost- lessly, do or undo any action of this type taken by the firm, simply by readjusting their portfolios). When real-world complexity (managerial discretion, taxes, asymmetric information, etc.) is introduced, the picture is considerably less clear. Thus:

(i) in practice there may be some tax advantages associated with such diversification, with the possibility that the firm may benefit from the particular ways that tax authorities deal with tax losses (more products means greater scope for offsetting tax losses)

(ii) diversification may also facilitate dividend smoothing, again something to be of interest to both managers and shareholders

(iii) managerial discretion theory suggests that managers' concerns also count-and fairly clearly, diversification is of benefit as it reduces the company's total risk and hence the risk to their jobs. Thus one would expect the some pressure for diversification from managers, even if this does not particularly advance the interests of the firm's owners

(iv) in practice, there may also be benefits in that the larger the enterprise, the lowerthe costsof raising finance (equity , debt issues etc) may be reduced.

Limits to Diversification?

All the above discussion suggests there may be benefits to increasing the size of the firm-to increasing the number of products produced under one umbrella. So why is there not a single global firm? What limits the boundaries of the firm? The answer is usually that there are also diseconomies associated with organization, and these eventually become significant as size increases.

Cost and Demand Categorization

When there are economies of scope, there is an incentive to set up a multi-product firm. With common provision and use of common facilities, it is quite likely that the cost function will feature some degree of interdependency in the sense that the marginal cost of producing each product may be affected not only by its own output level, but also by that of the other products in the product range. Likewise, because products in the product range are often related and hence substitutes, demand interdependence is also common. Whenever there is interdependence on the cost or demand sides, profit-maximizing prices cannot be determined for products independently

Table : The multi-product pricing problem

		Demand	
		Independent (zero cross-price elasticities	Interdependent (non-zero cross price elasticities)
Cost	Independent (marginal cost independent of other product outputs)	Price each product separately	System solution required
	Interdependent (marginal cost varies with other product outputs)	System solution required	System solution required

Cost Dependence or Independence

Two products are cost-independent if, as the output of the first product is varied, the marginal cost of the second does not change. A set of products is said to be cost-independent if, when each output is varied, this variation does not affect the marginal costs of producing any of the other products in the set

A set of products is cost-interdependent if for each product in the set, its marginal cost depends on the output of at least one other product in the set.

Demand Dependence and Independence

The firm's products are often substitutes (and occasionally are complements) for each other, and hence have non-zero cross-price elasticities. Whenever the cross-price elasticity is non-zero, we say .there is demand interdependence.

The n-product Pricing Problem

If there is interdependence either on the cost or on the demand side, then the theoretical problem of setting prices in order to maximize profits requires the solution of a set of simultaneous equations (equal to the number of products). It is not possible to identify this optimum by setting prices for the various products either sequentially or independently. However, if there is independence on both the cost and demand side, then the products may be priced in isolation. To see this, we examine the mathematics of the problem. The necessary ingredients for optimizing prices for multiple products are estimates of the demand functions for each product and the cost function which describes how cost varies as the output mix and volume is varied.

Suppose the firm manufactures n products. Ordinary demand functions (assumed to be differentiable functions) for these take the form

$$q_i = f_i(p), \qquad i = 1, ..., n, \qquad \text{eq (1)}$$

where q_i , $i = 1, ..., n$ are the quantities demanded and

$p=(p_1,p_2,.....,p_n)$ are the prices set by the firm.

The formulation in eq.(1) indicates that the prices of each of the firm's n products may have an influence on the sales of each product (although typically the own price will be the major determinant of an individual product's sales). The total cost of producing output $q = (q_1, q_2, \dots, q_n)$ is assumed to be a smooth function C(q). The firm's profits are thus given as

$$\pi = (\Sigma\, p_i q_i) - C(q)$$

Given the ordinary demand function eq(1), the first-order necessary conditions for maximum profits are most easily obtained through analysis in price space. This treats the n prices as choice variables; the first-order conditions are thus

$$\partial\pi / \partial p_j = q_j + \Sigma(p_i - \partial C(q) /\partial p_i) (\partial q_i/\partial p_j) \qquad i=1,\ldots,n$$
$$= 0 \qquad j= 1,\ldots,n.$$

In fact, so long as the demand and cost functions are reasonably well behaved, these n equations, in conjunction with the demand equation , suffice to identify the optimum prices, outputs, and attainable profit for the firm. However, this may not be immediately obvious; the following numerical example illustrates the solution process.

EXAMPLE Consider a simple two-product firm whose cost function takes the simple linear form

$C(q_1, q_2) = 100 + 10q_1 + 20q_2$ .....(i)

(so costs are independent) and whose demand functions are also linear and given as

$q_1 = 100 - p_1 + p_2$ .....(ii)

$q_1 = 50 + p_1 - 2p_2$. .....(iii)

The profit function can then be written as

$\pi = p_1q_1 + p_2q_2 - 100 - 10q_1 - 20q_2$. .....(iv)

Using (ii) and (iii), this can be written as

$\pi = (p_1 - 10)(100- p_1 + p_2) + (p_2 - 20) (50 + p_1 - 2p_2) - 100$ ... (v)

Differentiating this with respect to the two choice variables gives the first-order conditions as follows : (expand (v) first if you find it easier to then perform the differentiation):

$\partial\pi/\partial p_1 = (100 + p_1 - p_2) - (p_1 - 10) + 2(p_2 - 20)$

$= 90 - 2p_1 + 24p_2 = 0$ ....(vi)

$\partial\pi/\partial p_2 = (p_1 - 10) + (50 + p_1 - 2p_2) - 2(p_2 - 20)$

$= 80 - 2p_1 + 4p_2 = 0$ ....(vii)

Solving this pair of equations gives optimal prices $p_1 = 130$ and $p_2 = 85$. Substituting these values into (ii) and (iii) gives quantities $q_1 = 55$ and $q_2 = 10$, and substituting the prices into (v) gives profit level 7150.

Note in above Example that, with two products, the first-order conditions generate twô equations in the two unknowns p_1 and p_2. This observation can be generalized; with n products, there are n equa- tions which, if well behaved, can be solved for the n prices p1, ...pn. The simple linear form of the cost and demand functions makes the analytic solution process fairly straightforward in the above example (and linear systems such as this can always be viewed as approximations to more complex non- linear systems in the region of the optimum). More generally, however, the equations obtained may be non-linear and complex in structure. In such cases, a variety of algorithms exist which can be used to obtain the optimal solution.

Multiple Products and Organizational Structure

Typically, multi-product firms, particularly large firms, may be organized such that individual sections or divisions of the firm are responsible for individual products, or subsets of the total set of products manufactured by the firm. There are many reasons for this. Divisionalization helps to keep jobs manageable and can stimulate competition amongst managers or divisions, leading to improvements in the productivity of both production and marketing practices. However, there is a potential problem when the products being sold by the divisions are related in demand (either as substitutes or as complements): if a manager is concerned only with her own profit, she will ignore the spillover effects of the pricing decision for this product on the other products manufactured by the firm (and the same point applies to related decisions, such as advertizing and marketing decisions generally). Thus, the manager of the division selling the jth product, if concerned only with her own performance, will compute a price using the mark-up rule.If the products are substitutes, as is usually the case for a product line of similar goods, then this suggests that individual managers/divisions will tend to set their prices too low.

The danger is thus that product managers get drawn into competing against each other, while the firm as a whole benefits only if they co-operate. Each product manager sees the demand for their product as relatively elastic (because of the presence of competition from the rest of the product line) and is inclined to set too low a price. This ignores the fact that although raising price does lose sales, it also increases the sales of other managers/ divisions.

In principle it is organizationally possible to over- come this type of problem, so long as managers meet, exchange the relevant information, and agree on an overall set of prices which maximizes the .firm's profits as a whole. Indeed, if one argues that bargaining (etc.) costs are small, it can be argued that the divisions will take into account spillover effects, and will come to some form of agreement. In practice, however, such agreements are costly to implement; there is considerable asymmetry of information and much scope for game-playing. For example, there are elements of a prisoners' dilemma about the pricing situation. Individual product managers may initially agree to setting higher prices, but will then have an incentive to cheat on that agreement. That is, once the agreement has been reached, individual managers will have an incentive to sell more product by (secretly) offering discounts and price reductions to customers. This may be individually rational but can lead to a general erosion of prices and adverse profit con- sequences for the firm as a whole.

Organizationally, therefore, it would appear beneficial to choose product groupings such that products within a group manifest demand and/or cost interdependency, whilst between groupings there are relatively low-order demand and/or cost interdependencies. Managers looking after such product groups would then be motivated to internalize the form of within-group externality described above. However, if the product groupings turn out to be too large for a single decision-maker to manage, then the communication problems of the type described above may need to be faced. This suggests that, quite apart from any other considerations, cost and demand interdependencies give rise to organizational trade- offs in the choice of product groupings.

Questions:

1. 'Whether products are produced by a single firm, or by separate single-product firms, depends solely on whether there are economies of scope or not.'According to theory, is this true?, Discuss.
2. A monopolist produces two goods labelled a and b. The cost of producing quantities qa and qb of a and b is given by $C = (q_a + q_b)^2$. The inverse demand schedules are estimated to be pa = 10 - q_a and $p_b = 20 - 2q_b$ respectively.
   (a) If the firm wishes to maximize profits, what prices and output levels should it adopt? What is the attainable level of profit?
   (b) If the firm faces a per unit tax of r on good a, how does this affect its price and output choices? (Hint: first write down an expression for the firm's after-tax profits; the tax payment is simply rq).
   (c) There is an impact on both product prices of imposing the tax in (b). Explain intuitively the direction of the impact of the tax on product prices. (Hint: consider the type of - product interdependence involved in this model.)
3. 'Price discrimination is simply a special case of multi-product pricing.' True or false? Discuss.

Optimizing Economic Order Quantity (EOQ) Definition: That quantity derived from a mathematical technique used to determine the optimum (lowest) total variable costs required to order and hold inventory.

Inventory models for calculating optimal order quantities and reorder points have been in existence long before the arrival of the computer. When the first Model T Fords were rolling off the assembly line, manufacturers were already reaping the financial benefits of inventory management by determining the most cost effective answers to the questions of When? and How much?. Long before JIT, TQM, TOC, and MRP, companies were using these same (then unnamed) concepts in managing their production and inventory. So why is it that, in these days of advanced information technology, many companies are still not taking advantage of these fundamental inventory models? Part of the answer lies in poor results received due to inaccurate data inputs. Accurate product costs, activity costs, forecasts, history, and lead times are crucial in making inventory models work. Ironically, software advancements may also in part to blame. Many ERP packages come with built in calculations for EOQ which calculate automatically. Often the users do not understand how it is calculated and therefore do not understand the data inputs and system setup which controls the output. When the output appears to be "out of whack" it is simply ignored. This sometimes creates a situation in which the executives who had purchased the software incorrectly assume the material planners and purchasing clerks are ordering based upon the systems recommendations. Many operations will find these built-in EOQ calculations inadequate and in need of modifications to deal with the diversity of their product groups and processes.

Corporate goals and strategies may sometimes conflict with EOQ. Measuring performance solely by inventory turns is one of the most prolific mistakes made in the name of inventory management. Many companies have achieved aggressive goals in increasing inventory turns only to find their bottom line has shrunk due to increased operational costs.

EOQ is essentially an accounting formula that determines the point at which the combination of order costs and inventory carrying costs are the least. The result is the most cost effective quantity to order. In purchasing this is known as the order quantity, in manufacturing it is known as the production lot size.

While EOQ may not apply to every inventory situation, most organizations will find it beneficial in at least some aspect of their operation. Anytime the firms have repetitive purchasing or planning of an item, EOQ should be considered. Obvious applications for EOQ are purchase-to-stock distributors and make-to-stock manufacturers, however, make-to-order manufacturers should also consider EOQ when they have multiple orders or release dates for the same items and when planning components and sub-assemblies. Repetitive buy maintenance, repair, and operating (MRO) inventory is also a good application for EOQ. Though EOQ is generally recommended in operations where demand is relatively steady, items with demand variability such as seasonality can still use the model by going to shorter time periods for the EOQ calculation. Just make sure your usage and carrying costs are based on the same time period.

Doesn't EOQ conflict with Just-In-Time? A common misunderstanding is JIT means all components should arrive in the exact run quantities "just in time" for the production run. JIT is actually a quality initiative with the goal of eliminating wasted steps, wasted labor, and wasted cost. EOQ should be one of the tools used to achieve this. EOQ is used to determine which components fit into this JIT model and what level of JIT is economically advantageous for the firm's operation. As an example, let us assume the firm is a lawn equipment manufacturer and the firm produce

100 units per day of a specific model of lawn mower. While it may be cost effective to have 100 engines arrive on the firm's dock each day, it would certainly not be cost effective to have 500 screws (1 days supply) used to mount a plastic housing on the lawn mower shipped to the firm daily. To determine the most cost effective quantities of screws or other components the firm will need to use the EOQ formula.

The basic Economic Order Quantity (EOQ) formula is as follows:

$$EOQ = \sqrt{\frac{2(\text{Annual usage in units})(\text{Order cost})}{(\text{Annual carrying cost per unit})}}$$

The Inputs

While the calculation itself is fairly simple the task of determining the correct data inputs to accurately represent the firm's inventory and operation is a bit of a project. Exaggerated order costs and carrying costs are common mistakes made in EOQ calculations. Using all costs associated with the firm's purchasing and receiving departments to calculate order cost or using all costs associated with storage and material handling to calculate carrying cost will give the firm highly inflated costs resulting in inaccurate results from the firm's EOQ calculation. One should not use benchmarks or published industry standards in calculations. As the firm prepare to undertake this project keep in mind that even though accuracy is crucial, small variances in the data inputs generally have very little effect on the outputs. The following breaks down the data inputs in more detail and gives insight into the aspects of each.

Annual Usage

Expressed in units, this is generally the easiest part of the equation. The firm simply input its forecasted annual usage.

Order Cost

Also known as purchase cost or set up cost, this is the sum of the fixed costs that are incurred each time an item is ordered. These costs are not associated with the quantity ordered but primarily with physical activities required to process the order.

For **purchased items,** these would include the cost to enter the purchase order and/or requisition, any approval steps, the cost to process the receipt, incoming inspection, invoice processing and vendor payment, and in some cases a portion of the inbound freight may also be included in order cost. It is important to understand that these are costs associated with the frequency of the orders and not the quantities ordered. For example, in the firm's receiving department the time spent checking in the receipt, entering the receipt, and doing any other related paperwork would be included, while the time spent repacking materials, unloading trucks, and delivery to other departments would likely not be included. If the firm have inbound quality inspection where the firm inspect a percentage of the quantity received the firm would include the time to get the specs and process the paperwork and not include time spent actually inspecting, however if the firm inspect a fixed quantity per receipt the firm would then include the entire time including inspecting, repacking, etc. In the purchasing department the firm would include all time associated with creating the purchase order, approval steps, contacting the vendor, expediting, and reviewing order reports, the firm would not include time spent reviewing forecasts, sourcing, getting quotes (unless the firm get quotes each time the firm order), and setting up new items. All time spent dealing with vendor invoices would be included in order cost.

Associating actual costs to the activities associated with order cost is where many an EOQ formula runs afoul. Do not make a list of all of the activities and then ask the people performing the activities "how long does it take you to do this?" The results of this type of measurement are rarely even close to accurate. It is more effective to determine the percentage of time within the department consumed performing the specific activities and multiplying this by the total labor costs for a certain time period (usually a month) and then dividing by the line items processed during that same period.

It is extremely difficult to associate inbound freight costs with order costs in an automated EOQ program and it should be taken only if the inbound freight cost has a significant effect on unit cost and its effect on unit cost varies significantly based upon the order quantity.

In **manufacturing,** the order cost would include the time to initiate the work order, time associated with picking and issuing components excluding time associated with counting and handling specific quantities, all production scheduling time, machine set up time, and inspection time. Production scrap directly associated with the machine setup should also be included in order cost as would be any tooling that is discarded after each production run. There may be times when the firm wants to artificially inflate or deflate set-up costs. If the firm lack the capacity to meet the production schedule using the EOQ, the firm may want to artificially increase set-up costs to increase lot sizes and reduce overall set up time. If the firm has excess capacity it may want to artificially decrease set up costs, this will increase overall set up time and reduce inventory investment. The idea being that if the firm are paying for the labor and machine overhead anyway it would make sense to take advantage of the savings in reduced inventories.

For the most part, order cost is primarily the labor associated with processing the order, however, the firm can include the other costs such as the costs of phone calls, faxes, postage, envelopes, etc.

Carrying cost

Also called Holding cost, carrying cost is the cost associated with having inventory on hand. It is primarily made up of the costs associated with the inventory investment and storage cost. For the purpose of the EOQ calculation, if the cost does not change based upon the quantity of inventory on hand it should not be included in carrying cost. In the EOQ formula, carrying cost is represented as the annual cost per average on hand inventory unit. Below are the primary components of carrying cost.

Interest: If the firm had to borrow money to pay for the firm's inventory, the interest rate would be part of the carrying cost. If the firm did not borrow on the inventory, but have loans on other capital items, the firm can use the interest rate on those loans since a reduction in inventory would free up money that could be used to pay these loans. If by some miracle the firm are debt free the firm would need to determine how much the firm could make if the money was invested.

Insurance: Since insurance costs are directly related to the total value of the inventory, the firm would include this as part of carrying cost.

Taxes: If the firm is required to pay any taxes on the value of the firm's inventory they would also be included.

Storage Costs: Mistakes in calculating storage costs are common in EOQ implementations. Generally companies take all costs associated with the warehouse and divide it by the average inventory to determine a storage cost percentage for the EOQ calculation. This tends to include costs that are not directly affected by the inventory levels and does not compensate for storage characteristics. Carrying costs for the purpose of the EOQ calculation should only include costs that are variable based upon inventory levels.

If the firm is running a pick/pack operation where the firm have fixed picking locations assigned to each item where the locations are sized for picking efficiency and are not designed to hold the entire inventory, this portion of the warehouse should not be included in carrying cost since changes to inventory levels do not effect costs here. The firm's overflow storage areas would be included in carrying cost. Operations that use purely random storage for their product would include the entire storage area in the calculation. Areas such as shipping/receiving and staging areas are usually not included in the storage calculations. However, if the firm have to add an additional warehouse just for overflow inventory then the firm would include all areas of the second warehouse as well as freight and labor costs associated with moving the material between the warehouses.

Since storage costs are generally applied as a percentage of the inventory value the firm may need to classify the firm's inventory based upon a ratio of storage space requirements to value in order to assess storage costs accurately. For example, let's say the firm have just opened a new E-business called "WeSellEverything.com". The firm calculated that overall the firm's annual storage costs were 5% of the firm's average inventory value, and applied this to the firm's entire inventory in the EOQ calculation. The firm's average inventory on a particular piece of software and on 80 kg bags of concrete mix both came to Rs10,000. The EOQ formula applied a Rs 500 storage cost to the average quantity of each of these items even though the software actually took up only 1 pallet position while the concrete mix consumed 75 pallet positions. Categorizing these items would place the software in a category with minimal storage costs (1% or less) and the concrete in a category with extreme storage costs (50%) that would then allow the EOQ formula to work correctly.

There are situations where the firm may not want to include any storage costs in the firm's EOQ calculation. If the firm's operation has excess storage space of which it has no other uses it may decide not to include storage costs since reducing the firm's inventory does not provide any actual savings in storage costs. As the firm's operation grows near a point at which the firm would need to expand the firm's physical operations it may then start including storage in the calculation.

A portion of the time spent on cycle counting should also be included in carrying cost, remember to apply costs which change based upon changes to the average inventory level. So with cycle counting, the firm would include the time spent physically counting and not the time spent filling out paperwork, data entry, and travel time between locations.

Other costs that can be included in carrying cost are risk factors associated with obsolescence, damage, and theft. Do not factor in these costs unless they are a direct result of the inventory levels and are significant enough to change the results of the EOQ equation.

Variations

There are many variations on the basic EOQ model. The most useful ones are listed below.

- Quantity discount logic can be programmed to work in conjunction with the EOQ formula to determine optimum order quantities. Most systems will require this additional programming.
- Additional logic can be programmed to determine max quantities for items subject to spoilage or to prevent obsolescence on items reaching the end of their product life cycle.
- When used in manufacturing to determine lot sizes where production runs are very long (weeks or months) and finished product is being released to stock and consumed/sold throughout the production run the firm may

need to take into account the ratio of production to consumption to more accurately represent the average inventory level.

• The firm's safety stock calculation may take into account the order cycle time that is driven by the EOQ. If so, the firm may need to tie the cost of the change in safety stock levels into the formula.

Implementing EOQ

There are primarily two ways to implement EOQ. Both methods obviously require that the firm have already determined the associated costs. The simplest method is to set up the firm's calculation in a spreadsheet program, manually calculate EOQ one item at a time, and then manually enter the order quantity into the firm's inventory system. If the firm's inventory has fairly steady demand and costs and the firm can probably use this method once per year. If the firm has higher variability in demand and costs the firm will need to program the EOQ formula into the firm's existing inventory system. This allows the firm to quickly re-calculate EOQ automatically as often as needed. The firm can also use a hybrid of the two systems by downloading the firm's data to a spreadsheet or database program, perform the calculations and then update the firm's inventory system either manually or through a batch program. Whichever method the firm use the firm should make sure to follow the following steps:

• **Test the formula**. Prior to final implementation the firm must test the programming and setup. Run the EOQ program and then manually check the results using sample items that are representative of the variations of the firm's inventory base.

• **Project results**. The firm will need to run a simulation or use a representative sampling of items to determine the overall short-term and long-term effects the EOQ calculation will have on warehouse space, cash flow, and operations. Dramatic increases in inventory levels may not be immediately feasible, if this is the case the firm may temporarily adjust the formula until arrangements can be made to handle the additional storage requirements and compensate for the effects on cash flow. If the projection shows inventory levels dropping and order frequency increasing, the firm may need to evaluate staffing, equipment, and process changes to handle the increased activity.

• **Maintain EOQ**. The values for Order cost and Carrying cost should be evaluated at least once per year taking into account any changes in interest rates, storage costs, and operational costs.

A related calculation is the **Total Annual Cost** calculation. This calculation can be used to prove the EOQ calculation. Total Annual Cost = [(annual usage in units)/(order quantity)(order cost)]+{[.5(order quantity)+(safety stock)]*(annual carrying cost per unit)}. This formula is also very useful when comparing quotes where vendors offer different minimum order quantities, price breaks, lead times, transportation costs.

The EOQ calculation is "Hard Science", if the firm have accurate inputs the output is the most cost-effective quantity to order based upon the firm's current operational costs. To further increase inventory turns the firm will need to reduce the order costs. E-procurement, vendor-managed inventories, bar coding, and vendor certification programs can reduce the costs associated with processing an order. Equipment enhancements and process changes can reduce costs associated with manufacturing set up. Increasing forecast accuracy and reducing lead times which result in the ability to operate with reduced safety stock can also reduce inventory levels.

Cost Benefit Analysis

Background

Cost-Benefit Analysis (CBA) estimates and totals up the equivalent money value of the benefits and costs to the community of projects to establish whether they are worthwhile. These projects may be dams and highways or can be training programs and health care systems.

Principles of Cost Benefit Analysis

One of the problems of CBA is that the computation of many components of benefits and costs is intuitively obvious but that there are others for which intuition fails to suggest methods of measurement. Therefore some basic principles are needed as a guide.

There Must Be a Common Unit of Measurement

In order to reach a conclusion as to the desirability of a project all aspects of the project, positive and negative, must be expressed in terms of a common unit; i.e., there must be a "bottom line." The most convenient common unit is money. This means that all benefits and costs of a project should be measured in terms of their equivalent money value. A program may provide benefits which are not directly expressed in terms of rupees but there is some amount of money the recipients of the benefits would consider just as good as the project's benefits. For example, a project may provide for the elderly in an area a free monthly visit to a doctor. The value of that benefit to an elderly recipient is the minimum amount of money that that recipient would take instead of the medical care. This could be less than the market value of the medical care provided. It is assumed that more esoteric benefits such as from preserving open space or historic sites have a finite equivalent money value to the public.

Not only do the benefits and costs of a project have to be expressed in terms of equivalent money value, but they have to be expressed in terms of rupees of a particular time. This is not just due to the differences in the value of rupees at different times because of inflation. A rupee available five years from now is not as good as a rupee available now. This is because a rupee available now can be invested and earn interest for five year and would be worth more than a rupee in five years. If the interest rate is r then a rupee invested for t years will grow to be $(1+r)^t$. Therefore the amount of money that would have to be deposited now so that it would grow to be one rupee t years in the future is $(1+r)^{-t}$. This called the discounted value or present value of a rupee available t years in the future.

When the rupee value of benefits at some time in the future is multiplied by the discounted value of one dollar at that time in the future the result is discounted present value of that benefit of the project. The same thing applies to costs. The net benefit of the projects is just the sum of the present value of the benefits less the present value of the costs.

The choice of the appropriate interest rate to use for the discounting is a separate issue that had to be considered.

CBA Valuations Should Represent Consumers or Producers Valuations As Revealed by Their Actual Behavior

The valuation of benefits and costs should reflect preferences revealed by choices which have been made. For example, improvements in transportation frequently involve saving time. The question is how to measure the money value of that time saved. The value should not be merely what transportation planners think time should be worth or even what people say their time is worth. The value of time should be that which the public reveals their time is worth through choices involving tradeoffs between time and money. If people have choice of parking close to their destination for a fee of Rs 10 or parking farther away and spending 5 minutes more walking and they always choose to spend the money and save the time and effort then they have revealed that their time is more valuable them than Rs 5 per minute. If they were indifferent between the two choices they would have revealed that the value of their time to them was exactly Rs 5 per minute.

The most challenging part of CBA is finding past choices which reveal the tradeoffs and equivalencies in preferences. For example, the valuation of the benefit of cleaner air could be established by finding how much less people paid for housing in more polluted areas which otherwise was identical in characteristics and location to housing in less polluted areas. Generally the value of cleaner air to people as revealed by the hard market choices seems to be less than their rhetorical valuation of clean air.

Benefits Are Usually Measured by Market Choices

When consumers make purchases at market prices they reveal that the things they buy are at least as beneficial to them as the money they relinquish. Consumers will increase their consumption of any commodity up to the point where the benefit of an additional unit (marginal benefit) is equal to the marginal cost to them of that unit, the market price. Therefore for any consumer buying some of a commodity, the marginal benefit is equal to the market price. The marginal benefit will decline with the amount consumed just as the market price has to decline to get consumers to consume a greater quantity of the commodity. The relationship between the market price and the quantity consumed is called the demand schedule. Thus the demand schedule provides the information about marginal benefit that is needed to place a money value on an increase in consumption.

Gross Benefits of an Increase in Consumption is an Area Under the Demand Curve

The increase in benefits resulting from an increase in consumption is the sum of the marginal benefit times each incremental increase in consumption. As the incremental increases considered are taken as smaller and smaller the sum goes to the area under the marginal benefit curve. But the marginal benefit curve is the same as the demand curve so the increase in benefits is the area under the demand curve

Some Measurements of Benefits Require the Valuation of Human Life

It is sometimes necessary in CBA to evaluate the benefit of saving human lives. There is considerable antipathy in the general public to the idea of placing a rupee value on human life. Economists recognize that it is impossible to fund every project which promises to save a human life and that some rational basis is needed to select which projects are approved and which are turned down. The controversy is defused when it is recognized that the benefit of such projects is in reducing the risk of death. There are many cases in which people voluntarily accept increased risks in return for higher pay, such as in the oil fields or mining, or for time savings in higher speed in automobile travel. These choices can be used to estimate the personal cost people place on increased risk and thus the value to them of reduced risk. This computation is equivalent to placing an economic value on the expected number of lives saved.

The Analysis of a Project Should Involve a With Versus Without Comparison

The <u>**impact**</u> of a project is the difference between what the situation in the study area would be with and without the project. This that when a project is being evaluated the analysis must estimate not only what the situation would be with the project but also what it would be without the project. For example, shows the importance of considering the impacts of a project and a with-and-without comparison. Suppose an irrigation project proposes to increase cotton production in Arizona. If the United States Department of Agriculture limits the cotton production in the U.S. by a system of quotas then expanded cotton production in Arizona might be offset by a reduction in the cotton production quota for Mississippi. Thus the impact of the project on cotton production in the U.S. might be zero rather than being the amount of cotton produced by the project.

Cost Benefit Analysis Involves a Particular Study Area

The impacts of a project are defined for a particular study area, be it a city, region, state, nation or the world. In the above example concerning cotton the impact of the project might be zero for the nation but still be a positive amount for Arizona.

The nature of the study area is usually specified by the organization sponsoring the analysis. Many effects of a project may "net out" over one study area but not over a smaller one. The specification of the study area may be arbitrary but it may significantly affect the conclusions of the analysis.

Double Counting of Benefits or Costs Must be Avoided

Sometimes an impact of a project can be measured in two or more ways. For example, when an improved highway reduces travel time and the risk of injury the value of property in areas served by the highway will be enhanced. The increase in property values due to the project is a very good way, at least in principle, to measure the benefits of a project. But if the increased property values are included then it is unnecessary to include the value of the time and lives saved by the improvement in the highway. The property value went up because of the benefits of the time saving and the reduced risks. To include both the increase in property values and the time saving and risk reduction would involve double counting.

Decision Criteria for Projects

If the discounted present value of the benefits exceeds the discounted present value of the costs then the project is worthwhile. This is equivalent to the condition that the net benefit must be positive. Another equivalent condition is that the ratio of the present value of the benefits to the present value of the costs must be greater than one.

If there are more than one mutually exclusive projects that have positive net present value then there has to be further analysis. From the set of mutually exclusive project the one that should be selected is the one with the highest net present value.

If the funds required to carry out all of the projects with positive net present value are less than the funds available this means the discount rate used in computing the present values is too low and does not reflect the true cost of capital. The present values must be recomputed using a higher discount rate. It may take some trial and error to find a discount rate such that the funds required for the projects with a positive net present value is no more than the funds available. Sometimes as an alternative to this procedure people try to select the best projects on the basis of some measure of goodness such as the internal rate of return or the benefit/cost ratio. This is not valid for several reasons.

The magnitude of the ratio of benefits to costs is to a degree arbitrary because some costs such as operating costs may be deducted from benefits and thus not be included in the cost figure. This may be done for some projects and not for others. This manipulation of the benefits and costs will not affect the net benefits and it will not raise the benefit cost ratio which is less than one to above one.

An Example

To illustrate how CBA might be applied to a project, let us consider a highway improvement such as the extension of Highway. The local four-lane highway which carried the freeway and commuter traffic into santiago did not have a median divider and inordinate number of fatal head-on collisions occur there The improvement of the highway would lead to more capacity which produces time saving and lowers the risk. But inevitably there will be more traffic than was carried by the old highway.

The following is a highly abbreviated analysis using hypothetical data.

TRIP DATA	No Extension	Extension
Rush Hours		
Passenger Trips (per hour)	3,000	4,000
Trip Time (minutes)	50	30
Value of Time ($/minute)	$0.10	$0.10
Nonrush Hours		
Passenger Trips (per hour)	500	555.55
Trip Time (minutes)	35	25
Value of Time ($/minute)	$0.08	$0.08
Traffic Fatalities (per year)	12	6

The data indicates that for rush-hour trips the time cost of a trip is $5 without the project and $3 with it. It is assumed that the operating cost for a vehicle is unaffected by the project and is $4.

The project lowers the cost of a trip and the public responds by increasing the number of trips taken. There is an increase in consumer surplus both for the trips which would have been taken without the project and for the trips which are stimulated by the project.

For trips which would have been taken anyway the benefit of the project equals the value of the time saved times the number of trips. For the rush-hour trip the project saves $2 and for the nonrush-hour trip it saves $0.80. For the trips generated by the project the benefit is equal to one half of the value of the time saved times the increase in the number of trips.

The benefits per hour are:

TYPE	Trips Which Would Be Taken Anyway	Trips Generated By the Project	Total
Rush Hour	6,000.00	1,000.00	7,000.00
Nonrush Hour	400.00	22.22	422.22

To convert the benefits to an annual basis one multiplies the hourly benefits of each type of trip times the number of hours per year for that type of trip. There are 260 week days per year and at six rush hours per weekday there are 1560 rush hours per year. This leaves 7200 nonrush hours per year. With these figures the annual benefits are:

TYPE	Trips Which Would Be Taken Anyway	Trips Generated By the Project	Total
Rush Hour	$9,360,000	$1,560,000	$10,020,000
Nonrush Hour	$2,880,000	$160,000	$3,040,000
Total	$12,240,000	$1,720,000	$13,960,000

The value of the reduced fatalities may be computed in terms of the equivalent economic value people place upon their lives when making choices concerning risk and money. If the labor market has wages for occupations of different risks such that people accept an increase in the risk of death of 1/1,000 per year in return for an increase in income of $400 per year then a project that reduces the risk of death in a year by 1/1000 gives a benefit to each person affected by it of $400 per year. The implicit valuation of a life in this case is $400,000. Thus benefit of the reduced risk project is the expected number of lives saved times the implicit value of a life. For the highway project this is 6x$400,000= $2,400,000 annually.

The annual benefits of the project are thus:

TYPE OF BENEFIT	VALUE OF BENEFITS PER YEAR
Time Saving	$13,960,000
Reduced Risk	$2,400,000

Let us assume that this level of benefits continues at a constant rate over a thirty-year lifetime of the project.

The cost of the highway consists of the costs for its right-of-way, its construction and its maintenance. The cost of the right-of-way is the cost of the land and any structures upon it which must be purchased before the construction of the highway can begin. For purposes of this example the cost of right-of-way is taken to be $100 million and it must be paid before any construction can begin. At least part of the right-of- way cost for a highway can be recovered at the end of the lifetime of the highway if it is not rebuilt. For the example it is assumed that all of the right-of-way cost is recoverable at the end of the thirty-year lifetime of the project. The construction cost is $200 million spread evenly over a four-year period. Maintence cost is $1 million per year once the highway is completed.

The schedule of benefits and costs for the project are as follows:

TIME (year)	BENEFITS ($millions)	RIGHT-OF -WAY ($millions)	CONSTRUCTION COSTS ($millions)	MAINTENANCE ($millions)
0	0	100	0	0
1-4	0	0	50	0
5-29	16.36	0	0	1
30	16.36	-100	0	1

The benefits and costs are in constant value dollars; i.e., there was no price increase included in the analysis. Therefore the discount rate used must be the real interest rate. If the interest rate on long term bonds is 8 percent and the rate of inflation is 6 percent then the real rate of interest is 2 percent. Present value of the streams of benefits and costs discounted at a 2 percent back to time zero are as follows:

	PRESENT VALUE ($millions)
Benefits	304.11
Costs	
Right-of-Way	44.79
Construction	190.39
Maintenance	18.59
Net Benefits	50.35

The positive net present value of $50.35 million and benefit/cost ratio of 1.2 indicate that the project is worthwhile if the cost of capital is 2 percent. When a discount rate of 3 percent is the benefit/cost ratio is slightly under 1.0. This means that the internal rate of return is just under 3 percent. When the cost of capital is 3 percent the project is not worthwhile.

It should be noted that the market value of the right-of-way understates the opportunity cost of having the land devoted to the highway. The land has a value of $100 million because of its income after property taxes. The economy is paying more for its alternate use but some of the payment is diverted for taxes. The discounted presented value of the payments for the alternate use might be more like $150 million instead of $100 million. Another way of making this point is that one of the costs of the highway is that the local governments lose the property tax on the land used.

Summary

By reducing the positive and negative impacts of a project to their equivalent money value Cost-Benefit Analysis determines whether on balance the project is worthwhile. The equivalent money value are based upon information derived from consumer and producer market choices; i.e., the demand and supply schedules for the goods and services affected by the project. Care must be take to properly allow for such things as inflation. When all this has been considered a worthwhile project is one for which the discounted value of the benefits exceeds the discounted value of the costs; i.e., the net benefits are positive. This is equivalent to the benefit/cost ratio being greater than one and the internal rate of return being greater than the cost of capital.

Points to remember

Cost-Benefit Analysis

Cost-Benefit Analysis is one of the major basis of determining whether a project,

e.g. road, mass transit, job-training program etc, should be implemented or not.

The decision rule is: allocate resources to a project as long as marginal social

benefit > marginal social cost.

Some Concepts used in cost benefit analysis

Present value: of a future amount of money is the maximum amount you would be willing to pay today for the right to receive the money in the future.

e.g. to receive Rs100 next year how much are you willing to pay today? Clearly less than Rs100.

PV of Rs100 (you receive next year) = 100/(1 + r), where r = interest rate. In general, the PV of Rs R you receive after t years = $R/(1 + r)^t$.

If you have a stream of benefits each year (e.g. your earnings) R0, R1, R2,... RT until you retire at t = T, what is the PV of your earnings?

PV = R0 + R1/(1 + r) + R2/(1 + r)2 +........+ RT/(1 + r)T, where r = discount rate and

(1+r)t = discount factor.

Net Present Value

If streams of benefits are B0, B1, B2,... BT and streams of costs from any projects

are C0, C1, C2,... CT then Net present value

NPV= (B0 - C0) + (B1 - C1)/(1 + r) + (B2 – C2)/(1 + r)2 +........+ (BT – CT)/(1 + r)T

Decision Rules based on Net Present Value (NPV)

(1) A project is admissible only if NPV > 0.

(2) When two projects are mutually exclusive, then chose the one with higher NPV.

Discount rate plays a crucial role in the decision rule of C-B analysis.

(1) different values of r can lead to very different conclusion about the admissibility of projects.

Example: R&D vs. Oil well

Year	R&D	Oil well	*r*	NPV (R&D)	NPV (Oil well)
0	-1000	-1000	0	150	200
1	600	0	0.01	128	165
2	0	0	0.03	86	98
3	550	1200	0.05	46	37

Here, Oil well has a higher NPV when r = 0.01, but when r = 0.05 R&D has a higher NPV. It is clear from this example that a high discount rate disfavors the project with higher benefits on in the distant future (but lower benefits in the near future)

(2) Internal Rate of Return (IRR)

It is the discount rate, r, that makes NPV of a project = 0. In other words, IRR is an implicit solution to NPV(r) = 0

Admissibility criteria based on IRR:

(1) Accept the project if its IRR > firm's opportunity cost of funds.

e.g. if IRR = 4% while the firm can earn < 4% on other alternative investment opportunities, then accept the project.

Problems with IRR as the basis of selecting projects:

(a) IRR criterion does not consider the size of the projects. However, NPV criterion does consider the size of projects.

(b) May not produce a unique solution.

(3) Benefit-cost Ratio

C-B ratio = B/C

where

B=benefits and C= costs

If B – C > 1, admit the project

If B – C < 1, reject the project.

Problems with C-B ratio

a) does not consider sizes of projects. e.g. 200/100 = 2000/1000 = 2. Having the information on B/C = 2, one cannot say whether the project's B/C = 2000/1000 or 200/100.

b) In certain situation B may be taken as a negative of cost. In such a case depending on how we consider the negative of cost (i.e., add to B or reduce from C), B/C ratio can be different.

Public Sector Discount Rate

What is the appropriate value of r?

1) *Private sector rate*

public sector investment is at the expense of private sector.

r(government) = r(private before tax) if the fund comes at the expense of private investment.

r(government) = r(private after tax) if it comes at the expense of private consumption.

r(government) = w1x r(before tax)+ w2 x r(after tax), where w1 = % of funds coming from investment and w2 = % of funds coming from consumption.

(2) Social Discount Rate

It is the valuation society places on consumption that is sacrificed today. But why should society's view of opportunity cost of foregoing consumption differ from opportunity cost revealed in the market? The following are the major reasons behind such discrepancy.

a) *Concern for future generation*:

private sector devotes too few resources to the future savings. That basically boils down to that private section places too high discount rate to future returns.

b) *Paternalism*:

Not farsighted enough to adequately weigh future benefits. Paternalistic view says future benefits should be weighted adequately.

c) *Market inefficiency*:

Investment causes positive externality. Therefore investment is underprovided by private market. By applying lower r, government can correct this inefficiency.

Cost-benefit Analysis Games C-B Analysts Play

Chain-Reaction Game

In order to increase the admissibility of a public project, C-B analysts often count

secondary benefits:

In the case of road projects, for example,

Primary benefits: reduction in transportation costs.

Secondary benefits: profits to local restaurants, motels, gas station and to grocery stores, bed linen, gasoline producers. Most of these secondary benefits are merely transfers, however. e.g. increase in gasoline price is nothing more than a transfer from consumers to producers. So if secondary benefits are counted, it is likely that many public projects will pass the NPV test which otherwise would not.

Labor game

Government project "creates" employment. But some labor may come from leaving jobs in other sectors. Even those who were unemployed (before the govt. project) may not remain unemployed for a long time (in the absence of government project). So the actual number of new employments < number of employments in the public sector.

Double counting

e.g. irrigation, C-B analyst may count both (1) the increase in the value of land (2)PV of stream of benefits from farming the land.

The problem with such benefit accounting is that a farmer can either farm the land or sell the land, not both.

Distributional Consideration

There is a view that if NPV > 0, undertake the project regardless of who benefits from it (or who loses). According to this view, the losers can be compensated by the gainers as long as NPV > 0. Thus there is a potential for Pareto improvement as long as NPV > 0 (This criterion of project selection is often called Hicks-Kaldor criterion).

Uncertainty and Project Selection

Project x: net B = $1000 with 100% certainty.
Project y: net B = $0 with 50% and $2000 with 50%
Then expected B from project y = 0*(1/2)+200*(1/2) = $1000
Which one will you choose?

a) risk averse, choose x.

b) risk neutral, indifferent

c) for a risk averse person, project y may be preferable only if expected B > $1000.

Valuing Project Benefits and Costs.

Social benefits and costs may not be reflected in market prices.

a) Market prices: in a competitive market, market prices can be used to evaluate B and C.

Problems: market imperfections such as monopoly, externalities etc. In such cases, market prices may not reflect the true opportunity costs (or shadow prices) of inputs or outputs.

b) Adjusted market price: If there is monopoly in input market then the price of input > marginal cost of its production. In C-B analysis

i) if production of inputs increases by the amount of government purchase, then social price of input = marginal cost of production.

ii) if government' use of inputs is at the expense of private consumption, then price of input = market price.

(c) Taxes: purchasers' price = sellers price + tax

Which one to use?

i) if production of input is expected to expand, then for the purpose of C-B analysis use input price = supply price

ii) if government's use is at the expense of private consumption, then price = demand price (i.e., purchase's price)

Questions

Q.1. Why multi product firms exists? Also explain how pricing is done for multi product firms.

Q.2. hat is social cost benefit analysis? How is it different from financial analysis . Discuss briefly the steps involved in social cost benefit analysis of a project.

Q 3. Explain the concept of economic order quantity.

Glossary

Adaptive Forecasting

A method of forecasting which is easy to revise and in doing so corrects for earlier differences between a forecast and the actual volume of sales. Moving Average and Exponential Smoothing are the examples of such forecasting.

Allocative Efficiency

Production of goods and services in close accordance with consumer demand.

Amortisation

Process of writing off or liquidating an asset or loan periodically on an instalment basis.

Barrier to Entry

Any advantage which firms in an industry have over new .trrivals or potential entrants.

Barrier to Exit

Any limit on asset redeployment from one line of business or industry to a any factor which makes it expensive for a firm to leave an industry.

Benefit-Cost Ratio Analysis.

The present value of marginal social benefits per rupee of marginal social costs.

Black Market

A market in which goods are sold illegally at prices which violate legal restriction , on prices.

Branding

Attaching a brand mark or brand name to a product in order to distinguish it from other product variants.

Budget Line

All combinations of a product which can be bought for a given rupee amount.

Business Profit

Also called Accounting Profit. it refers to residual of sales revenue minus the explicit accounting costs of doing business.

Capital Deepening

Increasing the ratio of capital to labour. .,;

Capitalism

National resources are allocated by private holders.

Clustering

A business strategy whereby many firms serving the same industry (say, automobile industry) tend to get together. Sometimes localised and sometimes dispersed to explore the economies of scalê and scope.

Collusion

A covert informal agreement among firms in an industry to fix prices and output levels.

Command Economy

An economy in which the decision of the Central Authority (as distinguished from households and firms) exert the major influence over allocation of resources and distribution.

Use of central authority, usually the government to decide on key questions faced by every economy: What? How? and For Whom? Heavy reliance placed on central planning and administrative allocation of resources.

Concentration

The extent to which industrial activity is in the hands of a small number of firms.

Concentration Ratio

Fraction of the total market sales controlled by the largest group of sellers.

Conglomerate

Where firms carrying on business in unrelated sectors come together. Also called *diversified* merger.

Consumer Sovereignty

Buyer supremacy in the market place.

Contestable Markets. Theory of

Baumol's Theory of Contestable Markets suggests that the threat of entry coupled with the possibility of exit is sufficient to restrain even a single incumbent producer In the market from reaping monopoly profits. It is the threat of entry that acts as a regulator.

Control loss Cost increases attributable to management inability to monitor and control the performance of subordinates.

It,

Countervaillng Power

Buyer market power that offsets seller market power, and *vice versa.*

Firm. Theory of

The theory of firm is the basic model of business. The theory of firm states that owner-manager aims at profit maximixation.

Five Forces Approach

Developed by Porter. where the structure of competition In an industry is analysed in terms of five major forces, viz.. intensity of rivalry among existing firms, threat of entry, threat of substitutes, power of buyers and power of suppliers.

FMCG Multinationals

Fast moving consumer goods multinationals, viz., Hindustan Lever.

Freebies

Free shopping gifts by marketers to consumers, for example, free Breeze soap with Brook Bond Tea Packet, tax-free cigarettes and wines in European Union.

Goodness of Fit

A degree to which a model fits the observed data in a regression analysis. The goodness of fit is measured by the coefficient of determination (R squared).

Hidden Preferences Problem

The difficulty of determining the demand for public goods.

Horizontal Merger

Where two or more firms in the same industry, and at the same stage of the distribution process join together.

HR Value

Human Resources Value is the present value of future earnings upto retirement age.

Inc

Corporate sector of a country, e.g., India Inc. Japan Inc. meaning India's and Japan's corporate sector respectively.

Inferior Goods

Products for which consumer demand declines as income rises. Their demand is said to be *countercyclical.*

Inflection Point

A point of maximum slope.

Information Agreements,

Agreements between firms to share information on issues like price in order to establish a tacit form of collusion.

Frictional Profit Theory-It refers to abnormal profits earned following unanticipated changes in demand or cost conditions leading to market disequilibrium.

Innovation profit theory'-It refers to above-normal profits that follow successful invention, innovation or modernization.

Monopoly Profit Theory-It refers to above normal profits caused by barriers to entry that restrict competition.

Private Good

Products or services where consumption by one individual precludes or limits consumption by other~.

Public Good lmi

Products or services where consumption by one individual does not reduce the amount available for others.

Question Marks

Businesses which have low market shares but rapid market growth.

Qualitative Forecasts ,

These are subjective forecasts based on intuition, personal experiences and judgement and opinion

Quantitative Forecasts

These employ a variety of statistical methods and mathematical models using historical data and/or causal variables ,to forecast demand.

Ramping

Ramping means retailer or distributor or the channel member taking away gift or freebie meant for consumer, e.g.. a mug given free or a tea jar, sold by the retailer separately. That is, it means the final consumer not getting consumer freebie and it is eaten up by someone else in the pipeline.

R&.D

Research and Development

Relative Distance Method

Graphic technique used to solve linear programming problems.

Reservation Demand

A producer would himself like to retain a part of his own produce for self-consumption. e.g., a farmer. This is called Reservation Demand.

Risks

Unpredictable changes that can be insured against.

Business Risk-Chance of loss associated with a given managerial decision. *Credit* Risk-Chance that another party will fail to abide by its contractual obligations.

Cultural Risk-Chance of loss because of product market differences due to distinctive social customs making it difficult to predict which products might do well in foreign markets.

Currency Risk-Loss due to changes in the domestic currency value of foreign

profits.

Expropriation Risk-Danger that business property located abroad might be seized by host governments.

Government Policy Risk -Chance of loss to global investors because foreign

government grants of monopoly franchises. tax concessions, favoured nation status, etc. can be tenuous.

Inflation Risk-Danger that a general increase in price level will undermine the real economic value of any legal agreement that involves a fixed promise to pay over a period of time.

Interest Rate Risk-Market risk due to the fact that changing interest rates affect the value of any agreement involving a fixed promise to pay over a period of time.

Liquidity Risk-Difficulty of selling corporate assets or investments that have only a few willing buyers or are otherwise not easily transferable at favourable prices under typical market conditions.

Market Risks-Chances that a portfolio of investments can lose money because of swings in the financial markets as a whole.

Political Risk-The possible endangerment that an MNC might face when conducting overseas due to political instablity in the host country.

Risk Aversion

A desire to avoid or mini mise risk.

Risk Premium

Investor reward for risk-taking. Also, the added expected return for a risky asset over that of a riskless asset.

Risk-Return Trade-off

This refers to the relationship between risk and required rate of return. There is direct relationship between risk and return: low risk has low returns and high risk has high returns.

Risk Seeking

A preference for speculation

Safety-Stock

The minimum level of inventory which provides a cushion against the possibility of being out of stock as a result of change in demand.

Sensitivity Analysis

The analysis of the effect of change in certain variable on an outcome, to estimate the variability of the outcome or risk associated with a project or a situation.

Scope

The range of activities, industries, market and countries in which the firm is involved.

Social Costs

Extemal costs passed on to persons not directly involved in the activity and so passed on to society (opposed to private costs).

Social Discount Rate

A discount rate for public investment

Span of Control

The number of individuals under the direct control of another individual.

Spreading of Overhead Cost

Decreasing average fixed cost.

**Spreadsheet **

A table-of electronically stored data.

Stars

Businesses which have both large market share and rapid market growth.

Tailoring the Product

Developing a product or altering the old product according to preferences and purchasing power of potential consumers.

Technological Forecasting

Technological forecasting is the process of identifying and assessing future threats and opportunities arising from the development of relvant technology.

Trend

Long-run pattem of increase or decrease.

Trend Analysis

It involves characterizing long-run pattem of increase or decrease in a series *of* economic data.

Growth Trend *Analysis'—This* assumes constant percentage change over time.

Linear Trend *Analysis-This* assumes constant unit change over time.

Unbundling

Unbundling means separation of activities in which economies *of* scale are not important. Separation of electricity generation from transmission and distribution is an example of vertical unbundling. Separation of value-added services (e.g. radio-based cellular services) from basic telephone services is an example *of* horizontal unbundling in telecom sector.

Value Added

The value of a firm's output minus the value of inputs that it purchases from other firms.

Value of the Firm

It means the present value of the firm's expected future net cash flows.

Vertical Integration

When a single company controls various links in the production chain from basic inputs to final output.

Vertical Relation

Where the ouput of one division or company is the input to another.

White Goods

Fridge and washing machines.

Windfall Profit

Economic profit due to unwarranted good fortune.

Workable Competition

Most desirable form of competition selected from those that are possible.

X -inefficiency

Where a firm incurs higher costs than are necessary; given the set of plant and equipment in use and its level of capacity utilization.

Zero-sum Game

A game in which the gains to the winners are exactly equal to loser.